DESPERATE SUNSET

DESPERATE SUNSET

JAPAN'S KAMIKAZES AGAINST ALLIED SHIPS, 1944–45

MIKE YEO

OSPREY PUBLISHING
Bloomsbury Publishing Plc
PO Box 883, Oxford, OX1 9PL, UK
1385 Broadway, 5th Floor, New York, NY 10018, USA
E-mail: info@ospreypublishing.com
www.ospreypublishing.com

OSPREY is a trademark of Osprey Publishing Ltd

First published in Great Britain in 2019

© Mike Yeo, 2019

Mike Yeo has asserted his right under the Copyright, Designs and Patents Act, 1988, to be identified as Author of this work.

All rights reserved. No part of this publication may be reproduced or transmitted in any form or by any means, electronic or mechanical, including photocopying, recording, or any information storage or retrieval system, without prior permission in writing from the publishers.

A catalogue record for this book is available from the British Library.

ISBN: HB 978 1 4728 2941 2; eBook 978 1 4728 2942 9; ePDF 978 1 4728 2943 6; XML 978 1 4728 2944 3

19 20 21 22 23 10 9 8 7 6 5 4 3 2 1

Edit and photo captions by Tony Holmes
Maps and diagrams by Bounford.com
Index by Fionbar Lyons
Originated by PDQ Digital Media Solutions, Bungay, UK
Printed and bound in India by Replika Press Private Ltd.

Front cover: Firefighters aboard the aircraft carrier USS *Hancock* (CV-19) hose down damage caused by a kamikaze attack. (Photo by Time Life Pictures/US Navy/The LIFE Picture Collection via Getty Images)
Spine: An A6M5, clearly damaged by antiaircraft fire, plummets towards the sea. (*NARA*)
Back cover and flap: Smoke billows from USS *Ward* (APD-16) following a kamikaze attack. (*NARA*)

Artwork on pages 200 and 266 by Chris Davey, © Osprey Publishing, originally published in ACE 75: *Royal Navy Aces of World War 2*.

Artwork on pages 66–67 by Ian Palmer, © Osprey Publishing, originally published in NVG 180: *Kamikaze*.

All other artwork by Jim Laurier, © Osprey Publishing. Five plates originally published in the following books: (pages 32, 158 and 278) DUE 76: *US Navy Ships vs Kamikazes 1944–45*; (pages 206 and 280) COM 119: *Nakajima B5N 'Kate' and B6N 'Jill' Units*.

Osprey Publishing supports the Woodland Trust, the UK's leading woodland conservation charity.

To find out more about our authors and books visit www.ospreypublishing.com. Here you will find extracts, author interviews, details of forthcoming events and the option to sign up for our newsletter.

CONTENTS

CHAPTER 1 INTRODUCTION — 6
CHAPTER 2 TACTICS AND AIRCRAFT — 20
CHAPTER 3 THE PHILIPPINES — 68
CHAPTER 4 OTHER THEATERS — 148
CHAPTER 5 OKINAWA — 190

Bibliography — 341
Index — 343

CHAPTER 1
INTRODUCTION

By mid-1944, Imperial Japan's armed forces found themselves in an increasingly desperate situation. The Imperial Japanese Army Air Force (IJAAF) and Imperial Japanese Naval Air Force (IJNAF) had suffered terrible losses in the grinding aerial battles over the Solomons in 1942–43, while the Imperial Japanese Navy (IJN) was a shadow of the force that had so successfully attacked Pearl Harbor on December 7, 1941. The battle of the Philippine Sea on June 19–20, better known to high-scoring US Navy fighter pilots in the immediate aftermath of the campaign as the "Marianas Turkey Shoot," effectively sounded the death knell for the IJNAF. An attempt to forestall the US amphibious invasion of the Mariana Islands had seen the IJNAF wiped out as a fighting force, losing between 550 and 650 aircraft (estimates vary), along with most of what remained of its cadre of combat-experienced pilots. Little damage had been inflicted on the US Navy's Pacific Fleet in return.

Among the hundreds of pilots lost during this one-sided battle was Lt Cdr Takashige Egusa, who had led the D3A "Val" dive-bombers of the second wave attack on Pearl Harbor and had personally bombed the battleship USS *Nevada* (BB-36). He subsequently hit the cruiser HMS *Dorsetshire* and the carrier HMS *Hermes* as the Japanese swept across the Pacific and Southeast Asia. However, by June 1944 off Guam, in the Northern Mariana Islands, it was a vastly different war, and on the 15th of that month Egusa found himself leading a small force of land-based Yokosuka P1Y "Frances" twin-engined torpedo-bombers against a powerfully defended carrier task force. His entire formation was unceremoniously shot down before they reached their targets.

A *Zuikaku* D3A1 "Val" dive-bomber that was hit by antiaircraft fire is seen here moments before it crashed into USS *Hornet* (CV-8) in a jibaku strike during the battle of Santa Cruz. A *Shokaku* B5N "Kate" can also be seen flying over the doomed carrier, having just launched its torpedo at *Hornet*. Two B5N2s from *Shokaku* and one from *Junyo* scored torpedo hits on CV-8, leaving it immobilized and listless in the water. *Hornet* was subsequently abandoned and sunk by torpedoes launched from two Japanese destroyers on October 27, 1942. This photograph was taken from the heavy cruiser USS *Pensacola* (CA-24). (*Naval History and Heritage Command*)

DESPERATE SUNSET

Acknowledged throughout the IJNAF as its finest dive-bomber leader, Lt Cdr Takashige Egusa led the D3A "Val" dive-bombers of the second wave during the attack on Pearl Harbor on the morning of December 7, 1941, and also presided over the sinking of British cruisers HMS *Cornwall* and HMS *Dorsetshire* in the Indian Ocean in April 1942. He fell in battle on June 15, 1944 leading a small force of land-based P1Y1 "Frances" bombers of the 521st Kokutai against a US Navy carrier task force off the Northern Mariana Islands. (*Tony Holmes collection*)

When he died in combat, Egusa was among the last aircrew survivors from the men who had attacked Pearl Harbor two-and-a-half years earlier. The ranks of this once elite force had been drastically thinned during the carrier clashes in the battles of the Coral Sea and Midway and then utterly decimated in the war of attrition that followed in the Solomons. As an example, the tactical "victory" won by the IJN at the battle of Santa Cruz on October 26, 1942 – its carrier-based aircraft sank USS *Hornet* (CV-8) and badly damaged USS *Enterprise* (CV-6) in exchange for two Japanese carriers being heavily damaged – came at a horrific cost in aircrew. No fewer than 148 pilots and observers/gunners, including two dive-bomber group leaders, three torpedo-bomber squadron leaders, and 18 section or flight leaders were lost, together with 99 of the 203 aircraft committed by the IJNAF to the battle.

Things were little better for land-based units of the IJAAF either, as they too had endured heavy attrition in New Guinea and the Solomons in 1942–43 in a forlorn attempt to wrest aerial supremacy back from increasingly powerful Allied air forces in-theater following initial successes in the early days of the Japanese campaign in Southeast Asia and the western Pacific.

In spite of such reversals in fortune, both the IJNAF and the IJAAF had one last desperate, and deadly, card to play. By October 1944 senior naval officers were openly discussing forming Tokubetsu Kogekitai (shortened to tokko-tai) units to fly serviceable, bomb-laden aircraft and crash them into enemy ships. Faced with a severe lack of skilled, experienced airmen able to accurately bomb or torpedo Allied vessels using conventional methods, Vice Admiral Takijiro Onishi (soon to be appointed commander of 1st Air Fleet in the Philippines) requested approval from the Chief of the Naval General Staff to form a Special Attack unit to carry out suicide strikes on the US Navy's Pacific Fleet.

Although initially opposed to the idea of such attacks when first briefed on them, Onishi had quickly realized that conventional attacks had little chance of success against the overwhelming firepower of the US forces being massed for the imminent invasion of the Philippines. It was duly decided the best way to inflict maximum damage on the enemy forces approaching Japan was to get the poorly trained IJNAF and IJAAF pilots to crash their aircraft into their targets, thus essentially becoming guided bombs.

The use of tai-tari (body-crashing) tactics was not a new phenomenon, with Japanese pilots whose aircraft were badly hit being known to have attempted to crash into Allied ships as early as May 1942. However, these were individual actions taken by pilots who decided that there was no way their badly damaged aircraft could have returned to base. The formation of Tokubetsu Kogekitai and the employment of Special Attack tactics would be a different thing altogether, for it would entail pilots setting out specifically to crash their aircraft onto enemy ships, with no intention of returning home.

That the Japanese should turn to such tactics out of desperation should not have come as a great surprise to the Allies. Indeed, there had been numerous occasions throughout the Pacific War when Japanese pilots facing an imminent crash in a stricken aircraft had opted to adopt jibaku (Japanese term for the act of suicide) tactics and attempted to strike an enemy vessel, with varying degrees of success.

In February 1942, following the fall of Rabaul, on the South Pacific island of New Britain, to Japanese forces, the Allies were concerned that the IJN would turn it into a major base that could pose a threat to the vital California–Australia sea lane supply route. A raid was quickly planned

This dramatic image was a still frame taken from a cine film shot by a sailor on board USS *Lexington* (CV-2) during the aborted raid on Rabaul by TF 11 on February 20, 1942. In an early example of jibaku, FCPO Chuzo Watanabe, flying G4M1 "Betty" F-348 of the 4th Kokutai, decided to crash into *Lexington*. He missed and flew into the sea just off the carrier's port bow after the "Betty" had been repeatedly hit by antiaircraft fire from other US Navy ships escorting CV-2. Minutes earlier, and just prior to bomb release, the G4M1 had had its port engine and nacelle completely shot off by VF-3 fighter pilot Lt Edward H. "Butch" O'Hare, flying an F4F-3 Wildcat from *Lexington*. (NARA)

against Rabaul, with the US Navy's Task Force (TF) 11, centered on the aircraft carrier USS *Lexington* (CV-2), ordered to carry out the attack scheduled for February 21. TF 11 was detected by a patrolling IJNAF flying boat on the morning of the 20th, with Rabaul still out of range, and the decision was made to call off the raid soon after. However, by then, the IJNAF had already sortied 17 G4M1 "Betty" bombers of the newly arrived 4th Kokutai from Rabaul's Vunakanau airfield to attack the ships.

Nine aircraft from the 4th Kokutai's 1st Chutai and eight from the 2nd made contact with TF 11 in the afternoon. An epic fighter action in defense of the carrier duly ensued, with F4F Wildcats of VF-3 shooting down or damaging three 1st Chutai aircraft before they could reach the ship. Among the successful pilots was Lt Edward "Butch" O'Hare, who was awarded a Medal of Honor following this engagement. One of the damaged "Bettys" was the mount of Kokutai commander Lt Cdr Takuzo Ito, the aircraft being flown by FCPO Chuzo Watanabe. It had had its port engine and nacelle completely shot off by O'Hare just prior to bomb release, and Watanabe subsequently decided to crash into *Lexington*. He missed and flew into the sea off the carrier's port bow after the "Betty" had been repeatedly hit by antiaircraft fire from US Navy ships.

The next known jibaku attempt met with more success. Following the crippling of the IJN's carrier force with the sinking of four of its "flattops" during the battle of Midway in early June, American forces started their counteroffensive soon after. This included the surprise invasion of Guadalcanal, in the Solomon Islands, on August 7 and the subsequent occupation of a newly built Japanese airfield there. The seizure of the island had a twofold objective. Firstly, the Allies hoped to prevent the IJNAF and IJAAF from using the airfield as a base for aircraft tasked with threatening supply and communication routes between the USA, Australia, and New Zealand. Secondly, the Allies saw Guadalcanal as a key location from which to neutralize the strategically important Japanese stronghold of Rabaul.

The Japanese response to the amphibious assault on Guadalcanal was instantaneous and predictably fierce. Air attacks from Rabaul against the invasion fleet started the very day the US Marine Corps came ashore. One of the ships to survive the attacks on August 7 was USS *George F. Elliott* (AP-13), a Heywood-class transport acquired from civilian service by the US Navy in 1940. It had arrived off Guadalcanal with the main invasion fleet on D-Day, and among the Marines it disembarked that day was Robert Leckie, author of the book *Helmet for my Pillow*, which was subsequently used as the basis of the television mini-series *The Pacific*.

Like many of the transports involved in this operation, *George F. Elliott* was awaiting the order to resume sending the balance of its cargo ashore due to congestion on the beachhead on the morning of the 8th when more G4M1s were detected on radar. A total of 23 torpedo-armed "Bettys" were closing on Guadalcanal, 14 from the 4th Kokutai and nine from the Misawa Kokutai. Some 26 bombers had originally taken off from Vunakanau, but three aircraft from the 4th Kokutai had aborted before reaching the target area.

Upon receiving word of the impending attack, *George F. Elliott*'s crew weighed anchor and got the vessel underway, heading out into the open waters of nearby "Ironbottom Sound" as they prepared to meet the oncoming threat. The 16,400-ton ship was spotted by "Betty" bomber pilot Lt(jg) Takafumi Sasaki of the 4th Kokutai's 2nd Chutai, who bored in from its starboard side just above the wavetops.

George F. Elliott's gunners blazed away at the bomber with the ship's paltry antiaircraft armament, which consisted of a single five-inch gun, four three-inch weapons, and eight 0.50-caliber machine guns. Several hits were scored without apparent effect, although at some point in his torpedo run Sasaki decided that a jibaku attack was the only option left open to him. The bomber struck the ship just aft of the superstructure, showering its topsides with burning fuel and debris. The bulk of the damage inflicted on the transport was caused by the G4M1's twin engines, which penetrated the thin skin of the ship and severed the rear fire mains, starting a massive blaze in the cargo hold in the process. The resulting conflagration soon raged out of control, with the crew forced to fight the fire with a bucket brigade because of the severed mains.

With neighboring ships unable to provide assistance due to the ongoing air attack, the crew of *George F. Elliott* realized they were fighting a losing battle when a damaged bulkhead failed, releasing bunker fuel

The 16,400-ton transport ship USS *George F. Elliott* (AP-13) was struck by the "Betty" flown by Lt(jg) Takafumi Sasaki of the 4th Kokutai's 2nd Chutai while underway in "Ironbottom Sound," off Guadalcanal, on the morning of August 8, 1942. Most of the damage was caused by the G4M1's twin engines, which penetrated the thin skin of the ex-merchant ship and severed the rear fire mains, starting a massive blaze in the cargo hold in the process. The crew was told to abandon ship shortly thereafter, and the burning hulk was scuttled by the destroyer USS *Hull* (DD-350).

into the rear hold that literally fueled the flames. The order to abandon ship was given soon after 1300hrs, and later that evening the burning hulk was scuttled by the destroyer USS *Hull* (DD-350).

From the Japanese perspective, the mission on August 8 was an unmitigated disaster. Aside from *George F. Elliott*, the only other vessel to be hit, by a torpedo, was the destroyer USS *Jarvis* (DD-393) – it was sunk with all hands the following day during an attack by 31 IJNAF aircraft. This was a poor return for the loss of 18 "Bettys" and 125 aircrew, many of them veterans of earlier campaigns who took with them their irreplaceable experience.

BELOW
The heavy cruiser USS *San Francisco* (CA-38) was another victim of a "Betty" jibaku off the Solomons in 1942, the vessel being hit on November 12 off Guadalcanal while escorting Allied transports carrying much-needed supplies and fresh troops for the land campaign. One of 19 torpedo-bombers to target TF 67.4, the G4M1 crashed into *San Francisco's* aft main battery control station, swung around that structure and plunged over the port side into the sea. Fifteen crew were killed, 29 wounded, and one listed as missing. Maneuvering behind the already burning cruiser is the attack transport USS *President Jackson* (AP-37), this dramatic photograph being taken from the latter vessel's sister-ship USS *President Adams* (AP-38). *(NARA)*

The invasion of Guadalcanal marked the start of a series of air and naval actions carried out by both sides in support of their respective ground forces in the Solomons. The primary objective of the IJN and Allied navies was to resupply and reinforce their troops' positions on Guadalcanal itself, while simultaneously trying to deny their adversary a hold on the island.

On November 12 yet another Allied convoy reached Lunga Point, on the northern coast of Guadalcanal, with much-needed supplies and fresh troops for the bitter, grinding land campaign that continued to be fought for control of the island. The transports were escorted by Rear Admiral Daniel Judson Callaghan's TF 67.4, which comprised the heavy cruisers USS *San Francisco* (CA-38) and USS *Portland* (CA-33), the light cruisers USS *Helena* (CL-50) and USS *Juneau* (CL-52), and six destroyers. The force had been sighted and shadowed by Japanese reconnaissance floatplanes soon after departing Espiritu Santo, in the New Hebrides, two days before, and just after noon on the 12th Allied beachcombers further up the Solomons chain had sent a warning that a force of IJNAF bombers were on their way. At 1408hrs a force of 19 bombers attacked.

These were once again torpedo-armed "Bettys" from Rabaul, although mounting losses among the G4M1 units committed to the campaign in the Solomons meant that this force was made up of aircraft from the 703rd, 705th, and 707th Kokutai (the former Chitose, Misawa, and Kisarazu Kokutai, respectively). The bombers made their way down Indispensable Strait before swinging south, using the hills of Florida Island and Tulagi to mask their approach towards the ships off Guadalcanal. Among the sailors to spot the "Betty" torpedo-bombers minutes before they attacked was Lt(jg) John George Wallace on board *San Francisco*:

> Over these hills came the 30 [actually 19, as mentioned above] "Bettys," fanning out to disperse the defensive firepower from our ships. They skimmed down so that they were only a few feet from the water, and when they got within range of the ships they dropped their "fish." By then the ships had opened fire, some, including *San Francisco*, using their big eight-inch main battery guns as well as their antiaircraft guns. Since the big eight-inch guns had contact shells, not shells with fuzes in them that would explode in the air near an aircraft, we aimed the guns at a point in the water ahead of an incoming plane. We were hoping that when the shell

struck the water, it would explode and disable the plane – or that the turbulence caused by the water splash would tend to make the planes drop into the water. No planes were shot down in this manner, but the Japanese pilots wiggled their planes to avoid the splashes.

Wallace's battle station was in the ship's aft main battery control station for the cruiser's eight-inch main guns, from where he observed the action:

> As the planes approached, I was standing in the door looking out to starboard, with communication headphones strapped over my head. I was ready to take control of the main battery guns should the forward station, containing the Gunnery Officer, become disabled. I saw plane after plane drop torpedoes, and for a while it didn't look as if we were going to shoot any of them down. Finally, planes got hit and started to drop in the water or skid in and flop over. One came in from our starboard bow and, for the longest time, it didn't get hit. It dropped its torpedo, and I was sure this would hit *San Francisco* forward on the starboard side.

This photograph (onto which white circles were drawn to highlight areas damaged by the "Betty") was taken upon CA-38's arrival at Mare Island Navy Yard, north of San Francisco, on December 11, 1942, where it remained for almost three months while being repaired. *(NARA)*

The torpedo missed, but the crew of the bomber was not done yet. Wallace continued:

> About the time I expected that torpedo to hit – it missed – our antiaircraft 20mm guns behind me, right outside my battle station, started to really kick them out. I looked out toward the starboard quarter, and what I saw was a "Betty" bomber coming right at me with its starboard engine smoking. I just had time to duck inside the outer door when a tremendous explosion knocked me all the way up to the forward side of the secondary conn, after which I lost consciousness.

The stricken bomber crashed into *San Francisco*'s aft main battery control station, swung around that structure and plunged over the port side into the sea. Fifteen crew were killed, 29 wounded, and one listed as missing. Wallace was among those to be wounded, suffering burns to his face and legs and subsequently earning a Navy Cross for his actions that day. The bomber demolished the cruiser's aft main battery control station, while its secondary command post, "Battle Two," was burned out but was reestablished that same evening. *San Francisco*'s after antiaircraft director and radar were also put out of commission, while three of the ship's 20mm antiaircraft mounts were destroyed.

In between these two actions off Guadalcanal, other US Navy vessels had endured impromptu jibaku attacks. Indeed, on October 26, 1942 during the battle of the Santa Cruz Islands, *Hornet* was struck by two flak-damaged D3A "Val" dive-bombers during a series of carrier-borne air attacks mounted by both sides on each other's carriers throughout the engagement. The hulk of the abandoned *Hornet* was eventually sunk by four Long Lance torpedoes fired by IJN destroyers after the carrier withstood all attempts by the US Navy to scuttle it.

The destroyer USS *Smith* (DD-378) was also damaged in a jibaku hit on October 26, the ship being hit in the forecastle by a B5N "Kate" torpedo-bomber. The aircraft's torpedo reportedly exploded shortly after the "Kate" had struck the ship, resulting in 57 sailors being killed or listed as missing and 12 wounded. Despite the damage, the destroyer retained its position in the TF 17 cruiser-destroyer screen protecting larger vessels from aerial attack. Its gunners were credited with downing six IJNAF aircraft prior to the vessel being sent to Noumea for temporary repairs and then on to Pearl Harbor for a four-month yard overhaul. *Smith* was awarded a Presidential Unit Citation for its exploits during the battle of the Santa Cruz Islands.

GENESIS

Fast-forward to the summer of 1944, and by the time of Lt Cdr Takashige Egusa's death in June of that year, the discussion about whether to formally use suicide tactics or not was already in progress. Ironically, given the fact that the IJNAF was the first to employ organized tokko tactics in October 1944 off the Philippines, it was the IJAAF that initially mooted the idea of such attacks. The genesis of it was a fact-finding mission to New Guinea in early 1944 by Lt Col Koji Tanaka from the Imperial General Headquarters. Once in-theater, he found that IJAAF units were facing various operational, training, and serviceability problems with their aircraft. More importantly, Tanaka also learnt that there had been occasions where pilots, faced with considerable difficulty in downing USAAF B-17 Flying Fortress and B-24 Liberator heavy bombers with their lightly armed Ki-43 "Oscar" and Ki-61 "Tony" fighters, had resorted to using ramming tactics against the "heavies."

Tanaka also recommended to the Imperial General Headquarters following his return to Japan that such tokko attacks be formally adopted as official operational tactics. However, the IJAAF leadership felt that Special Attacks should be strictly voluntary, rather than being seen as part of a mandate, which in turn meant that no orders were issued to train pilots in such tactics. Nevertheless, in July 1944, flight school superintendents and IJAAF unit commanders were asked to submit lists of volunteers for tokko missions, and soon after 50 "volunteers" were selected from the Hitachi, Akeno, Hamamatsu, and Hokota flight training schools, with 60 more following soon after.

Despite being described as "volunteers," it appears that the pilots assigned to tokko operations had little choice but to put their hands up when senior officers asked for personnel to carry out Special Attack missions, given the existing culture prevalent in Japan and the military at the time. Several testimonies attest to this, and the phenomenon of pressure being applied on pilots or trainees to "volunteer" for tokko operations only increased as the campaign ramped up and the ranks of available pilots naturally thinned out.

The initial batch of volunteer trainees was soon being schooled in tokko tactics, and this tuition was still in progress when the invasion of the Philippines commenced on October 20, 1944. Shortly thereafter, the pilots were formed into the Hakko-tai units that they would deploy with to the Philippines, and they were expended in tokko attacks between November 1944 and January 1945 (see Chapter 3).

The impending invasion of the Philippines had also prompted the IJNAF to develop its own tokko program, although it took an altogether shorter and more ad hoc path. It appears that Rear Admiral Masafumi Arima, commander of the Manila-based 26th Koku Sentai (Air Flotilla), was the initiator of the service's move into tokko attacks. He attempted to crash a D4Y "Judy" dive-bomber into a fast carrier – possibly USS *Franklin* (CV-13) – on October 15, 1944, having personally led a strike

Rear Admiral Masafumi Arima was the initiator of the IJNAF's move into dedicated tokko attacks, rather than ad hoc jibaku. An IJN veteran with almost 30 years of service to his country, he had been captain of the carrier *Shokaku* from late May 1942 through to his promotion to rear admiral one year later – he had seen action with the vessel off Guadalcanal and during the battles of the Eastern Solomons and the Santa Cruz Islands. When leading a strike against TF 38 off Luzon in October 1944, Arima attempted to crash his D4Y into a fast carrier. (*Tony Holmes collection*)

Takijiro Onishi

The individual seen as the father of kamikaze attacks was Vice Admiral Takijiro Onishi, commander of the First Air Fleet in the Philippines in October 1944. His resolve to begin suicide attacks culminated a year's worth of theoretical discussions among the IJN's leadership on how to overcome Japan's growing inferiority against the US Navy. (*Tony Holmes collection*)

Takijiro Onishi is generally credited with being the father of kamikaze operations, being a long-time aviator and advocate of naval aviation. His early war career included a role in planning the Pearl Harbor attack and command of the naval air forces on Taiwan, which supported the invasion of the Philippines in 1941. In 1944, he was the head of the Aviation Department of the Ministry of Munitions. After the battle of the Philippine Sea, Onishi was ordered to take over the First Air Fleet (on October 2) and defeat the expected American invasion of the Philippines.

Before leaving for his new assignment, he had informed the Chief of the Naval General Staff and the Navy Minister of his intention to form "Special Attack" units to target the American invasion force. Although this was not worded in such a way to explicitly state he was forming suicide units, his intent was clear. Onishi was advised only to make sure all the pilots were volunteers.

Onishi arrived in the Philippines on October 17, just as US forces were making preliminary landings near Leyte. Upon reaching Mabalacat two days later, he found that his air fleet possessed only 100 aircraft. The size of this meager force convinced Onishi that suicide tactics were his only chance for success. On October 20 he spoke to the pilots who had volunteered for tokko missions:

Japan is in grave danger. The salvation of our country is now beyond the power of the ministers of the state, the General Staff and lowly commanders like myself. It can come only from spirited young men such as you. Thus, on behalf of your hundred million countrymen, I ask of you this sacrifice and pray for your success.

You are already gods, without earthly desires. But one thing you want to know is that your own crash-dive is not in vain. Regrettably, we will not be able to tell you the results. But I shall watch your efforts to the end and report your deeds to the Throne. You may all rest assured on this point.

I ask you all to do your best.

The die was cast for a campaign of suicide attacks.

Onishi was ordered to leave the Philippines on January 10, 1945 and relocate his headquarters back to Formosa. He continued in command of the First Air Fleet until May, when he was ordered to return to Japan to take up the position of Vice Chief of the Naval General Staff. Even at this late stage of the war Onishi continued to advocate for a bitter fight to the end, despite the seemingly inevitable American invasion that would lay waste to Japan.

Having ordered so many young men to their deaths, Onishi elected to take his own life after the announcement from the Emperor that Japan would surrender. On August 16, 1945 he committed ritual suicide, but botched the attempt. He died a painful death from his wounds over a period of 15 hours since he would not allow others to hasten his ritual death.

against TF 38 off Luzon. Aircraft from the US Navy task force were in the process of attacking targets in Formosa and the Philippines prior to the invasion of the latter five days later. A subsequent Japanese account of Arima's attack noted that "This act of self-sacrifice by a high flag officer spurred on the flying units in forward combat areas and provided the spark that touched off the organized use of suicide attacks in the battle for Leyte."

Confusingly, IJNAF records state that Arima crashed his A6M "Zeke" (rather than a D4Y) into *Franklin*. However, US Navy records do not bear this out, with *Franklin* itself reporting being attacked by two "Oscars" and a "Judy" at 1045hrs. All three aircraft dropped bombs, resulting in the carrier being hit once and suffering two near misses. One of the attacking "Oscars" was shot down by the carrier, without any indication that its pilot had attempted to crash into the ship.

Two days after Arima's death, the newly appointed commander of the First Koku Kantai (Air Fleet), Vice Admiral Takijiro Onishi, arrived in the Philippines. On October 19, during his visit to Mabalacat West airfield (known today as Clark air base), north of Manila, Onishi "suggested" to the leadership of the resident 201st Kokutai that tokko attacks were the only way to defeat the enemy. Although he had previously been opposed to such tactics, he told the 201st's pilot cadre that as they were going to die in combat operations in any case, then their deaths should not be futile. The tactics to be employed were quickly agreed upon, and soon volunteers were selected to form the Dai-ichi Kamikaze Tokubetsu Kogekitai (1st Kamikaze Special Attack Corps) to carry out the IJNAF's first dedicated tokko attacks. The stage was set.

CHAPTER 2
TACTICS AND AIRCRAFT

TACTICS

Although the tactics behind flying an aircraft into a ship seemed straightforward enough once the pilot involved got past the psychological barrier of being killed in the resulting crash, as it turned out, throughout the tokko campaign both sides constantly reassessed and refined their offensive (IJNAF and IJAAF) and defensive (Allied ships and defending fighters) tactics in an effort to maximize success. For the Japanese, the challenge was to get the pilot and his bomb-laden aircraft past Allied fighter combat air patrols (CAPs) and antiaircraft fire and into a position whereby he could crash into a moving, maneuvering target. For the Allies, they simply had to try and prevent the enemy pilot from doing so.

In practice, it turned out that the challenge for both sides was more difficult that it appeared. The increasingly poorly trained Japanese pilots found it more and more difficult to break through the massed ranks of fighters and intense antiaircraft fire that they encountered as their adversaries woke up to the tokko threat. Ships' gunners and Allied fighter pilots alike quickly discovered that scoring numerous hits on a tokko aircraft, and even setting it alight, often proved insufficient when it came to stopping a Japanese pilot already committed to his death dive. As a direct result of these factors, the tactics adopted by both sides evolved considerably from when the tokko first appeared off Leyte to the last such operations on August 15, 1945 – the day that hostilities ended in the Pacific.

At the start of the tokko campaign, the Japanese typically used two different flight profiles when approaching the target. The first saw the aircraft attack at low level, closing on their targets at wavetop heights. This had the advantage of making it more difficult for ships' radar to detect the incoming aircraft, as well as increasing

On April 11, 1945, the battleship USS *Missouri* (BB-63) was hit amidships on its starboard side by a Zero-sen while sailing off Okinawa. Here, gun crews watch the aircraft approach, which, when it hit, exploded in a large fireball but caused no real damage to the heavily armored battleship. Low-level attacks were initially favored by tokko pilots. *(NARA)*

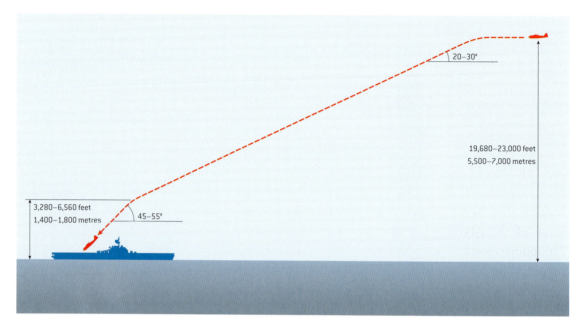

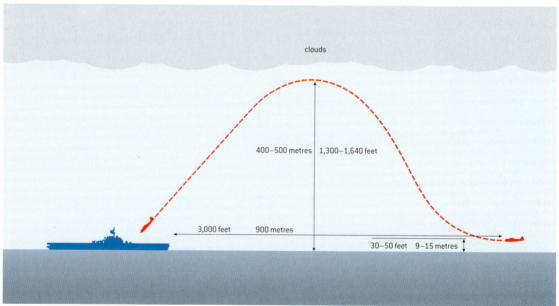

the risk of vessels' defensive fire hitting friendly ships nearby (something that happened on occasion). This attack profile also made it more difficult for defending fighters to intercept tokko aircraft, even if they had been detected during their approach. Allied pilots attempting intercepts would have to divide their attention between shooting down their target aircraft and avoiding hitting the water while doing so.

DIAGRAMS LEFT
These diagrams show the two most commonly employed tokko attack profiles. The high-altitude approach was the preferred profile for inexperienced pilots. More challenging for both the suicide pilot and the defender was a low-altitude approach, which, if flown low enough, could evade radar detection. Usually before executing his final dive, the low-altitude attacker would perform a pop-up maneuver to acquire a target. Occasionally, however, tokko would fly all the way to the target at low altitude.

This method of approach was possible during the first attacks that took place in late October 1944, for the Japanese aviators involved in these one-way missions were still relatively experienced and skilled. Indeed, they had completed the standard pilot training courses, with some of the IJNAF pilots selected for early tokko operations in the Philippines even having combat experience under their belts. This method of attack was also used by the Formosa-based tokko on occasion during the battle of Okinawa, which commenced on April 1, 1945, underlining their reputation among their opponents that they were more skilled in kamikaze attacks than their Japan-based counterparts.

A tokko pilot conducting a low-level attack needed to possess sufficient flying skills to maintain a consistently low altitude (as low as 30–50ft above the waves) on approach, and then be able to "pop up" to 1,300–1,640ft before diving onto the target at an angle of 45 degrees or steeper. This approach could be combined with the use of nearby landmasses that created "ground clutter" on ships' search radar screens to further cloak the attackers' presence. Such tactics were often used during tokko missions against US Navy vessels sailing off Leyte and Luzon, in the Philippines. Due to the pilot's need to maintain a visual reference with the target, the terminal dive following "pop up" was sometimes done with the aircraft inverted. Such a maneuver required an even greater degree of skill.

The tokko pilots were also taught to approach their target from the stern whenever possible owing to the reduced concentration of antiaircraft guns in the after part of the ship. In an attempt to counter this tactic, ships under attack would turn so that their beams faced the oncoming aerial threat. While this presented a bigger target for the Japanese pilots to aim at, Allied navies judged that this was a risk worth taking as it allowed the crew to bring its full battery of antiaircraft guns on one side of the ship into play.

The other flight profile attempted by tokko pilots was to attack from high altitude. This entailed approaching the targeted ship at an altitude of at least 20,000ft, before losing height and picking up speed in a shallow

20–30-degree dive prior to finally entering a steeper 45–55-degree dive in the terminal phase of the attack. While simpler to execute, this approach still required a fair amount of skill. In practice, although more damage could be done by an aircraft crashing into the target at a higher speed, it also made it harder for pilots to successfully hit a relatively small target turning at speed. When closing on a maneuvering ship at speeds in excess of 400mph, the pilot had little time available to make fine adjustments to his aim. Furthermore, his aircraft was less responsive to control inputs at higher speeds due to the airflow forces being exerted on its ailerons and rudder.

Both profiles were tried in the Philippines, although by the time of the battle of Okinawa the Japanese tended to approach mostly at low-to-medium altitudes ranging anywhere from 1,500ft up to 10,000ft. Both wavetop and high-altitude approaches were still very occasionally attempted, however. The virtual abandonment of these original attack profiles was forced upon the Japanese when pilot quality deteriorated to a point where, for the most part, they were unable to effectively fly either.

The adoption of simpler attack profiles coincided with a dramatic increase in the number of aircraft being committed to tokko missions compared to the initial attacks. With the latter, only a solitary aircraft or pair of attackers would target ships off Leyte. However, when low-to-medium altitude profiles were flown, ever larger formations of aircraft were

BELOW
A group of Japanese aircraft flies high above the escort carriers USS *St. Lo* (CVE-63) and USS *Kitkun Bay* (CVE-71) on October 25, 1944. The sailors on board these ships could not know that this was no conventional attack, but the beginning of a whole new phase of the war. Targeting Allied ships from high altitude was one of the two forms of tokko attack most commonly seen in the Pacific War. *(NARA)*

IJNAF pilots study a map of Luzon during a pre-mission briefing in early January 1945. Taking off in total darkness, the aviators would circle overhead until first light, when they would launch their attacks from the west. Approaching Allied vessels from this direction made it difficult for crews – particularly gunners manning antiaircraft weapons – to spot their attackers in the darkness. *(NARA)*

being sent out against Allied ships to the point where waves of tokko were detected on Allied radar screens during the numbered Kikusui (Floating Chrysanthemum) operations off Okinawa. Such attacks were mounted in order to overwhelm the defenders, ensuring that at least some of the tokko would "leak" through the defenses to achieve hits on Allied warships.

Eventually, the time of day that attacks were mounted also became a deciding factor in their success. Shortly after the US Army commenced its amphibious assault on the main Philippine island of Luzon on January 9, 1945, the IJNAF and IJAAF, with the Allied naval vessels just offshore from their main tokko bases, started targeting ships at dawn. In order to be in the correct location to mount such attacks, aircraft were taking off from their bases while they were enveloped in darkness. Pilots would then circle overhead until first light, when they would launch their attacks from the west. Approaching Allied vessels from this direction made it difficult for crews to spot their attackers against the dark western skies, while the ships themselves were perfectly silhouetted against the brightening skies to the east.

On January 9 and 10, 1945, the destroyer escorts USS *Hodges* (DE-231) and USS *LeRay Wilson* (DE-414) were attacked at dawn, most likely by IJAAF Kawasaki Ki-45 "Nick" fighters or Mitsubishi Ki-67 "Peggy" twin-engined bombers. Fortunately for the crews on board both ships, the pilots just missed their respective targets (see Chapter 3 for

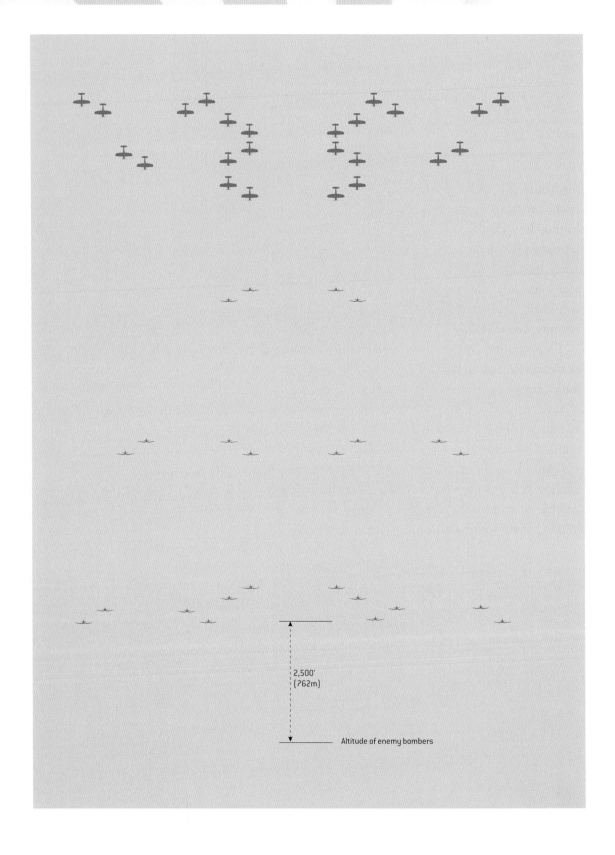

TACTICS AND AIRCRAFT   27

DIAGRAM LEFT
CAPs were usually under the direction of a Fighter Director Officer on board a radar picket destroyer. Fighters would stay closed up in one of four prescribed formations as they approached the intercept point to avoid confusing the radar operators. The formations were designed to place the main intercepting force some 2,000–3,000ft above the estimated height of the enemy tokko formation so as to give naval aviators superiority of position, with a part of the formation flying above to provide high cover. Formation sizes varied based on visibility and the probable composition of the enemy formation.

---

further details), although six of *LeRay Wilson*'s gunners were killed by the starboard wing of the crashing aircraft as it glanced the ship prior to hitting the water. These dawn attacks had the added advantage of allowing Japanese pilots to avoid marauding Allied fighters, as CAPs could only be safely mounted during the hours of daylight. Nightfighter CAPs were also increasingly flown in response to the tokko threat, but they were considerably fewer in number than daylight CAPs and appreciably less effective due to the primitive nature of Air Intercept radar in 1944–45.

From around the halfway point during the battle of Okinawa, this tactic was turned on its head in that the Japanese now started mounting dusk attacks by aircraft that were not operating as part of a massed Kikusui operation. The longer distance from their bases in Japan and Formosa and the decreasing skills of poorly trained pilots meant that the tokko were unable to carry out night overwater flights to reach Okinawa at dawn. They would take off from Kyushu and Formosa in the mid-afternoon instead, timing their attacks on shipping off the invasion beaches to coincide with the sun being at its lowest point in the sky. Making their approach from the west, the tokko forced the defending

A B6N2 from the Kikusui-Tenzan Kokutai (formerly the 131st Kokutai) departs Kanoya on a dusk tokko mission in late May 1945, the crew having taken off during the mid-afternoon so as to arrive off Okinawa shortly after sunset. "Jills" armed with Type 91 air-dropped torpedoes routinely carried out lone attacks such as this, rather than participating in massed Kikusui operations. Kanoya served as the focal point of the IJNAF's kamikaze efforts, and was the primary airfield from which the IJNAF launched such strikes. The "Jill" officially carried out its first tokko missions in early January 1945. *(Photo by Yasuo Tomishige/The Asahi Shimbun via Getty Images)*

gunners to shoot with the setting sun directly in their eyes, or in the rapidly fading light – conditions that made it difficult for them to identify aerial targets. Again, this approach method had the added advantage of leaving the attackers relatively unmolested by fighters, with the day CAP having already left their patrol stations and the nightfighter CAP yet to arrive overhead.

SEARCHES AND REPORTING ATTACKS

The Japanese also made extensive use of their excellent long-range reconnaissance aircraft to search for targets prior to attacks being mounted, tokko pilots awaiting word from Ki-46 "Dinah," C6N "Myrt," and D4Y "Judy" crews that vessels had been sighted. Upon discovery of a suitable warship, the scout would transmit course, speed, and composition of the target back to airfields on Formosa or mainland Japan. This would in turn prompt kamikaze pilots to man their aircraft and take off, having first received details on what course to steer in order to reach their target interception point. Whenever possible, the scout would shadow the ship for as long as it could so as to give the attackers the best chance of finding their target. Such a tactic came with an element of risk for the scouts, which were occasionally intercepted and shot down by enemy fighters despite the excellent speed and high-altitude performance of aircraft such as the "Dinah" and "Myrt."

The C6N "Myrt" high-altitude reconnaissance aircraft was frequently used in support of tokko missions, scouting for targets and reporting their locations for fighters and bombers following in its wake. Thanks to the "Myrt's" outstanding range, the aircraft could also remain in the area and report on the results of the ensuing attacks. Less than 500 C6Ns were delivered to the IJNAF by Nakajima. (NARA)

Upon reaching the expected interception point, a variety of methods were used by the attackers to locate their target. The groups comprising better-trained pilots would split up to mount a search pattern shaped like a Japanese fan, with individual aircraft undertaking sector search on pre-assigned headings until the target was located. This information was then relayed to the rest of the attacking aircraft, which would all head independently towards the located target before attacking individually.

This tactic was used on several occasions off Okinawa, including on April 11, 1945 when 13 "Zekes" of the 5th Kenmu-tai targeted TF 58. The aircraft, each carrying a 1,102lb bomb, split up as they arrived over Kikaijima Island north of Okinawa and commenced a fan-shaped search to the south. A number of pilots reported that they had located their targets and were going in to attack Allied ships, although only two managed to strike the destroyer USS *Kidd* (DD-661) and the battleship USS *Missouri* (BB-63) at 1410hrs and 1443hrs, respectively (see Chapter 5 for details).

The Japanese also refined their tactics after studying accounts from pilots whose sole job it was to observe and then report on kamikaze attacks. Most of the time, aviators undertaking such missions flew a fighter that was part of a group of aircraft providing close escort for tokko, and they observed attacks from a distance. However, on occasion, the aircraft involved were dedicated reconnaissance types or scout-bombers. The latter also took on the role of lead navigator thanks to them being multi-crewed, guiding the inexperienced tokko pilots to their targets. Very rarely, they too became tokko themselves.

By reporting on attacks and making it back to be debriefed, these aviators and crewmen were able to describe the results of the attacks, the enemy's response, and the effectiveness, or otherwise, of the actions taken by the attackers and defenders. Such accounting allowed the Japanese to know what worked and what did not, giving tokko units the chance to refine or adjust their tactics for future attacks. Unfortunately, these reports, for whatever reason, tended to overinflate the success of the attacks. This had historically been a problem for the Japanese since the opening days of the Pacific War, and it frequently resulted in ships that had not been attacked at all being listed as damaged, while light damage was often exaggerated to the point where vessels were noted as having been sunk. In the case of the tokko campaign, this led the Japanese high command to believe the kamikaze

30 DESPERATE SUNSET

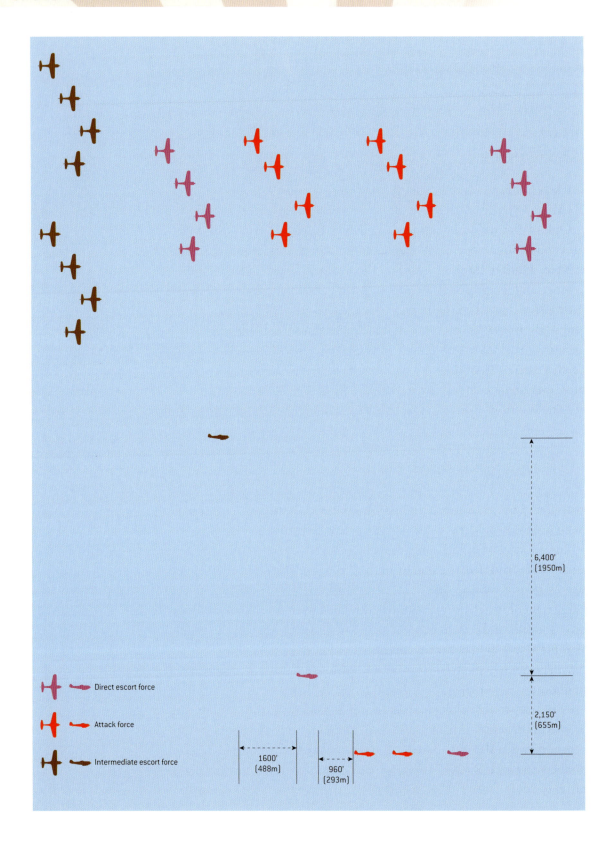

DIAGRAM LEFT
The fighter escorts had three objectives to fulfill when escorting tokko unit formations. Because so many of the kamikaze pilots were inexperienced, the escorts would guide them to their targets. The direct escort force would fly alongside or among the tokko aircraft as guides. The intermediate escort force and the direct escort force would attempt to clear a path for the tokko aircraft through the Allied CAPs. Assuming the tokko aircraft made it through to their targets, the escort force was instructed to observe and report on the results achieved, before returning to base.

---

attacks were more effective than they really were, and encouraged the IJNAF and IJAAF to increase the scope of the campaign.

One of the refinements to tokko tactics based on experience with earlier operations was the use of increased numbers of attackers whenever possible. During the early part of the campaign, particularly in late October and early November 1944, the Japanese sometimes regularly sortied small numbers of aircraft to attack, with predictably meager results. By the latter part of November the numbers of attackers per operation had started to increase, and the Japanese started to pool together aircraft from different tokko units to form a larger, coordinated force, eventually culminating in the massed, numbered Kikusui attacks off Okinawa from April 6 through to June 22, 1945.

TOKKO ORDNANCE

From the outset, it was determined that the aircraft tasked to carry out tokko attacks would need to carry explosive ordnance to improve the results of a successful crash into an enemy vessel. As the early tokko strikes quickly demonstrated, an aircraft hitting even a relatively small warship such as a destroyer or destroyer escort did relatively little damage, given that it was constructed much more lightly than the vessel it was crashing into. Indeed, only the aircraft's heavy engine block, in the right circumstances, could penetrate through steel hulls or decks. Nevertheless, this still was not enough to put a ship out of action or, on most occasions, significantly impair its fighting ability.

Therefore, aircraft assigned to tokko operations almost always carried explosive ordnance. This was mostly bombs, although on occasion torpedoes were also carried if the aircraft was cleared to do so. The numbers and type of bomb depended on what the aircraft was capable of carrying, the range to the target, and what was available at the time.

A6M5 "Zeke" Type 99 No. 25 Model 1 551lb Bomb

The A6M5 model "Zeke" could carry ordnance weighing up to 1,102lb on a single centerline rack. Typically, however, the aircraft would be armed with a single Type 99 No. 25 Model 1 551lb bomb as seen here. The body of this weapon consisted of one piece of machine-forged steel three-quarters of an inch in thickness. It was threaded in the nose to receive a fuze. The after end of the body was threaded internally to accommodate a male base plate. The latter was drilled centrally to receive the tail fuze. The weapon's tail cone was secured to the base plate by six screws. Four fins were welded to the tail cone and braced by a single set of box-type struts. The bomb body was filled with Type 91 (Trinitroanisol) explosive. Designed in 1938 and adopted by the IJNAF the following year, the Type 99 No. 25 Model 1 bomb was capable of penetrating 50mm of armor before exploding. (Artwork by Jim Laurier, © Osprey Publishing)

The most common ordnance employed by the tokko was the 551lb class bomb, of which the Japanese had several sub-types. The IJNAF called a weapon of this weight class the No. 25 Model 1 Bomb, which was further divided into five sub-types with various small differences between them. Although nominally in the 551lb weight class, the sub-types varied slightly in size, with the most common being the Type 98 No. 25 Land Bomb and Type 99 No. 25 Ordinary Bomb.

The Type 98 No. 25 Land Bomb entered service in 1938 alongside the original No. 25 Model 1 Bomb, before replacing it altogether in the IJNAF arsenal soon after the Pacific War began in late 1941. The weapon's explosive power was derived from 211lb of Picric acid or Type 98 explosive inside its 72in. body, which was made of welded and riveted half-inch steel. As its name suggests, this 532lb weapon was primarily designed for attacking land targets. Out at sea, however, it was used as a high-explosive bomb, and in the early stages of the war IJNAF doctrine dictated that part of its dive-bomber strike force would carry the Type 98 No. 25 Land Bomb into action on anti-shipping missions as a flak suppression weapon for destroying shipboard antiaircraft guns or incapacitating their crews.

Despite its name, the Type 99 No. 25 Ordinary Bomb was a more specialized weapon. Also known as the semi-armor-piercing bomb, this 551lb weapon was developed to sink ships. The one-piece, machine-forged bomb body was made of three-quarter-inch-thick steel and could penetrate two-inch armor, which made it suitable for attacking the armored deck of enemy warships. As a result of its armor-piercing function, the bomb housed less explosives than the Type 98, containing 132lb of Trinitroanisol (Type 91 explosive).

The IJAAF had its own class 551lb bombs. The most common were the Types 1 and 92 high-explosive bombs, although the service also developed its own specialized anti-shipping bombs in the form of the Type 3 and Type 4. The Type 3 had full length sheet steel tail struts welded to fins, as well as a bolted internal reinforcing plate at the junction of the barrel and cone. Most IJAAF aircraft carried 551lb class weapons, although the Ki-61 "Tony" fighter was only able to carry two 220lb weapons on each of its underwing hardpoints.

Less common than the 551lb bomb was the 1,102lb weapon. The IJNAF's Type 2 No. 50 Model 1 Ordinary Bomb was a teardrop-shaped armor-piercing weapon that was sometimes carried by A6M5 Type 52 "Zekes" during the battle of Okinawa. It was also used by D4Y "Judy" dive-bombers throughout the tokko campaign. Consisting of a one-piece, machine-forged body, the Type 2 No. 50 Model 1 Ordinary Bomb was the weapon that caused such carnage on board USS *Bunker Hill* (CV-17) on May 11, 1945, when one of the bombs from the two "Zekes" that hit the carrier off Okinawa exploded inside its hangar bay among fueled and armed aircraft, killing almost 400 sailors and wounding more than 260 (see Chapter 5).

The heaviest weapon carried by the tokko was the 1,764lb Type 2 No. 80 Mk 5 Land Bomb. Not to be confused with the better-known 1,641lb armor-piercing Type 99 No. 80 Mk 5 weapon that was specially manufactured from 16in. naval shells for the Pearl Harbor attack, the No. 80 Mk 5 Land Bomb was capable of penetrating 16 inches of concrete. Designed in 1939 and issued to front-line units from 1942, this high-explosive weapon carried 842lb of Picric acid or Type 98 explosive inside its 113in. body, which was made from welded and riveted half-inch steel.

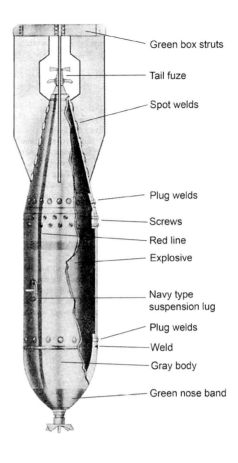

This diagram, taken from the US Army's *Technical Manual 9-1985-4 Japanese Explosive Ordnance (Army Ammunition, Navy Ammunition)*, identifies the parts that made up a 551lb Type 98 No. 25 Land Bomb – the most common weapon employed by the tokko. As per most Japanese land bombs of World War II, the Type 98 was little more than an explosive-filled thin-walled steel cylinder with a nose and tail screwed and welded on. *(NARA)*

Groundcrew cheer as the pilot of a bomb-toting A6M5 "Zeke" taxis out prior to takeoff. The official US Navy caption for this shot states that the photograph was taken during the send-off for a tokko mission in the Philippines in 1944. However, the "Zeke" is armed with a 1,102lb Type 2 No. 50 Model 1 Ordinary Bomb, which was not used by the A6M until the ill-fated defense of Okinawa in the spring of 1945. *(NARA)*

The Type 2 No. 80 Mk 5 Land Bomb was used by a number of IJNAF tokko aircraft types including the B5N "Kate," B6N "Jill," B7A "Grace," and P1Y "Frances" torpedo-bombers. This weapon was also employed on occasion by D4Y "Judy" dive-bombers, although its carriage would require the aircraft's bomb-bay doors to be removed. It was most likely a "Judy" carrying such a weapon that narrowly missed the Royal Navy carrier HMS *Victorious* on May 9, 1945, although the tremendous underwater explosion that ensued further damaged the vessel's already battered hull and eventually sent it back to Australia to be repaired in a drydock.

The Type 2 No. 80 Mk 5 Land Bomb even found itself adopted by the IJAAF, with the Kawasaki Ki-48 "Lily" and Nakajima Ki-49 "Helen" sent on tokko operations in the Philippines carrying the weapon. The twin-engined bombers were specially modified for these operations, with long metal poles protruding from the front of the aircraft that would act as a fuze-extender to trigger the weapon carried within the bomb-bay when the tokko hit its intended target.

Other types of bombs and explosive ordnance were also used during tokko operations, although on a smaller scale than those listed above. These included 132lb and 220lb bombs that were carried on occasion. Type 91 air-dropped torpedoes were also used on some tokko operations, most notably during the attack by "Jills" of the 2nd Mitate-tai on Allied warships off Iwo Jima in February 1945 (see Chapter 4). Crews flying

This lone, land-based, B6N2 was photographed just as the pilot launched his torpedo during a dusk attack on USS *Essex* (CV-9) on October 14, 1944 on the eve of the battle of Leyte Gulf. The weapon ultimately missed its target and the "Jill" fell victim to the carrier's intense antiaircraft fire. Such attacks by solitary B6N2s became more frequent following the amphibious landings on Okinawa in April 1945. *(NARA)*

these aircraft were expected to launch their torpedoes at their targets before following up with a tokko attack, instead of crashing into a ship without first dropping their ordnance like most bomb-carrying kamikaze. None of these torpedo-carrying tokko were known to be effective, and although the radar picket destroyer USS *Twiggs* (DD-591) was sunk on the night of June 16, 1945 after being hit by a torpedo and then crashed into by the bomber that dropped the weapon (see Chapter 5), this was most likely a case of an improvised jibaku attack rather than a preplanned tokko operation.

There were also some rarely seen and improvised weapons that were used a handful of times. On January 13, 1945, for example, the attack transport vessel USS *Zeilin* (APA-3) was hit off Luzon by an aircraft that left more than 100 "incendiary missiles of gas pipe construction" scattered on board, starting numerous fires that were rapidly put out (see Chapter 3). It is not known for certain what type of weapon this was, although the description fitted some types of aerial fragmentation bombs designed to be dropped over heavy bomber formations to destroy or scatter them. Another unusual modification for use in the tokko role was seen in a widely reproduced photograph of Tachikawa Ki-9 "Spruce"

These Ki-9 "Spruce" trainers were found abandoned at Kikushi airfield, near Nagasaki, after VJ Day. They had been crudely prepared for suicide missions through the installation of a drum probably full of gasoline in the rear cockpit. The aircraft closest to the camera has been marked with a typical kamikaze emblem – the cherry blossom – on its tail, along with the Kana symbol "To" for tokko and the Kazekaoru inscription "Rise on a perfumed breeze, fall in a rain of cherry blossoms." Aircraft such as these proved difficult to detect on radar due to their material composition and low-level attack profiles. They were also hard to shoot down, for both machine gun and cannon rounds simply passed through their wood and fabric fuselage and wings. (*NARA*)

biplane trainers of the IJAAF at Kikushi airfield, near Nagasaki, following the end of the war. The trainers had been found carrying single 55-gallon drums, filled with an unknown volatile fluid intended to be used as a post-crash accelerant following a tokko attack, in their rear cockpits.

DAMAGE VECTOR

Tokko pilots were trained to target the vital parts of a ship in their attacks, being taught to fight their natural instinct to close their eyes prior to the crash in order to ensure that they were clearly able to see their aiming point. The latter included the flightdeck of an aircraft carrier (a hit would impede flying operations) and the bridge or funnel(s) of other warships so as to disrupt the vessel's command and control or knock out its propulsion system. Damage to either or both would seriously affect the ship's fighting capabilities.

As previously noted in this chapter, the impact of a lightly built aircraft (or even several) was usually not enough to inflict severe damage on a ship, let alone sink it. This was particularly the case when targeting heavy cruisers and battleships. One notable exception was the unarmored flightdecks of an American carrier, which a diving Japanese aircraft could usually penetrate prior to burying itself in the hangar bay. Instead, the severity of the damage inflicted usually depended on other factors, such as the location of the hit, the explosion of the bomb or other ordnance carried by the attacker, the fire that ensued, and the triggering of secondary explosions from volatile materials such as fuel or ammunition on board the target ship. The location of the hit (or near miss, which could nevertheless cause underwater damage), and whether vital functions were affected by the resulting explosion and/or fire, also had to be taken into account when assessing the success of an attack.

The number of publicly available US Navy damage reports following tokko attacks means there is no shortage of detailed material to draw from when analyzing the effectiveness of the kamikaze campaign, and trends quickly become clear. With carriers, serious damage usually resulted from the tokko penetrating through to the hangar bay and the aircraft's bomb exploding among fueled and armed fighters and bombers chained down there, waiting to be sent up to the flightdeck for launching. Burning fuel from the tokko added to the carnage by inducing further explosions from the aircrafts' bombs, bullets, and torpedoes within the hangar bay. Just such a chain reaction caused the loss of several escort carriers and inflicted terrible damage and mass casualties on *Bunker Hill* when one of two "Zekes" that hit the vessel off Okinawa on May 11, 1945 plowed through the flightdeck and into the hangar bay, where its 1,102lb bomb detonated.

The escort carrier USS *Ommaney Bay* (CVE-79) burns furiously after being struck by a tokko (probably a Ki-45) in the Sulu Sea on January 4, 1945. The fires raged out of control and eventually detonated ordnance in the hangar deck, triggering further explosions that sunk the vessel. Tokko pilots frequently targeted carriers because their flightdecks provided them with a large area to aim for and they were poorly armored compared to other Allied warships. *(NARA)*

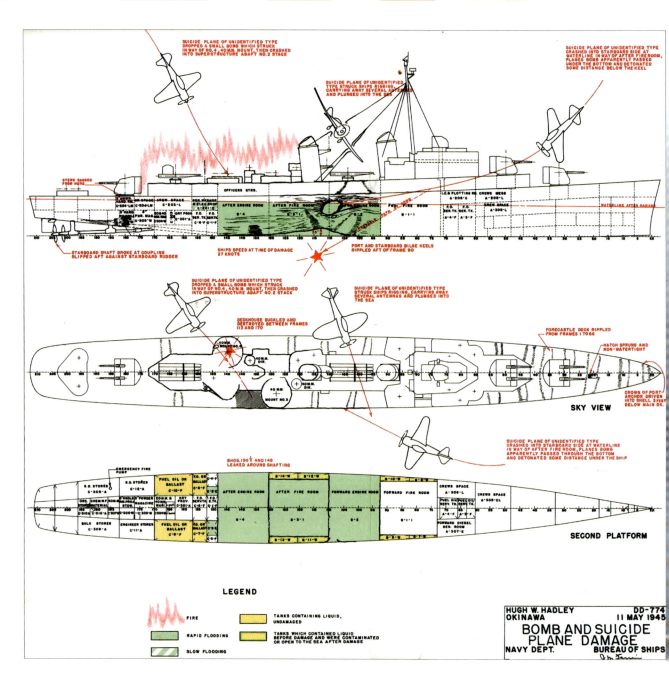

ABOVE

The US Navy produced detailed damage reports for the vessels that were hit by tokko, with this chart coming from the multi-page document created in the wake of the attack on the destroyer USS *Hugh W. Hadley* (DD-774) on May 11, 1945 while the ship was manning Radar Picket Station 15 north of Okinawa. DD-774 was hit by a bomb, two aircraft, and an Ohka, killing 30 crew. *Hugh W. Hadley*'s gunners in turn claimed 12 kamikazes destroyed. Although the destroyer survived the engagement, it was declared a constructive total loss after being towed back to San Francisco and subsequently scrapped. (*NARA*)

In contrast, USS *Randolph* (CV-15) was patched up and repaired within a month of being hit by a larger twin-engined "Frances" torpedo-bomber carrying a heavier 1,764lb bomb on March 11, 1945. The aircraft, which had flown more than 700 nautical miles from mainland Japan, crashed through the carrier's flightdeck while it was at anchor in Ulithi Atoll, in the Caroline Islands. Fortunately for *Randolph*'s crew, the "Frances" was critically short of fuel when it hit the carrier. Furthermore, CV-15's hangar bay contained aircraft that were barely fueled and not armed.

For smaller ships, such as destroyers and destroyer escorts, a direct hit often caused significant damage. Unfortunately for sailors on board these vessels, it was the "tin can" warships that bore the brunt of tokko attacks while manning the vital, but highly dangerous, radar picket stations off Okinawa, or while carrying out their general screening duties for carriers and capital ships. Very often, the impact of the aircraft and the explosion of its bomb, or the shock of a near miss, knocked out the ship's boilers and/or turbines, which in turn impeded damage control efforts and exacerbated the damage caused by a tokko strike.

Several ships were lost this way, including the destroyer escort USS *Oberrender* (DE-344), which was so badly damaged by fire off Okinawa

The US Navy's fast fleet carriers proved to be just as vulnerable to tokko as the smaller, slower, escort carriers, although unlike the latter, none were ever sunk by kamikazes. This photograph provides a graphic illustration of just how much damage a bomb-laden aircraft could inflict on a carrier and its embarked air group. Only the engines remain of more than 20 Corsairs from VF-84, VMF-221, and VMF-451 following a tokko attack by two bomb-laden "Zekes" on USS *Bunker Hill* (CV-17) on May 11, 1945 that killed 393 men and knocked the vessel out of the war. (*NARA*)

ABOVE
Unlike carriers, cruisers and battleships usually suffered only moderate materiel damage when struck by tokko, although losses among the crew (particularly gunners and, on occasion, officers and ratings on the bridge) could be high. The light cruiser USS *Columbia* (CL-56) was targeted by a Ki-51 from either the Tesshin-tai or the Sekicho-tai in Lingayen Gulf on January 6, 1945. Despite a bomb from the aircraft penetrating two decks before it exploded, the ship remained in action after this attack.

Although the fireball that engulfed *Columbia* seemed to portend severe damage, even light cruisers were protected sufficiently to make them difficult targets for tokko to sink. The typically large explosions after such impacts were caused by aviation fuel, and were not as deadly as they appeared for larger warships – with the exception of aircraft carriers. *Columbia* suffered 13 dead and 44 wounded during this attack, and it stayed on station for a further three days until it was hit again. The second strike killed a further 23 crew and wounded 97. It also inflicted sufficient damage on the battered vessel to force it to return to Philadelphia to be repaired. *(NARA)*

following a kamikaze hit on May 9, 1945 that it was deemed beyond repair and eventually sunk as a target. The escort carrier USS *Ommaney Bay* (CVE-79) was also ravaged by an uncontrollable fire following a tokko attack on January 4, 1945 while underway in the Sulu Sea, southwest of the Philippines. Several hours after the vessel had been hit, the order to abandon ship was given and the carrier sunk off Luzon by a torpedo fired by USS *Burns* (DD-588).

The smaller size of the destroyers and destroyer escorts also meant that being struck by a tokko could result in underwater damage being inflicted on the hull by the aircraft itself or exploding ordnance. In an unusual case, USS *William D. Porter* (DD-579) sank on June 10, 1945 following out of control fires and flooding caused by an underwater explosion from the bomb of an aircraft identified by the crew as a "Val" that had crashed into the sea almost immediately beneath the destroyer.

Cruisers and battleships tended to fare the best when pitted against the tokko, and hits usually inflicted little more than scant damage on these well-armored vessels. For example, the Royal Australian Navy's heavy cruiser HMAS *Australia* and the light cruiser USS *Columbia* (CL-56) both endured multiple hits while sailing off Luzon in January 1945 and continued their duties on the line. They were only replaced when the attrition suffered by the ships' personnel meant that their antiaircraft guns were left short-handed

In fact, casualties among the crew tended to be the major concern for such ships when facing the tokko – the light cruiser USS *Nashville* (CL-43) suffered 133 dead (including several senior US Army officers) and 190 wounded when it was hit while acting as the flagship of the escorts screening the Mindoro invasion force on December 13, 1944. The "Oscar" that struck the vessel's bridge was armed with two bombs, which exploded when the aircraft hit *Nashville*. Fuel from the fighter and shrapnel from its ordnance rained down onto the main deck and fully manned antiaircraft gun mounts immediately below the point of impact, resulting in more explosions from the ready ammunition stored nearby.

THE AIRCRAFT

It has often been said that the IJNAF and IJAAF used elderly and obsolete aircraft to mount tokko operations. While there is indeed an element of truth to this assertion, a look at Japanese records shows that some of the latest, most capable aircraft types then in front-line use were also utilized in the kamikaze role. These include the IJNAF's Yokosuka P1Y "Frances" twin-engined torpedo-bomber and Nakajima B6N "Jill" torpedo-bomber, while the IJAAF regularly threw Nakajima Ki-84 "Frank" fighters into the fray as tokko, both in the Philippines and off Okinawa.

NEXT PAGES
The light cruiser USS *Nashville* (CL-43) sustained heavy casualties when it was hit by a tokko during the campaign to liberate the Philippines, the vessel being struck by a bomb-armed Ki-43 "Oscar" while acting as the flagship of the escorts screening the Mindoro invasion force on December 13, 1944. No fewer than 133 crew were killed and 190 wounded when the IJAAF fighter struck the bridge and its ordnance exploded. (*NARA*)

This remarkable photograph reveals just how ineffective smaller tokko could be against warships of a certain size, even if they hit them directly. The heavy cruiser HMS *Sussex* was targeted by two Ki-51s on July 26, 1945, one of which was shot down by gunfire during its attack run. The other managed to crash into the starboard side of the ship abaft its "Y" turret just above the waterline. However, the cruiser's 4.5in. belt armor, together with the "Sonia's" light construction, meant the damage sustained by the ship was limited to dents, scrapes, and scorch marks on the side of the hull. *(Donor L. Jackman/AWM)*

At the other end of the scale, obsolete types including biplane trainers were also used, with the IJAAF's Mitsubishi Ki-51 "Sonia" army cooperation aircraft and the Nakajima Ki-27 "Nate" fighter, long replaced in front-line service by more modern machines, being routinely seen in tokko attacks. As the Okinawa campaign continued into the early summer of 1945 and aircraft shortages continued to bite, even more obsolete aircraft such as the Kyushu K11W and Yokosuka K5Y "Willow" trainers were drafted into the tokko role, and although their limited performance meant they were restricted to night attacks only, these slow-flying types were, perhaps counterintuitively, quite successful.

In addition to single-engined types, the Japanese also employed twin-engined aircraft as tokko. The IJAAF's fast-flying Ki-45 "Nick" interceptor was relatively successful over the Philippines and again off Okinawa. However, the same cannot be said for the other twin-engined types used for tokko operations, which ranged from the IJAAF's obsolete Ki-48 "Lily" light bomber to the more modern Ki-67 "Peggy" heavy bomber and the IJNAF's P1Y "Frances" torpedo-bomber. They suffered heavy losses due to their poorer performance and maneuverability, which made them more vulnerable to interception by enemy fighter CAPs and easier for antiaircraft gunners to shoot down.

Finally, the dreaded MXY7 Ohka manned aerial bomb made an appearance off Kyushu and Okinawa from March 1945, this weapon – which had the potential to be the ultimate tokko – having been conceived of desperation in the fall of 1944.

The following entries provide concise information on the wartime use of some of the more common types expended in tokko attacks.

Mitsubishi A6M "Zeke"

Unquestionably the most famous Japanese aircraft of World War II, the A6M Zero-sen (Allied reporting name "Zeke") was the standard IJNAF carrier- and land-based fighter throughout the war in the Pacific. Indeed, it participated in all the key battles fought by the IJNAF from Pearl Harbor through to the ill-fated defense of the Home Islands, with almost 11,000 examples having been built by war's end.

Development commenced on the fighter just as its predecessor, the Mitsubishi A5M "Claude," was entering service in early 1937. First seeing action over China in September 1940, the A6M was a low-wing cantilever monoplane that featured a retractable wide-track undercarriage and enclosed cockpit. Designed for long-range operations and blessed with superb maneuverability, the Zero-sen lacked pilot armor or self-sealing fuel tanks – it traded protection and robustness for agility and endurance. Nevertheless, the aircraft packed a respectable punch, with a pair of rifle-caliber machine guns alongside two wing-mounted 20mm cannon in the A6M2/3 and more powerful weaponry in later models (A6M5/7).

Despite it already being a known quantity following reports of its activity over China, the Zero-sen's excellent performance and maneuverability still gave the Allies a rude shock when they first encountered it in the skies over Southeast Asia and the western Pacific. The fighter quickly gained a fearsome reputation among Allied flyers facing their well-trained Japanese opponents. However, the Zero-sen's weaknesses were soon laid bare with the capture and recovery of a handful of nearly intact examples. Coupled with the attrition of the elite pre-war core of IJNAF aircrew, the A6M increasingly found itself outclassed by American fighters as the war went on. Despite the introduction of new, improved variants in 1943–44, the "Zeke" was essentially little different from the aircraft the Japanese went to war with in December 1941. As a direct result of this, IJNAF fighter pilots increasingly became little more than cannon fodder when engaged by their better-trained Allied counterparts in aircraft that easily outperformed the Zero-sen.

As the mainstay of the IJNAF during the war, it was not surprising that the "Zeke" should be heavily utilized for tokko missions. In fact a number of the ships sunk by kamikazes were struck by bomb-armed Zero-sens according to US Navy reports. Furthermore, the very first tokko missions were undertaken by A6M5s of the Yamato-tai off the

War-weary A6M2 "Zekes" armed with 551lb bombs, escorted by drop tank-equipped A6M5s, taxi out at Davao, on Mindanao Island, on October 25, 1944 to signal the start of the tokko campaign. After several aborted attempts over previous days, during which no targets were found, the first successful attacks took place on this date when the escort carriers of "Taffy 1" and "Taffy 3" were hit hard. (Tony Holmes collection)

Philippines in mid-October 1944 – these aircraft had been stripped of armament, radios, and other unnecessary weight and armed with a single 551lb bomb. Days later, on October 25, Zero-sens registered the first hits in tokko attacks when aircraft targeted escort carriers during the battle of Leyte Gulf. They hit USS *St. Lo* (CVE-63), which holds the unhappy distinction of being the first ship sunk in a kamikaze attack, and damaged USS *Santee* (CVE-29).

Other famous victims of "Zekes" operating as tokko include the fast carriers *Bunker Hill* and *Enterprise*, both of which were knocked out of the war after being damaged in separate strikes in May 1945. It was perhaps fitting that the last ship to be struck by a tokko – the fast attack transport USS *La Grange* (APA-124) on August 13, 1945 – was hit by a bomb-armed Zero-sen off the southern coast of Okinawa two days before the end of hostilities.

Nakajima Ki-43 "Oscar"

The "Oscar" was essentially the IJAAF equivalent of the "Zeke," sharing the latter type's general layout. Serving as the IJAAF's principal fighter throughout the Pacific War, it was first encountered by Allied forces as the Japanese swept down through Burma, Malaya, Singapore, and the Philippines. Like the Zero-sen, the Ki-43 quickly acquired a reputation for being a nimble, if somewhat fragile, opponent.

Lacking the Zero-sen's long range, the "Oscar" was also more lightly armed than its IJNAF counterpart – the fighter was initially fitted with just two cowling-mounted Type 89 7.7mm machine guns. Despite this, the "Oscar" was a popular mount among IJAAF pilots thanks to its outstanding agility. The Ki-43 quickly replaced the fixed-undercarriage Ki-27 "Nate" fighter in front-line service, seeing action in every theater to which the IJAAF was committed. Almost 6,000 "Oscars" were eventually built.

The Ki-43 was also constantly refined as the war went on, with Nakajima focusing on improving the aircraft's survivability. Compared to the IJNAF, the IJAAF was relatively quick to rectify the lack of pilot armor and self-sealing tanks fitted in its aircraft, these being added to the Ki-43 from late 1942. The revised "Oscar" not only featured Ho-103 12.5mm machine guns in place of the 7.7mm weapons, but also underwing shackles for the carriage of two 551lb bombs or fuel tanks – a capability that stood the type in good stead when the IJAAF started tokko operations.

Newly completed Ki-43-III aircraft were among the first to be used in kamikaze attacks off the Philippines in late 1944, "Oscars" equipping no fewer than seven of the 12 specially formed tokko units (each assigned

The Ki-43 eventually became the most numerous IJAAF tokko. After an uncertain start in the Philippines because of its unwillingness to commit experienced aircrew to suicide operations, the IJAAF increased the scale of its kamikaze operations in the defense of Okinawa. In this famous photograph, taken on April 12, 1945 (the day on which Kikusui No. 2 commenced), high-school girls from Chiran, in Kagoshima Prefecture, wave farewell with cherry blossom branches to kamikaze pilot 2Lt Toshio Anazawa of the 22nd Shinbu-tai. His aircraft is a Ki-43-III armed with a 551lb bomb. *(Tony Holmes collection)*

between ten and 12 aircraft) that saw action during the early stages of this ill-fated campaign. IJAAF fighter units in-theater also utilized the Ki-43 on several tokko missions in the opening stages of the invasion of Luzon, and together they achieved several successes. "Oscars" are known to have hit the battleships USS *Colorado* (BB-45) and USS *Maryland* (BB-46) and the cruisers USS *Montpelier* (CL-57), *Nashville,* and USS *St. Louis* (CL-49), as well as several destroyers and other ships.

The use of the "Oscar" as tokko continued over Okinawa, with the type operating from bases in southern Kyushu as well as Formosa. Based on available records, the Ki-43 notched up further successes there, with one damaging USS *Indianapolis* (CA-35) off Okinawa just before the landings took place on April 1, 1945. On the evening of May 20, a total of five ships were hit by "Oscars" from two tokko units flying from Kyushu and Formosa.

Aichi D3A "Val"

A key part of the IJNAF carrier-borne attack force that swept all before it in the six months following the Pearl Harbor raid, the D3A "Val" constituted the dive-bomber arm embarked in the carriers of the IJN's Kido Butai (Mobile Force). Its effectiveness as a precision bomber helped the IJNAF achieve victory after victory from December 1941 through to June 1942, as the Japanese rapidly expanded its sphere of influence in Southeast Asia and the western Pacific.

The D3A stemmed from a 1936 IJN requirement for a new monoplane dive-bomber to operate from its expanding fleet of carriers. The resulting design from Aichi featured thick elliptical wings complete with dive-brakes, and a fixed, spatted undercarriage. It was officially designated the Navy Type 99 Carrier Bomber. One of the drawbacks of the D3A was its relatively modest bombload, with the aircraft only capable of carrying a single 551lb bomb on the centerline or four 132lb weapons under the wings. However, the IJNAF's dominance of the skies during the early months of the Pacific War meant that the "Val's" bombload was not that much of a factor, as the Japanese were able to concentrate all facets of their naval air power (torpedo-bombers, level bombers, and dive-bombers) against weaker opponents during the heady days of 1941–42.

Like the Zero-sen, the D3A1 reached front-line units in 1940, and subsequently took part in operations over China before joining the Kido

Butai on its sweep across the Pacific from December 1941 until the disastrous defeat at the battle of Midway in early June 1942. By the time of the Solomons campaign the D3A was recognized as being obsolete, and the IJN's carrier air wings had discarded the aircraft in favor of the D4Y "Judy" as they attempted to work back up to strength following the losses at Midway.

During the early summer of 1942 Aichi commenced flight-testing of the D3A2, which featured a more powerful version of the Kinsai radial engine and increased fuel tankage. Despite the "Val" having been replaced on carrier decks, Aichi still built more than 1,000 D3A2s over the next three years. Relegated to shore-based operations and anti-submarine patrols, the "Val" gained a new lease of life as a tokko, being extensively used both off the Philippines and Okinawa. The D3A was also frequently misidentified as an attacker during this period when American sailors mistook it for the similar-looking IJAAF Ki-51 "Sonia" ground attack/tactical reconnaissance aircraft and Ki-27 "Nate" fighter – all three types had fixed, spatted undercarriages.

Nevertheless, the "Val" still claimed its share of successful strikes during the tokko campaign, including the sinking of the destroyer USS *Abner Read* (DD-526) off the Philippines on November 1, 1944 and several other ships off Okinawa. A Formosa-based D3A also badly damaged the destroyer escort USS *England* (DE-635), which had sunk six IJN submarines in just 12 days in May 1944, on May 9, 1945. Deemed to be not worthy of repairing, DE-635 was scrapped in November 1946.

In addition to its record as a tokko, the "Val" was also credited with the sinking of 14 Allied warships in conventional dive-bombing attacks, including the British cruisers HMS *Dorsetshire* and HMS *Cornwall*, the

The most recognizable Japanese tokko aircraft after the Zero-sen, the "Val" had been the scourge of the Allies during the early stages of the war in the Pacific. Although an outstanding dive-bomber in 1941–42, the D3A was obsolete as a front-line combat type by the summer of 1943. Having been relegated to shore-based operations (this particular D3A1 of the 33rd Kokutai is seen here being used as a pilot trainer) and anti-submarine patrols, the "Val" gained a new lease of life as a tokko off both the Philippines and Okinawa. (*Tony Holmes collection*) carrier HMS *Hermes*, the US Navy destroyers USS *Sims* (DD-409), USS *De Haven* (DD-469), and USS *Aaron Ward* (DD-483), and the RAN destroyer HMAS *Vampire*. "Vals" also played a part in the sinking of the carriers USS *Yorktown* (CV-5) during the battle of Midway and *Hornet* during the battle of the Santa Cruz Islands.

Mitsubishi Ki-51 "Sonia"

The Ki-51 "Sonia" was a two-seat ground attack/tactical reconnaissance aircraft utilized on all fronts by the IJAAF throughout the war. First flown in June 1939 and designated the Army Type 99 Assault Aircraft, it was widely deployed in support of Imperial Japanese Army (IJA) operations in the opening years of the war before obsolescence and the loss of air superiority saw the type relegated to second-line roles such as liaison and patrolling in areas devoid of Allied fighters. Almost 2,400 examples were built between September 1939 and July 1945.

Well-armored, highly maneuverable, easy to fly and maintain, and capable of being operated from small airfields, the "Sonia" proved to be a fairly effective tokko platform. Designed to carry small bombs (totaling 441lb) on multiple wing stations when supporting troops in the front line, aircraft pressed into use as tokko were frequently modified to instead carry a single 551lb bomb on a centerline station.

As previously noted in this chapter, the Ki-51's long canopy and fixed undercarriage often led to it being misidentified as the IJNAF's "Val"

The Ki-51 "Sonia" was a two-seat ground attack/tactical reconnaissance aircraft utilized on all fronts by the IJAAF throughout the war, Mitsubishi building almost 2,400 examples between September 1939 and July 1945. The Ki-51's long canopy and fixed undercarriage frequently led it to being misidentified as the IJNAF's "Val" dive-bomber by Allied sailors enduring the terrifying experience of a kamikaze attack. (*NARA*)

dive-bomber by sailors during the horrific experience of a kamikaze attack. This was totally understandable, as the aircraft looked similar when viewed from head-on in the heat of battle. Another possible reason for this frequent misidentification was the fact that Allied sailors had rarely encountered the "Sonia" prior to the tokko campaign, unlike the "Val," which had been used in the anti-shipping role as a dive-bomber from the very start of the Pacific War.

The Ki-51, therefore, has rarely been given the credit it deserves for several successful tokko attacks that included the sinking of the tanker USS *Porcupine* (IX-126) off Leyte on December 30, 1944. "Vals" were blamed for the vessel's destruction. Another successful kamikaze strike undertaken by the type was the sinking of the minesweeper HMS *Vestal* off Thailand on July 28, 1945 – the only British ship sunk in a tokko attack, and the last Royal Navy vessel to be lost in action in World War II. Its demise will be studied in more detail later in this book.

Nakajima Ni-27 "Nate"

The Ki-27 became the first monoplane fighter to enter service with the IJAAF in late 1937, Nakajima's design having been chosen over rival aircraft from Kawasaki and Mitsubishi to fulfill a requirement for an advanced monoplane interceptor issued in 1935. Like all Japanese fighters of this period, its principal attribute was maneuverability.

A low-wing monoplane with a fixed, spatted undercarriage, the Ki-27 was powered by a 650hp Nakajima Ha-1a nine-cylinder radial engine that drove a two-bladed variable-pitch propeller. Among its unique features were "butterfly" or "combat" flaps, which Nakajima fitted to all of its wartime fighters to improve their maneuverability. Further modest improvements (including the fitment of a rearward-sliding canopy and increased wingspan) were made to the fighter when it entered series production in December 1937.

By March 1938 the Ki-27 was in action over northern China, and it was swiftly recognized as an excellent fighter as the aircraft wrested control of the skies from the Chinese. The Ki-27 further proved itself in the summer of 1939 when the Japanese fought the Soviet Union in the region called variously Khalkin-Gol or Nomonhan, on the Manchukuo/Outer Mongolia border. Again, the type gave a good account of itself when pitted against well-flown Soviet Polikarpov monoplane and biplane fighters.

The Ki-27 "Nate" was another front-line type that was thoroughly obsolete by 1944, the fixed-undercarriage fighter serving mainly as an advanced trainer when the tokko campaign commenced. However, with more than 2,000 examples having been built, the IJAAF had a ready supply of "Nates" – as well as less-powerful open-cockpit Mansyu Ki-79b trainers (1,329 built) based on the Ki-27 – available for use as tokko off Okinawa. The Ki-27s were duly modified to carry a single 551lb or 1,102lb bomb to attempt to increase their ability to damage enemy ships. (*Tony Holmes collection*)

However, even though five "Nate"-equipped units were deployed with great success in support of the campaigns in the Philippines, Malaya, Burma, and the Dutch East Indies during the early months of the Pacific War, and the fighter continued to serve in China and provide the main air defense for the Japanese Home Islands until 1943, the type was thoroughly obsolete by 1944 and serving mainly as an advanced trainer when the tokko campaign commenced.

Despite this, "Nate" fighters, along with less-powerful open-cockpit Mansyu Ki-79b trainers based on the Ki-27, were pressed into service as suicide attackers off Okinawa. The aircraft were modified to carry a single 551lb or 1,102lb bomb like the "Sonia" in an effort to increase their ability to damage enemy ships. This modification meant both performance and maneuverability were adversely affected, although the type still managed to strike successful blows on the rare occasions that they evaded the attention of marauding fighters. For example, the damage sustained by the USS *Gregory* (DD-802), USS *Sterett* (DD-405), and USS *Rall* (DE-304) off Okinawa in mid-April 1945 was as a result of "Nate" hits during tokko attacks.

Yokosuka D4Y "Judy"

Intended as a replacement for the D3A "Val," the D4Y "Judy" was one of the fastest dive-bombers to see service during the war. Development began in 1938, and the aircraft was beset with problems principally with

its Aichi AE1 Atsuta inline engine (a license-built version of the Daimler-Benz DB 601A) but also with wing flutter that caused wing spar cracks during dive-bombing test flights. The latter issues prevented the D4Y1 from being used as a dive-bomber when it entered service in 1942.

The first handful of production aircraft joined the IJNAF in time to take part in the battle of Midway, with a pair embarked on board the carrier *Soryu* as reconnaissance aircraft (both were lost when the vessel was sunk). The D4Y1 was finally cured of its wing flutter issues through the fitting or reinforced wing spars and improved dive-brakes, which meant that the type was accepted into service as a dive-bomber in late April 1943. Ongoing reliability and servicing issues with the Atsuta finally saw the IJNAF instruct Yokosuka to replace the inline engine with a Mitsubishi MK8P Kinsei 62 radial in early 1944, resulting in production of the D4Y3 from May of that same year.

In service, and following the modifications previously noted, the "Judy" proved to be an excellent dive-bomber. It carried a much heavier bombload than the "Val," with the internal bomb-bay being able to carry a 1,102lb bomb (the dedicated D4Y4 tokko variant could even accommodate a 1,764lb weapon following the removal of its bomb-bay doors – 246 examples were built between February and August 1945). Flight performance was also good, with the type capable of outpacing the F4F Wildcat, although not the later generation of American fighters – namely the F4U Corsair, F6F Hellcat, P-38 Lightning, P-47 Thunderbolt, and P-51B/C/D/K Mustang.

The "Judys" based in the Philippines were heavily committed to tokko attacks at the start of the campaign in October 1944. Indeed, they were responsible for hits on the fast carrier USS *Essex* (CV-9), the escort carrier USS *Kitkun Bay* (CVE-71), and the heavy cruiser USS *Louisville* (CA-28). In February 1945, IJNAF Special Attack (Kamikaze) Unit D4Y3 construction number 3957 was one of a number of "Judys" captured by US forces after they had seized Clark Field, north of Manila. Rebuilt over a period of several months, this aircraft was eventually flight tested by USAAF and US Navy pilots in the Philippines prior to being scrapped there. (*NARA*)

By the time the "Judy" entered fleet service in adequate numbers Japan's fortunes were already inexorably waning in the Pacific. Despite its qualities, the type suffered high losses due to the overwhelming superiority of American fighters in-theater combined with the poor quality of IJNAF aircrew training – carrier-based D4Y units were decimated during the battle of the Philippine Sea in June 1944. Nevertheless, the "Judy" enjoyed a modicum of success as a conventional dive-bomber, primarily flying from land bases in the Marianas, Formosa, the Philippines, and Japan.

When the tokko campaign started, the Philippines-based D4Ys were heavily committed to the initial attacks, where they were responsible for hits on the fast carrier USS *Essex* (CV-9), the escort carrier USS *Kitkun Bay* (CVE-71), and the heavy cruiser USS *Louisville* (CA-28). The type was also involved in attacks off Okinawa, Iwo Jima, and the Japanese Home Islands, with a Formosa-based "Judy" helping to send the carrier *Victorious* to the drydock after the underwater explosion from its 1,764lb bomb caused severe damage to the vessel's already battered hull off Okinawa on May 9, 1945.

Nakajima B5N "Kate"

The B5N was the result of a 1935 specification issued by the IJNAF for a monoplane torpedo-bomber to replace the biplane Yokosuka B4Y. Nakajima's prototype completed its first flight in January 1937, and the aircraft was ordered into production shortly thereafter, following its selection over the Mitsubishi B5M1 torpedo-bomber in competitive trials.

In addition to serving as a torpedo-bomber, the B5N was also used as a conventional (horizontal) bomber. Indeed, the type made its operational debut in this role in 1938 during the Sino-Japanese War, where combat experience revealed several weaknesses in the original B5N1 production model – principally a lack of protection for the crew and fuel tanks. However, instead of adding armor to the B5N, which would have had an adverse impact on performance, the IJNAF instead ordered Nakajima to fit a more powerful 1,000hp Sakae 11 engine in an attempt to make the resulting B5N2 faster than its adversaries.

Although the changes only offered minimal improvements in performance, and its weaknesses remained, this version replaced the B5N1 in production and service from 1939. It was the type Cdr Mitsuo Fuchida, leader of the Pearl Harbor strike force, flew in during the attack

An obsolete B5N1 hastily pulled from a training unit departs from an undisclosed airfield at the start of its final flight – a tokko mission against a US aircraft carrier task force off Okinawa in the spring of 1945. Being slow, especially when armed with a torpedo, and not overly agile, the "Kate" was not well suited to the role of kamikaze aircraft. Indeed, officially at least, the aircraft's first dedicated Special Attack mission occurred as late as April 1945, although B5N2s had in fact conducted ad hoc tokko attacks on US Navy warships during the defense of the Philippines. (Tony Holmes collection)

in December 1941. Furthermore, it was a B5N2 that was responsible for delivering one of the 1,764lb armor-piercing bombs the Japanese had had specially machined for the raid that hit the battleship USS *Arizona* (BB-39) and penetrated its magazine, triggering the explosion that sunk the battleship.

Known to the Allies by its codename "Kate," the B5N was also instrumental in the IJNAF's success in the opening months of the Pacific War. Carrier-borne examples torpedoed *Lexington*, *Yorktown*, and *Hornet* at the battles of Coral Sea, Midway, and the Santa Cruz islands, respectively, all three vessels subsequently sinking.

By 1944 the "Kate" had been replaced in front-line service by the B6N "Jill," although it continued to provide sterling service in second-line roles such as long-range reconnaissance, anti-submarine warfare, and crew training. Although not officially committed to the tokko effort until April 1945, B5N2s conducted ad hoc kamikaze attacks on US Navy warships during the liberation of the Philippines. Both B5N1s and 2s were expended off Okinawa on at least 20 separate occasions in the final months of the war, with as many as 16 specially formed kamikaze units including varying numbers of "Kates" within their ranks. It was almost certainly a bomb-laden B5N2 that hit USS *Zellars* (DD-777) during Kikusui No. 2 on April 12, 1945, forcing the destroyer to return to the USA for repairs.

Nakajima B6N "Jill"

The IJNAF had issued a request for a replacement for the B5N as early as 1939, seeking a three-seat carrier-borne torpedo-bomber with a top speed of 288mph and a range of 1,000 nautical miles with a 1,764lb bombload. The new aircraft, designated the B6N by the IJNAF, was aerodynamically similar to the B5N, but its Nakajima NK7A Mamoru 11 14-cylinder air-cooled radial engine produced 1,870hp – 80 percent more than the Sakae 11 in the "Kate."

Constrained by carrier stowage restrictions, Nakajima's design team was forced to use a wing that was similar to the B5N's in both span and area, despite the new aircraft (given the Allied reporting name "Jill") being considerably heavier than the "Kate." This meant that the B6N would suffer from a high landing speed and wing loading, restricting its fleet use to larger carriers. Flight testing commenced in the spring of 1941, whereupon it was soon found that the design was plagued by serious engineering flaws – including directional stability issues caused by the powerful torque of the aircraft's four-bladed propeller. To solve the latter problem, Nakajima had to move the vertical tail surfaces two degrees to the left. Teething troubles with the Mamoru 11 engine also delayed the test program, which meant that the B6N1 was not accepted for production until February 1943.

After completing just 133 B6N1s through to July 1943, Nakajima was instructed by the Ministry of Munitions to cease production of the Mamoru 11 to allow the company to concentrate on building the more

Among the many aircraft used by the IJNAF for tokko attacks was the B6N2 Carrier Attack Bomber. Designed as a carrier-based aircraft to replace the B5N "Kate," it was capable of torpedo or bombing attacks. With a top speed of 299mph and the ability to carry a 1,764lb payload, the "Jill" was a capable kamikaze platform. Here, a Type 91 air-dropped torpedo-equipped B6N2 from the Kikusui-Tenzan Kokutai is having its engine run up to full power prior to taking off from Kanoya airfield on a tokko mission in May 1945. *(Photo by Yasuo Tomishige/The Asahi Shimbun via Getty Images)*

widely used Sakae and Homare engines. Fitted with the Mitsubishi MK4T Kasai 25 rated at 1,850hp, the re-engined "Jill" was designated the B6N2. A total of 1,133 B6N2s would be completed by Nakajima between June 1943 and August 1945.

When the B6N finally became operational, in New Guinea, from December 1943 it proved to be largely ineffective due to the air superiority established by advanced US Navy carrier-borne fighters. Land-based "Jills" fought in the Marshall and Gilbert islands, in the defense of Truk and in the First Battle of the Philippine Sea. Carrier-based units also participated in the latter action in June 1944, losing a considerable number of aircraft in the "Great Marianas Turkey Shoot." Surviving examples were brought together four months later for the IJN's final carrier action during the Second Battle of the Philippine Sea (also known as the battle of Leyte Gulf), and again losses for the IJNAF were catastrophic. Formosa-based B6N2 units continued to attack Allied ships until late October 1944, when most remaining "Jills" were sent to the Philippines in an effort to repel invading American forces.

Like the "Kate," many surviving "Jills" were used as kamikaze platforms by at least eight tokko units during the final ten months of the Pacific War. Indeed, the B6N2 proved to be more effective in this role than its predecessors thanks to its increased top speed. "Jills" were known to have sunk at least three destroyers and badly damaged the veteran carrier USS *Saratoga* (CV-3) – the latter, targeted on February 21, 1945 during the battle of Iwo Jima, was hit by five bombs dropped in a conventional attack by six "Jills," three of which then flew into the vessel.

Yokosuka P1Y "Frances"

The development of what would become the P1Y "Frances" fast medium bomber commenced in 1940 following the issuing of a specification by the IJNAF for an aircraft capable of carrying out low-altitude, torpedo- and dive-bombing attacks. The Dai-Ichi Kaigun Koku Gijitsusho was tasked with producing a bomber that rivaled the performance of the Junkers Ju 88, North American B-25 Mitchell, and Martin B-26 Marauder. The aircraft was expected to have a top speed of more than 345mph, and unlike previous IJNAF bombers, it would be fitted from the start with protected fuel tanks – eight in total, with a further six unprotected. Armor for the three-man crew consisted of a single 20mm

The P1Y1 fast medium bomber was used both conventionally and as a kamikaze platform, enjoying some success in the latter role during the campaign in the Philippines. A handful of examples also took part in the one-off long-range night mission that saw crews target US Navy vessels at anchor in Ulithi Atoll, 700 nautical miles from mainland Japan, on March 11, 1945. *(NARA)*

plate behind the pilot's head, and unlike its German and American contemporaries, the P1Y had only single flexibly mounted guns in the nose and rear cockpit positions. Capable of carrying either a single 1,764lb torpedo semi-internally beneath the fuselage or two 1,102lb bombs in a ventral bomb-bay, the P1Y, like the de Havilland Mosquito, had to rely on speed for its survival.

Powered by a pair of 1,820hp Nakajima Homare 11 18-cylinder radial engines, the first of six prototype P1Ys was completed in August 1943 and made its maiden flight shortly thereafter. The aircraft's impressive top speed and maneuverability proved popular with test and service pilots alike, and principal constructor Nakajima immediately commenced production of the P1Y1. However, the bomber's hydraulic system and immature engines proved troublesome for groundcrews, resulting in the IJNAF refusing to accept the P1Y1 for service use until October 1944 – by then 453 aircraft had been built.

Among the changes made to the P1Y1 in an attempt to improve its reliability was the fitment of two 1,825hp Homare 12 radials, but the engines remained problematic. The weapons installed in the aircraft also varied, with flexible 20mm Type 99 Model 1 cannon being fitted in the nose and dorsal positions on some airframes, and others featuring 13mm Type 2 machine guns on single or twin mountings.

Five kokutai would eventually be equipped with the P1Y1, flying missions from land bases in China, Formosa, the Marianas, the Philippines, the Ryukyu Islands, Shikoku, and Kyushu from late 1944. The bomber was used both conventionally and as a kamikaze platform, and had some success in the latter role during the Philippines campaign. A more unusual tokko attack involving the P1Y1 saw a handful of examples sent on a long-range night mission to target US Navy vessels at anchor in Ulithi Atoll on March 11, 1945. Having flown more than 700 nautical miles from mainland Japan, the crews dropped their ordnance before one aircraft was flown through the flightdeck of the fast carrier *Randolph*. More P1Ys were expended from April 1945 during the largescale tokko attacks synonymous with the Okinawa campaign.

Nakajima Ki-84 "Frank"

Even as the Ki-43 was entering service in 1941, the IJAAF set about looking for a replacement fighter, recognizing the need to combine the agility of the Ki-43 with performance and firepower to match the latest western fighters that were under development. Nakajima, the manufacturer of the "Oscar," was assigned this task, and its Ki-84 first flew in March 1943 – a little more than 18 months after its predecessor had made its combat debut.

Codenamed "Frank" by the Allies, the Ki-84 addressed the most common complaints emanating from the front line about the popular and highly maneuverable Ki-43 – insufficient firepower, inadequate defensive armor, and a poor rate of climb. The most common armament fit for the "Frank" comprised two 12.7mm Ho-103 fuselage-mounted,

A formation of Ki-84s from the 101st Sentai prepares to take off on a mission from Miyakonojo, on the island of Kyushu, in 1945. The 101st was heavily involved in escorting IJAAF tokko-tai targeting ships off Okinawa. *(Dr. Yasuho Izawa)*

heavy machine guns and a pair of 20mm Ho-5 cannon in the wings. Some even heavier armament fits were tried (with four cannon in the wings), but these were not produced in significant numbers.

The compact, but powerful, Nakajima Ha-45-21 Homare radial engine was supercharged, with water injection for boost, turning a four-bladed propeller that saw the second prototype reach a speed of 387mph in level flight during testing. In the spring of 1945 a captured late-production example tested by the USAAF in the Philippines attained 422mph using 92 octane fuel and aided by methanol injection. Defensive armor was also fitted for the pilot and self-sealing fuel tanks installed in the wings – both rare luxuries for a Japanese combat aircraft.

While the design itself was sound, growing difficulties in securing high quality fuel and materials, and lack of adequate manufacturing facilities as the tide of the war turned against the Japanese often prevented the aircraft from reaching its full potential in the field. By January 1945 surviving aircraft in the Philippines were being rapidly expended into tokko operations, with the last ship to be hit in-theater – the escort carrier USS *Salamaua* (CVE-96) – being struck by a "Frank" carrying two 551lb bombs on the morning of January 13, 1945. The resulting damage was extensive enough for the vessel to have to be sent to San Francisco to be repaired.

The Ki-84 continued to be used in tokko operations off Okinawa, equipping specially formed dedicated kamikaze units as well as ad hoc flights established within regular IJAAF fighter regiments. Three of the four ships hit on the night of April 27 were almost certainly attacked by Formosa-based "Franks," while the battleship USS *New Mexico* (BB-40) was hit by a Japan-based aircraft on the evening of May 12. A quick-fire attack in the space of a few minutes saw four more Ki-84s from another Japan-based tokko unit sink two ships (although one was a gutted victim of a previous tokko attack) and badly damage a third on the evening of June 21.

Kawasaki Ki-61 "Tony"

With the distinction of being the only mass-produced Japanese fighter to use a liquid-cooled inline engine, the Ki-61 was designed in response to a late 1939 IJAAF request for two new fighters, each to be built around the Daimler-Benz DB 601A engine. Production aircraft would use a license-built DB 601 known as the Kawasaki Ha-40. When the IJAAF

decided to proceed with the Nakajima Ki-44 "Tojo" as its main high-speed, high-altitude interceptor, the heavier Ki-60 was abandoned and Kawasaki was ordered to focus its efforts on the smaller Ki-61. This aircraft was intended for use mainly in an offensive, air superiority role at low-to-medium altitude.

The first prototype of the Type 3 Fighter, Model 1 made its maiden flight in December 1941, and although test pilots were enthusiastic about its self-sealing fuel tanks, upgraded armament, and good performance in a dive, the aircraft was viewed with some skepticism by many of the IJAAF's senior officers. They still believed there was a place for light, highly maneuverable and modestly armed fighters. In response, Kawasaki staged flight trials between two Ki-61 prototypes and the Ki-43, a pre-production Ki-44-I, a defector-flown Soviet LaGG-3, a German Messerschmitt Bf 109E-7, and a captured Curtiss P-40E Warhawk. The Ki-61 emerged as the fastest of all of these fighters, and it was inferior only to the Ki-43 in respect to its maneuverability.

Some of the early pre-production examples were encountered by B-25 crews during the Doolittle raid on Tokyo on April 18, 1942, where they tried, unsuccessfully, to intercept the American bombers. Deliveries of

Initially, the Ki-61 was used exclusively as a conventional fighter by the IJAAF during the campaign in the Philippines. However, in the wake of the American amphibious landings on Okinawa in April 1945, Formosa- and Japan-based tokko units immediately employed the "Tony" in attacks on Allied ships. With its enhanced protection and performance, the Ki-61 proved to be relatively successful in tokko operations, although the fighter's destructive force was restricted by its inability to carry larger bombs on its underwing stations. (Dr. Yasuho Izawa) aircraft to front-line units commenced in February 1943, and the Ki-61 (given the Allied reporting name "Tony") first saw combat two months later in New Guinea. Here, the extreme weather conditions associated with operations in-theater, coupled with a lack of spare parts and the usual "teething" issues associated with operating a new type quickly undermined the efficiency of both men and machines.

The main problem afflicting the Ki-61 was its engine, which required even more precise and sophisticated manufacturing standards in order for it to run properly than its German-built progenitor. Attaining these standards proved difficult for Japanese manufacturers hamstrung by raw materials of variable quality. Furthermore, front-line units were forced to run their Ha-40s on low-octane fuel and keep them lubricated with poor quality oil. Poor serviceability of the high-performance engine duly ensued, particularly in New Guinea.

Nevertheless, the Ki-61 gave a good account of itself in combat when not afflicted by mechanical problems, with its impressive performance allied with a decent armament fit that typically included two wing-mounted 12.7mm Ho-103 machine guns and a pair of 20mm Ho-5 cannon in the nose. However, with the Japanese stretched thin, the air war in New Guinea inevitably came to an end when attrition grounded all remaining Japanese air assets in-theater. The "Tony" also saw extensive service during the disastrous defense of the Philippines, although only as a conventional fighter. Like the rest of the Japanese air power committed to this campaign, the Ki-61 units were wiped out. Other Special Attack units, serving in the Home Defense role against the B-29s that began appearing over Japan from the late summer of 1944, started using the "Tony" in ramming attacks against the bombers. By the time the Okinawa campaign commenced, Formosa- and Japan-based tokko units had also started using the type against Allied ships.

With its enhanced protection and performance, the Ki-61 proved to be relatively successful in tokko operations, even though it was restricted to carrying smaller bombs on its underwing stations. The "Tony" was responsible for sinking the Landing Ship (Medium) *LSM-135* on May 25, 1945, and Ki-61s also damaged the escort carrier USS *Sangamon* (CVE-26), the troop transport USS *Gilmer* (APD-11), the high-speed destroyer minesweeper USS *Macomb* (DMS-23), and the Landing Ship (Tank) *LST-599*, as well as several other ships.

Kawasaki Ki-45 "Nick"

In response to the emergence in Europe of twin-engined heavy fighters such as the Messerschmitt Bf 110, the IJAAF ordered development of a similar two-seat fighter in 1937, with Kawasaki assigned the task of developing an aircraft to meet the requirement. The first Ki-45 prototype flew in January 1939, but it failed to meet the expectations of the IJAAF due to its underpowered, failure-prone Ha-20 Otsu radial engines. Despite this, development continued, and eventually resulted in further improvements, including the fitment of the powerful 1,080hp Mitsubishi Ha-102. The Ki-45 Kai (Improved) entered service in February 1942 as the Type 2 Two-Seat Fighter, being given the Allied reporting name "Nick." A total of 1,700 Ki-45s would be built through to July 1945.

The IJAAF, like other air arms utilizing twin-engined, two-seat fighters as long-range bomber escorts, quickly found the Ki-45 poorly suited to that role. It was subsequently used as a ground attack and anti-shipping aircraft in theaters such as New Guinea and the Philippines, where it was marginally more successful. However, like the Bf 110 in Europe, the "Nick" found its greatest success as an interceptor of heavy bombers, with its heavy cannon armament (single 37mm Ho-203 and 20mm Ho-3 weapons and a flexible 7.92mm machine gun) being especially effective.

This Ki-45 KAIc nightfighter, fitted with two obliquely mounted upward-firing 20mm Ho-5 cannon in the center fuselage, was found at Clark Field along with a number of other "Nicks" when the base fell to US Army troops in early February 1945. The Ki-45 was one of the most effective types to be employed on tokko operations by the IJAAF, with the aircraft being responsible for the sinking of several ships and inflicting serious damage on a handful of other vessels off the Philippines and Okinawa. *(NARA)*

When USAAF B-29s started to attack Japan in the late summer of 1944, the "Nick" was again found to be relatively ineffectual due to the altitudes at which the Superfortresses operated, bar some successful interceptions that included ramming attacks.

The Japanese utilized several twin-engined types as tokko from the inception of the campaign to the end of the war, again with limited success. They tended to be bombers (mostly Ki-48s, Ki-67s, and P1Ys, along with a handful of assorted nightfighter or reconnaissance aircraft), although these proved to be highly vulnerable to Allied CAPs when sortied on Special Attack missions. The exception was the "Nick," which sank a number of ships and damaged several more off the Philippines and Okinawa. This was likely due to its smaller size and greater agility in comparison with other twin-engined types and, being fitted with self-sealing fuel tanks and crew armor, it was harder to bring down.

Comparing Japanese and American reports, it can be surmised that the escort carrier *Ommaney Bay*, the high-speed troop transport USS *Ward* (APD-16), and the destroyers USS *Mahan* (DD-364) and USS *Drexler* (DD-741) were all sunk as a result of being hit by Ki-45s on tokko missions. The type was also almost certainly responsible for the damage inflicted on the escort carrier *Sangamon* as well as the destroyer USS *Hughes* (DD-410) and the destroyer escort USS *Sederstrom* (DE-31), in addition to several other ships. This list of successes proves that the Ki-45 was one of the most effective types to be employed on tokko operations.

Yokosuka MXY7 "Baka"

By the late summer of 1944, the Japanese cause in World War II had become so desperate that it resorted to the development of specialized suicide or kamikaze aircraft to repel Allied invasion fleets. The IJNAF requested the creation of a rocket-powered, manned flying bomb that was to be air-launched from a G4M2e Model 24J "Betty" or other heavy bombers. This revolutionary weapon became known as the Yokosuka MXY7 Ohka ("Cherry Blossom"), which was given the Allied reporting name "Baka" ("Fool" or "Idiot") bomb. The MXY7, which was the brainchild of the 405th Kokutai's Ens Mitsuo Ohta and the University of Tokyo's Aeronautical Research Institute, successfully performed an unpowered (glide) flight in October 1944 and a successful powered flight the following month.

TACTICS AND AIRCRAFT

The MXY7 first saw combat during the US invasion of Okinawa, examples being air-launched via "Betty" bombers at the US invasion fleet with the intent of sinking or badly damaging as many capital warships as possible. While the "Bakas" were successful in sinking several destroyers and badly damaging a minesweeper, they failed to score any hits on larger vessels due to the US Navy's timely application of defensive measures. These included the effective deployment of vectored carrier fighter aircraft to intercept and shoot down the "Betty" parent aircraft carrying the MXY7s and the use of barrage antiaircraft fire from radar picket destroyers to prevent the rocket-propelled suicide aircraft from scoring direct hits on aircraft carriers, battleships, or cruisers.

On April 12, 1945, nine "Betty" bombers launched a successful "Baka" attack on the US fleet off Okinawa, sinking the destroyer USS *Mannert L. Abele* (DD-733) and causing so much damage to the high-speed destroyer minesweeper USS *Jeffers* (DMS-27) that it was put out of commission. Twenty-two days later, a "Betty" air-launched MXY7 scored a direct hit on the bridge of the destroyer minelayer USS *Shea* (DM-30), badly damaging the ship and inflicting a heavy loss of life among its crew. Finally, on May 11, another "Baka" attack resulted in the destroyer USS *Hugh W. Hadley* (DD-774) being put out of commission. A total of 852 MXY7s had been built by war's end.

This MXY7 Ohka was one of a number of fully assembled manned aerial bombs found in jungle hideaways by the US Marine Corps following the capture of Yontan airfield, on Okinawa. Several destroyers were sunk and a minesweeper badly damaged by Ohkas that had been air-launched from "Betty" bombers at the US invasion fleet off Okinawa. Although Yokosuka had built 852 MXY7s by war's end, only a small percentage of the rocket-powered manned aerial bombs had been expended in combat. *(NARA)*

MXY7 Ohka

SPECIFICATIONS

Crew – one pilot

Allied codename – "Viper" or "Baka" (popular nickname)

Length – 20ft

Wingspan – 16ft 5in.

Weight – 4,416lb

Propulsion – Glider with three electrically ignited Type 4 Mark 1 Mod 20 rockets

Fuel – 500 Special FDT-6 monoperforated, double-base solid propellant

Rocket thrust – 1,500lb average, 4,500lb maximum, 9.7-second duration

Warhead – Tekkou armor-piercing steel case warhead

Warhead fuzes – A-3 nose fuze, Model 1 base impact fuze, and Model 2 all-way action fuze

Warhead weight – 2,645lb, with 1,135lb of Type 91 Trinitroanisol explosive

Range – maximum 48 nautical miles when released from 27,000ft; average range in combat was 3.5–5.25 nautical miles

Speed – 540–600mph in terminal phase

(Artwork by Ian Palmer, © Osprey Publishing)

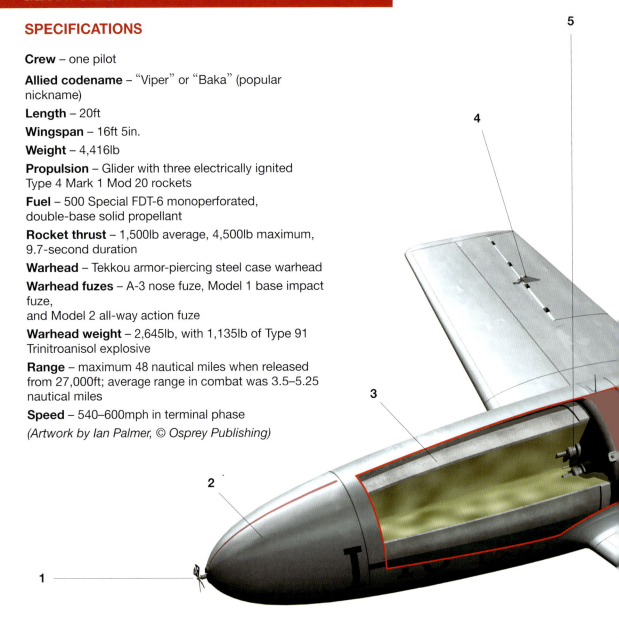

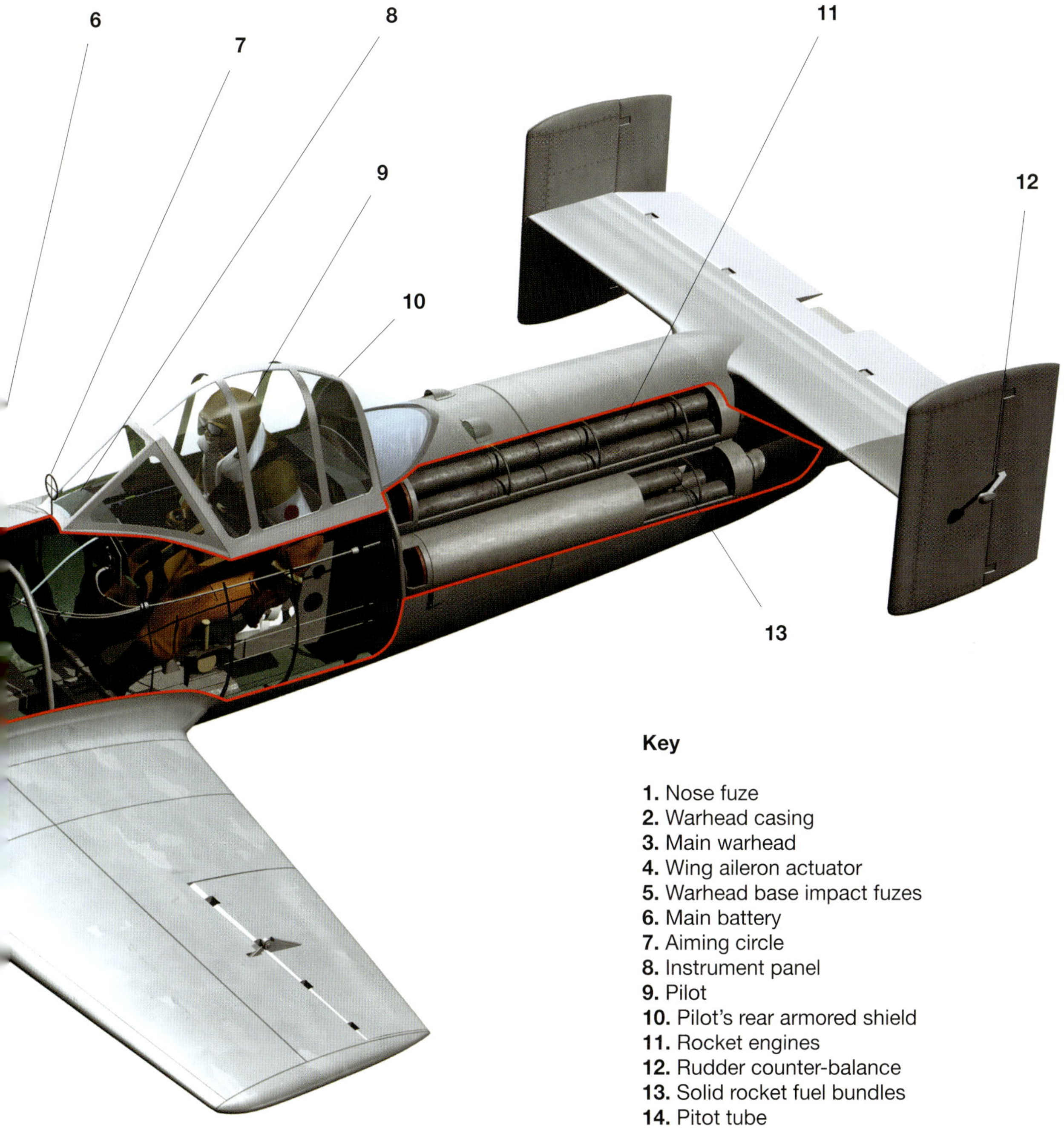

TACTICS AND AIRCRAFT

Key

1. Nose fuze
2. Warhead casing
3. Main warhead
4. Wing aileron actuator
5. Warhead base impact fuzes
6. Main battery
7. Aiming circle
8. Instrument panel
9. Pilot
10. Pilot's rear armored shield
11. Rocket engines
12. Rudder counter-balance
13. Solid rocket fuel bundles
14. Pitot tube

CHAPTER 3
THE PHILIPPINES

By September 1944, American forces were less than 270 nautical miles southeast of Mindanao, the largest island in the southern Philippines, and were able to attack Japanese positions there using long-range bombers flying from recently captured airfields in western New Guinea. Troops under Gen Douglas MacArthur, Supreme Commander of Allied Forces in the Southwest Pacific Theater of Operations, had either overrun, isolated, or bypassed all of the remaining IJA strongholds in New Guinea and the Admiralty Islands.

Meanwhile, American naval forces under Admiral Chester W. Nimitz, Commander in Chief, US Pacific Fleet, and Commander in Chief, Pacific Ocean Areas, had advanced across the central Pacific Ocean, capturing the Gilbert Islands, some of the Marshall Islands, and most of the Mariana Islands. With US Navy submarines taking a frightful toll of Japanese merchant shipping at the same time, it meant that garrisons like Rabaul could be bypassed and left "to wither on the vine," with no source of supplies and military capability.

The Allies were now ready for the next stage of the campaign against Japan. Senior officers in the US Navy wanted to seize the port of Amoy, on China's east coast, along with Formosa, while MacArthur was adamant that the Philippines had to be the priority. In July 1944, President Franklin D. Roosevelt met with MacArthur and Nimitz in Hawaii, where the decision was made to invade the Philippines. The Joint Chiefs of Staff ordered MacArthur to plan an attack on the southern Philippines for the end of 1944, with Luzon to follow in early 1945.

Over the summer and fall of 1944, following the invasion and seizure of the Marianas, aircraft from carriers of the US Navy's Third Fleet, commanded by Admiral William F. Halsey, carried out several successful missions over the Philippines and found Japanese resistance to be decidedly lacking. Halsey then recommended a direct strike on

The damage inflicted by the tokko that hit *Australia's* foremast at 0605hrs on October 21, 1944 can be seen in this photograph taken shortly after the attack. Fortunately for the ship, the bulk of the wrecked aircraft fell into the sea after clipping the cruiser's superstructure. *(Royal Australian Navy)*

Having led the US Navy's Third Fleet in several key actions in the Pacific during the summer and early fall of 1944, Admiral William F. Halsey was in charge of TF 38 throughout the campaign to liberate the Philippines. He recommended a direct strike on Leyte ahead of other planned operations, with October 20, 1944 chosen as the date of the main landing. *(NARA)*

Leyte ahead of other planned operations, with October 20 chosen as the date of the main landing. Preliminary operations in preparation for the assault began early that same month, with the US Navy's fast carrier-equipped TF 38 (previously TF 58 when part of Fifth Fleet), again under Halsey, gathering off the southeastern coast of Formosa. It duly carried out a series of air strikes against airfields around Takao that were aimed at reducing the ability of the Japanese to fly reinforcements to the Philippines.

Unsurprisingly, the IJNAF in particular retaliated ferociously, with daily attacks against TF 38 between October 10 and 14. These met with little success, however. At twilight on the 13th, the Essex-class carrier *Franklin* was recovering eight fighters from a CAP when five bombers identified as "Bettys" were sighted emerging from a rain squall on its port side at an altitude of between 50 and 75ft. These were almost certainly from either the 703rd or 708th Hikotai of the 763rd Kokutai, which expended its entire strength in similar attacks between October 12 and 14. One "Betty" was driven off by gunfire from the carrier's escorts, but the remaining four pressed home their torpedo attacks, two torpedoes narrowly missing their mark.

The first of the attackers approached on a relative bearing of 270 degrees, and although it was hit repeatedly by the ship's antiaircraft batteries and set on fire, the bomber continued to close on the carrier and released a torpedo at a distance of about 500 yards that passed under the fantail. Although his aircraft was burning fiercely, the pilot of the "Betty" attempted to crash into *Franklin*. Striking the ship "on the flightdeck just abaft the island, the bomber slid across the flightdeck and appeared to explode upon striking the water on the starboard beam." The carrier emerged from this attack virtually unscathed, however, with its damage report noting that "the flightdeck was gouged in several places by the propeller of the plane as it skidded across the deck and three 20mm guns were temporarily put out of commission," adding that "necessary repairs were made by the ship's force."

The escorting Atlanta-class light cruiser USS *Reno* (CL-96) was also hit by a torpedo-bomber, identified as a B6N "Jill," on its fantail at

1711hrs the following day, although it too suffered only light damage that included the No. 6 twin five-inch turret being partially incapacitated.

The main invasion of Leyte proper began a week later on October 20, with a force of four cruisers and six destroyers of Commodore John Collins' RAN/US Navy TF 74 being part of the invasion fleet that included the heavy cruisers HMAS *Australia* and HMAS *Shropshire* as well as the destroyers HMAS *Warramunga* and HMAS *Arunta*. The ships had shelled targets ashore from dawn on the 20th in the lead up to the amphibious landings, and once the latter commenced they positioned themselves to provide gunfire support and attack targets of opportunity throughout the day,

The next morning saw the task force covering the landings from a position just off the invasion beaches when, out of the predawn murk, a small group of aircraft were spotted approaching against the still-dark skies to the west from the direction of Leyte Island. They were promptly engaged by *Shropshire* at 0600hrs, which claimed hits on at least one aircraft that the ship's lookouts reported skimmed the water before recovering and heading back westward.

At 0605hrs this aircraft, or another from the same group, was sighted by lookouts on board *Australia* diving at an angle of ten to 15 degrees from about 2,000 yards astern. The shallow approach angle meant that most of the heavy cruiser's antiaircraft weapons could not be trained low enough at sufficient speed to hit the aircraft. Nevertheless, a handful of gunners scored several hits on the attacker, which was identified as a "Val," prior to it tearing into the foremast of the ship and the bulk of the wreckage falling into the sea. In the words of *Australia*'s official history, "there was a large explosion and an intense fire was started in the air defense position and bridges. Type 273 radar hut and lantern fell onto the compass platform; both H.A. [High Angle] Directors and D.C.T. [Director Control Tower] were put out of action and the port strut of the foremast was broken."

Although the fire itself was swiftly brought under control, 30 of *Australia*'s officers and crew had been

The bridge and forward superstructure of the heavy cruiser HMAS *Australia* in September 1944. This area was badly damaged when a tokko (described as a "Val" by eyewitnesses) collided with the ship on October 21, 1944 while it was sailing off Leyte. The ship's commanding officer, Capt Emile Dechaineux (seen here in the white uniform, facing right), was among the 30 officers and crew who were either killed or mortally wounded in the attack. *(Gordon Herbert Short/AWM)*

killed or mortally wounded, including Capt E. F. V. Dechaineux (who was disembowelled by shrapnel and died several hours later). A further 65 were wounded to varying degrees, among them Commodore Collins – he did not resume his command until July 1945.

Some historians have claimed that this was the first ever tokko attack, although more recent research has refuted this, ascribing the TF 74 strike to six IJAAF "Sonia" light attack aircraft from the 6th Hikodan (Flying Brigade) based at San Jose airfield on the island of Mindoro, some 240 nautical miles northwest of Leyte. As noted in the previous chapter, the more famous D3A and the virtually unknown Ki-51 and obsolescent Ki-27 were frequently misidentified by Allied sailors in the heat of battle.

Following the attack, *Australia* headed for the Kossol Passage, in Palau, in company with *Warramunga* and the damaged light cruiser USS *Honolulu* (CL-48), which had been hit by an aerial torpedo during the Leyte invasion – they were escorted by the destroyer USS *Richard P. Leary* (DD-664). On October 24 the Australian ships proceeded to Manus, in the Admiralty Islands, and then Espiritu Santo for repairs, rejoining the Allied fleet off the Philippines in early December. *Australia* subsequently endured more tokko attacks, and these are detailed later in this book.

October 21 was also the day the Dai-ichi Kamikaze Tokubetsu Kogekitai (First Kamikaze Special Attack Group) began operations. Unlike the novice pilots who were expended in later attacks, the aviators of the Dai-ichi Kamikaze Tokubetsu Kogekitai had seen varying degrees of combat. Among its ranks was the ranking IJNAF ace WO Hiroyoshi Nishizawa, although he was not selected to be one of the tokko pilots. This new unit was further subdivided into smaller flights, with one of these, the Yamato-tai, moving south to Cebu in preparation for its first attacks. This was mounted by a single A6M5 flown by Lt(jg) Yoshiyasu Kuno against US Navy vessels located east of Leyte Gulf. Kuno took off from Cebu at 1625hrs on the 21st and nothing further was heard from him, nor were any Allied ships hit by

Two four-inch Mk XVI turrets (foreground), a 40mm Mk VIII "pom-pom," and what appears to be a solitary four-inch Mk V high-angle gun can all be seen pointing skyward as HMAS *Shropshire* bombards Biak Island with its eight-inch MK VIII weapons in May 1944. Observers on board the heavy cruiser claimed that the ship's gunners hit the tokko prior to it striking *Australia* on October 21. "It was taken under fire and retired westward. The aircraft was reportedly hit and touched the water, but it then recovered. It then turned east again, and although under heavy fire, passed up the port side of *Australia* and crashed into the ship's foremast at 0605hrs." (Royal Australian Navy)

The RAN heavy cruisers HMAS *Shropshire* (left) and HMAS *Australia* (right), with an unidentified US Navy heavy cruiser behind, were photographed through a ring gunsight on board USS *Phoenix* (CL-46) shortly after the tokko attack off Leyte on October 21, 1944. *(NARA)*

tokko that day (*Australia* had been struck early in the morning). On the 23rd another "Zeke" from the Yamato-tai, flown by CPO Kaoru Sato, left Cebu on a tokko mission, although he returned to the airfield after failing to locate any targets.

The following day the 33-year-old fleet tug USS *Sonoma* (AT-12) became the first ship to be sunk directly as a result of being hit by an aircraft. This unfortunate vessel had entered Leyte's San Pedro Bay as part of Task Unit (TU) 78.2.9 on October 20. Allied ships had been repeatedly attacked by Japanese aircraft since the invasion had begun, and on the morning of the 24th a flight of "Bettys" attacked the fleet – this was not a planned tokko strike. One headed straight for *Sonoma*, which was lashed alongside the Liberty ship SS *Augustus Thomas* taking on fresh water. The tug's crew tried desperately to cast off as both ships opened fire on the bomber with their antiaircraft guns, setting the aircraft aflame as it aimed for the vessel.

According to eyewitnesses, the burning "Betty" clipped *Sonoma*'s stack and crashed into the water, its bombs exploding as it did so. The underwater explosion holed both ships, and the aviation fuel that drenched *Sonoma* caught fire. The blaze was soon raging out of control, and although a landing craft and harbor tug attempted to assist in fighting the fire as *Sonoma*'s crew tried to beach the tug, it sank in shallow water before it could be run aground.

On the morning of October 24, 1944, the 33-year-old fleet tug USS *Sonoma* (AT-12) became the first ship to be sunk directly as a result of being hit by an aircraft (albeit in a jibaku attack rather than a pre-planned tokko strike) when vessels from TU 78.2.9 were targeted by "Betty" bombers in Leyte's San Pedro Bay. Holed by a bomb that exploded nearby and set ablaze by aviation fuel from the crashing G4M, *Sonoma* was quickly engulfed in flames despite the best efforts of its crew and assistance from fleet tug USS *Chicksaw* (ATF-83) and USS *LCI(L)-72*. (NARA)

Despite the loss of the veteran vessel, a greater disaster was averted as the *Augustus Thomas* was carrying 3,000 tons of ammunition and 1,000 barrels of high octane fuel at the time of the attack. Had these exploded, the results could have been devastating for other vessels in San Pedro Bay. Thanks to the skill of its crew, the freighter was successfully beached with no fatalities, despite the engine room having been flooded after a hole was punched into the hull beneath its waterline from the "Betty's" exploding ordnance. The identity of the attacking G4M2A remains unknown, and its demise was almost certainly the result of an impromptu jibaku attack rather than a planned tokko mission.

The dedicated Special Attackers did not have to wait long to claim their first scalp, however. Together with the remnants of the IJN's once proud surface fleet, the tokko units took part in what is known today as the battle of Leyte Gulf on October 25. Under the overall strategy known as the Sho-1 plan, the Japanese fleet was flung against the powerful invasion forces arrayed around the Leyte Gulf in a bid to derail the

invasion of the Philippines. The ships were backed up by whatever air power could be mustered by the IJNAF.

During the predawn hours the first waves of tokko took to the air tasked with finding enemy ships. Elements of the 1st Kamikaze Special Attack Corps at Davao swung into action at 0630hrs with five A6M5s being sent aloft, each armed with a Type 99 No. 25 Model 1 551lb on its centerline. Asahi-tai (a single aircraft flown by PO2c Keiichi Ueno), Yamazakura-tai (two "Zekes" flown by PO2cs Kenichi Miyahara and Mitsuo Takizawa), and Kikusui-tai (two "Zekes" flown by PO2cs Toyofumi Kato and Masa Miyakawa) disappeared into the darkness in search of targets.

Off Leyte, first light saw the escort carriers and their accompanying destroyers and destroyer escorts of Task Group (TG) 77.4, under the command of Rear Admiral Thomas Sprague, sailing east of the Philippines as they provided close air support for the invasion force. TG 77.4 was split into three Escort Carrier Task Units known as "Taffys," with each "Taffy" consisting of four to six "baby flattop" escort carriers and a

Vice Admiral Shigeru Fukudome (right), commander of land-based naval air forces in the Philippines, toasts some of the first tokko pilots sent into action during the last week of October 1944. Hopelessly isolated from Japan and with few aircraft and no hope of survival, pilots readily volunteered for Special Attack missions during the campaign in the Philippines. *(Tony Holmes collection)*

number of screening destroyers. They were to have been covered by the fast carriers of TF 38, but Admiral Halsey had taken all five of them and five light fleet carriers (with more than 600 aircraft between them), six fast battleships, eight cruisers, and more than 40 destroyers north to engage what turned out to be a Japanese decoy force, leaving the invasion fleet to fend for itself.

The southern component of the three sub-groups, TU 77.4.1 or "Taffy 1" under the direct command of Rear Admiral Sprague himself, found itself off the northeastern coast of Mindanao Island that morning. At 0545hrs "Taffy 1," consisting of the escort carriers *Sangamon*, *Santee*, USS *Suwannee* (CVE-27), and USS *Petrof Bay* (CVE-80), launched an air strike against the remnants of the IJN's Southern Force that had been severely mauled overnight during the battle of Surigao Straits. At 0658hrs an urgent message came from TG 77.4's northern component, "Taffy 3," that Japanese surface forces had been sighted and assistance was required for it was coming under attack from what turned out to be the battleships, cruisers, and destroyers of Admiral Takeo Kurita's Center Force.

At 0702hrs permission was given for "Taffy 1's" outgoing strike to attack this new target instead, and four minutes later additional aircraft were launched to engage the Center Force. This meant that by 0740hrs, when the first tokko spotted the carriers of "Taffy 1," the latter had been totally shorn of air cover. Moments later, according to official Japanese records, the Asahi-tai aircraft flown by Ueno slammed into *Santee*'s flightdeck just forward of its elevator, starting fires both here and in the hangar bay. A torpedo fired by the Japanese submarine *I-56* caused further damage to the vessel, although *Santee* had declared itself operational again by 0900hrs.

Immediately after the tokko struck *Santee*, both *Sangamon* and *Petrof Bay* were near-missed by other attackers, with the former's tokko being hit by gunfire from *Suwannee* while in its death dive. At 0759hrs *Suwannee* engaged another aircraft sighted flying astern of the carrier at 8,000ft, the tokko then rolling over and diving into its flightdeck. The resulting explosion and fire caused serious damage to the flightdeck and hangar bay, although the fires were rapidly extinguished and the vessel made operational again by 1030hrs.

The aircraft that targeted "Taffy 1" that morning were almost certainly the five A6M5s that had taken off from Davao before dawn, the tokko pilots having taken Sprague's vessels by surprise. Although they had inflicted damage on two escort carriers and killed a number of crew on both ships as the kamikaze drew first blood, far worse was to come for "Taffy 3" to the north.

It had already endured a torrid morning under the guns of Kurita's Center Force, which included the super-battleship *Yamato*. Only a tenacious fight by TU 77.4.3, which included the valiant self-sacrifice of some of its screening destroyers, dogged air attacks by aircraft from all three "Taffys" and hesitation on the part of Kurita enabled "Taffy 3" to escape total annihilation. But survive it did. In fact TU 77.4.3 actually managed to dish out more damage to the Center Force than it received during what became known as the battle off Samar, sinking three IJN heavy cruisers in exchange for the loss of the escort carrier USS *Gambier Bay* (CVE-73), the destroyers USS *Hoel* (DD-533) and USS *Johnston* (DD-557), and the destroyer escort USS *Samuel B. Roberts* (DE-423).

In the immediate aftermath of this engagement "Taffy 3's" aircraft complement had been significantly reduced because many of the fighters, dive-, and torpedo-bombers launched against the Center Force that

OPPOSITE
Vice Admiral Takijiro Onishi (left), commander of the First Air Fleet in the Philippines in October 1944, was also on hand to provide words of encouragement for one of the early groups of tokko pilots flying from Mabalacat West airfield. *(NARA)*

78 DESPERATE SUNSET

MAP LEFT

The Japanese first employed tokko in their ill-fated defense of the Philippines from October 1944 through to January 1945. Initial attacks concentrated on US Navy forces located in Leyte Gulf and to the east. In December the US Navy moved into Ormoc Bay, to the west of Leyte, and immediately came under repeated tokko attack. Moving through the Sulu Sea, the Americans landed on Mindoro on December 15. This invasion force was also subjected to an intense kamikaze reaction. The heaviest suicide attacks of the campaign, however, came against the US Navy's large invasion fleet undertaking the amphibious landings on Luzon in January 1945. For ten days warships were subjected to numerous suicide attacks as they entered Lingayen Gulf. The last attacks of the campaign were conducted on January 13, after which the IJNAF and IJAAF had exhausted their supply of aircraft.

---

morning had had to land at Leyte's Tacloban airfield to refuel and rearm. This meant that the Casablanca-class escort carriers USS *Fanshaw Bay* (CVE-71), USS *St. Lo* (CVE-63), USS *White Plains* (CVE-66), USS *Kalinin Bay* (CVE-68), and *Kitkun Bay* were short of fighter CAPs (and screening destroyers, following the loss of *Hoel* and *Johnston*) when, at 1050hrs, spotters on board CVE-71 sighted five aircraft headed for "Taffy 3" at low altitude, crossing the carrier's bow from port to starboard.

These were the "Zekes" of the Shikishima-tai, which had taken off from Mabalacat at 0725hrs under the leadership of Lt Yukio Seki. Each of the five tokko was carrying a single 551lb bomb, and they were escorted by four more A6M5s, one of which was flown by ace WO Hiroyoshi Nishizawa. The attackers, a mixed force of older A6M2s and new A6M5s drawn from the 201st Kokutai, were immediately fired upon after being sighted, and the tokko pilots responded by climbing rapidly before initiating their final dives on their individual targets. A single attacker went after *Kitkun Bay*, the pilot rolling his fighter onto its back at the top of its climb and aiming for the carrier's island, firing

This amazing photograph was taken during the late morning of October 25, 1944 when the IJNAF commenced its tokko attacks on the escort carriers of "Taffy 3." This bomb-armed "Zeke" was one of two that targeted USS *White Plains* (CVE-66), their attack runs being thwarted by the carrier's antiaircraft fire and deft maneuvering – note how the flightdeck is angled to port, indicating a late turn to starboard to throw the pilot's aim off. The latter had approached the vessel from the starboard quarter, and is seen here in the process of turning to the right in an attempt to hit the carrier. The aircraft missed the ship, but hit close aboard along the portside. The shock from the "Zeke's" exploding 551lb bomb was severe enough to force the combat-weary carrier home for repairs. *(NARA)*

A6M2 "Zeke" of the Shikishima-tai, Mabalacat, Luzon, October 25, 1944

This aircraft, armed with a Type 99 No. 25 Model 1 551lb bomb on a centerline mounting, was one of the A6M2 "Zekes" from the Shikishima-tai led aloft by Lt Yukio Seki to attack the escort carriers of "Taffy 3" on the morning of October 25, 1944. The aircraft's tail code 02-888 indicates that it was originally assigned to the 201st Kokutai. The war-weary A6M2s were escorted by four A6M5 fighters. (Artwork by Jim Laurier, © Osprey Publishing)

his guns as he did so. However, instead of hitting the island the "Zeke" struck a glancing blow on the ship's port catwalk before crashing into the sea about 25 years off the port bow, its bomb exploding as it hit the water. One sailor was killed and a further 16 were wounded when the aircraft hit the catwalk.

Two more tokko set their sights on *White Plains*, whose gunners threw up a hail of lead and caused one of them to break off his run. The remaining

USS *St. Lo* (CVE-63) is seen from USS *Kitkun Bay* (CVE-71) shortly after it was hit by a Zero-sen from the 201st Kokutai's Shikishima-tai on October 25, 1944. The pilot that targeted the escort carrier conducted a skilful attack, approaching over the stern and dropping his 551lb bomb before the aircraft hit amidships and skidded off the flightdeck. The bomb penetrated to the hangar and caused fires and explosions there, as shown in this view. Less than 30 minutes after being hit, the carrier rolled over and sank with the loss of 113 crew – a further 30 subsequently perished because of their injuries following the sinking. *St. Lo* was the first ship to be sunk in a dedicated tokko attack. (NARA)

pilot pressed on with his dive despite the gunfire directed at him, splashing into the sea just off the carrier's port stern and scattering fragments down its port side and across the flightdeck. These wounded 11 crewmen. This attack has been immortalized on film in a series of photographs taken from on board the ship, clearly showing the dark green Zero-sen in a slight diving turn to starboard as it attempted to strike the ship.

Minutes later the 201st Kokutai's Shikishima-tai inflicted its most significant hit of October 25 on *St. Lo*. One of the attacking "Zekes" had peeled off from the formation and turned towards the ship just as the remaining tokko flew abeam to its starboard side, and it was quickly taken under fire by the carrier's starboard gun batteries. The latter had no effect on the aircraft – identified as a "Zeke 52" – as it approached at very high speed and, according to the ship's loss report tabled by skipper Capt Francis J. McKenna, crossed the ramp at little more than 50ft. The pilot "appeared to push over sufficiently to hit the deck at about the No. 5 [arrestor] wire. There was a tremendous crash and flash of an explosion as one or both bombs [carried by the 'Zeke'] exploded. The plane continued up the deck, leaving fragments strewn about and its remnants went over the bow."

Capt McKenna's first impression following the hit was that no serious damage had been inflicted on his ship – there was a hole in the flightdeck with smoldering edges, which soon erupted into flames. However, he soon noted that:

USS *Kitkun Bay* (CVE-71) was more fortunate than its sister-ship *St. Lo* on October 25, the escort carrier only being struck a glancing blow by a "Zeke" in the attack that sunk CVE-63. A short while later a "Judy" made a run on *Kitkun Bay* from astern, although the carrier's antiaircraft batteries scored several hits on the diving bomber. The D4Y burst into flames, as seen here, and broke up just prior to falling into the sea close to the ship. Several fragments, including the aircraft's horizontal stabilizer assembly, hit the vessel. *(NARA)*

Still wearing his steel helmet, a gunner manning one of the deck edge 20mm Oerlikon guns on board *Kitkun Bay* stares intently at the severed tail section of the "Judy" tokko that he and his shipmates had shot down in flames a short while earlier. It appears that this aircraft had in fact been initially acting as a pathfinder/observer for the Shikishima-tai "Zekes" that attacked "Taffy 3" that day, prior to its pilot conducting an unsuccessful jibaku against CVE-71. *(NARA)*

Smoke was coming through the hole from below, and that smoke was appearing on both sides of the ship, evidently coming from the hangar. I tried to contact the hangar for a report, but was unable to do so. Within 60 to 90 seconds an explosion occurred on the hangar bay, which puffed smoke and flame through the hole in the deck and, I believe, bulged the flightdeck aft of the hole. This was followed in a matter of seconds by a much more violent explosion, which rolled back a part of the flightdeck and burst through aft of the original hole. The next heavy explosion tore out more of the flightdeck and also blew the forward elevator out of its shaft.

The first explosions after the initial hit were caused by three TBM Avengers that had only just been refueled and rearmed in the hangar bay when a bomb from the "Zeke" detonated. More fires and explosions followed shortly thereafter. By 1100hrs, less than ten minutes after the aircraft struck, Capt McKenna decided that the ship could not be saved. At that point in time, the after part of the carrier was barely discernible from the bridge through the smoke and flames, and all on-board communication had been lost except for the sound-powered phones and word of mouth among the crew. Orders were given to prepare to abandon ship and to stop all engines, with evacuations commencing minutes later.

By then the ship had taken on a heavy list to port. However, following further explosions (a total of eight explosions were recorded, including the initial one from the bomb carried by the "Zeke"), it rolled over to starboard and sank by the stern at approximately 1123hrs – almost exactly 30 minutes after it had been attacked. Off the 889-man crew on board, 113 were killed and a further 30 died of their injuries after the sinking. It has been said the Lt Seki himself was responsible for the sinking of *St. Lo* based on testimony from Nishizawa, although this has been disputed by other sources.

Within 15 minutes of *St. Lo* being sunk, more tokko had found and targeted "Taffy 3," with *Kalinin Bay* coming under attack from three "Zekes" just after 1100hrs. Having already borne the brunt of the Center

Force's attacks earlier that morning (it had sustained 15 shell hits that had caused substantial damage without affecting its watertight integrity or machinery spaces), CVE-68 had initially received further attention from a lone Shikishima-tai aircraft at around the same time as *St. Lo* was hit. The tokko was shot into the sea off the carrier's starboard bow by the ship's gunners.

This new trio of "Zekes" approached *Kalinin Bay* from the stern and began their attack runs one after the other. The first tokko was hit repeatedly by antiaircraft fire from the ship, and it was smoking when the fighter crashed through the port side of the flightdeck. According to the ship's action report, it created "two large holes and several small ones" in the flightdeck, wrecking two longitudinals below and starting several fires that were quickly extinguished. The second attacker approached in a steep glide and also successfully hit the carrier, wrecking the aft port stack and adjacent catwalks. The third pilot missed the carrier and crashed into the sea. Miraculously, despite the pounding the ship had been subjected to throughout the morning from both the IJN's Center Force and IJNAF tokko, casualties were light – five dead and 55 wounded.

USS *Kalinin Bay* (CVE-68) enters San Diego harbor on November 25, 1944, one month after narrowly escaping disaster off Samar when it survived 15 shell hits from IJN warships of the Central Force and being struck twice by tokko aircraft while assigned to "Taffy 3." Three "Zekes" had attacked CVE-68 from astern and the starboard quarter, with antiaircraft fire downing one of them close aboard. The second fighter crashed into the port side of the flightdeck, damaging it badly, and the third destroyed the aft port stack and adjacent catwalks. (NARA)

ABOVE
Crews manning quadruple Bofors 40mm cannon mounts on the light carrier USS *Independence* (CVL-22) undertake gunnery practice. The US Navy's standard intermediate-range antiaircraft weapon, the Swedish-designed Bofors gun was the best weapon of its type during the war and it had a solid record of being able to successfully engage aircraft undertaking conventional air attacks. Against tokko, however, the 40mm gun lacked the hitting power to be entirely successful. *(NARA)*

Just as the stricken *St. Lo* was sinking, yet another tokko targeted "Taffy 3" when a D4Y "Judy" made a run on *Kitkun Bay* from astern. Antiaircraft fire scored several hits on the diving bomber, which broke up as it fell into the sea close to the ship. Several fragments hit the vessel, including the aircraft's horizontal stabilizer assembly that landed on the flightdeck. Although *Kitkun Bay* had sustained little further damage, four more crewmen were added to the list of wounded from the earlier tokko attack.

It has frequently been assumed that all of the tokko attacks on "Taffy 3" that day were mounted by Shikishima-tai. However, the number of aircraft involved would seem to indicate that a second tokko unit was also involved. Based on Japanese records, the tokko that attacked *Kalinin Bay* and *Kitkun Bay* from astern were almost certainly from the Yamato-tai. Led by CPO Kazuo Otsubo, a handful of "Zekes" had departed Cebu at 0900hrs with a "Judy" acting as a pathfinder/observer.

The tokko action for October 25 was almost at an end following the D4Y attack on *Kitkun Bay*, save for "Taffy 1" reporting another failed suicide attack on *Santee* at 1220hrs that saw the aircraft "driven off by ships' gunfire." Japanese sources state the Wakazakura-tai carried out this particular attack, having despatched four "Zekes" from Cebu at 1140hrs – a fact seemingly corroborated by US Navy reports that this attack was carried out by a quartet of aircraft. With this action ended the first contact between the tokko units and their enemy, with the damage inflicted on the US Navy by this new tactic totaling one escort carrier sunk and four damaged to varying degrees. While a seemingly modest haul, this still represented a significant proportion of the losses suffered by the US Navy during the battle of Leyte Gulf. The results of October 25 would have also assured Vice Admiral Onishi and other proponents of the tokko that their decision to adopt such tactics had been more than justified.

Dawn the next day saw the battered Japanese fleet disengaging the scene of the battle, with the tokko now being exclusively tasked with taking the fight to the US Navy. Among the first examples thrown into action on October 26 were five A6Ms, and two pathfinders/escorts, of the Yamato-tai that launched again from Cebu in two waves at 1015hrs and 1230hrs. The formations were led by Ens Masahisa Uemura and CPO Tomisaku Katsumata, respectively.

The first wave found "Taffy 1" 70 nautical miles east of Surigao, and at 1240hrs *Suwannee*, having been hit the day before, suffered more

Even more than the 40mm Bofors gun, the 20mm Oerlikon cannon (the US Navy's standard light antiaircraft weapon) was found to be ineffective against tokko since its projectiles – which weighed just 0.27lb – were unable to break up incoming aircraft. Capable of targeting aircraft up to 10,000ft, the Oerlikon cannon had a rate of fire of 450 shells per minute. (NARA)

damage when one of the attackers slammed into its flightdeck near the forward elevator as the carrier was recovering Avengers. Several parked aircraft that had just landed back on board were destroyed by the "Zeke," which also inflicted yet more damage on the already-mauled escort carrier when its bomb exploded. The bridge and island structure were both damaged and, unlike the attack of the previous day, the flightdeck was put out of commission. The carrier was left dead in the water as more tokko tried, unsuccessfully, to hit *Petrof Bay* and *Sangamon*. Despite the damage, *Suwannee* was soon underway again, making five knots by 1300hrs and 18 knots less than 20 minutes later, by which time all the fires had been extinguished. Both *Suwannee* and *Santee* retired from the battle that night so that further repairs could be effected, and they would not rejoin the fleet until January 1945.

The Japanese launched several ineffectual tokko attacks on October 27–28 as TF 38's fast carriers mounted a series of strikes across Luzon. The IJNAF was more successful on the 29th when Rear Admiral Gerald F. Bogan's TG 38.2, comprising the carriers USS *Intrepid* (CV-11), USS *Hancock* (CV-19), USS *Bunker Hill* (CV-17), USS *Cabot* (CVL-28), and USS *Independence* (CVL-22), came under attack from "Vals" shortly after noon following air strikes on Mabalacat West airfield. Only *Intrepid* was hit, despite its attacker being picked up on radar as the dive-bomber approached. Sighted very late as it bore in from the ship's starboard quarter, the D3A was only engaged by the carrier's lighter 20mm cannon. Nevertheless, gunners managed to hit the "Val" repeatedly, causing it to partially disintegrate. The pilot lost control at this point in his attack, which almost certainly threw off his aim. The "Val" skimmed the flightdeck, its right wing hitting Gun Tub No. 10 on the port side of the ship before crashing into the water.

Intrepid's Gun Tub No. 10 was a segregated battery of 20mm guns manned by African American steward's mates under the command of a Mexican American non-commissioned officer. The "Val's" wing killed ten and wounded six, although the damage caused by the tokko was restricted to that area. A fire started by the strike was quickly extinguished and five of the six guns that were knocked out had been repaired within an hour of the vessel being hit. *Intrepid* had had a lucky escape on this occasion, although over the course of the next few months more tokko would make CV-11 the most frequently targeted Allied ship of World War II.

Japanese records for that day indicate that a total of 18 aircraft ("Zekes," "Vals," and "Judys") from seven tokko units took off from Nichols Field, south of Manila, and targeted TG 38.2. Ten of the D3As were from the 2nd Kamikaze Attack Corps' Shisei-, Jinmu-, and Shinpei-tai, with the four "Vals" from Shisei-tai having taken off before *Intrepid* was attacked. The remaining six D3As departed Nichols Field at around 1500hrs.

Like all the other tokko units sent into action on October 29, Shisei-tai's target was a carrier task force "to the east [bearing 80 degrees] 175 nautical miles from Manila" according to Japanese records, which corresponds closely to the position noted for the strike on TG 38.2 and *Intrepid*. The latter is listed in US Navy records as having been at 15.07N 124.01E when it came under attack. This means that it was almost certainly a "Val" from Shisei-tai that struck the vessel's Gun Tub No. 10 just after noon, the dive-bomber having likely been a part of the second wave of three aircraft that departed Nichols Field at 1040hrs (a solitary Shisei-tai aircraft had previously taken off at 0945hrs). Japanese records also note that WO Yasunori Sasa's D3A was the only tokko that failed to return from this sortie.

The following day, Hazakura-tai's CPO Sei Sakita led six bomb-laden "Zekes" (with five more A6M5s as escorts) aloft from Cebu in the early afternoon and headed in the direction of a carrier task force that had been spotted 40 nautical miles from Suluan Island. They soon found Rear

Firemen and damage control parties work feverishly to simultaneously fight the raging blaze on the flightdeck of USS *Belleau Wood* (CVL-24) and move undamaged Avengers and Hellcats towards the bow and away from the flames. The vessel had been struck by a lone "Zeke" during the afternoon of October 30, 1944, just moments after the fleet carrier *Franklin* (seen here off the port side of the CVL-24 also trailing smoke) had been hit by a bomb-laden A6M. Twelve of the carrier's TBMs and F6Fs were also destroyed in the attack, adding to the 33 aircraft wrecked on board *Franklin*. (NARA)

Admiral Ralph E. Davison's TG 38.4 sailing off the Leyte invasion beaches about 90 nautical miles east of Samar Island (which roughly corresponds to the official Japanese position report), standing by to provide naval gunfire and air support on call to shore operations.

Built around the fast carriers *Enterprise* and *Franklin*, along with the light carriers USS *Belleau Wood* (CVL-24) and USS *San Jacinto* (CVL-30), TG 38.4 picked up the incoming raiders on radar at 1410hrs at a distance of 32 nautical miles just as CV-13 was in the midst of launching 12 fighters via catapult to assist a nearby fleet tanker force that was being subjected to a conventional air attack. The launch of the fighters was completed at 1420hrs, soon after which General Quarters sounded and "Material Condition Able" was declared at 1423hrs – such a declaration by a warship assured its watertight integrity and combat readiness.

This had been achieved just in time, for the first attack commenced shortly thereafter when five of six attackers penetrated the CAP to make their runs on the task group. Three "Zekes" headed for *Franklin*, with the first fighter crashing into the sea about 20ft from the port side abreast frame 120. However, CV-13's luck then ran out, with the second Zero-sen smashing into the after part of the flightdeck following a shallow dive. It plowed through the flight and gallery decks, at which point its centerline-mounted 551lb bomb detonated, before coming to rest in the hangar bay. The "Zeke" and its ordnance had by then blown a 12ft by 35ft hole in the flightdeck right of the centerline, bulging the surrounding deck area outwards.

The impact of the crash had also wrecked the aft deck elevator and started fires raging among the aircraft on the flightdeck and hangar bay, the flames being fed by leaking fuel from airframes holed by the bomb

With the barrels of their 20mm Oerlikon cannon pointing skyward, members of the Marine Detachment on board USS *Enterprise* (CV-6) shield their eyes from the sun as they scan the skies for more tokko on October 30. Fellow TG 38.4 carriers *Franklin* and *Belleau Wood* are burning furiously behind them, having already been struck by suicide attackers. *Franklin* was out of action until March 1945 and suffered 56 dead and 60 wounded, while *Belleau Wood* recorded 92 killed and 54 wounded. The light carrier did not return to action until February 1945. *(NARA)*

The weather on October 30 was fine and clear, which meant the smoke created by the burning carriers could be seen for many miles. This photograph of gunnery crews manning their 20mm Oerlikons while transfixed by the blazing vessels (*Belleau Wood* on the left and *Franklin* on the right) behind them was taken on board an unidentified escorting destroyer. *(NARA)*

blast and flying shrapnel. Fortunately for the ship, no bombs or torpedoes were in the hangar bay at the time, nor were any gasoline vapor explosions induced by the flames. The fires were eventually extinguished two hours after the carrier had been hit, by which point 56 crewmen were dead and 60 wounded.

The third attacker also made a run at the ship, although the fighter dropped its bomb prematurely and the weapon landed harmlessly in the sea off *Franklin*'s starboard bow. In his action report, the captain of the nearby Independence-class light carrier *Belleau Wood*, sailing just off CV-13's starboard bow, said the "Zeke" then leveled off on a course roughly parallel to that of TG 38.4, whereupon it became the target of fierce antiaircraft fire. As it reached a position off the port bow of CVL-24, the aircraft made a hard starboard turn towards the light carrier and approached it in a gentle glide. Despite his fighter being struck

D3A2 "Val" of the Tempei-tai, 2nd Kamikaze Attack Corps (Attack 102nd Hikotai/701st Kokutai), Nichols Field No. 1, Luzon, November 1, 1944

Attack 102nd Hikotai was reassigned to the 701st Kokutai on October 1, 1944 and deployed to the Philippines three weeks later. It hastily formed five tokko units on the 26th, and these began flying sorties the next day. This aircraft, flown by Lt(jg) Kazuo Tsuchiya (observer/commander) and PO Genshichi Eguchi (pilot), made its attack on warships of TG 77.1 off Tacloban on November 1, 1944 as part of the Tempei-tai (Heavenly Soldier Unit). In keeping with standard practice at that time, the tail code reflects the last two digits of the hikotai designation, rather than those of the parent kokutai. The aircraft carries a Type 99 No. 25 Ordinary Bomb Model 1 on the centerline and four Type 99 No. 6 Ordinary Bomb Model 1s, two under each wing, for its one-way mission. (Artwork by Jim Laurier, © Osprey Publishing)

repeatedly by the barrage of antiaircraft fire thrown up by the vessel's gunners, the pilot pushed the "Zeke's" nose down sufficiently enough to careen into a group of aircraft spotted aft on the flightdeck.

Even though the tokko had (fortunately) already dropped its bomb, the Zero-sen nevertheless managed to wreak havoc on board *Belleau Wood* by triggering explosions that holed its flightdeck and started an intense fire that was also fueled by the aircraft on board. Casualties were again heavy, with 92 killed and 54 wounded. Twelve of the vessel's aircraft complement were destroyed in the attack, adding to the 33 aircraft wrecked on board *Franklin*.

Both carriers were forced to head to the floating base at Ulithi Atoll, where they were temporarily patched up by Service Squadron 10 prior to heading back to the USA for further repairs and general refitting that would keep them out of action until early 1945.

The remaining two attackers from the Hazakura-tai targeted *San Jacinto*, although both "Zekes" crashed into the sea without inflicting any damage on the carrier.

The next successful tokko missions were flown on November 1, and the action on this day provides a perfect illustration of how difficult it can

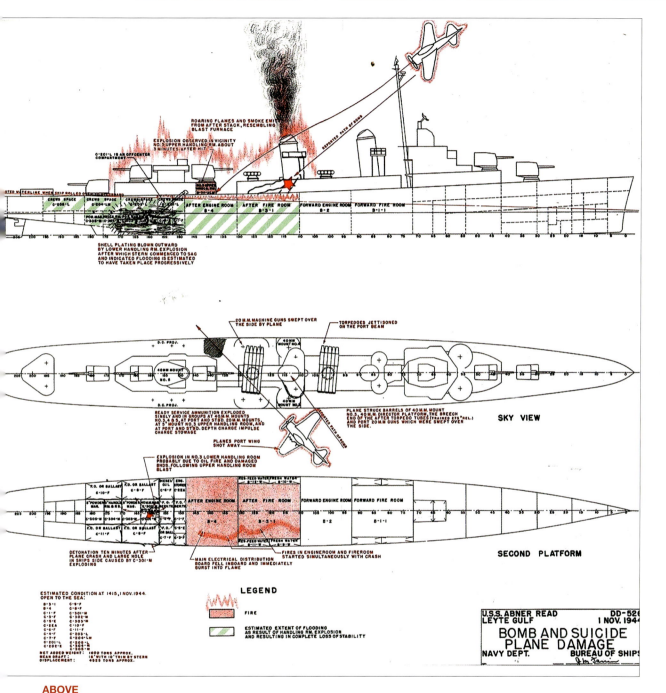

ABOVE
Another example of a detailed damage report created by the US Navy for one of its vessels hit by a tokko. In this particular case, the Fletcher-class destroyer USS *Abner Read* (DD-526) was sunk by one of two "Vals" that attacked it at 1340hrs on November 1, 1944 in Leyte Gulf. Although the impact of the D3A that hit the vessel caused little structural damage, it triggered an intense blaze – fed by the spilt fuel from the "Val" – in the after fireroom which eventually culminated in a tremendous explosion at the stern of the ship about ten minutes after the aircraft had struck. *(NARA)*

be to try to attribute responsibility for individual attacks – particularly with pilots becoming increasingly more intent on jibaku strikes even when not part of a dedicated tokko unit. This was probably because the results being achieved by the Special Attackers were now receiving growing attention in the Japanese press. That day saw TG 77.4's Fire Support Group operating within Leyte Gulf itself. Unsurprisingly, from mid-morning, it became the target of numerous conventional air attacks and tokko. By the end of the day, the destroyers *Abner Read*, USS *Ammen* (DD-527), USS *Claxton* (DD-571), and USS *Anderson* (DD-411) had been hit by enemy aircraft, with *Abner Read* sunk and the rest having suffered varying degrees of damage.

The action started just before 1000hrs. *Ammen* had already fired at several aircraft when its gun crews shifted their attention to a P1Y "Frances" twin-engined bomber approaching from the ship's port beam. Several hits set the aircraft on fire, although this did not deter the pilot and he duly struck the destroyer 15ft from the bridge, tearing off a searchlight and two stacks as the "Frances" deflected off the ship into the sea. It had caused considerable topside damage and inflicted 26 casualties, including five dead.

At around the same time that *Ammen* was hit, *Claxton* was targeted by a single "Val" that had originally gone after the nearby Australian cruiser *Shropshire*. The pilot inexplicably broke off his attack and disappeared into low cloud, before catching the destroyer's crew by surprise moments later when he emerged in a dive heading for *Claxton*. The IJNAF aircraft was hit repeatedly by antiaircraft fire, which deflected the pilot off his attack run and resulted in the "Val" slamming into the water alongside the destroyer. Unfortunately for *Claxton*, the aircraft's single bomb – believed to be a 551lb weapon – exploded as it hit the water, riddling the starboard quarter with fragments and opening up a hole in the hull near the upper handling room for the three aft five-inch guns that rapidly flooded the after part of the ship.

Five men were killed and 23 wounded on board *Claxton*, and the crew spent the next few hours attempting to pump out the water so that the damage repair team could plug the hole. The latter was partially filled by mattresses that had been tied together, the ship's pumps then being used to expel water from the flooded compartments faster than it was coming in via the hole in its hull. *Abner Read* pulled alongside to assist shortly thereafter, and the ship's medical and damage control personnel were sent over to *Claxton*.

At about 1340hrs DD-526 was itself struck by one of two "Vals" that targeted the destroyer less than 11 nautical miles from where *Ammen* and *Claxton* had been damaged that morning. The aircraft hit *Abner Read*'s starboard side amidships and, according to the ship's action report, its bomb entered "the forward starboard side of the after stack about five feet above the deckhouse top and exploded in the uptakes of the after fireroom." Although the impact itself caused little structural damage, it triggered an intense blaze – fed by the spilt fuel from the "Val" – in the after fireroom, after engine room, No. 3 upper handling room, and topsides from its after stack to the No. 3 five-inch main gun. The fire spread quickly and eventually culminated in a tremendous explosion at the stern of the ship about ten minutes after the aircraft struck.

The explosion, most likely triggered by detonating five-inch ammunition, opened a hole below the waterline and induced a sharp starboard list. The order to abandon ship was given, although this was quickly countermanded when the flooding seemed to douse some of the fires. However, it was given again at 1358hrs when the list worsened. The ship rolled over and sank at 1417hrs, with the loss of 14 of its crew.

At 1809hrs *Anderson* was sailing in the Surigao Strait off Panaon Island when its crew sighted three "Oscars" at 3000ft some five nautical miles away. The vessel's gunners opened fire a minute later without result, and at 1812hrs one of the Ki-43s was sighted passing down the ship's starboard side on a reverse course at a distance of approximately 5,000 yards. The antiaircraft batteries opened up once again, and although they succeeded in setting their target on fire, the pilot managed to crash into the destroyer's port side at the break of the forecastle deck. The impact started fires, knocked out two boilers (reducing DD-411's speed to 24 knots) and killed 16 crew, including the ship's doctor. With the assistance of USS *Bush* (DD-529), *Anderson*'s damage control team had the fires extinguished by 1855hrs.

IJNAF records indicate that on November 1 six tokko units despatched eight aircraft to target Allied warships off Leyte. At 0700hrs five "Vals" (from the Shisei-, Shinpei-, and Tenpei-tai) had taken off from Nichols Field, along with a solitary "Zeke" (from the Reisen-tai). A second A6M5 (from the Oka-tai) had departed Mabalacat at 1100hrs, with a third "Zeke" (from the Baika-tai) taking off from Nichols Field at 1520hrs. Of these aircraft, the "Val" crewed by WO Sadao Tsukamoto and PO1c Soichi Kato from the Shinpei-tai and one of the three D3As from the

The US Navy's 5in./38 dual-purpose gun with its large shell offered the best chance of defeating a tokko before it could damage a target. These are the forward twin mounts on USS *Intrepid* (CV-11), which downed a number of aircraft when they were called into action in 1944–45 as the carrier became the most frequently targeted Allied ship of World War II. The 5in./38 gun, which fired a 54lb shell, had an effective ceiling of 37,200ft. A well-trained crew could fire 15–20 shells per minute if required. *(NARA)*

Tenpei-tai, crewed by PO Takashi Arima and CPO Takashi Date, encountered mechanical problems en route, forcing them to divert to Cebu. Having taken off again at 1250hrs, these were almost certainly the aircraft that attacked and sank *Abner Read* less than an hour later, given the close proximity of Cebu to Leyte Gulf.

The fact that the destroyer's attackers made no attempt to drop bombs lends credence to them being tokko. This was also the case for *Claxton*'s attacker, which was identified by multiple sources as being another "Val." These included Lt Charlie Nelson, the vessel's Damage Control Officer at Leyte, who remembered "vividly seeing that round spinner on the prop and those two wheels that hung below the fuselage." That would mean *Claxton*'s attacker was either from the Shisei-tai or Tenpei-tai.

There were no "Frances" (or any other twin-engined aircraft) launched as tokko that day, so the P1Y that clipped *Ammen* was almost certainly an out-of-control aircraft or an IJNAF pilot intent on jibaku – a conclusion reinforced by the fact that the "Frances" had already dropped a bomb on or launched a torpedo at the destroyer USS *Killen* (DD-593) moments before crashing into *Ammen*.

Identifying exactly what aircraft targeted *Anderson* is more challenging. In the vessel's Deck Log, it is recorded that the destroyer was struck by an "Oscar," which was of course an IJAAF type. However, the IJAAF did not generate its first dedicated kamikaze missions – flown by "Oscars" – until late November following the arrival in the Philippines of specially raised tokko units from Japan earlier that same month. It is possible, therefore, that the pilot who hit DD-411 might have also been carrying out an impromptu jibaku attack. Another explanation could be that the aircraft involved was actually the solitary "Zeke" from the Baika-tai, flown by WO Haruo Ooshita (or Ooshimo). IJNAF records indicate that he had taken off from Nichols Field with two escorts at 1520hrs, which might explain why *Anderson*'s crew reported being attacked by just one aircraft, despite them initially spotting three.

By November 5 TF 38 was once again sailing off Luzon, with three of its four fast carrier task groups pounding airfields in and around the Manila area with a view to further eroding Japanese air power in the Philippines. The scale of these attacks can be measured by the fact that naval aviators claimed more than 400 Japanese aircraft destroyed in the air and on the ground in just 48 hours on November 5–6.

The inevitable Japanese response predictably included the tokko units, with five "Zekes" from the Sakon- and Byakko-tai, under the leadership of CPO Torao Otani and PO1c Takao Michizaka, respectively, taking off from Mabalacat soon after midday after they had been tasked with attacking the American carriers. They eventually found Rear Admiral Frederick C. Sherman's TG 38.3, composed of *Essex*, USS *Lexington* (CV-16), and USS *Ticonderoga* (CV-14), about 220 nautical miles northeast of Manila shortly after 1300hrs. The CAP only managed to shoot down one of the attackers, with the remaining four then commencing their attack runs. Two headed straight for *Lexington* at 1325hrs, and the lead "Zeke" was quickly shot down by antiaircraft fire – it crashed into the water about 1,000 yards from the vessel. The second aircraft headed for the carrier from almost dead astern, with the ship's action report noting that:

> The plane was also taken under fire and although hit many times by 20mm and 40mm shells, and afire, it managed to drop its bomb and hit the ship on the starboard side of the island structure aft. The bomb exploded against the armor plate of Battle Two, completely shattering it and destroying all of the Secondary Conn equipment and communications in the area. The plane completely disintegrated upon hitting the island. The resulting fragments and gasoline explosion, along with the bomb blast and bomb fragments, caused serious damage to the signal bridge, several 30mm [sic] and 40mm batteries and caused many casualties.

Prompt and effective action by the damage control parties meant that all the fires were put out within 20 minutes. However, casualties were heavy, with 50 killed and 132 wounded. *Lexington* was still capable of flight operations though, and it swiftly exacted revenge on the enemy when, soon after the tokko strike, the carrier air group targeted Japanese shipping in the Manila Bay area together with aircraft from *Ticonderoga*. They repeatedly hit the already-damaged IJN heavy cruiser *Nachi* with bombs,

The most severe challenge to the Essex-class carriers during the war was the tokko. These ships suffered 13 successful kamikaze attacks, but none were sunk. *Intrepid* was hit on three occasions by tokko (the most of any US Navy carrier), including twice by "Zekes" on November 25, 1944, when this photograph was taken. The carrier had just been struck in the flightdeck at 1255hrs while recovering its own air group, hence the large number of aircraft ranged forward towards the bow. *(NARA)*

torpedoes, and rockets as it struggled in vain to get underway, tearing the ship into three sections and sending it to the bottom with heavy loss of life among the crew.

The strikes against Luzon by the fast carrier groups started to develop a pattern during the month of November, with one or two carrier task groups hitting targets ashore every five days or so following replenishments at sea or brief visits to Ulithi Atoll. The tokko units usually responded to these strikes, although without success until November 25 when TGs 38.2 and 38.3 arrived off Leyte prior to its air groups again taking the fight to the

Gunners on board the battleship USS *New Jersey* (BB-62) remain at their stations while their compatriots on board CV-11 fight fires caused by two tokko hits in the space of just 30 minutes on November 25. "Big J" had been sailing directly ahead of *Intrepid* when the carrier was initially struck, after which the battleship moved to its starboard side to offer the vessel the protection of its extensive array of antiaircraft defenses – 20 5in./38 guns in ten dual mounts, 80 40mm Bofors guns, and 49 20mm Oerlikons. Even with such firepower to hand, BB-62 could not stop the second "Zeke" from hitting CV-11. *(NARA)*

enemy. Aircraft from the fast carriers sank yet another of the heavy cruisers crippled during the Leyte Gulf battles, this time *Kumano*, whose travails since late October are worthy of a book in itself. Also sunk was the escort ship *Yasoshima* (formerly the light cruiser *Ping Hai*, which had been the flagship of the Republic of China Navy until it was captured in 1938), along with several other auxiliaries and merchantmen.

In response, the tokko units appeared over TG 38.2 soon after noon, just as a wave of aircraft was returning from a mission. This initially caused confusion among the American ships, as with the air filled with aircraft, it was difficult to discern a small number of foes among so many friendly machines. Nevertheless, the CAP managed to engage "six Zekes" and claimed three. However, at 1233hrs, *Intrepid* reported that "an enemy plane was seen to attempt a suicide dive on *Hancock* at a diving angle of about 30 degrees. Next, another enemy plane was seen to dive on *Cabot*. Both of these appeared to be near misses."

In fact *Hancock*'s attacker broke up under fire just above its flightdeck, showering the ship in debris – one wing demolished a 20mm gun mount on the port side amidships and started a small fire that was quickly extinguished. Following an examination of IJNAF records, it seems likely that this attack was carried out by Dai-3 Kotoku-tai, which had sortied two bomb-laden "Zekes" (led by CPO Isao Uemura) at 1020hrs from Nichols Field. Three more A6M5s were also sent aloft as escorts, all five aircraft being sent to attack a carrier task force located 100 nautical miles to the north of Cape Naga.

At 1250hrs six more Japanese aircraft were detected approaching TG 38.2, and two minutes later a pair of attackers was sighted by the aft director approaching *Intrepid* from the starboard quarter at low level. By then they were only 8,000ft away, and the first "Zeke" broke up when hit by the carrier's antiaircraft artillery while still 1,500ft short of the ship. The second powered on, despite a landing Hellcat making a "gun run" on the jinking IJNAF fighter. The ship's action report stated that at "about 100 yards astern, this Zeke went into a power stall, did a wing-over from

The body of one of the unidentified "Zeke" pilots who hit *Intrepid* on November 25 was recovered from the wreckage of his aircraft. In this case, the sacrifice of one tokko pilot and his aircraft had cost the US Navy 66 killed and 35 wounded and forced the carrier out of fleet service until March 1945. *(NARA)*

ABOVE
This was the impact point of one of the "Zekes" that hit *Intrepid* on November 25. Although the damage inflicted on the lightly built flightdeck was not extensive, and the fires started here were put out in ten minutes, the bulk of the aircraft and its bomb crashed into the hangar bay. It was the devastation caused when the ordnance exploded that forced the carrier to return to San Francisco to be repaired. *(NARA)*

an altitude of about 500ft and crashed into our flightdeck at 1255hrs. Just as he did his wing-over he received many hits from our automatic weapons and caught on fire, but he was too close to be stopped."

The aircraft and its 551lb bomb penetrated the flightdeck, whereupon the weapon exploded in the gallery deck area immediately below, starting fires on the flightdeck and in the hangar bay. Fifteen crewmen were killed,

including six steward's mates manning one of the port aft 20mm guns that was closest to the "Zeke's" point of impact. It hit the ship immediately inboard of their station.

Intrepid's ordeal that day was far from over, however, for at 1257hrs two more "Zeke" pilots selected it as their target, this time approaching from the carrier's port quarter. The events of the previous attack were closely replicated, with the first fighter being shot down by antiaircraft fire and the second aircraft pressing home its attack. Having jinked furiously to avoid as much of the defensive fire as possible, the pilot then briefly climbed before performing a wingover and starting his final dive. Again, the "Zeke" was hit by the ship's gunners as it began the wingover, and again it was too late, for the aircraft struck the carrier amidships. The bomb carried by the "Zeke" penetrated the flightdeck before exploding in the hangar bay, inflicting yet more carnage. The fires started by the tokko took two hours to put out, by which point 66 crewmen had been killed and scores more wounded. With its flightdeck holed in two places, *Intrepid* was unable to operate aircraft. The carrier was forced to detach from TF 38 and head back to San Francisco to be repaired.

The tokko were not yet done with TG 38.2, for two other "Zekes" successfully targeted *Cabot* as *Intrepid* was being attacked. The first struck port side forward, wrecking several gun mounts and a Mk 51 fire-control system director and gashing the flightdeck, while the second exploded just off the carrier's port side, damaging its hull plating in the process. In between these two attacks a third A6M was shot down by gunfire from *Cabot*, although it is not clear if this aircraft could have been one of those also claimed by *Intrepid*.

Damage to *Cabot* was not serious, with flight operations resuming in short order so that returning aircraft could be recovered. However,

One of the IJNAF's most effective tokko aircraft was the D4Y "Judy," which could carry a 1,764lb bomb in a suicide role. This particular D4Y3, flown by Lt(jg) Masa Tanabe (pilot) and Ens Taro of the 701st Kokutai's Katori-tai, was photographed moments before it hit the deck of *Essex* on November 25, 1944. One of two kamikazes that targeted the ship, this aircraft was the only one to succeed in its mission, striking the carrier's flightdeck. The resulting explosion started a fire that killed 15 and wounded 44. *(NARA)*

ABOVE
This image was taken by a combat cameraman on board USS *Ticonderoga* (CV-14), which was sailing to the port side of *Essex* when the carrier came under attack by the D4Y3s of Lt(jg) Tanabe (pilot) and Ens Taro, and CPOs Yoshinori Yamaguchi (pilot) and Masa Sakaki. This still image taken from the motion picture footage clearly shows numerous aircraft spotted on the after part of CV-9's flightdeck that were missed by the "Judy." Had they been hit, the damage inflicted on the carrier would almost certainly have been far worse as these machines were both fueled and armed. (*NARA*)

BELOW
A billowing cloud of smoke and flame marks the spot where the D4Y3 struck *Essex* on November 25. Note the plumes of spray ahead of the carrier where parts of the aircraft had hit the water following its impact with the ship. One of these was almost certainly caused by the "Judy's" single bomb, which was flung overboard without exploding. The ship's after action report suggested that the lack of serious damage inflicted on CV-9 was due to the "Judy" being unarmed. However, IJNAF records indicate that both aircraft were indeed carrying a single 1,102lb Type 2 No. 50 Model 1 Ordinary Bomb each. (*NARA*)

casualties were heavy, with 36 sailors killed among its gun crew and a further 14 seriously wounded. IJNAF records indicate that this attack was the work of the Yoshino-tai, led by CPO Seiji Kawauchiyama, which had despatched six bomb-laden "Zekes" from Mabalacat at 1130hrs. The pilots of these aircraft were tasked with attacking a carrier group located approximately 100 nautical miles from the base on a heading of 75 degrees.

The human cost of the tokko offensive is depicted in this image. When *Essex* came under attack on November 25, the suicide aircraft crashed inboard from the aft port 20mm gun galleries. One of the Oerlikons was manned by six stewards, who fired their weapon until the last moment and were all killed. An undercarriage leg from the "Judy" can be seen at the top of the photograph. *(NARA)*

This was the gash inflicted on *Essex*'s portside flightdeck edge by the Katori-tai "Judy" on November 25. The carrier was repaired locally, allowing CV-9 to be back in action in just over two weeks. *(NARA)*

TG 38.3, operating some 50 nautical miles from TG 38.2, also came under attack in the early afternoon when two aircraft appeared off *Essex*'s starboard quarter at 1255hrs just as the carrier was in the midst of launching its air group on a strike mission. Both tokko were immediately fired upon by the carrier's antiaircraft batteries until they disappeared into a nearby cloud bank, only to reappear separately minutes later in

The cost to the US Navy was high every time a tokko hit a ship, with the average number of casualties caused by a successful kamikaze attack being 40. In this view, some of the 15 crewmen killed on board *Essex* on November 25 are buried at sea the following day. It was common practice to bury men at sea if they were killed in action. (NARA)

their attack dives. Although the lead aircraft had its port wing set alight (as seen in a series of spectacular photographs taken from on board the ship as the tokko inexorably closed on its target), the pilot succeeded in hitting *Essex* on its port side amidships and exploded in a fireball. Fifteen crewmen were killed and 44 wounded, most of them manning a number of 20mm guns that were destroyed on the port side of the ship. The explosion inevitably started a fire, although this was quickly doused before it could cause any structural damage.

The second aircraft had crashed harmlessly into the sea 800 yards away after it was repeatedly struck by antiaircraft fire.

Essex's crew identified their attackers as "Jill" or "Grace" torpedo-bombers, although the previously mentioned photographs of the lead aircraft plunging into the ship from astern shot show it clearly to be a late-model D4Y3 "Judy" dive-bomber bearing the number "17" on its tail. Identifying the culprit behind this attack is thus relatively straightforward, given there was just a single tokko unit that launched "Judys" that day. This was the 701st Kokutai's Katori-tai, which sent off two aircraft from Mabalacat at 1130hrs. The lead D4Y3 was crewed by Lt(jg) Masa Tanabe (pilot) and Ens Taro, while CPOs Yoshinori Yamaguchi (pilot) and Masa Sakaki were in the second aircraft. They had been tasked with attacking an enemy carrier task group approximately 150 nautical miles east-southeast of Mabalacat.

Several sources attribute the hit on *Essex* to Yamaguchi. However, given that the ship's crew reported CV-9 being hit by the lead aircraft, it would seem that it was Lt(jg) Tanabe's "Judy" that exploded upon crashing into the port side of the carrier.

Aside from the still photographs taken from on board *Essex*, this attack was also immortalized on film by a combat cameraman filming from the nearby *Ticonderoga*. His motion picture footage shows numerous aircraft spotted on the after part of CV-9's flightdeck which were missed by the "Judy." Had they been hit, the damage inflicted on the carrier would

THE PHILIPPINES

invariably have been far worse. The ship's action report suggested that the lack of serious damage caused by the "Judy" was due to it not carrying a bomb. However, IJNAF records indicate that both aircraft were armed with a single 1,102lb Type 2 No. 50 Model 1 Ordinary Bomb each. Given that the D4Y3 hit very near the port edge of the flightdeck, the bomb itself was clearly flung overboard without exploding.

These were not the only tokko attacks mounted on November 25, for four more "Zekes" from the Kasagi-tai and four "Frances" bombers from the Shippu- and Kyofu-tai also took off later that day to target both carrier task groups, although without further success. The four P1Ys were probably the aircraft intercepted off the east coast of Luzon by a pair of F6Fs from VF-80 flown by Lt Patrick Fleming and Ens Paul Beaudry at about 1350hrs. Flying from *Ticonderoga*, they shot down three bombers and sent the last aircraft fleeing in the direction of Luzon.

IJAAF OPENS ITS ACCOUNT

The IJAAF had actually started flying tokko missions in early November, following the arrival of dedicated kamikaze unit Fugaku-tai in the Philippines in late October. It was equipped with specially modified Ki-67-I KAI "Peggy" twin-engined bombers that had had all their defensive armament removed (by the Tachikawa Dai-Ichi Rikugan Kokusho), thus reducing both the aircraft's weight and crew – the latter from eight to just three. Fitted in their place were a pair of 1,760lb bombs or a special explosive charge weighing 6,393lb that gave the "Peggy" (officially christened the To-Go) what would have been a devastating punch should one of them have actually managed to hit a ship.

The Ki-67-I KAI was the tokko version of the "Peggy" bomber fitted with a pair of 1,760lb bombs or a special explosive charge weighing 6,393lb that gave the aircraft (officially christened the To-Go) what would have been a devastating punch should one of them have actually managed to hit a ship. The nose-mounted probe seen protruding from this aircraft – found abandoned at Clark Field by the US Army – contained a fuze to ensure the detonation of the explosive charge upon impact with the target. However, when the weapon was used against the Allies in early November, it was without result. *(NARA)*

However, in practice, the To-Go was an abject failure, with no recorded results when the Fugaku-tai attempted to target Allied ships on November 7, 11, 13, and 15. The unit attempted more tokko attacks in December and January off Luzon, and it appears that the closest the To-Go got to hitting an enemy vessel were two near misses.

The Fugaku-tai was joined in tokko attacks in the Philippines by the Banda-tai on November 12 and 15, the unit flying elderly Ki-48 "Lilys" drawn from IJAAF units based in-theater. Although several transport vessels were hit off Leyte by tokko on the 12th – including the repair ship USS *Achilles* (ARL-41), which had 33 crew killed when it was struck by a "Zeke" while moored off Samar Island – none of the victims identified their attackers as having been twin-engined bombers. No ships were struck by tokko on the 15th.

As the men and aircraft of the Fugaku-tai started operations, other IJAAF tokko units were forming in Japan. Known collectively as the Hakko-tai, these were subdivided into 12 sub-units and each given individual names, with their pilots drawn from graduating students of Japan-based training units. Typical of these was the second Hakko-tai, which was established on November 5 as the Hakko Dai 2-tai, Ichyu-tai and staffed by pilots from the Hitachi Kyodo Hikoshidan (Hitachi Instructional Air Unit). Led by 1Lt Kyoichi Kurihara, it left for the Philippines after receiving brand new Ki-43 "Oscars," arriving at Laoag airfield on Luzon on the 19th and flying on to Mabalacat 24 hours later. On November 23 the unit moved again, this time to Silay airfield on Negros Island, although five pilots and their aircraft, including that of 1Lt Kurihara, were lost en route and never seen again.

The next day saw the first mission flown by the Hakko-tai, with a single "Oscar" from the third Hakko unit, the Yasukuni-tai, undertaking a mission to attack Allied shipping off Manicani Island, in Leyte Gulf, without result. US Navy fighter sweeps wrought havoc with the IJAAF's tokko missions on November 25, when Hellcats intercepted a pair of Banda-tai "Lilys" and their Ki-43 escorts from the 20th Sentai on the ground at Caloocan, in Manila. Both bombers and no fewer than 11 "Oscars" were destroyed in a series of devastating strafing passes. The same fate befell three of five Yasukuni-tai Ki-43s caught by USAAF P-38s the next day, leaving only the aircraft of 1Lt Kazuo Demaru and 2Lt Masahiro Tanigawa to carry out the intended mission to attack shipping off Leyte. Both men missed their targets.

ABOVE
On the morning of November 27, while escorting troop transports supporting the Leyte invasion, USS *Colorado* (BB-45) suffered a direct hit from one of two bomb-equipped "Oscars" that targeted the battleship. These 1st Hakko-tai aircraft were part of a force of 11 Ki-43s that had been sortied from Fabrica, on Negros Island. The tokko managed to knock out one of BB-45's portside 5in./51 casemate guns and punch a hole in the deck, killing 19 crew and wounding a further 71 in the process. Nevertheless, the heavily armored battleship remained very much in the fight. *(NARA)*

These setbacks did not deter the IJAAF, with the 1st Hakko-tai launching 11 "Oscars" from Fabrica, on Negros Island, at 1045hrs on November 27. Led by 1Lt Hideshi Tanaka, their target was by now a familiar one for all tokko pilots – Allied warships in Leyte Gulf. One of the aircraft crash-landed back at Fabrica shortly after taking off after suffering engine trouble, but the remaining ten pilots spotted TG 77.2 – a force of four battleships, four cruisers, and 16 destroyers covering troop transports supporting the Leyte invasion – at 1130hrs. Lookouts on board the vessels sighted the approaching aircraft at much the same time as they headed east for the task group, whose ships were taking turns in refueling from the tanker USS *Caribou* (IX-114).

The Ki-43s split into three attack groups and proceeded to dive on their targets. The light cruiser *St. Louis*, whose crew had made the first visual sighting of the aircraft, bore the brunt of the ensuing attack, being dived on by no less than six tokko. Only the first one managed to hit the light cruiser, however, killing 15 sailors, with one more listed as missing in action, and wounding 43. The vessel was so badly damaged that it was sent back to California for repairs, which had been completed by the end of February 1945.

The battleship *Colorado* and the light cruiser *Montpelier* were also damaged during this attack, the former being struck by one of two aircraft that targeted it. One of BB-45's port-side five-inch guns was destroyed, killing 19 crewmen and wounding a further 71. The heavily armored battleship remained in the fight, however, while *Montpelier* was only slightly damaged by a near miss.

Sailors on board *St. Louis* reported that their attackers were "Judys," "Vals," and "Hamps" (clipped-wing A6M3s, as opposed to A6M2/5 "Zekes," which had rounded wingtips). However, on that day, the IJNAF was involved in a general all-out attack on US forces that were fighting in the city of Tacloban, on Leyte. Furthermore, its own records note that the nine tokko and 26 other aircraft that had been sent into action that day had failed to carry out their planned attacks due to poor weather over Tacloban and the intervention of enemy fighters.

St. Louis's action report noted that among the wreckage of its attacker strewn about the ship was the pilot's back armor and material from self-sealing fuel tanks. These items effectively ruled out the light cruiser having been hit by an IJNAF type, as neither armor nor self-sealing tanks were installed in any of them. They were, however, present in late-model Ki-43-IIIs similar to the ones operated by the IJAAF's tokko units in the Philippines, which together with the timeline and number of attacking aircraft seen approaching the US Navy ships means that TG 77.2 was indeed targeted by "Oscars" from the 1st Hakko-tai that morning.

There was a postscript to the attacks on November 27. As TG 77.2 battled with its own tokko attackers, the 110ft-long, 95-ton submarine chaser *SC-744* was 20 nautical miles to the southwest, escorting a tug towing a fuel-laden barge from the main invasion beaches down the west coast of Leyte to Liloan, on the island of Cebu, where a PT boat base was being established. Soon after noon the chaser's crew sighted what was identified as a "Zeke" heading towards the ship, pursued by two USAAF P-38s. According to eyewitness reports, the pilot of the enemy fighter suddenly "snap-rolled" onto the tail of one of the Lightnings and shot it down, after which the second P-38 then seemingly abandoning the fight as *SC-744* became the focus of attention.

The Japanese pilot commenced a strafing run on the submarine chaser, whose crew succeeded in damaging their opponent as it bore in. Moments later the aircraft slammed into the ship just aft of the bridge. Although there was no fire or explosion from any ordnance that the fighter was carrying in the wake of the impact, it had, nevertheless, badly damaged *SC-744*. The vessel immediately lost all power and was soon awash by the stern as it quickly flooded. The 21-man crew, save for four officers and crew assigned to try and save the ship, were evacuated by the tug they had been escorting. The personnel that remained on board eventually managed to stop the flooding, allowing another tug to tow *SC-744* back to Tacloban. Despite their sterling efforts, the submarine chaser sank off Tacloban two days later when an emergency seal over one of the many holes in the hull failed and water flooded the vessel's engine room.

According to IJAAF records, the 1st Hakko-tai tokko were escorted that day by two "Oscars" from the 54th Sentai. Aside from providing the kamikaze aircraft with a modicum of protection from marauding American fighters, the pilots from the 54th Sentai were also tasked with assessing the results of the tokko attacks. The unit duly reported that both aircraft and their pilots were lost in combat with P-38s, and it is highly likely that one of these Ki-43-IIs, misidentified as a very similar-looking "Zeke" by the crew of *SC-744*, was the fighter that struck the submarine chaser in a jibaku attack after being damaged by the vessel's antiaircraft guns.

After a 24-hour break due to bad weather, the IJAAF's tokko units were back in action on November 29, with the Yasukuni-tai mustering six bomb-laden "Oscars" under the leadership of 2Lt Akira Otsubo for another crack at the Allied ships in the Leyte Gulf. Again, TG 77.2 was the target as it continued to sail in the confined waters between Leyte and Samar Island, to the northeast. Shortly after 1700hrs the battleship *Maryland* and the destroyers USS *Aulick* (DD-569) and USS *Saufley*

Three "Oscars" of the Ichyu-tai and seven "Sonias" from the 6th Hakko's Sekicho-tai wrought havoc among a flotilla of landing vessels and their escorts in the Surigao Strait or off nearby Suluan Island on December 5, 1944. Three ships were hit, with *LSM-20* sinking 20 minutes after it had been struck aft of the pilothouse on the starboard side just above the waterline. In this dramatic photograph, a sailor can be seen on the verge of jumping as the vessels slides into the water stern first. *LCI(G)-1017* is standing by to rescue the crew. Eight sailors were killed and nine wounded. *(NARA)*

(DD-465) were all hit. The latter two vessels were assigned radar picket duty at the entrance of the Leyte Gulf, with each ship patrolling the northern and southern ends of this hotly disputed body of water looking for enemy aircraft or warships. They may have been selected as targets due to their isolation, the destroyers not being able to rely on the collective protection of the task group's antiaircraft fire.

Maryland was struck between main turrets Nos. 1 and 2, with fragments piercing the forecastle, main, and armored decks. The "Oscar's" 551lb bomb had blown a hole in the four-inch steel plating when it exploded, the ordnance killing 31 crewmen and wounding 30 more. Nevertheless, the battleship remained on station, supporting troops ashore as if it had never been hit.

The same could not be said for *Aulick*, which had suffered a near miss from the lead Ki-43 (its bomb had also exploded close to the vessel) and then been hit by a second "Oscar." The aircraft struck the starboard side of the bridge with its wingtip, before continuing forward and downward until its bomb exploded near the bow just above the main deck. The No. 2 five-inch gun and handling room were immediately set on fire. Metal fragments from the explosion had killed several crewmen on the bridge and flying bridge, with *Aulick* having a total of 31 killed, 64 wounded, and one listed as missing in action. The ship was sent to San Francisco to be repaired, not returning to the Philippines until mid-April 1945. The lightly damaged *Saufley* suffered only a single fatality.

There followed a pause in attacks as the land campaign on Leyte ground on, with Japanese troops offering up typically stubborn resistance. In the predawn hours of December 5, a small US Army force comprising both tanks and infantry leapfrogged south down the Leyte coast and positioned itself east of Balogo in anticipation of the planned landings south of Ormoc City, on Leyte's west coast, by the US Army's 77th Infantry Division two days later. That same day more tanks and troops were despatched to Leyte on board a small convoy of eight landing craft, escorted by four destroyers under the command of Capt William M. Cole embarked in USS *Flusser* (DD-368). The vessels were slowly transiting north along the Surigao Straits when, at 1100hrs, they came under attack from what the crew of the destroyer USS *Drayton* (DD-366) reported were eight "Vals" and "Oscars" (other ships reported between 12 and 15 attackers).

Although these aircraft were savaged by four P-38s performing CAP duties over the convoy and the ships' gunfire, they still succeeded in hitting three vessels – *Drayton*, *LSM-20*, and *LSM-23*. The 1,095-ton *LSM-20* was struck three feet above the waterline just aft of the conning tower, the aircraft's bombs exploding in the engine room. These caused both a large fire and widespread flooding, consigning *LSM-20* to a watery grave just 20 minutes after it had been hit. Eight enlisted men were killed and two officers and seven sailors wounded.

The remaining two ships suffered only moderate damage, although *LSM-23* had to be taken under tow and *Drayton* was forced to leave the convoy and seek the closest port so that repairs could be made. The convoy continued northward, now at an even slower speed than before because of the issues with *LSM-23*.

A Ki-51 from the Sekicho-tai takes off from Bacolod, on the island of Negros, at the start of a tokko mission during December 1944. Often mistaken for a "Val" by Allied crews enduring attacks on their ships, the bomb-armed "Sonia" proved to be an effective weapon during the bitter fighting in the Philippines and off Okinawa. (*Tony Holmes collection*)

At approximately 1710hrs the vessels came under attack from four more aircraft, which crews stated were "Vals." One of them slammed into the destroyer USS *Mugford* (DD-389) near its after funnel, wrecking the fireroom, knocking out all power, starting several fires (which were quickly extinguished), and killing eight crewmen and wounding a further 14. Restoring power took three hours, and the damage inflicted on the ship kept *Mugford* out of the war until March 1945.

IJAAF records indicate that three *tokko* units took to the air on this day, and they all targeted ships either in the Surigao Strait or off nearby Suluan Island. Three "Oscars" of the Ichyu-tai and seven "Sonias" from the 6th Hakko's Sekicho-tai took off from Bacolod, on the northwest coast of Negros Island, that morning, and it was these aircraft that were responsible for the attacks on *Drayton*, *LSM-20*, and *LSM-23*. The vessels, however, reported being attacked and hit by "Vals," an "Oscar," and a "Val," respectively.

Three more Ki-51s from the 5th Hakko's Tesshin-tai sortied from Caloocan, in Manila, that afternoon, these aircraft being flown by 1Lt Hiroshi Matsui, 2Lt Keiji Nishiyama, and Cpl Kiyoshi Nagahama. The number of attackers and the types reported by both the IJAAF and the US Navy appear to loosely match each other's, allowing for the fact that the "Sonias" were once again wrongly identified as "Vals."

December 5 also saw a convoy of 41 merchant ships, with five armed escorts, bringing in supplies from New Guinea endure a day of attacks from Japanese aircraft as it sailed towards Leyte. The IJNAF targeted the convoy with every aircraft it could muster from Davao and Cebu, with most of the attacks being conventional in nature. The crews involved claimed six transport vessels sunk and three more damaged, although in reality only the SS *Antoine Saugrain* was sunk – it was struck by two torpedoes dropped from B6N2 "Jills" in the early afternoon, the Liberty ship sinking the next day while under tow.

Soon after 1500hrs the Liberty ships SS *Marcus Daly* and SS *John Evans* were struck by "Zekes" in quick succession northeast of Mindanao, with the former sustaining substantial damage to its superstructure and losing 65 killed while the latter got off with light damage when its attacker fell into the water next to the vessel before exploding. It was not clear if the fighters were tokko from the 11th Shomu-tai that had departed Cebu soon after 1300hrs or impromptu jibaku attackers that may or may not have been misidentified as "Zekes."

ABOVE
The fast transport USS *Ward* (APD-16) sits motionless in the water off Ormoc Bay, smoke billowing from fires burning within its hull, after being hit by what was almost certainly a Ki-45 "Nick" of the Kinno-tai on December 7, 1944. Three years earlier to the day, *Ward* had become the first American warship to fire a shot in anger at Pearl Harbor. In a cruel twist of fate, its captain on December 7, 1941, now-Cdr William W. Outerbridge, was in command of the destroyer USS *O'Brien* (DD-725) which was ordered to scuttle *Ward* after the fires on board could not be brought under control. *(NARA)*

Two days later, on the morning of December 7, the 77th Infantry Division made an amphibious landing at Albuera, three nautical miles south of Ormoc City on the west coast of Leyte. Commanded by Maj Gen Andrew D. Bruce, the US Army division had been tasked with opening up a second line of advance on Leyte and cutting off the steady stream of Japanese reinforcements that had been using this area as a disembarkation point after being shipped in from nearby islands. Japanese resistance on the beaches was negligible, the defenders having been caught unprepared by this sudden turn of events. It was a different story out at sea, however, with the tokko about to enjoy their most successful day of the Philippine campaign.

Three years to the day after Pearl Harbor had been attacked by the IJNAF, the ship that fired the first American shot of the Pacific War, the former destroyer now turned high-speed troop transport *Ward*, found

Ki-45 KAIc "Nick" of the 8th Hakko-tai, Kinno-tai, Bacolod airfield, Negros, December 1944

Designed as a twin-engined heavy fighter, the "Nick" was well protected against enemy fire, unlike other more lightly constructed Japanese aircraft types. Consequently, Allied antiaircraft gunners found the Ki-45 difficult to bring down when used as tokko. On December 7, 1944 the Kinno-tai attacked vessels involved in the Ormoc Bay landings, striking the destroyer USS *Mahan* (DD-364) three times and the high-speed troop transport USS *Ward* (APD-16) once. Both ships were badly damaged, leading to their scuttling later that day. (Artwork by Jim Laurier, © Osprey Publishing)

itself involved in the landings at Ormoc. The vessel was tasked with putting 108 officers and men of the 77th Infantry Division ashore, before taking up station at the mouth of the bay along with the destroyer USS *Mahan* (DD-364) and two minesweepers to undertake anti-submarine and radar picket duties.

Shortly before 0950hrs a force of approximately nine twin-engined aircraft and four fighters were sighted closing in on *Mahan*'s port bow. The destroyer had a fighter director team on board who quickly vectored in USAAF P-38s covering the invasion. The Lightnings intercepted the enemy aircraft, and several of them were either shot down or driven off by the P-38s or antiaircraft fire from the US Navy warships. Unfortunately for *Mahan*, however, three twin-engined "leakers" slipped past the fighters and defensive gunfire and struck the ship in rapid succession around its bridge and forward stack, starting fires that could not be controlled. At 1020hrs the destroyer's forward magazine, which could not be flooded due to a break in the fire main, exploded and the decision was taken to abandon ship. USS *Walke* (DD-723), which had been assisting with rescue efforts, together with USS *Lamson* (DD-367) then scuttled the stricken *Mahan* with gunfire and torpedoes.

Nearby, *Ward* had opened fire on the tokko targeting *Mahan* as they started their attack runs. With *Mahan* hit repeatedly, three more twin-engined aircraft turned their attention to APD-16. The lead machine, identified as a "Betty," hit *Ward* on its port amidships, rupturing fuel tanks and igniting a fire that rapidly raged out of control. Once again, the painful decision was made to scuttle the ship, with the task falling to the destroyer USS *O'Brien* (DD-725). In what was one of those cruel coincidences war occasionally throws up, the CO of *O'Brien* that day, Cdr William W. Outerbridge, had been in command of *Ward* during its action off Pearl Harbor three years earlier.

The twin-engined aircraft that attacked both ships had made no attempt to drop ordnance on *Mahan* and *Ward*, and it would be reasonable to conclude, therefore, that they were from a dedicated tokko unit. Despite being identified as "Bettys" by *Ward*'s crew, IJNAF records show that none were assigned to tokko missions that day. In fact, no G4Ms carried out tokko missions throughout the Philippines campaign. Instead, the makeup of this force and the time of the attack suggest that the Ki-45 "Nicks" of the 8th Hakko-tai's Kinno-tai were responsible for the sinking of *Mahan* and *Ward*.

Nine "Nicks," led by 1Lt Takumi Yamamoto, had taken off at 0700hrs from Bacolod with five Ki-44 "Tojo" fighters of the 29th Sentai as escorts. Heading directly to the Ormoc beachhead, their success in sinking *Mahan* and *Ward* came at a price for all the attackers and their escorts were lost – including the 29th Sentai's commanding officer, Capt Masatsugu Tsuchihashi.

The tokko were not done yet, for at 1400hrs *Lamson*, which had assumed *Mahan*'s role as fighter director following the latter ship's scuttling, was departing Ormoc Bay with the rest of the convoy following the completion of landing operations when more Japanese aircraft appeared. A twin-engined machine, reported as a Mitsubishi Ki-46 "Dinah" (a type usually employed as an unarmed reconnaissance aircraft), dropped a bomb that narrowly missed *Lamson* before being shot down by defensive fire from the ship.

Minutes later, according to the vessel's action report:

> A Tony came around from behind Himuquitan Island and made a low, fast approach on our starboard quarter. Control managed to get on the plane at about a range of 1,000 yards, but guns one and two were in the blind [masked by the ship's superstructure]. The plane came in weaving and strafing. Its approach was on our starboard quarter 30ft off the water, but it crossed

Ki-43-III "Oscar" flown by 2Lt Joji Tanaka of the Hakko Dai 2-tai, Ichyu-tai, Silay airfield, Negros, November 1944

The Ichyu-tai arrived in the Philippines from Japan in late November and advanced to bases near Leyte later that month. The unit flew tokko missions on December 5, 7, and 13, with three, two, and one aircraft, respectively, with 2Lt Tanaka taking part in the operation against American ships in Ormoc Bay on the 7th. That day the destroyers USS *Lamson* (DD-367) and USS *Edwards* (DD-619) were both targeted by single-engined IJAAF fighters (including Ki-43s), with the former being badly damaged. (*Artwork by Jim Laurier, © Osprey Publishing*)

slightly to amidships as we went hard left. It hit No. 2 stack with its right wing and spun around, crashing into the after port corner of the transmitter room, and drove on in until the propeller was imbedded on the outside of the after Control bulkhead.

The hit, and subsequent fire, killed 21 of the ship's crew and almost resulted in *Lamson* being abandoned and sunk, with Capt William M. Cole, commander of Destroyer Squadron 5, deciding that preparations should be made to sink it as well. However, firefighting efforts proved to be successful, and the vessel was subsequently towed to safety.

A number of accounts detailing the *Lamson* attack agree with the ship's action report that its attacker was a Ki-61, with others identifying it only as a "single-engined fighter." IJAAF records indicate that no "Tonys" – readily identifiable by their inline engines, which were rarely used by Japanese aircraft – undertook tokko attacks on December 7, or indeed at any point during the entire campaign in the Philippines.

One possibility is that *Lamson*'s attacker could have been an early-model "Judy," as both the D4Y1 and 2 were powered by the Aichi Atsuta inline engine before later models switched to the more reliable Mitsubishi MK8P Kinsei 62 radial engine. There were several other tokko units in action that day, with a single "Judy" from the Chihaya-tai (accompanied

LSM-318 burns after being hit by a tokko off Ormoc Bay, Leyte, on December 7, 1944. Its crew reported that they had been attacked by an "Oscar," although it appears that the vessel had in fact been hit by a "Zeke" from the Luzon-based Gufu-tai. It was the detonation of the aircraft's solitary 551lb bomb on board following the crash that eventually sunk the 1,095-ton Landing Ship Medium. (NARA)

by four "Zeke" escorts) taking off from Mabalacat soon after midday – it is not known whether the D4Y was an early or late-model aircraft. Another possibility could be the *Lamson*'s attacker was one of ten "Oscars" from either the IJAAF's Hakko-, Ichyu-, Yasukuni-, or Gokoku-tai. The destroyer USS *Edwards* (DD-619) reported being attacked (unsuccessfully) by five single-engined fighters, each carrying a pair of wing-mounted bombs, at the same time as *Lamson* was struck.

Unlike the IJNAF, which recorded times and locations of their tokko sorties, the IJAAF generally failed to note this information other than in some specific cases, thus making it difficult to pinpoint exact attribution of hits by its tokko aircraft.

Seven "Zekes" and five "Frances" from the Gufu-tai were also sent into action that day, departing Luzon at noon. The A6Ms duly sank *LSM-318* and damaged the high-speed troop transport USS *Liddle* (APD-60) and *LST-737* to round off a miserable day for the US Navy.

Three days later, on December 10, the Kinno-tai was in action again when it sortied three "Nicks," the aircraft being joined by six "Oscars" from the 7th Hakko's Tanshin-tai – more Ki-43s from the 20th Sentai provided escort for the tokko. They found the destroyer USS *Hughes* (DD-410) on radar picket duty in the Surigao Straits shortly after 1700hrs, and one of the Ki-45s (identified in the ship's action report as a "Betty") crashed into the destroyer's port side amidships, despite being hit repeatedly by antiaircraft fire. Badly damaged, with one engine room demolished and much of its other machinery destroyed, *Hughes* was only spared further destruction when friendly fighters arrived to chase off the remaining Japanese aircraft just as a second tokko started its attack run.

This group was not to be denied, however, and they soon found more targets further up the Leyte Gulf in the form of the 41-ship convoy from New Guinea that had been previously attacked on December 5. The vessels were in the process of unloading their cargo south of Dulag when they were attacked by a group of four aircraft. SS *Marcus Daly*, which had been attacked and hit five days earlier during its transit to Leyte, was targeted again while craning its cargo onto nearby landing craft tank *LCT-1075*. This time the ship's attacker (described erroneously as a "Zeke" or "Tojo," when it was almost certainly a Tanshin-tai "Oscar") was hit while diving on the ship, although the fighter still managed to slam into its port side, scattering aircraft parts and spraying fuel all over the Liberty ship and down onto *LCT-1075*. The vessel was not heavily damaged, however, and fires were quickly extinguished.

The landing craft was not so fortunate, being turned into an inferno. Two crewmen were killed and a further nine wounded, with the 320-ton *LCT-1075* being deemed beyond saving and beached.

Liberty ship SS *William S. Ladd* was also targeted, the vessel carrying a lethal combination of fuel and 150 tons of ammunition. Its crew reported coming under attack by "Vals" at about the same time that SS *Marcus Daly* and *LCT-1075* were hit. One plowed through *William S. Ladd*'s aft mast and bounced off the amidships house before falling into the No. 4 cargo hold, the tokko's bomb or bombs exploding as it did so, shattering the engine room bulkhead and triggering a series of explosions in the Nos. 4 and 5 holds. The ensuing fire soon burned out of control, and after two hours the ship was abandoned, sinking later that evening. Miraculously, no one was killed, although eight crew were wounded.

On December 11 a convoy of 13 amphibious craft and six destroyers was spotted heading to Ormoc Bay by Japanese aircraft. The CAP protecting the vessels numbered just four fighters, and they could not cope with the 12 tokko that targeted the convoy. These overwhelmed the destroyer USS *Reid* (DD-369), which managed to down two of its attackers but was hit by three more in quick succession. A bomb carried by the last aircraft to hit the ship exploded in the after magazine, opening up its stern while DD-369 was still doing 20 knots. The destroyer rolled violently and sank in less than a minute, taking 103 crewmen with it. *Reid* was almost certainly attacked by "Oscars."

PT boat PT-323 of Motor Torpedo Boat (MTB) Squadron 21 was also sunk on this date, the vessel being underway in company with PT-327 in Leyte Gulf when they were attacked by four Japanese aircraft. PT-327 turned one way and PT-323 maneuvered in the opposite direction until it was hit amidships – the wooden-hulled 80ft Elco MTB was virtually cut in half by the unidentified tokko near Hingatungan Point, on southern Leyte. The boat's captain, Lt(jg) Herbert Stadler, was killed, and second officer Ens William I. Adelman listed as missing in action. Its remaining 11 crewmen, all of them wounded, were rescued by PT-327.

MINDORO LANDINGS

There were a few more tokko attacks off Leyte in the following days, but by this time the Japanese high command had realized the island was lost. Concurrently, the Americans started preparing for the invasion of Mindoro Island, codenamed Operation *Love III*. With the newly captured airfields on Leyte too far from Luzon, and specifically Manila, to allow land-based USAAF aircraft to support the invasion of this key island in the Philippines, Mindoro was deemed to be the logical choice for the next amphibious assault thanks to its coastal plains and minimal Japanese presence. An area near the town of San Jose at the southwestern tip of the island was chosen as the spot for the initial landings, scheduled for December 15.

The seaborne invasion forces were located by Japanese reconnaissance aircraft a full two days before the planned landings as they traversed the Bohol Sea and entered the Sulu Sea between the islands of Mindanao and Negros. However, with both IJNAF and IJAAF air power in-theater now on the wane, the response was low key. The IJNAF despatched four Cebu-based "Zekes," and a fifth fighter as an escort/observer, from the 2nd Kongo-tai, the aircraft being led aloft by Lt(jg) Hiroshi Komatsu. The IJAAF managed to sortie just one "Oscar" from the second Hakko unit, the Ichyu-tai, flown by 2Lt Masayoshi Ono, as well as an unknown number of "Lily" bombers from the Kyoko-tai – a tokko unit that had been created by the 75th Sentai at Lipa airfield, near Manila.

The Kyoko-tai had been formed on December 8 with 12 (or ten according to some sources) crews from the 75th Sentai and three from the Ki-48-equipped 208th Sentai, the tokko unit being led by 2Lt Naga Mikyo. One week later a second tokko unit was created, the

Wakazakura-tai including five 75th Sentai crew. It was commanded by 2Lt Tsumura Masao. Both units were issued with specially modified Ki-48-II KAIs that initially carried one unjettisonable 1,760lb bomb and had three ten-foot-long nose-mounted rods with contact fuses on their tips. However, the Aviation Arsenal in Manila modified some of these aircraft for tokko missions so that they could jettison the large bombs. They also reduced the number of rods in the nose to just one.

Both tokko units were especially active during the efforts to stop the Mindoro Attack Force, the Kyoko-tai making its combat debut on December 13. However, this mission proved to be an abject failure as the crews involved failed to spot the invasion force.

Even with depleted numbers, the remaining tokko still claimed scalps. At 1500hrs 2Lt Ono encountered Rear Admiral Arthur Dewey Struble's TG 78.3 as it sailed past the narrowest point of the Bohol Sea between the islands of Negros and Mindanao, escorting the vulnerable transports carrying men and materiel of the Mindoro Attack Force. He managed to elude the CAP, made up of FM-2 Wildcats from the escort carriers of Rear Admiral Felix B. Stump's Heavy Covering Group and the F4U Corsairs of Marine Air Group 12, and targeted Struble's flagship, the light cruiser *Nashville*.

Diving from 5,000ft, the Ki-43, which was correctly identified as carrying a bomb under each wing, leveled out and bore in from almost dead astern. This limited the number of antiaircraft guns that could be brought to bear on the attacker before Ono slammed into *Nashville*'s main deck port side amidships near the admiral's cabin. His "Oscar"

Two other destroyers from TU 77.12.7 stand by to assist USS *Haraden* (DD-585) after it was hit by a tokko on December 13, 1944 as the vessel transited the Bohol Sea while accompanying the Mindoro invasion force. Its crew identified their attacker as an "Oscar," although IJNAF records indicate that the aircraft involved was almost certainly one of four "Zekes" from the 2nd Kongo-tai that had taken off from Cebu. Note that DD-585 is missing its forward funnel, blown overboard when the fighter struck the starboard side of the destroyer. (NARA)

Shorn of their masts, the destroyers *Lamson* and *Haraden* sit side by side in the drydock at Puget Sound Navy Yard in Washington awaiting repair in early 1945. *Lamson* had been struck by a tokko (either a "Judy" or an "Oscar") while departing Ormoc Bay on December 7, 1944. The hit, and subsequent fire, killed 21 of the ship's crew and almost resulted in the destroyer being abandoned and sunk. Both vessels returned to the Pacific theater in May 1945. *(NARA)*

immediately exploded, as did its two bombs, starting a huge fire fed by the aircraft's fuel and, subsequently, exploding antiaircraft ammunition.

Typical of the many tokko strikes against well-armored cruisers and battleships, the damage inflicted on CL-43 was not severe beyond the antiaircraft guns immediately affected by the explosion and fire, and the ship was never in danger from sinking. It was, nevertheless, knocked out of the war until April 1945. However, the loss of life was disproportionately heavy, with 133 dead and 190 wounded. Among the latter was US Army Brigadier-General William C. Dunckel, commander of the Mindoro landing forces, while both his and Struble's chiefs of staff (Col Bruce C. Hill and Capt E. W. Abdell) were killed, as was Col John T. Murtha, CO of the USAAF's 310th Bombardment Wing.

A little over two hours later, it was the turn of Stump's escort carriers and their screening vessels to come under attack. The destroyer USS *Haraden* (DD-585) of TU 77.12.7, which was in turn part of Stump's Heavy Covering Group heading for Mindoro, was targeted by the quartet of "Zekes" from the 2nd Kongo-tai that had taken off 30 minutes earlier from Cebu. Three managed to elude the CAP and attack the ships, with the battleship USS *West Virginia* (BB-48) and another destroyer shooting down one apiece before the third (which the ship's crew identified erroneously as an "Oscar") slammed into the starboard side of *Haraden*, knocking out the pilot house and torpedo director and blowing its forward funnel overboard. The forward fireroom was also wrecked. Although 14 crewmen were killed and 24 wounded, the situation was

TOP RIGHT
On December 15, 1944, as American forces landed on Mindoro, the invasion fleet TU 78.34 was attacked by 12 "Zekes" and a solitary "Judy" from the 9th Kongo-tai. The tokko hit a total of five ships, including *LST-738* shown here, which was eventually abandoned and scuttled after being gutted by fire following the strike. USS *Moale* (DD-693) closed up alongside the tank landing ship in an effort to help save the vessel, but four explosions – one of which holed the destroyer's bow and killed a sailor – forced DD-693 to abandon this course of action. *(NARA)*

RIGHT
LST-472 was also sunk by a tokko off Mindoro on December 15. Various vessels tried to save the tank landing ship, including the Patrol Craft Escort *PCE(R)-851* and the destroyers *O'Brien* and USS *Hopewell* (DD-681), but the raging fire on board *LST-472* could not be brought under control and it had to be scuttled by USS *Hall* (DD-583) after the crew had abandoned ship. *(NARA)*

BELOW
The bulk of *LST-472*'s crew have gathered in the prow of the vessel while damage control parties and firefighters attempt to control the blaze aft. The ship was typically manned by 13 officers and 104 enlisted personnel, and it could also accommodate 163 troops. Five Seebees were killed and seven seriously wounded in the attack on *LST-472*. *(NARA)*

quickly brought under control with the help of the destroyer *Twiggs*. Like *Nashville*, *Haraden* was now also out of the fight, being sent back to Puget Sound Navy Yard in Washington for repairs, where it too remained until April 1945.

Several attempted tokko and conventional attack sorties by the Japanese on December 14 resulted in no hits on the Mindoro Attack Force in the Sulu Sea. Instead, ten "Tojos" of the 246th Sentai, returning to Zablan airfield, near Manila, after a long-range escort for a tokko unit, were bounced by US Navy Hellcats on yet another fighter sweep of Luzon just as the IJAAF fighters entered the landing pattern. In the one-sided action that ensued, virtually all of the Ki-44s were either shot down or written off in emergency landings, with two pilots killed.

Japanese records indicate that the sole IJAAF Special Attackers active that day were nine Ki-49 "Helen" twin-engined bombers from the Kikusui-tai – a unit formed using aircraft and crews from the 74th and 95th Sentai based at Clark. The unit was ordered to attack an enemy carrier task force (Stump's TU 77.12.7, which consisted of six escort carriers and their escorts) in the Sulu Sea that was carrying out strikes on nearby Negros and Panay islands, and at 0943hrs the Kikusui-tai reported that they had been intercepted by enemy fighters en route. All aircraft, along with 47 crewmen, were lost, with two claimed by 1Lt Ellis Baker of the 40th FS/35th FG in his P-47 Thunderbolt.

Tokko units would enjoy more success on the morning of December 15 as the invasion of Mindoro began. With the fleet mostly sitting off San Jose, both the IJNAF and IJAAF despatched whatever air power they could muster – five groups of tokko aircraft were sent aloft, four from the IJNAF and one from the IJAAF (a solitary Ki-48-II from the Kyoko-tai, escorted by fighters). Only three of these groups were sent against the invasion fleet, however. It was the 9th Kongo-tai force, consisting of 12 "Zekes" and a solitary "Judy," from Mabalacat under the command of Lt Susumu Aoki that was almost certainly responsible for the damage inflicted on the escort carrier USS *Marcus Island* (CVE-77) and the destroyers USS *Howorth* (DD-592) and USS *Paul Hamilton* (DD-590), and the sinking of *LST-472* and *LST-738*.

Another IJNAF tokko unit, the 1st Kusanagi-tai based at Degos airfield on the southern coast of Mindanao, sortied two "Frances" at 0720hrs under the command of Ens Katsumi Nishimura that encountered Stump's escort carriers off Mindoro. Both aircraft were shot down during

P1Y1 "Frances" of the 1st Kusanagi-tai, Degos airfield, Mindanao, December 15, 1944

This was the aircraft caught in a series of 11 photographs as it was shot down while attacking the escort carrier USS *Ommaney Bay* (CVE-79) off Mindoro, on December 15, 1944. The tail code 763-29 indicated that the fast medium bomber had originally come from the IJNAF's 763rd Kokutai. The "Frances" was committed to tokko operations both off the Philippines and off Okinawa, its ability to carry two 1,102lb bombs in a ventral bomb-bay making the aircraft a potentially deadly opponent for Allied ships. It proved vulnerable to antiaircraft fire, however, as it was not as well armored as the slightly smaller Ki-45. (*Artwork by Jim Laurier, © Osprey Publishing*)

---

the course of their attack runs, with one of them, 763-29, becoming the unwitting subject of a series of 11 photographs taken from *Ommaney Bay* as it flashed across the carrier's stern with its port engine on fire before plunging into the water.

No Allied ships were hit by the tokko on the 16th, although this was not due to a lack of effort on the part of the Japanese. The IJNAF's 11th and 12th Kongo-tai, with 12 and two attackers, respectively, sortied from Mabalacat and Davao at 0650hrs and 1335hrs for the San Jose beachhead and northern Sulu Sea, but all aircraft returned home following a fruitless search for targets. Meanwhile, the IJAAF had launched two "Sonias" from the 5th Hakko's Tesshin-tai, along with a single "Peggy" and "Lily"

A Ki-43-III Ko "Oscar" formerly of the 33rd Sentai (which switched to the Ki-84 just prior to the Allied offensive to retake the Philippines) and now assigned to an unidentified tokko unit takes off on a mission in late 1944. Note that the aircraft is carrying a 551lb high explosive bomb beneath its right wing, this weapon greatly increasing the lethality of the otherwise lightweight "Oscar" when employed as a kamikaze. Bombs of this size were always carried in conjunction with a 200-liter drop tank beneath the opposing wing, the latter being used both to extend the fighter's range and to offset the weight of the bomb. (*Tony Holmes collection*)

In one of the iconic photos of the Pacific War, a P1Y1 "Frances," already on fire, flies over the escort carrier *Ommaney Bay* in the Sulu Sea on December 15, 1944. This aircraft, from the 1st Kusanagi-tai at Degos airfield on the southern coast of Mindanao, missed, but on January 4, 1945 a lone tokko (probably a Ki-45) attacked *Ommaney Bay* without warning. A perfectly placed bomb exploded in the ship, destroying all power and starting a devastating fire in the hangar bay that led to the carrier's loss. *(NARA)*

from the Fugaku- and Kyoko-tai, respectively. None of these aircraft registered any hits.

The morning of December 17 saw the departure of the Heavy Covering Group, leaving the Mindoro beachhead to be protected by smaller craft such as PT boats. The sudden lack of sizeable targets did not deter the tokko, and PT-75 was narrowly missed by aircraft as it patrolled off Mindoro. Its attacker was either one of two "Oscars" from the 7th Hakko's Tanshin-tai or a Ki-84 "Frank" of the Seika-tai. By this time the IJAAF's ranks in the Philippines had been decimated, and the 4th Kokugun (Air Army) hastily formed the Seika-tai for tokko missions, with aircraft drawn from the remnants of the fighter Sentai in the Philippines – hence the widespread employment of the IJAAF's best fighter in the kamikaze role from then on.

The next day, PT-300 came under attack from what its crew reported were three "Vals" off San Jose, the MTB being hit squarely amidships by one of them. It immediately broke in half and sank, resulting in the deaths of eight crewmen, with seven more wounded. The IJNAF did not launch any sorties that day, so it is highly likely that PT-300 was sunk instead by an IJAAF "Sonia." Indeed, a single example of just such an aircraft, from the Tesshin-tai, took off from Caloocan with

Sgt Maj Kumao Nagao at the controls and headed for shipping off Mindoro. The discrepancy between the number of attackers launched and that observed by PT-300's crew cannot be explained, however.

On December 19 the first Mindoro resupply convoy departed Leyte, and on the 21st it was making its way north through the Sulu Sea off Panay when the tokko attacked. Soon after 1700hrs the convoy of 25 ships, 14 LSTs, six chartered freighters, and 11 destroyers sighted a number of "Oscars" and "Tojos" that proceeded to dive on the ships. The Liberty ship SS *Juan de Fuca* shot down one of the attackers, but others proceeded to hit it, *LST-460*, and *LST-749*. *Juan de Fuca* was lightly damaged and proceeded to Mindoro, but both LSTs were abandoned and sunk when the fires started by the tokko and their detonating bombs could not be brought under control.

The identification of the attackers by the ships' crew appears to be partially correct, for five "Oscars" from the tenth Hakko unit, the Jungi-tai, led by 1Lt Shinji Tsuruga were indeed sent after the convoy that day. There were no "Tojos" involved, however, with the type being used in the Philippines solely in its intended fighter role. The Jungi-tai was instead accompanied by a solitary "Sonia" flown by 2Lt Yasuo Koizumi of the Koizumi-tai (a tokko unit formed by the Philippines-based 83rd Sentai) and another Ki-48-II KAI from the Kyoko-tai at Bacolod. The latter aircraft was possibly the same "Lily" claimed shot down by the destroyer USS *Foote* (DD-511) at 1738hrs as the attack petered out.

The previous day, according to IJAAF records, solitary Ki-48s from the Wakazakura- and Banda-tai and two Ki-84s belonging to the Seika-tai, escorted by three fighters, took off at 1500hrs from Manila and attacked ships in Lingayen Gulf off Luzon, sinking one transport vessel – no Allied vessels were recorded as lost on this date. The Wakazakura-tai Ki-48 was flown by Cpl Yomura Goro, the aircraft having been the personal mount of the 75th Sentai CO, Doi Tsutomu. It was carrying a 1,760lb bomb.

The convoy reached Mindoro on the morning of December 22, at which point the destroyers formed a circular screen about four nautical miles from the beach to cover the unloading of the remaining landing ships. At 0945hrs USS *Bryant* (DD-665) sighted what its crew identified as a "Zeke" commencing a diving attack, and the destroyer immediately proceeded to turn to starboard at flank speed in an effort to unmask its antiaircraft guns. The latter registered hits on the incoming fighter, although it continued with its dive and narrowly missed a 40mm mount

OPPOSITE
Crewmen wearing anti-flash clothing while manning the port side amidships 5in./25, 20mm, and 40mm antiaircraft guns strain to identify an aircraft flying overhead the light cruiser *Phoenix* on December 18, 1944 during the Mindoro invasion. The gunners on board the ship were some of the most effective during the campaign to liberate the Philippines, downing a handful of aircraft and preventing the cruiser from ever being struck by a tokko. Three days prior to this photograph being taken, the crew of one of the 5in./25 batteries had downed a circling aircraft at a range of 8,500 yards (25,500ft). *(NARA)*

before splashing into the sea 50 yards away. A bomb carried by the aircraft exploded as it sank, showering the ship with fragments of the tail assembly that wounded a crewman. Although identified as a "Zeke," DD-665's attacker was almost certainly one of two "Oscars" from the Jungi-tai that were following up on the unit's attacks on the convoy the previous day. The aircraft were flown by 2Lt Minao Hino and Sgt Yotsugi Hayashi, who had been tasked with attacking shipping west of Panay.

The next resupply convoy for Mindoro was south of Negros on December 28 when it came under attack from astern by six aircraft at 1020hrs. Three broke through the gunfire and plowed into *LST-750* and the Liberty ships SS *William Sharon* and SS *John Burke*. The LST dropped out of formation, later taking another hit from an aerial torpedo that caused the crew to abandon the 4,080-ton vessel. It was eventually scuttled. *William Sharon* suffered 11 dead (six civilian crew and four US Navy personnel and a US Army officer), with a similar number wounded in the attack, and was also abandoned. The ship did not sink, however, and it was eventually towed to Leyte and patched up before sailing back to California to be properly repaired.

John Burke would not enjoy a similar reprieve. Loaded with ammunition, the Liberty ship erupted in a tremendous explosion seconds after being struck. The eruption, which was filmed by medical officer Lt George Johnson from the destroyer *Bush* on his 16mm camera, showed a huge cloud of vapor from the humid tropical air followed by an even bigger mushroom cloud from the explosion that followed. No sign of the ship or its 68 crewmen were found after the smoke and debris cleared, with an unidentified US Army Freight and Supply ship nearby also sinking when it was caught up in the explosion. Also damaged by the shock wave from the detonation was the tanker *Porcupine* (which was spared a similar fate when a tokko was shot down as it made a run on the ship) and the PT boat PT-332. The MTB had its seams opened to the sea, despite being 500 yards away from *John Burke*.

Most sources attributed this attack to "Vals," although IJNAF records show that none were launched as tokko on that day. Three "Zekes" from the 14th Kongo-tai that departed Cebu at 0950hrs and a solitary Nakajima J1N "Irving" nightfighter from the Gekko-tai were the only Special Attackers to engage the enemy on December 28. It would seem likely, therefore, that the D3As involved in this action were conventional dive-bombers carrying out an impromptu jibaku attack. This would explain why *Bush*'s crew spotted two surviving aircraft withdrawing after the explosion of *John Burke*.

The 29th saw no ships hit by the tokko, although the destroyer USS *Pringle* (DD-477) was attacked and narrowly missed by what its crew identified as a "Zeke" that flew in between the vessel's stacks soon after 1700hrs as the ship screened a resupply convoy. If this is indeed correct, it means that DD-477 was targeted by an A6M from the 15th Kongo-tai, the unit having sortied four fighters from Batangas, on Luzon, at 1600hrs. IJAAF tokko units were also active that day, with the 5th Hakko's Tesshin-tai and the 10th Hakko's Jungi-tai contributing three "Sonias" and an "Oscar," respectively, while the Kyoko-tai sent one of its few remaining "Lilys" against the fleet off Mindoro.

During the early hours of December 30 the resupply convoy reached Mindoro and commenced unloading just as dawn broke. By mid-afternoon the tokko had once again made an appearance overhead, and at 1530hrs *Pringle*, which had had a lucky escape 24 hours earlier, was struck in its No. 5 40mm gun mount by an aircraft that had opened fire on the destroyer just before it slammed into the ship. Although damage was slight, 11 crewmen were killed and 20 wounded.

Minutes later the destroyer USS *Gansevoort* (DD-608), the tanker *Porcupine*, and the PT boat tender USS *Orestes* (AGP-10) were also hit. *Gansevoort*'s action report stated that a fighter dropped bombs on *Porcupine* at 1548hrs before turning its attention to DD-608, crashing into its port side and causing extensive damage that saw two boilers destroyed, 17 crewmen killed, and 15 wounded. Knocked out of the war, and with temporary repairs in situ only completed in February 1945, the vessel subsequently departed for San Francisco via Leyte, Ulithi Atoll, and Pearl Harbor.

The other ships reported that their attackers were "Val" dive-bombers, with *Porcupine* coming off worst. Soon after *Gansevoort*'s eventual attacker had attempted to drop bombs on the destroyer, without scoring any hits, another aircraft struck the luckless tanker with its ordnance and finished off the ship by crashing into the main deck aft of the deckhouse at 1555hrs as the vessel waited its turn to unload. The bomb and the crashing tokko ruptured three of *Porcupine*'s tanks and started a fire that rapidly spread out of control, fueled by the tanker's volatile cargo. It was quickly abandoned, after which an attempt was made by the crew of the damaged *Gansevoort* to scuttle the tanker. This failed, however, due to the shallow waters off Mindoro affecting the run of the weapon fired by the destroyer. Seven of *Porcupine*'s crew were declared missing, presumed dead, and a further eight wounded in the attack. The ship eventually burned down to the waterline, with the hulk settling on the sea bed.

The heaviest casualties were on board *Orestes*, with 59 killed and 106 wounded after its attacker struck starboard amidships at 1600hrs. The bomb carried by the aircraft detonated inside the ship, causing severe damage and starting fires. Nevertheless, it survived the attack and was towed to Leyte for temporary repairs, before heading back to San Francisco. *Orestes* eventually re-entered service in August 1945, arriving back in the Philippines the following month just as Japan surrendered.

While the crewmen aboard the trio of ships targeted again identified their attackers as being "Vals," IJNAF records showed that its Special Attackers were not active that day. Only the IJAAF's tokko units engaged Allied ships, with five "Sonias" from the 12th Hakko's Shinshu-tai taking off from Marikina, on Luzon. A single Oka-tai "Nick" from nearby Zablan was also sent aloft at this time. The latter tokko unit had been formed from the aircraft and personnel of the 45th and 208th Sentai, who contributed ten and five pilots, respectively. The Oka-tai was led by 1Lt Sadao Ikeuchi of the 45th Sentai.

Thus, the attacks on *Orestes, Porcupine*, and *Pringle* can almost certainly be attributed to the Ki-51s of the Shinshu-tai, the IJAAF aircraft having once again been mistaken for similar-looking "Vals." This leaves only the identity *Gansevoort*'s attacker in doubt, as the ship's action report identified it as a "fighter." This pilot's attempt to bomb *Porcupine* before crashing into the destroyer suggests it may have been a jibaku strike, given that there was a conventional air attack going on at about the same time the other ships were hit. *Bush* had in fact noted in its action report that at 1546hrs "enemy aircraft attacked shipping in the bay at widely separated points, launching bombs."

FOCUS ON LUZON

By late December 1944, the situation on Mindoro had stabilized, and with the capture and refurbishment of two airfields (by US Army engineers), the focus of the campaign shifted to the main prize of Luzon. The invasion of the largest and most densely populated island in the Philippines, which was also the location of its capital, Manila, was

Ommaney Bay explodes following the attack by a lone tokko on January 4, 1945, this photograph being taken shortly after nine aerial torpedoes detonated in the aft end of the hangar bay at 1818hrs. Just six minutes earlier, the vessel's commanding officer, Capt Howard L. Young, was the last man off the escort carrier. The explosion of the torpedoes, caused by the raging fire started by the tokko, collapsed the after flightdeck and induced a list to starboard. *Ommaney Bay* was scuttled by USS *Burns* (DD-588) a short while later. (NARA)

scheduled for January 9, 1945. Exactly one week earlier, the first ships of the assembled invasion force weighed anchor from Leyte.

Among the first to leave due to its slow speed was the Minesweeping and Hydrographic Group comprising 72 assorted vessels under the command of Cdr Wayne R. Loud, which found itself in the Bohol Sea approaching the entrance to the Sulu Sea on the morning of the 3rd. Among these was the 22,231-ton Type T2 fleet tanker USS *Cowanesque* (AO-79), which at 0728hrs was hit by a tokko identified yet again as a "Val." Although it caused minimal damage, two crewmen were killed and a similar number wounded.

According to Japanese records, the only tokko in action that day were indeed IJNAF aircraft, although none were "Vals." Furthermore, all of them had taken off between 1600hrs and 1750hrs and targeted convoys in the Bohol Sea, with no results attained. The aircraft involved consisted of a solitary "Judy" from the Kyokujitsu-tai, a pair of "Zekes" from the 30th Kongo-tai and a solitary "Irving" from the Gekko-tai. Thus, *Cowanesque* was probably the victim of another jibaku attack, which almost certainly explains why the oiler did not report a bomb detonation after being struck.

January 4 began relatively quietly as the convoys started entering the Sulu Sea and heading north for Luzon. Among the vessels involved in the operation were Rear Admiral Felix B. Stump's escort carriers of TU 77.4.2, which were part of Vice-Admiral Jesse B. Oldendorf's powerful Bombardment and Fire Support Group. CAPs by fighters from these vessels, together with aircraft from the other escort carrier task units, successfully kept the steady stream of tokko at arm's length from the fleet for much of the day.

However, this all changed in the late afternoon when, at 1712hrs, *Ommaney Bay*, which had been missed by a previous tokko in the same area barely three weeks earlier, was targeted by a twin-engined aircraft diving out of the sun from almost directly ahead of the ship. Firing at the carrier as it zeroed in, the tokko slammed into the right side of the flightdeck amidships, destroying the after part of the vessel's open bridge and starting fires among the fueled and armed aircraft. More fires broke out among other fueled machines in the forward part of the hangar bay, triggered by an exploding bomb carried by the kamikaze aircraft. The explosion knocked out boilers Nos. 1 and 2, with the former also being ruptured along with steam lines from the forward boiler room.

The ship had been caught by surprise, and as a result the damage control parties were not fully prepared when *Ommaney Bay* was hit. Coupled with the failure of power and fire mains pressure in the forward part of the ship as a result of the forward boiler room being knocked out of commission by the hit, the fires raged unchecked, particularly in the hangar bay. Attempts by the accompanying destroyers to come alongside to assist in fighting the fires were hampered by the intense heat of the blaze in the hangar bay, and by 1750hrs the order to abandon ship had been given as the wounded were being lowered over the side. At 1812hrs Capt Howard L. Young was the last man off *Ommaney Bay*, and six minutes later nine aerial torpedoes, stored at the aft end of the hangar bay, detonated with a violent explosion, collapsing the after flightdeck and inducing a list to starboard. The vessel was beyond saving, and at 1940hrs the destroyer *Burns* was ordered to sink the gutted escort carrier – a task it carried out at 1958hrs. A total of 93 crewmen had been killed and 65 wounded in the attack.

The twin-engined aircraft that struck *Ommaney Bay* would appear to have been one of an unknown number of Ki-45s from the Oka-tai that sortied for Mindoro that day. The "Nick," unlike the "Lily," "Helen," and "Peggy" bombers that were also sent on tokko missions in the Philippines by the IJAAF, was comparatively successful in this role, having scored hits on several ships during the campaign, with more victims to come off Okinawa (see Chapter 5).

Soon after *Ommaney Bay* was struck, the Liberty ship SS *Lewis L. Dyche* was off San Jose when it too was hit by an aircraft (reported in some quarters to be a "Val"). Like the unfortunate *John Burke* barely a week earlier, the vessel was also carrying a lethal cargo of ammunition and fuzes, and it too was almost instantaneously vaporized in a tremendous explosion. The 71 men on board stood no chance, and at least one sailor on a nearby ship was also killed along with several more wounded. The Liberty ship SS *Kyle V. Johnson* was lightly damaged too, and it would be targeted again eight days later.

The "Val" that struck *Lewis L. Dyche* could have possibly been yet another "Sonia" – a single aircraft from the Shinshu-tai, flown by Sgt Naoyuki Kobayashi, had undertaken a sortie that day. The sinking of *Ommaney Bay* and *Lewis L. Dyche* was a bad start to the campaign for Luzon, and marked the first day of a final spasm of ferocious assaults against the invasion fleet by the tokko units that was only surpassed by the massed Kikusui attacks off Okinawa that spring.

The sheer volume of the attacks that saw conventional aircraft mixed in with kamikazes, coupled with the (understandably) questionable accuracy of the aircraft identification by the crewmen on the vessels being targeted, means that attribution of the tokko attacks off Luzon in the next few days is an almost impossible task. With IJAAF and IJNAF air power in-theater virtually at its end and the defenders in the Philippines almost totally cut off from Japan, there was also the possibility that official records of tokko operations at this juncture are incomplete. This further complicates any attempts to attribute attacks with any degree of accuracy.

January 5 saw the first elements of the invasion force arrive off central Luzon after traversing the Mindoro Strait. Numerous enemy aircraft were plotted on the radars, and many of them were intercepted by CAPs that had been launched by the numerous escort carriers of TU 77.4.2. USS *Savo Island* (CVE-78) was included in this force, and the pilots of its embarked Fleet Composite (VC) Squadron 27 (equipped with both FM-2 Wildcats and TBM Avengers) would claim 61.5 aerial victories during the Philippines campaign – the highest number of kills credited to a Fleet Composite Squadron. The majority of these successes were over kamikazes, and on January 5 the unit would tally 15 enemy aircraft destroyed. VC-27's CO, and nine-victory ace, Lt Ralph Elliott and Ens Robert Pfeifer (4.5 victories) were in the thick of the action, the former leading a division of FM-2s on a CAP at 17,000ft, with a second division led by Lt Roger Mulcahy at 12,000ft.

At 1645hrs many bogies were reported approaching the Bombardment and Fire Support Group, and in the ensuing interceptions the two divisions became separated. Elliott and his wingman, Ens James Manfrin, were vectored out and found a Ki-61 "Tony" flying at 3000ft. The two pilots made multiple passes on the Japanese aircraft, and its pilot used skillful maneuvering to avoid getting hit for as long as possible. Finally, Elliott managed to get onto the "Tony's" tail and send it crashing into the sea. Elliott and Manfrin then spotted a Mitsubishi J2M3 "Jack," and they bracketed the IJNAF fighter and made repeated runs on it until it too plunged into the sea. Ordered to return to their carrier, Elliott and Manfrin spotted what they identified as a "Jill."

A short while later squadronmate Lt Mulcahy spotted several "Zekes" approaching the Bombardment and Fire Support Group and led his division in to attack them from the stern. However, when he pressed the gun button to open fire he found that his weapons had frozen. Breaking off his attack, Mulcahy ordered Ens Robert Pfeifer to take the lead. In only a few minutes Pfeifer managed to shoot down four "Zekes." Describing the combat in the squadron's action report, Pfeifer recalled:

> I was not in the best position at the beginning of this run, so kicking a little right rudder, I shot a burst of tracers off to the Zeke's right and he immediately turned to port, putting me in a beautiful position for a shot from "seven o'clock above." I got in a long burst that struck the port wing and cockpit vicinity, and the aircraft began to smoke, finally bursting into flames and crashing into the sea. I surprised another "Zeke," catching him about 50ft off the water and hitting him from "six o'clock above." He immediately rolled over onto his back and then crashed into the sea. No fire or smoke was observed, and it is believed that the pilot was killed on this run or that he lost control of his aircraft in a desperate attempt to lose me.
>
> I then retired westward, with Lt(jg) Uthoff on my wing. I spotted another "Zeke" a few minutes later attempting to make a stern run on Uthoff. Uthoff and I weaved towards each other and I made a flat side run on the "Zeke," shooting from "two o'clock slightly above." Lt(jg) Uthoff observed the aircraft nose over and crash into the sea. Lt(jg) Uthoff made a head-on run

on another "Zeke," and he got in a short burst with no effect. Following Uthoff on this head-on run, I got in a long accurate burst from "twelve" to "two o'clock," hitting the airplane on the port side of the engine and cockpit. The engine and cockpit began to disintegrate and the aircraft began to smoke and burn. It was last observed going into a sharp wingover to the left, before crashing into the water.

I had closed to point blank range – approximately 30ft – when firing at the last "Zeke," and after retiring to my carrier, I found my windshield and engine covered with human flesh, hair and blood stains.

These "Zekes" were the only IJNAF aircraft sent into action that day, the 201st Kokutai contributing no fewer than 17 "Zekes" (15 tokko from the 18th Kongo-tai under the command of Lt Shinichi Kanaya and two escorts). Taking off from Mabalacat just before 1600hrs, there is little doubt as to the identity of their targets – Rear Admiral Felix B. Stump's escort carriers and the nearby anti-submarine hunter-killer group under Capt J. C. Cronin, which the remnants of the 18th Kongo-tai formation encountered shortly after it had been mauled by VC-27.

The next few minutes saw several of the escort carriers and their screening vessels being targeted, with photographers on board the carriers USS *Manila Bay* (CVE-61) and USS *Natoma Bay* (CVE-62) clearly capturing on film what were bomb-laden "Zekes" in their death dives. In short order *Manila Bay*, *Savo Island*, and the destroyer escort USS *Stafford* (DE-411)

The US Navy's entry into Lingayen Gulf prompted an intense Japanese reaction that resulted in no fewer than 13 ships being hit on January 5, 1945, including the heavy cruiser USS *Louisville* (CA-28). As seen in this view, the suicide aircraft (probably a Ki-43 from the 9th Hakko's Ichisei-tai) is just about to strike the cruiser. Fortunately for the ship's crew, the aircraft hit the heavily armored face of No. 2 turret, which confined the damage to that area and resulted in only one sailor being killed and 59 wounded. *(NARA)* were all hit and damaged to varying degrees (*Savo Island* escaped with a glancing blow, *Manila Bay* suffered 66 casualties, including 14 killed, and *Stafford* had to return to San Francisco to be repaired) by the 18th Kongo-tai. Also hit was the RAN's heavy cruiser *Australia*, which was part of Oldendorf's Bombardment and Fire Support Group sailing nearby. The vessel turned out to be quite the tokko magnet, having encountered a "Sonia" on a jibaku mission during the Leyte campaign as detailed earlier in this chapter and subsequently being hit several more times in Lingayen Gulf over the next few days.

The IJAAF was also active on January 5, with the destroyer USS *Helm* (DD-388) being clipped by what its crew reported was an "Oscar" from a force of five aircraft. Shortly afterwards, at 1705hrs, Oldendorf's Fire and Support Group was picked out as a target by three aircraft approaching the ships from their port bow. One near-missed the Australian destroyer *Arunta*, hitting the water close enough to its port side that the vessel was riddled with fragments, killing two crewmen and severing power to its steering motors for two hours.

A second aircraft from this group was shot down as it headed for another unidentified destroyer in the screen, while a third machine immediately behind it managed to avoid being hit by flak and headed for the heavy cruiser *Louisville*. Its crew held their fire until the aircraft cleared the unknown destroyer, although this in turn shortened the amount of time the ship's gunners had to fire on the tokko. The delay proved fatal as, despite the aircraft trailing smoke from numerous hits, it crashed into the *Louisville*'s No. 2 turret.

Twenty-four hours after being hit, *Louisville* was struck again by a tokko while sailing in Lingayen Gulf. A total of 41 crew were killed and at least 125 wounded when the D4Y1 of the Kyokujisu-tai crashed into the starboard signal bridge, the bulk of the casualties being caused by burning aviation fuel. Despite the damage, and with no functioning bridge, *Louisville* shelled the invasion beaches and shot down several enemy aircraft over the next 72 hours before withdrawing on January 9. The cruiser would return to the action off Okinawa in late April. *(NARA)*

Despite the heavy cruiser's after-action report describing the strike as little more than "a glancing blow," with "the plane continuing over the starboard side after the first impact," photographs show that the aircraft struck the turret relatively full on, exploding in a huge fireball. Its bomb (or bombs, according to some eyewitnesses) exploded and inflicted damage on the well-protected turret, while the ignited fuel from the tokko – including the contents of one wing that was blown onto the forward shield of the open bridge – started a fire, which was quickly contained. Little real damage was done to the ship, although one crewman was killed and 59 wounded, including its commanding officer, Capt R. L. Hicks.

The tokko were identified as "Zekes," but if the reports of *Louisville*'s attacker carrying two bombs and the number of aircraft involved are accurate, it would make the three "Oscars" of the 9th Hakko's Ichisei-tai the most likely culprits. The group, led by 1Lt Hiroshi Tsuru, had departed Del Carmen field that afternoon along with four "Sonias" from the Sekicho-tai (three aircraft) and Shinshu-tai (one).

Ships from the Minesweeping and Hydrographic Group, out in front of the main force, were also attacked that day at 1730hrs, with the seaplane tender USS *Orca* (AVP-49), tug USS *Apache* (ATF-67), and Landing Craft, Infantry (gunboat) *LCI(G)-70* all receiving minor damage. Their attackers were identified as "Vals," and gunners on board ATF-67 claimed to have shot four of them down.

January 6 turned out to be the climax of the tokko offensive off Luzon, with Japanese records indicating a total of 44 aircraft (38 IJNAF and six IJAAF) being sent against the invasion fleet as vessels started arriving in Lingayen Gulf. Starting before noon and continuing throughout the day, the IJNAF's 19th, 20th, 22nd, 23rd, and 30th Kongo-tai sortied 35 "Zekes," with two "Judys" from the Kyokujitsu-tai and a single "Jill" from the Hachiman-tai rounding out the service's contribution that day. The more modest IJAAF contribution included two "Sonias" from the Tesshin-tai and one from the Sekicho-tai, along with single "Nicks" from the Oka-tai and the 11th Hakko's Kokon-tai.

The attackers hit in roughly three separate waves – the first just before noon, the second at around 1430hrs, and the third from 1730hrs onwards. A total of 15 ships were struck, with the high-speed destroyer minesweeper USS *Long* (DMS-12) being sunk after completing its first sweep of Lingayen Gulf. Targeted by two "Zekes" while sailing at

A remarkable view of the approaching A6M5 that struck the battleship USS *New Mexico* (BB-40) on January 6, 1945 off San Fernando, in Lingayen Gulf. The aircraft hit the port side of the bridge moments later, killing the ship's commanding officer, Capt Robert Fleming, and Prime Minister Winston Churchill's representative with Gen MacArthur's HQ, Lt Gen Herbert Lumsden, along with 29 others. A further 87 crewmen were wounded. *(NARA)*

25 knots, the vessel was hit on the port side below the bridge by one of these aircraft shortly after noon. The crew was soon ordered to abandon ship due to an uncontrollable fire amidships. Although *Long* remained seaworthy after the first hit, it was finished off during the mid-afternoon attack by a second tokko that destroyed the bridge and broke DMS-12's back.

Long's sister-ship USS *Brooks* (APD-10) was also permanently knocked out of the war that same day when it too was struck on the port side by a "Zeke," starting a fire amidships. Initially built as a destroyer, and a veteran of almost 25 years' service, APD-10 was subsequently towed back across the Pacific to San Pedro, California, and eventually decommissioned eight months after it had been attacked.

The numerous tokko, together with the stream of conventional air attacks, led to a very confused picture of the battle that took place that day. A lack of information regarding the takeoff times of some of the attackers combined with contradictory information from witnesses and action reports (for example, was the battleship USS *California* (BB-44) hit by a "Zeke" or twin-engined "Irving" in the late afternoon?) means that attribution for most of the strikes on this day is close to impossible. It is known, however, that the ships hit around noon were attacked by "Zekes" from the 22nd Kongo-tai, whose aircraft departed Angeles airfield at 1100hrs and were the sole group of tokko to sortie before midday. Furthermore, the minesweepers *Long* and *Brooks* were the first ships hit that day, with their crews stating that they had been attacked by "Zekes."

Confusingly, the destroyer *Richard P. Leary*, which was also targeted at this time, noted in its action report that the vessel had been clipped by a twin-engined "Irving" – none, however, were listed in the Japanese records of the tokko launched that day. Finally, the battleship *New Mexico* (which had been hit in the bridge and suffered 31 fatalities, one of whom was its commanding officer, Capt R. W. Fleming, and 87 wounded) and the destroyers USS *Allen M. Sumner* (DD-692) and *Walke* did not identify their noon attackers.

Two-and-a-half hours later, the light cruiser *Columbia* and destroyer *O'Brien* were both hit. They had almost certainly fallen victim to the 19th Kongo-tai, which had taken off from its base at Mabalacat just before 1300hrs. A photograph taken from on board *Columbia* backs this up, clearly showing that its attacker was a "Zeke." At 1729hrs the light cruiser was hit yet again, this time by a "Val" according to the ship's action report. Once again, no D3As had been used as tokko that day, and the famous series of photographs showing the aircraft crashing into *Columbia* clearly reveal that it was in fact a "Sonia" from either the Tesshin-tai – its two aircraft were flown by 2Lt Satoshi (or possibly Akira) Iwahiro and Sgt Maj Takehito Ogawa – or the Sekicho-tai (flown by 2Lt Naoki Okabe). The unfortunate *Australia* also reported that the aircraft that slammed into it at 1734hrs was yet another "Val," when the tokko was almost certainly a "Sonia" from either of these units.

Another repeat victim of a kamikaze attack on this day was the heavy cruiser *Louisville*, whose crew reported being attacked by a "Kate" and a "Val" at 1730hrs, with the former crashing into its starboard signal bridge – 41 sailors were killed and 125 wounded. A piece of wreckage that appears to have been an inner landing gear door was recovered by crewman John Duffy, and it was adorned with kanji stenciling that when translated read "Suisei Model 11, Aichi 156x" (last number unclear). This means that the vessel was actually struck by a D4Y1 "Judy," making it likely that the attacker was the Kyokujisu-tai aircraft that took off from Mabalacat crewed by Lt(jg) Kuni Fukino and Ens Seisaku Miyake. Despite having been extensively damaged by two tokko hits in 24 hours, and with no functioning bridge, *Louisville* shelled the invasion beaches and shot down several enemy aircraft over the next 72 hours before withdrawing on January 9 and proceeding to Mare Island Navy Yard, north of San Francisco, for repairs. It would return to the action off Okinawa in late April.

The number of attacks and the damage sustained on this day worried the US Navy to the point that TF 38, which had been in the Bashi Channel conducting strikes on Formosa, redirected its attention towards the airfields

Among those to die following the tokko strike on *Louisville* on January 6 was 50-year-old Rear Admiral Theodore E. Chandler, commander of Cruiser Division 4 and a US Navy veteran of 30 years. Minutes after his flagship had been hit, Chandler had jumped from the cruiser's bridge to the signal bridge – despite having been horribly burned by gasoline flames – to help deploy hoses alongside enlisted men as the latter fought to contain the fire. He then waited his turn for first aid with the same sailors he had just manned the hoses with. The Admiral's lungs had been so severely scorched that he was beyond help, however, and he died the following day in spite of the efforts of medical personnel on board the cruiser. *(NARA)*

ABOVE
This group portrait of the gun crew of a four-inch Mk V high-angle (HA) antiaircraft weapon on board *Australia* was taken during the campaign in the Philippines. In the back row, second from left, is Able Seaman William Robert Fisher, who was killed in action during a tokko attack (probably by a "Sonia") on *Australia* on January 6, 1945. Fourteen sailors died in total, with a further 26 being wounded. (AWM)

on Luzon during a three-day aerial campaign from January 7. This successfully suppressed Japanese air activity during that time, and although 11 aircraft from six tokko units still managed to take to the air that day, it was a far cry from the number generated on the 6th. No ships reported being hit.

January 8 saw the IJAAF get off to an early start, with 15 aircraft from five tokko units targeting the fleet massing in Lingayen Gulf soon after sunrise. The Kokon-tai sortied three "Nicks" from Angeles South at 0640hrs, and at least one of the "Oscar" tokko units joined it in a dawn attack. Two "Sonia" units were also possibly involved as well, although IJAAF records are not clear on this. Again, it was the heavy cruiser *Australia* that incurred the wrath of the tokko, its crew reporting two near misses that morning as the vessel sailed into Lingayen Gulf as the "tail-end Charlie" of the Bombardment Group. The first attacker, reported as a "twin-engined bomber," was shot down by Wildcat fighters flying a CAP as it bore in from *Australia*'s port side. The aircraft splashed into the water 20 yards from its target and skidded into the side of the heavy cruiser at 0720hrs, with a second attacker suffering a near-identical fate at 0739hrs, with the exception that it was antiaircraft fire that brought it down.

Australia clearly shows the damage inflicted following attacks by five tokko in four days off Luzon on January 5, 6, 8, and 9, 1945 while helping to protect the invasion fleet in Lingayen Gulf. The vessel had previously been hit by either a "Val" or a "Sonia" off Leyte on October 21, 1944 in what was probably an impromptu jibaku attack. Some 39 sailors were killed and 56 wounded during the tokko strikes off Luzon. *(NARA)*

The damage inflicted on *Australia* on January 9 was caused by a lone Ki-43 from the Ichisei-tai, which hit the heavy cruiser's mast strut and forward funnel, before crashing overboard. The aircraft also knocked out the ship's radar and wireless systems. Despite this final tokko hit causing no casualties among the crew, the decision was made to pull the battered vessel out of line and send it home to Sydney, New South Wales. It was given the task of escorting transport vessels back to Leyte, in company with several other Allied warships damaged by kamikaze strikes, on the evening of January 9. Temporary repairs were made to the cruiser at Manus, prior to it sailing to Australia. *(AWM)*

However, a bomb carried by the second tokko exploded against the warship's port flank near its waterline, opening up a 14ft-by-8ft hole in the hull and causing sufficient flooding to create a five-degree list, but inflicting no casualties.

The first attack was almost certainly carried out by one of the Kokon-tai "Nicks," although no information is available as to the identity of the second attacker – it may have been another Ki-45, as the aircraft could carry two 551lb bombs externally. At 0751hrs, just 12 minutes after *Australia* had been hit by a bomb, the escort carrier USS *Kadashan Bay* (CVE-76), tasked with providing air cover for the invasion convoy together with *Marcus Island*, was struck by an "Oscar" on its starboard side near the waterline. The impact caused flooding to its aviation fuel pump room, which meant the carrier was unable to continue flight operations. The vessel was subsequently forced to return to San Francisco to be repaired.

The other tokko units sent into action during the course of the day included the Sekicho- and Shinshu-tai, with three and two "Sonias," respectively, and the Ichisei- and Seika-tai with two "Oscars" each – the latter unit drew its aircraft from the Philippines-based 31st Sentai.

That evening at 1857hrs, the escort carrier *Kitkun Bay*, which was part of the luckless "Taffy 3" targeted by the very first organized tokko strikes back in late October, was hit again by one of two aircraft reported as "Oscars." They had initially been part of a group of six Ki-43s that had been whittled down by FM-2 Wildcats from CVE-71 and USS *Shamrock Bay* (CVE-84). The carrier was struck on its port side near the waterline, which, as with *Kadashan Bay*, caused flooding and precluded further flight operations. At virtually the same time the ship was hit by an errant five-inch shell on its starboard side, this having been fired at the tokko by one of the nearby screening destroyers, or possibly CVE-84. Good damage control work soon brought the resultant fires and flooding under control, by which point 16 crewmen were dead and 37 wounded. The following day *Kitkun Bay*, having by then developed a list and with only one engine running, withdrew from "Taffy 3" and proceeded by stages first to Leyte, then

Manus, Pearl Harbor and on to San Pedro, arriving there on February 28. The carrier would not return to Third Fleet until late June.

The action on January 9 also started early, with a twin-engined aircraft knocking the foremast off the destroyer escort *Hodges* before plunging into the sea without doing further damage at 0700hrs. This was almost certainly the solitary "Nick" from the Oka-tai, flown by 1Lt Sadao Ikeuchi, that took off from Zablan at 0530hrs and was listed in IJAAF records as having encountered the enemy fleet at 0610hrs.

That day also saw *Columbia* and *Australia* attacked yet again. The former, already three feet down by the stern and with its two rear main batteries out of commission from the "Sonia" hit three days earlier, was close inshore to start the day's bombardment when the tokko struck at 0745hrs. Surrounded by smaller landing craft, the light cruiser was hit by a single-engined fighter carrying a bomb. The resulting explosion blew its forward main battery director overboard and knocked out the forward SK air search and SG surface search radars. Sixteen crewmen were killed and seven listed as missing, the latter mostly trapped inside the battery director. A further 97 were wounded.

This attack, though attributed to a "Tojo" in *Columbia*'s action report, was probably carried out by PO1c Shigeru Kojima in a "Zeke" from the 24th Kongo-tai, which had taken off from Nichols Field at 0650hrs. The cumulative damage from three tokko strikes in four days finally forced CL-56 out of the line and back to the US for repairs. It returned to Leyte in mid-June and was in action again shortly thereafter.

As with *Columbia*'s crew, *Australia*'s complement had been depleted by the series of tokko attacks – 39 sailors had been killed and 56 wounded from the hits and near misses over the past four days. The losses had primarily come from its antiaircraft gun crews, exposed at their stations during attacks. By January 9 there were only enough trained personnel to man one of the two twin four-inch gun mounts situated on either side of the cruiser

At 1311hrs, while shelling targets in preparation for the amphibious landings in Lingayen Gulf, both *Australia* and the battleship USS *Mississippi* (BB-41) were hit in rapid succession by a pair of aircraft identified by the crew of the latter vessel as "Vals." The tokko that hit the heavy cruiser caught a mast strut and the forward funnel before crashing overboard. Aside from the damage caused to the funnel, the aircraft also knocked out the ship's radar and wireless systems. Despite causing no casualties among

Dressed in their winter blue sailor suits, ratings on board *Australia* carry a propeller and other parts from the aircraft that hit the ship on October 21, 1944. This photograph was probably taken shortly after the battered cruiser reached Sydney. (*Naval Historical Collection/AWM*)

the crew, the decision was made to pull the battered vessel out of the line and send it home to Sydney, New South Wales, so that the ship could be permanently repaired in the dockyard at Cockatoo Island. However, with Australian shipyards having been told to prioritize repairs to British Pacific Fleet vessels, the heavy cruiser had to sail to Plymouth, in Devon, to be overhauled. This refit was not completed until December 1945.

Mississippi was also lightly damaged, although it was less lucky in respect to casualties, with 23 killed and 63 wounded. Again, the hardest hit were the exposed antiaircraft gunners. IJNAF records list the 25th and 26th Kongo-tai as having each sortied a pair of "Zekes" from Tuguegarao, in northeastern Luzon, that day at 1200hrs and 1600hrs, respectively. The IJAAF's tokko contribution consisted of just two "Oscars" from the Ichisei-tai, and it is believed that these aircraft were responsible for the attack on *Australia* and, given that the vessel was attacked at the same time, *Mississippi*.

On January 10 TF 38 departed the waters off Luzon for a series of strikes against enemy targets in Indochina, having successfully curtailed Japanese air activity in-theater for the time being. This meant that there was relatively little tokko activity over the next 48 hours, with only two ships being hit by aircraft on the 10th and none on the 11th.

At about 0710hrs on the 10th the destroyer escort *LeRay Wilson* was conducting an anti-submarine patrol off the western entrance to Lingayen Gulf when its crew spotted a twin-engined bomber emerging out of the gloom of the western sky. The ship had little time to react, for the bomber was first observed just 1,000 yards off its port bow, approaching from almost dead ahead and flying just above the surface of the sea. Identified as a "Betty," this was most likely the modified To-Go "Peggy" bomber flown by Capt Kunio Soga of the Fugaku-tai that had taken off from Clark Field at 0400hrs.

To its crews' credit, *LeRay Wilson* responded admirably to the threat, despite its close proximity. Quickly engaging the bomber with antiaircraft fire, they scored several hits and set its port wing aflame, causing the pilot to veer off his intended flightpath. The last detail was crucial in securing the survival of the 1,350-ton warship, for it would have been unlikely to have survived a direct hit from the explosive-packed "Peggy." Instead, the bomber's wing clipped the two 20mm mounts on the port side amidships and plunged into the sea beyond. The broken wing released burning fuel onto the exposed surfaces of the ship and started a fire that took several hours to contain, although the vessel was never in any danger of sinking and was underway again by 1000hrs. Eight crewmen were killed and three others lost at sea, with two more wounded.

Later that day the IJAAF's Seika- and Gokoku-tai launched four and one "Oscars," respectively, while the Kokon-tai sortied a solitary "Nick" against the Allied ships off Luzon. The attack transport USS *DuPage* (APA-41) was hit by what its crew identified as a "Nick" at 1915hrs as the vessel departed Lingayen Gulf. Confusingly, the ship's action report stated that it was attacked by two aircraft, which would seem to rule out Kokon-tai's singleton.

Finally, *LST-610* and the destroyer USS *Robinson* (DD-562) both suffered modest damage from unidentified tokko that crashed into the water after just missing their targets.

January 12 saw the last massed attack by the tokko units in the Philippines, although by this time Japanese aerial resistance, save for the few remaining kamikaze aircraft, had by and large ended. Indeed, most pilots had by then evacuated anything that could be made flyable to Formosa. At 0645hrs the destroyer escort USS *Gilligan* (DE-508) was performing yet another anti-submarine patrol at the mouth of Lingayen Gulf when its radar picked up a "bogey" at a distance of approximately ten nautical miles approaching from the still-dark western sky. At 0658hrs the contact was sighted at less than 1,000 yards off the starboard beam, and all guns on board the ship opened fire as the tokko rapidly closed on DE-508.

The attack on *Gilligan* closely mirrored that suffered by *LeRay Wilson* two days earlier. It too was targeted by a twin-engined bomber, and following hits scored by the antiaircraft guns, the plane only managed to clip the ship (this time the aft 40mm twin mount) instead of scoring a direct hit. As with *LeRay Wilson*, the tokko's burning fuel covered the ship and caused an extensive fire from the torpedo tubes all the way to the fantail, but in this instance the blaze was under control by 0715hrs and damage assessment could then be undertaken. The hit had taken away the aft 40mm weapon and its mounting, the gun director and a stub mast and its radio antennae. The subsequent fire had wrecked the torpedo tubes, their control mechanism, and the torpedo crane hoist. Twelve sailors were killed (ten were lost at sea) and 13 wounded.

Shortly after *Gilligan* had been hit, the destroyer escort USS *Richard W. Suesens* (DE-342) left the inner anti-submarine ring (having been reassigned from the outer ring due to an earlier sonar failure) and moved alongside DE-508 to assist its crew in fighting the fire. While doing so, the vessel also came under attack, being narrowly missed by a crashing aircraft (reported as a "Val" by *Gilligan* but identified as a "Hamp" by *Richard W. Suesens*) at 0731hrs. The near miss riddled DE-342 with shrapnel fragments and wounded 11 men, but otherwise did little damage.

Twenty minutes later, it was the turn of the veteran destroyer-turned-high-speed transport USS *Belknap* (APD-34) to be targeted by the tokko. Undertaking antiaircraft screening duties at the mouth of Lingayen Gulf that morning, it had received a somewhat premature "all clear" signal at 0748hrs, only for lookouts on board the ship to spot four "Tonys" almost directly overhead two minutes later. *Belknap*'s action report noted that these aircraft had most likely eluded radar detection by following a Catalina flying boat that had passed over the ships immediately before they were seen. These tokko commenced their attack dives shortly thereafter.

Only the first pilot penetrated the storm of fire thrown up from the ship, whose gunners, according to the action report, knocked one of the "Tony's" bombs into the sea 500 yards from *Belknap* and set the attacker on fire. Despite this, the aircraft was carried on by its momentum and slammed into the ship's No. 2 stack, destroying it. The crash and detonation of the remaining bomb caused severe damage to *Belknap* that included knocking the vessel's Nos. 1 and 2 boilers offline and rendering its No. 2 five-inch gun inoperable, as well as killing 38 crewmen and wounding 49. APD-34 was subsequently towed to Manus and patched up, before heading back to Philadelphia Navy Yard, via California, in June. Deemed surplus to requirements and not repaired, the 26-year-old warship was decommissioned in early August and sold for scrap in November.

Gilligan, *Richard W. Suesens*, and *Belknap* were just three of the eight vessels hit on January 12, with the remaining five being transports and Liberty ships. Indeed, the latter bore the brunt of further attacks later in the day from 30 tokko sent into action by the IJAAF, although as with the

Pilots and crewmen from the IJAAF's Kyoko-tai tokko unit receive a farewell toast from their commanding officer before heading off on a kamikaze mission from Lipa airfield, near Manila, in mid-December 1944. This unit (consisting of airmen from the 75th and 208th Sentai) flew specially modified Ki-48-II KAI "Lily" light bombers on several missions during the final stages of the campaign in the Philippines. Four of the Kyoko-tai's aircraft can be seen parked behind the taxiing Ki-43 in the background. *(Tony Holmes collection)*

strikes six days earlier, attempting to reconcile Japanese records with Allied ones when there were so many attacks is an extremely difficult, if not impossible, task.

Among the ships to be struck was SS *Kyle V. Johnson*, which had been lightly damaged by a near miss eight days earlier. Carrying 500 US Army troops and 2,500 tons of vehicles and gasoline in drums, it was part of a 100-vessel convoy that consisted of cargo ships and LSTs. During an attack by six or more aircraft, one of the tokko targeted *Kyle V. Johnson* and was hit by 20mm gunfire just prior to crashing into the starboard side of the ship near the No. 3 hatch. The aircraft's engine plowed through the hull plating into a between-decks area crowded with troops and then on into the lower hold. One of the survivors of this attack subsequently stated that "There was a blinding flash and an explosion so heavy it blew the steel hatch beams higher than the flying bridge." The ship quickly dropped out of the convoy to fight the fire, allowing its damage control parties to eventually extinguish the blaze and enable *Kyle V. Johnson* to rejoin the fleet. No fewer than 128 soldiers and one sailor had been killed and many more wounded by the kamikaze strike on the Liberty ship.

The known attackers that day included a single "Peggy" from the Fugaku-tai, the final five serviceable "Lilys" from the Kyoko-tai and a pair of "Nicks" from the Oka-tai, which could have been the "twin-engined bomber" that attacked *Gilligan*. However, its action report stated that the estimated wingspan of the aircraft, which was identified as a G4M "Betty" or Mitsubishi G3M "Nell" bomber, was 81ft – identical to that of the G4M. But no IJNAF twin-engined types were active that day, so it must have been a Ki-67 from the Fugaku-tai that targeted the destroyer escort.

The "Val" or "Hamp" (two aircraft that looked quite different from each other) that nicked *Richard W. Suesens* could well have been the single Koizumi-tai "Sonia" flown by WO Kunio Kusumi. Indeed, *Gilligan*'s crew claimed that DE-342 was hit by a "Val" – a type readily confused with the Ki-51. *Belknap*'s crew also seem to have misidentified their attackers, for no Ki-61s undertook dedicated kamikaze missions that day. An all-out tokko effort was made by the 4th Kokugun, however, the overall command element of the IJAAF in the Philippines dispatching 21 "Franks" from the Seika-tai against ships in Lingayen Gulf. These aircraft were drawn from the already-depleted ranks of the 1st, 11th, 72nd, and 73rd Sentai.

The Seika-tai tried to repeat its success the following day, although this time the unit only managed to sortie two "Franks" flown by 2Lt Osamu Yoshida of the 73rd Sentai and Cpl Shichinosuke Kajita of the 200th Sentai. Nevertheless, at least one found TU 77.4.1 off Lingayen Gulf, and at 0858hrs its pilot dove virtually unannounced into the escort carrier *Salamaua*. Indeed, the crew only spotted it during the terminal stage of the fighter's dive at the ship's flightdeck amidships.

One of the "Frank's" two 551lb bombs failed to explode and disappeared into the South China Sea after tearing a hole through the starboard side of the ship beneath the waterline. The other bomb, however, did detonate inside the ship after penetrating the flightdeck and hangar bay, leading to an immediate loss of power, steering, and communications. The fire on the flightdeck was rapidly extinguished, but the blaze in the hangar bay was a lot more serious as the carrier had lost mains pressure aft due to blast damage and could not use hoses to tackle the conflagration in this part of the ship as a result. Numerous bombs, torpedoes, and rockets meant for *Salamaua*'s aircraft had to be hastily jettisoned overboard from the hangar bay to avoid them "cooking off" by the spreading fire, which was only doused with hoses linked to still-functioning water pumps in the forward part of the ship. The tokko strike claimed the lives of ten crewmen, with five more lost overboard and 88 wounded.

The attack transport *Zeilin* was also struck earlier that morning as it departed Luzon, bound for Leyte. The ship's attacker was identified in its action report as "either a 'Frank' or [an IJNAF Aichi B7A] 'Grace' " due to the twin-row, 18-cylinder radial engine recovered on board following the attack. The crash caused little damage to the ship, with the ensuing fire extinguished by 0830hrs – little more than nine minutes after *Zeilin* had been hit.

The limited amount of damage done was due in no small part to, as the action report noted, its attacker not carrying a bomb. At this point, however, things get a little unusual, with the report adding that, rather than conventional ordnance, the aircraft was instead carrying "three-quarter-inch [diameter] incendiary missiles of gas pipe construction," adding that the missiles were "three inches in length and filled with incendiary material, possibly thermite." More than 100 of these were recovered on board, with some found as far away as 100ft from where the aircraft hit. It also noted that some of these were discovered burned out following the crash, others having been extinguished after starting fires and yet more that had failed to ignite altogether.

The description of these weapons matches the IJNAF's 70.5lb Type 99 No. 3 Mk 3 or 125lb Type 3 No. 6 Mk 6 aerial fragmentation bombs, although their choice as an anti-ship weapon would seem odd. The crew's identity of the aircraft that hit *Zeilin* is also highly questionable, for little more than 100 "Grace" torpedo-bombers were ever built and none of these saw service in the Philippines. The other possibilities are that APA-3 was attacked by an Kawanishi N1K1-J "George" fighter or a C6N "Myrt" reconnaissance aircraft on a jibaku mission, as both types, like the "Frank" and "Grace," were powered by 18-cylinder radial engines. Furthermore, the N1K1-J and C6N were present in the Philippines in modest numbers, with a handful of "Myrts" having served with the 201st Kokutai which undertook several tokko missions with "Zekes." "Georges" of the 341st Kokutai had been tasked with escorting tokko in the Philippines, although no records exist of the ultimate IJNAF fighter being used either here or elsewhere (in later N1K2-J form) as a dedicated kamikaze aircraft.

The hits on *Zeilin* and *Salamaua* on January 13 were the last successful attacks on ships in the Philippines, with IJAAF and IJNAF air power having been almost totally destroyed by this point in the campaign. However, the end of tokko operations in the Philippines only saw the threat materialize elsewhere. In fact, the use of suicide tactics amplified as the Japanese grew increasingly desperate in their attempts to halt the Allied advance on the Home Islands.

CHAPTER 4
OTHER THEATERS

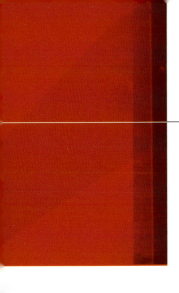

Although the vast majority of aerial tokko attacks occurred during the campaign to liberate the Philippines and the amphibious assault on Okinawa, a small number took place in other theaters as the Japanese sought to fight back with their increasingly limited means against overwhelmingly powerful Allied forces. Tokko-tai had been hastily formed throughout Japanese-occupied areas from late 1944, with units established in the southwest areas of the Empire, including Malaya and the former Dutch East Indies, as well as on Formosa, and in Japan itself.

FORMOSA

As the invasion forces established themselves on Luzon during the course of January 1945 and Japanese air activity over the Philippines dwindled into insignificance, TF 38 aircraft continued to conduct strikes against enemy-occupied territory in order to prevent the remaining troops on the island from being reinforced. On January 12 the fast carriers struck Indochina, before turning their attention on Formosa, Hong Kong, Hainan, and Canton on the 15th and 16th. After a break to refuel, they attacked targets on Formosa again on the 20th and 21st and Okinawa on the 22nd, before heading back to the floating base at Ulithi Atoll to prepare for the invasion of Iwo Jima.

The Japanese responded to these raids predominantly with conventional attacks, although a single tokko in the form of a "Zeke" from the 1st Niitaka-tai departed Taichu (Taichung), on the west coast of Formosa, at 1600hrs on January 20 in search of enemy ships reported south of Mako (Magong), on Penghu Island. No vessels

MAP LEFT USS *Franklin* (CV-13) is showered with debris as ordnance in the hangar bay explodes following an attack by a lone "Judy" on March 19, 1945. This photograph was one in a series taken by PHC Albert Bullock from the cruiser USS *Santa Fe* (CL-60), which was alongside assisting with firefighting and rescue work at the time. The carrier was just 44 nautical miles off mainland Japan when it was hit, the attack leaving the vessel dead in the water. As can be seen here, it quickly developed a dramatic 13-degree list to starboard – not because of battle damage, but owing to the large amount of water being used to fight the fires on board. *(NARA)*

ABOVE
USS *Ticonderoga* (CV-14) was hit by two tokko on January 21, 1945 while participating in TF 38's offensive against Japanese airfields on Formosa. The first aircraft slammed into the flightdeck amidships abreast of its No. 2 five-inch turret, starting fires in the gallery spaces forward of the bridge, the hangar bay, and among aircraft parked on the forward flightdeck. The vessel's commanding officer, Capt Dixie Kiefer, immediately changed course to keep the wind from fanning the blaze that erupted in the wake of the tokko strike. He also ordered the flooding of magazines and other compartments forward to prevent ordnance in these areas from exploding. The resulting induced ten-degree list to port helped drain blazing aviation fuel overboard and also jettisoned burning aircraft from the flightdeck. The second tokko struck the carrier's starboard side near the island, its bomb starting more fires among parked aircraft. Shrapnel riddled the flightdeck and killed or wounded many more sailors. Among the latter was Capt Kiefer. *(NARA)*

could be found, however. The following day three separate tokko-tai sortied in search of the enemy, the first pair of "Zekes" taking off at 1105hrs from Tainan. These aircraft were from the 1st Koku Kantai Reisen-tai (1st Air Fleet Zero Fighter Unit), with the lead fighter flown by Ens Yoshihide Horiguchi. They were instructed to attack enemy ships that had been spotted 80 nautical miles southeast of Taitung, on Formosa's east coast. The "Zekes" were followed aloft by five "Judys" from the 2nd Niitaka-tai, also based at Tainan. Led by Lt(jg) Kozo Nishida, the dive-bombers took off between 1130hrs and 1150hrs and were vectored towards another task force reported to be sailing 50 nautical miles east-southeast of Taitung. Finally, three more "Zekes" from the 3rd Niitaka-tai took off from Tuguegarao, in northern Luzon, with orders to attack an enemy fleet to the east of Formosa.

OTHER THEATERS 151

MAP LEFT
Both the IJNAF and the IJAAF had a large number of aircraft based on the island of Formosa in 1944–45, and they were frequently employed in tokko attacks on Allied ships following the invasion of Okinawa. Indeed, pilots flying aircraft from here appeared to be more skilled in kamikaze tactics than their Japan-based counterparts. Formosa-based tokko were particularly active against carriers of the British Pacific Fleet's TF 57 when they attacked airfields in the Sakishima Gunto archipelago in an attempt to stop kamikaze movements between Formosa and Okinawa.

The air attacks on TF 38 began soon after noon. A pair of aircraft approached out of the sun heading for the fast carrier *Ticonderoga* and the light carrier USS *Langley* (CVL-27) as the pair steamed 100 nautical miles to the east of Taitung with TG 38.3. One hit *Langley* with a bomb while the second aircraft slammed into *Ticonderoga*'s flightdeck amidships abreast of its No. 2 five-inch turret, starting fires in the gallery spaces forward of the bridge, the hangar bay, and among aircraft parked on the forward flightdeck. As the carrier induced a list to port and varied its speed and course in an effort to fight the various blazes, CV-14's antiaircraft batteries continued firing on enemy aircraft, claiming two other tokko shot down.

At 1258hrs the gunners took yet another aircraft under fire, and although they repeatedly hit it as it dove in at a shallow angle, the tokko plowed into the carrier's island from almost dead ahead and exploded. The flightdeck was showered with flaming fuel and splinters, which killed and wounded many crewmen caught in the open. In the island itself, skipper Capt Dixie Kiefer and his Executive Officer were wounded and left incapacitated, while the ship's Air and Gunnery Officers were both killed. No fewer than 143 sailors perished in these two attacks, with a further 202 being wounded.

Ticonderoga's action report identified its first attacker as a "Zeke," although *Langley*'s crew believed they were targeted by "Tojos." CVL-27's action report added that one of the enemy fighters dropped two small bombs in its attack, although only one exploded and caused minor damage on the flightdeck. *Langley* and nearby *Essex*, which had closed with the carriers following the sighting of enemy aircraft, reported that the ships were attacked by "Judys." Two were shot down, with the third aircraft being the one that hit *Ticonderoga*. TG 38.3's stated location tallies closely with that given to the "Zekes" of the 1st Koku Kantai Reisen-tai, and it is highly likely they were responsible for the initial attack, with the D4Ys of the 2nd Niitaka-tai following close behind.

The next ships to be targeted were the destroyers screening TF 38's carriers. USS *Maddox* (DD-731) and USS *Brush* (DD-745) were on radar picket duty 30 nautical miles northwest of TF 38 when, at 1310hrs, the former was hit by what its crew reported was a "Zeke" that had snuck in through broken cloud overhead and then got in among American aircraft returning from a strike. The ship was not seriously damaged, although seven sailors were killed and 33 wounded when the tokko hit. Had it struck the vessel ten feet further forward or aft, it could have detonated a magazine or broken the destroyer's back. As it was, *Maddox*

The second tokko to hit *Ticonderoga* (possibly a D4Y from the Formosa-based 2nd Niitaka-tai) struck the carrier's starboard side near the island, causing a fire that left the immediate area blackened and charred as seen here. The vessel was sent home to Puget Sound to be repaired, and it eventually rejoined the Fast Carrier Task Force as an element of TG 58.4 on May 22, 1945. *(NARA)*

was repaired and returned to service in March, and later gained greater fame (or infamy) as one of the main protagonists in the Gulf of Tonkin Incident in early August 1964 when it was attacked by communist torpedo-boats off the coast of North Vietnam. The ship's crew radioed for air support, which, in an amazing coincidence, was provided by aircraft from *Ticonderoga*.

IWO JIMA

Following a period of rest and refit at Ulithi Atoll in the wake of the mid-January strikes, TF 38 became TF 58 again, with the change in command seeing the fleet transferred from Third Fleet back to Fifth Fleet control as the US Navy prepared for the invasion of Iwo Jima. Part of the Volcano Islands group approximately halfway between the Mariana Islands and Japan's Home Islands, Iwo Jima had been increasingly reinforced since early 1944. This took on an added urgency following the loss of the Marianas in mid-1944 and the invasion of the Philippines in October.

The Americans, on the other hand, saw Iwo Jima as either a potential staging area for an invasion of Japan or a candidate for development into a forward fleet base. In the end, neither happened, although the island's Central and South Fields eventually became home to USAAF P-51 Mustang fighters undertaking Very Long Range missions as they escorted B-29 bombers targeting Japan. Its long runways also served as emergency divert fields for Superfortresses that were unable to make it back to the Marianas after bombing the Home Islands.

The invasion of Iwo Jima commenced on February 19, 1945. Despite the presence of two airfields on the islands and the partial completion of a third, there were no Japanese aircraft on Iwo Jima to oppose the operation. Instead, on the 18th, as the invasion fleet started to arrive offshore, preparations were made to send a tokko task force from Japan against the Allied warships. This mission fell to the 601st Kokutai at Katori, east of Tokyo, which scraped together a mixed force of 32 aircraft under the overall command of Lt Hiroshi Murakawa. Known as the 2nd Mitate-tai, the unit was composed of 12 D4Y3 "Judys" from the 1st Hikotai, an identical number of A6M5 "Zekes" from the 310th Hikotai, and eight B6N2 "Jills" from the 254th Hikotai. Facing this understrength force was an invasion fleet numbering more than 450 ships.

The 2nd Mitate-tai's D4Ys and B6Ns were divided between five units known as Kogekitai, with three of them made up of four "Judys" each armed with a 1,102lb Type 2 No. 50 Model 1 Ordinary Bomb and escorted by four "Zekes." The remaining two Kogekitai had four "Jills" each, with the aircraft from the fourth Kogekitai carrying a single centerline-mounted 1,760lb No. 80 Mk 5 Land Bomb each. The fifth Kogekitai was a conventional torpedo-bomber attack unit, and each of its "Jills" carried a Type 91 weapon when sent into action. Both B6N Kogekitai were manned by specialist night-attack crews.

The original plan was to attack the invasion force on February 20, but bad weather pushed this back a day to the 21st. With Iwo Jima more than 650 nautical miles away, the 2nd Mitate-tai had to refuel en route at Hachiro Jima, 175 nautical miles to the south of Katori. Once this had been successfully accomplished, the "Judys" took off from Hachiro Jima at 1400hrs and the "Jills" followed two hours later, their crews intending to time their attacks for the late afternoon and early evening. However, technical issues started bedeviling the 2nd Mitate-tai at this point. A "Judy" and two "Zekes" from the 2nd Kogekitai departed Hachiro Jima late, as did another A6M5 from the 3rd Kogekitai. A second "Zeke" from the latter unit was forced to return to Hachiro Jima after it was

On February 21, 1945 USS *Saratoga* (CV-3) was struck by four "Zekes" and "Judys" from the 2nd Kogekitai off Chichijima, the aircraft hitting the ship's forward flightdeck. Taking advantage of low cloud and *Saratoga*'s minimal three-destroyer escort, the tokko had scored two or three bomb hits on the carrier in just three minutes prior to the four aircraft being flown into the vessel. The forward flightdeck of the veteran carrier was wrecked, its starboard side holed twice, and large fires started in the hangar deck. *(NARA)*

CV-3's damage control party starts to clear away the sections of flightdeck that had been badly splintered and burned during the day's previous attacks, which had killed 123 crewmen and wounded a further 192. (NARA)

struck by mechanical problems, as were single "Jills" from each Kogekitai – one flew back to Hachiro Jima and the other to Chichijima.

The remaining "Judys" and their "Zeke" escorts were detected just before 1630hrs by the fleet off Iwo Jima as the aircraft approached on a gray, overcast afternoon. The tokko crews quickly singled out the veteran carrier *Saratoga* for attack, the ship having been detached from TG 58.5 that morning with a screening force of just three destroyers and sent to

This F6F-5 was just one of 36 aircraft (from a total complement of 70) assigned to Carrier Air Group (Night) 53 that were destroyed on February 21. Trained for nocturnal fighting, the specialized air group had only been in action for five days when the carrier *Saratoga* was so badly damaged that it was put out of combat commission for the remainder of the war. (NARA)

the northeast of Iwo Jima to provide night CAP over the island and undertake nocturnal "heckler" missions over Chichijima. The carrier was detected before it had reached its assigned station, however, with the six aircraft of the 2nd Kogekitai starting their attacks at 1700hrs. The ship's crew correctly identified their opponents as a mix of "Zekes" and "Judys," and four of them – along with two or three bombs – hit CV-3 in just a matter of minutes. *Saratoga*'s forward flightdeck was badly holed, leaving the carrier temporarily incapable of flight operations, and its hangar bay was also badly damaged. Upon landing his "Zeke" back at Chichijima, the solitary surviving pilot from this attack reported that the 2nd Kogekitai had sunk a carrier.

More tokko targeted the invasion fleet off Iwo Jima at 1720hrs, with the 6,250-ton net-laying ship USS *Keokuk* (AKN-4), *LST-477* and *LST-809* being attacked in quick succession as they steamed with similar vessels to the southeast of Iwo Jima. *Keokuk*'s crew identified the aircraft that approached from almost dead ahead as a "Jill," and despite it being set on fire, the B6N clipped the vessel's No. 1 20mm gun mount and forward searchlight and disintegrated as it tore through the ship's starboard side and amidships gig davit. Its bomb (estimated to be a 500lb weapon) exploded on *Keokuk*'s main deck to starboard moments later. The "Jill" and its detonating ordnance destroyed AKN-4's entire starboard gun battery, save for a single 20mm weapon, and started fires on board, although they had been extinguished by 1850hrs. Seventeen sailors were either killed or listed as missing, with 44 wounded. Prior to being struck by the B6N, the ship's gunners had been credited with shooting down one of the four aircraft sighted approaching the group.

The two LSTs both reported their attackers to be "Hamps," with *LST-809* narrowly avoiding serious damage when the tokko clipped the ship's mainmast before splashing into the water – it had severed two signaling halyards and damaged insulators on the ship's starboard mainmast stay. *LST-477* was less fortunate. Having previously encountered steering trouble that forced the vessel to drop behind the convoy, it proved to be an easier target for the lone tokko due to a lack of concentrated antiaircraft fire from other ships. The kamikaze pilot flew down the vessel's starboard side, barely missing the bridge, before slamming his aircraft into it amidships and exploding, together with its bomb. The attack left the LST dead in the water, although the fires were eventually put out and the vessel managed to get underway again. The ship landed its cargo – the US Marine Corps' 5th Tank Battalion – ashore on the invasion beaches at Iwo Jima on February 23, four days after the amphibious assault had taken place.

The 2nd Kogekitai reported encountering an enemy transport convoy at 1620hrs, and it is likely that it was this unit that attacked the LSTs and *Keokuk*. Sailors from the latter ship recovered two bodies from the wreckage of their attacker, which would suggest that it was a two-seat "Judy" and not a three-seat "Jill" that struck the vessel. The longer fuselage length of the "Judy" could make its wingspan appear relatively shorter, and this may be why the two LSTs misidentified their attackers as clipped-wing "Hamps" – a mistake that also occurred off the Philippines (see Chapter 3).

The remaining aircraft of the 3rd Kogekitai never reached their targets, as they were intercepted by US Navy Hellcats near Chichijima. Two "Judys" and two "Zekes" subsequently force-landed there due to battle damage. The solitary "Judy" and three "Zekes" that had taken off late from Hachiro Jima also ran into American fighters near Iwo Jima, with the D4Y being shot down and an A6M crashing as it also attempted to land at Chichijima. These were almost certainly the tokko intercepted by Hellcats from VF-53 embarked in *Saratoga*, the fighter pilots claiming three aircraft shot down and a fourth as a probable.

Following these attacks the US Navy declared the all-clear at 1815hrs, but this proved to be only a brief reprieve, for at 1846hrs more tokko appeared out of the rapidly fading light. "At least five planes" were sighted by the escort carrier USS *Lunga Point* (CVE-94), then operating as part of the Support Carrier Group TG 52.2. Four of them made attacking runs on the vessel, with three dropping torpedoes that missed before the fourth aircraft, already hit and burning, was aimed by its pilot directly at the carrier. The tokko's right wing clipped the island structure and then skidded across the flightdeck from the starboard side, its still-spinning propeller gouging grooves in the wooden planking prior to the torpedo-bomber plunging into the water on the port side.

The escort carrier USS *Bismarck Sea* (CVE-95) was hit by two tokko shortly after dusk on February 21, 1945 while taking part in the Iwo Jima operation with TG 52.2. It seems likely that the vessel, and its sister-ship USS *Lunga Point* (CVE-94), were targeted by "Jills" of the 4th and 5th Kogekitai. As this photograph – taken from USS *Saginaw Bay* (CVE-82) – clearly shows, *Bismarck Sea* was rocked by a series of explosions caused by detonating 20mm and 40mm shells that had been engulfed by the uncontrollable fire raging in the hangar bay. The call to abandon ship eventually went out, and shortly after 2100hrs CVE-95 sank, taking 318 crew with it. *Bismarck Sea* was the last American carrier to be sunk in World War II. *(NARA)*

Oerlikon 20mm Cannon

In this artwork, a 20mm cannon engages a "Zeke" fighter intending to crash onto a US Navy carrier. The single mount is firing from the gun gallery on the deck edge of the carrier. The 20mm Oerlikon was the most-produced antiaircraft gun in US Navy history, with more than 88,000 being made. The US Navy adopted the Swiss-designed cannon in 1941, and the weapon had much to recommend it – a fast rate of fire of 450 rounds per minute, an easily replaceable barrel, and a high degree of reliability that made jamming unlikely. The weapon was air-cooled and ammunition was provided by detachable magazines that held 60 rounds. The mount did not require power, making it easy to place the weapon anywhere with a clear firing arc.

Pointing and training was performed by the gunner using handlebars and shoulder rests. Guidance was originally provided by an open sight, and every fifth round was a tracer to aid spotting. In 1942, the open sight was gradually replaced by the Mk 14 gyro-stabilized gunsight, which dramatically increased the gun's effectiveness. All of this made the 20mm Oerlikon a capable weapon for engaging conventional attackers. However, the gun's 0.27lb projectile meant it was ineffective when it came to downing tokko. (*Artwork by Jim Laurier, © Osprey Publishing*)

At the same time that *Lunga Point* was being attacked, its sister-ship USS *Bismarck Sea* (CVE-95) was also engaged by a single enemy aircraft that was spotted approaching at very low level from the starboard side. The tokko slammed into the carrier abeam of its aft elevator, knocking it out and reducing water pressure on board to a mere trickle. Fighting the ensuing fire in the hangar bay with hoses run from forward spaces, the damage control parties had the blaze under control until another explosion occurred in the hangar bay immediately forward of the elevator that had originally been struck by the aircraft.

According to eyewitnesses, this second explosion was caused by another tokko crashing into the ship in a vertical dive. Many of the firefighters tackling the initial blaze were killed. Worse still, it also ignited several fueled fighters that had previously been struck down to the hangar bay to facilitate the recovery of airborne aircraft – including several from the already-crippled *Saratoga*. The conflagration at the rear of the ship raged out of control from this moment on, with exploding 20mm and 40mm ammunition adding to the devastation. Abandon ship was soon declared and *Bismarck Sea* sank after 2100hrs, taking 318 crew with it. CVE-95 was the last American carrier to be sunk in World War II.

Although the already-damaged *Saratoga* had sailed some distance away from Iwo Jima by the time the escort carriers were attacked, that did not prevent CV-3 from being targeted again. At 1846hrs at least three aircraft were spotted overhead, with the first two being shot down by the ship's gunners. The third tokko hit the carrier with a bomb prior to crashing into the water. The crew believed at least one of the tokko was a twin-engined "Betty." Similarly, sailors on board *Bismarck Sea* identified *Lunga Point*'s attackers as twin-engined "Bettys," although the aircraft that inflicted the damage on CVE-95 were not positively identified.

However, the crew of the nearby destroyer *Helm* claimed that the second tokko to hit the escort carrier was a "Judy." It seems unlikely that the D4Ys previously involved in attacks on the invasion fleet off Iwo Jima at 1720hrs had managed to stay in the area unchallenged for an hour, particularly given they had taken off four-and-a-half hours earlier from an airfield almost 500 nautical miles away. Instead, the dusk attackers were almost certainly the "Jills" of the 4th and 5th Kogekitai, with torpedo-equipped aircraft from the latter unit targeting *Lunga Point* – it was the only ship attacked at dusk to identify the tokko correctly, thanks in no small part to the starboard wing and landing gear left on the flightdeck by the B6N that struck the carrier. The poor light, along with the "Jills" carrying their unwieldy Type 91 air-dropped torpedoes, could have contributed to their being mistaken for larger "Bettys" by the other ships in TG 52.2.

The attacks on February 21 were the only serious attempts made by Japanese aircraft to disrupt the landings at Iwo Jiima. As a postscript to this operation, on March 1 a single "Judy" from the 2nd Mitate-tai, flown by WO Nao Kawasaki and CPO Yoshio Kobayashi (who had failed to complete their mission eight days earlier), left Chichijima intent on targeting shipping off Iwo Jima. No results were obtained.

OPERATION *TAN No. 2*

Many months before the invasion of the Philippines had led to the hurried creation of the tokko force, it was obvious to the Japanese that the initiative in the Pacific lay firmly with the Allies. The nation's inferior industrial capacity was increasingly unable to make good mounting losses in men and materiel, never mind match the Allied build-up of land, air, and sea forces in the Pacific. Nevertheless, the Japanese high command still harbored the desire to inflict a crushing blow on its enemies in a decisive battle. However, as the likelihood of that happening on the open seas became more remote, the IJN started formulating plans to attack the Pacific Fleet while it was at anchor. By February 1944, the Fifth Fleet's anchorage at Majuro, in the Marshall Islands, had been identified as the ideal target.

The initial plan was to have the IJN's First Mobile Force attack the anchorage with 500 carrier-borne and 300 land-based aircraft, as well as torpedo-armed amphibious tanks launched from submarines. Shore installations would be targeted by troops landed by other submarines. Codenamed *Yu-Go Sakusen*, the attack subsequently languished at the planning stage when one of its chief architects, Commander-in-Chief of the Combined Fleet Admiral Mineichi Koga, was killed when his Kawanishi H8K2 "Emily" long-range flying boat crashed after it flew into a typhoon on March 31, 1944.

More modest plans were subsequently developed by some of the IJNAF's most experienced surviving naval aviators, including Cdr Mitsuo Fuchida, who had led the attack on Pearl Harbor on December 7, 1941.

He proposed leading 27 torpedo-bombers in conjunction with Lt Cdr Takashige Egusa, who had led the second wave of dive-bombers at Pearl Harbor, in a precision attack on Majuro. Codenamed Operation *Tan*, the initial parts of the plan actually took place when Lt Cdr Takehiko Chihaya (yet another Pearl Harbor veteran who had led the dive-bombers from the carrier *Akagi*) sent two C6N "Myrt" long-range reconnaissance aircraft from the 121st Kokutai from Tinian, via Truk and Nauru, to reconnoiter the target on June 3, 1944.

Two days later, Chihaya personally participated in a follow-up mission flown by two more "Myrts," finding and photographing eight fleet and four escort carriers in the Majuro anchorage. He then flew back to Tinian to deliver the photographs to Fuchida, who tasked him with undertaking a third Majuro sortie on June 6 as the last mission to verify the presence of the targets prior to the commencement of *Tan*. That flight was delayed by American air strikes on Truk, and when the sortie was finally flown on June 9, Chihaya found the anchorage at Majuro devoid of ships. TF 58 had left for the invasion of the Marianas, forcing the cancelation of the operation

Fast-forward to late 1944, and despite terrible losses in the battle of the Philippine Sea and during the ill-fated defense of Peleliu and the Philippines, the IJN still hoped to deliver a comprehensive blow against anchored American fast carriers in an effort to turn the tide of the war. By this time the Pacific Fleet had set up shop in Ulithi Atoll in the western Caroline Islands, which boasted of an even bigger anchorage than Majuro or even Pearl Harbor – it was comfortably capable of accommodating more than a thousand ships. Combined Fleet Headquarters duly drew up a new plan for an attack on Ulithi, with Cdr Ryosuke Nomura incorporating tokko tactics, as were then being used with what the Japanese (mistakenly) thought was great success in the Philippines, in the latest iteration.

Now known as Operation *Tan No. 2*, the new plan called for an attack by bomb-laden "Frances" long-range bombers flying from Kyushu to Ulithi – a distance of more than 1,300 nautical miles – that would take more than ten hours to cover. Vice Admiral Matome Ugaki, then commander-in-chief of the IJNAF's Fifth Air Fleet, enthusiastically

Vice Admiral Matome Ugaki, commander of the Fifth Air Fleet, approved *Tan No. 2* – an attack by bomb-laden "Frances" long-range bombers flying from Kyushu on US Navy warships moored in Ulithi Atoll, in the western Caroline Islands. He later took charge of Kikusui operations off Okinawa, which ran from April 6 to June 22, 1945. (*Tony Holmes collection*)

approved *Tan No. 2* when it was presented to him, and it was originally scheduled to be carried out in late February. Indeed, on January 29, 1945, the unarmed transport submarine *I-366* departed Yokosuka for Truk laden with spares, aviation fuel, and other supplies in anticipation of the mission. The vessel only just made it to Truk on February 12, having endured technical problems and survived a close shave with enemy surface ships.

In early February seven "Myrts" from the 141st Kokutai had also been ordered to Truk from Kisarazu airfield, near Tokyo, as part of *Tan No. 2*. As with the aborted *Tan* operation, their job would be to fly reconnaissance missions over Ulithi as a prelude to the actual raid. Like *I-366*, the aircraft struggled to reach their destination, with two being forced to return to Kisarazu with technical issues, one ditching en route, and another being wrecked on landing at Truk.

Making good use of the supplies delivered by *I-366*, groundcrew at Truk prepared one of the "Myrts" for an early morning mission to Ulithi on February 13. Flying over the atoll at more than 40,000ft so as to avoid interception, the crew quickly discovered that there were no carriers in the anchorage at that time. This information was relayed directly to the commander-in-chief of the IJN's Fourth Fleet at Truk, Vice Admiral Chuichi Hara, who then passed it on to Admiral Soemu Toyoda at Combined Fleet Headquarters, whereupon it was decided to postpone the operation until early March.

Reconnaissance of Ulithi started again on March 5, and this time the "Myrt" crew found and photographed no fewer than 16 carriers. Things moved quickly from this point, and 48 hours later the Azusa Tokubetsu Butai (Special Attack Unit) was established with 24 aircraft and their crews from the 762nd Kokutai at Kanoya. A follow-up reconnaissance mission by another Truk-based "Myrt" on March 9 found six fleet and nine escort carriers at Ulithi, along with four more carriers entering the anchorage from the northeast. The stage was now set for *Tan No. 2* to proceed, and approval was duly given by Admiral Soemu Toyoda for the attack to take place on March 11.

While this was going on, other elements of the plan were being put in place. Two submarines – the transport *HA-106* and ocean-going *I-58* – were ordered to support the operation, with *HA-106* despatched to patrol off Minami-Daito Jima and pick up ditched aircrew, while *I-58* took up station off Okino-Torishima (Douglas Reef) and served as a navigational beacon via transmissions from its long-wave radio. *I-58* was only

ABOVE
An aerial view of the damaged flightdeck of USS *Randolph* (CV-15), seen here moored alongside the repair vessel USS *Jason* (ARH-1) the day after the carrier had been targeted in the audacious *Tan No. 2* raid on Ulithi Atoll. CV-15 had been hit by a solitary "Frances" twin-engined bomber from the Azusa Tokubetsu Butai. The paucity of fuel on board the aircraft, which had flown more than 1,300 nautical miles in a flight lasting in excess of ten hours, and the lack of exposed ordnance on board CV-15 reduced the damage done to the carrier. Indeed, *Randolph* was ready for action again a little over a month later. *(NARA)*

90 minutes away from launching four kaiten manned torpedoes in a planned underwater tokko attack on US Navy vessels anchored off Iwo Jima when the submarine received new orders on March 9. Its skipper, Cdr Mochitsura Hashimoto, jettisoned two of the kaiten and made haste for the submarine's new station, arriving on the evening of the 10th.

The "Frances" that hit *Randolph* slammed into the vessel's starboard side aft just below the flightdeck, killing 27 sailors and wounding a further 105. The subsequent explosion when the aircraft's single 1,764lb No. 80 Mk 5 Land Bomb detonated tore a large hole in the flightdeck. This photograph was taken prior to repair work being commenced by sailors from *Jason*. (NARA)

With these vessels in place, it was time for *Tan No. 2* itself to get underway the next morning. Vice Admiral Ugaki met with the men of the Azusa-tai immediately prior to their departure and told them that being chosen for the mission was a great honor. He also emphasized the importance of the mission, with "B-29s raiding our homeland every day." Ugaki also revealed to the aircrew that the defense of Iwo Jima was already doomed. He told the assembled men that there were 19 American ships at Ulithi, and that the key to success lay in achieving surprise. Finally, the admiral ended his impromptu briefing by telling the aircrew that they should not hesitate in returning to base if there was little chance of success. Clearly, this was not being viewed as a typical tokko mission.

As Ugaki spoke, five H8K2 "Emily" flying boats from the 801st Kokutai took off from nearby Kagoshima to provide both weather reconnaissance and pathfinder (navigational) assistance for the

24 Azusa-tai "Frances" bombers committed to the mission. The P1Y1s, each carrying a single 1,764lb No. 80 Mk 5 Land Bomb, followed suit from 0900hrs – they were led aloft by Lt Naoto Kuromaru. The formation passed *HA-106* off Minami-Daito Jima four hours later, and shortly thereafter aircraft started dropping out. Five bombers turned back because of engine problems, later landing on Minami-Daito Jima, while three more crashed or ditched at sea.

I-58 eventually detected what remained of the formation on its air-search radar and started sending out a continuous long-wave radio signal that was picked up by the pathfinder flying boats. It was also at this point that the "Emily" tasked with weather reconnaissance turned back, landing at Kagoshima at 1530hrs.

Bad weather now became a factor too, the formation having to climb and skirt around rain squalls as it continued south, lengthening the mission and burning precious fuel. Descending below the clouds eight hours after departure, the formation now found itself over Yap Island, 90 nautical miles west of Ulithi, just before sunset. More aircraft had since dropped out, including one of the pathfinding H8K2s, which simply disappeared. By the time the navigational error that took the bombers over Yap was corrected, the significant force of 24 bombers that took off was down to a mere two. The sun had set and it was almost dark when the crews of the "Frances" bombers radioed that they were attacking Ulithi.

As the mission planners had hoped, the arrival of the P1Y1s took the Americans by total surprise, the atoll being ablaze with lights and the defenses unprepared for attack. The first bomber picked the carrier *Randolph* as its target and slammed into the vessel's starboard side aft just below the flightdeck, killing 27 sailors and wounding a further 105. The subsequent explosion when the aircraft's bomb detonated tore a large hole in the flightdeck. However, owing to the "Frances'" lack of fuel, as well as limited fuel supplies on board the ship itself, only a small fire broke out following the crash. This was quickly dealt with by damage control parties.

This had been a grave miscalculation on the part of the Japanese, for although a carrier at anchor and at reduced readiness made for an easier target, it was devoid of highly flammable and fully armed aircraft that crowded flightdecks and hangar bays during operations at sea. Furthermore, the attacking bomber itself was also perilously short of fuel, which meant that there was little scope for inflicting more serious damage beyond that of the initial crash impact and bomb explosion.

This view of *Randolph*'s fantail was taken from a lighter circling the carrier. Note that some of the damaged deck panels have been removed prior to the stern area being repaired. (NARA)

Even at this late juncture, fate continued to deal *Tan No. 2* another cruel blow when the remaining "Frances" crew mistook a nearby islet for a ship and crashed into a lit baseball diamond, doing no damage beyond wounding a small number of American servicemen.

Combined Fleet's voice communications units picked up several plain language radio messages from the US Navy about an air raid on Ulithi, leading to hope that the mission had in fact succeeded. A "Myrt" was quickly despatched the following day from Truk on a post-strike assessment of the anchorage, and it noted that all the carriers previously seen were still there and no fuel was visible in the water to indicate that a ship, or ships, had been sunk. The results of this flight proved to the IJN that the audacious mission had been a dismal failure.

The lack of success enjoyed by *Tan No. 2* was squarely blamed on the unreliability of the Homare 12 engines fitted to the "Frances." While that was indeed true, and had led to a high number of aircraft dropping out, the plan itself was probably far too ambitious. Furthermore, the paucity of fuel remaining on board the two attacking P1Y1s, coupled with the lack of ammunition and fuel on board the carriers, meant there was no "chain reaction" of fire and explosions when *Randolph* was hit. As it was, the carrier was quickly repaired at Ulithi and participated in operations off Okinawa less than a month later.

Tan No. 2 had ultimately been a terrible waste of men and materiel that the IJNAF could ill afford at this late stage in the war, contributing nothing more than an interesting sideshow in the annals of the tokko.

KYUSHU

As the planned invasion of Okinawa (codenamed Operation *Iceberg*), scheduled for April 1, 1945, rapidly approached, TF 58's final task prior to the launch of the campaign was to strike the numerous airfields on Kyushu – the southwesternmost of Japan's three main islands. The US Navy knew full well that both the IJNAF and the IJAAF would mount their principal aerial response (including tokko) to the amphibious landings from these bases.

On March 14, just 72 hours after the failed P1Y1 attack on Ulithi, the warships of TF 58 weighed anchor and headed north for more strikes on Kyushu, without the damaged *Randolph*. Four days of operations against Kyushu, and beyond, commenced on the 18th, during which time carrier-based fighter pilots claimed almost 300 Japanese aircraft shot down. Many more were destroyed on the ground as their airfields were repeatedly attacked, effectively curtailing Japanese aerial activity in the two weeks leading up to the invasion of Okinawa.

The Japanese had tracked TF 58's progress as it headed toward Kyushu, and initially they were unsure if the US Navy was carrying out a carrier-based sweep of the area or launching an actual invasion. As it became clear that it was in fact the former, the IJNAF and IJAAF opted to limit their aerial counterattacks in order to save the bulk of their remaining aircraft for another day. A limited number of both conventional attacks and tokko were generated, although the small number of aircraft involved meant that the Japanese enjoyed only a modest return for their efforts. The most significant success by some margin was the bombing of *Franklin* on March 19 by a lone D4Y, the aircraft hitting the carrier with two

ABOVE
Tokko sporadically attacked TF 58 during its four-day offensive against airfields on Kyushu from March 18, 1945, the IJNAF and IJAAF opting to limit their aerial counterattacks in order to save the bulk of their remaining aircraft for another day once it became clear that the attacks were not the precursor to invasion. The IJNAF'S greatest success occurred on March 19, when a lone D4Y bombed *Franklin* – it was not a tokko attack, however, as the "Judy" crew did not crash into the vessel. The aicraft's two 551lb bombs caused a raging fire to break out on board that killed 807 crew and wounded 487. *Franklin*, which had only just returned to the Pacific Fleet following repairs to damage it had suffered when it was struck by a tokko off the Philippines on October 30, 1944, was knocked out of the war. *(NARA)*

551lb bombs. These caused a raging fire to break out on board that killed 807 crew (and wounded 487) and knocked the ship out of the war.

Kamikaze attacks came in the form of "Judy" and "Frances" bombers from the Kikusui Butai, which was the name that had been given to the tokko task force initially formed from Kyushu-based IJNAF Kokutai prior to the attacks by TF 58. The Azusa-tai, which had participated in the underwhelming *Tan No. 2* operation, was also part of this task force. With the strikes on Kyushu, more tokko-tai were established under the control of the Kikusui Butai, starting with the Suisei-tai and the Ginga-tai formed from the men and machines of the 701st and 762nd Kokutai, respectively. Known by the Japanese names for the "Judy" and "Frances," both units carried out attacks against TF 58 between March 18 and 21.

MAP ABOVE
As the southwesternmost of Japan's three main islands, Kyushu was home to the eight primary tokko bases used by IJNAF and IJAAF units, and their fighter escorts, during the numbered Kikusui missions mounted between April 6 and June 22, 1945. The airfields' relatively close proximity to Okinawa also made them a target for repeated attacks by carrier aircraft from TF 58, the latter undertaking several brief offensives against Kyushu both immediately before the commencement of Operation *Iceberg* (on April 1, 1945) and six weeks later in mid-May, when tokko were enjoying sustained success against Allied ships.

The destroyer USS *Halsey Powell* (DD-686) suffered the most tokko damage during the Kyushu operation. At 1454hrs on March 20, while sailing close alongside the carrier *Hancock* in order to receive fuel and transfer mail and personnel, an enemy aircraft was reported in the vicinity. As the destroyer hastily cast off the starboard side of the carrier, the latter opened fire at the Japanese aircraft approaching in a steep dive from the port side. Its gunners scored hits on the rapidly closing tokko, causing it to disintegrate as it passed over the carrier. However, a significant chunk of the airframe struck the destroyer's fantail and one of its wings clipped the after five-inch gun. A fire was started by the impact, which also caused some flooding and jammed the rudder at 15 degrees to port.

ABOVE
On March 20, 1945 USS *Halsey Powell* (DD-686) was alongside the aircraft carrier USS *Hancock* (CV-19) in order to receive fuel and transfer mail and personnel when Japanese aircraft attacked. As the destroyer was getting clear, a tokko (probably a "Judy" from the Suisei-tai) overshot the carrier and struck DD-686. With the vessel's steering gear jammed, only alert action with the engines by the crew averted a collision with the considerably larger CV-19. *(NARA)*

RIGHT The fires started on board *Halsey Powell* were quickly put out, but the ship's steering gear could only be temporarily patched after it had been hit by a significant chunk of the airframe that penetrated the destroyer's fantail as seen here. One of its wings also clipped the after five-inch gun. Nine crew were killed and 30 wounded by the tokko strike, with the bulk of the casualties being in the stern of the ship. The badly damaged destroyer reached Ulithi on March 25, where DD-686 was patched up for its voyage to San Pedro, California. *Halsey Powell* returned to the Pacific Fleet on July 19 after being repaired. *(NARA)*

After nearly being run over by *Hancock* as the destroyer strayed across the carrier's bow, *Halsey Powell* came to a stop so that its crew could assess the damage. Having temporarily left the task group's protective screen, the vessel relied on the assistance of other destroyers to help effect emergency repairs. DD-686 subsequently rejoined TF 58 once it was found that the crew could steer the ship by varying engine speeds. Despite considerable damage being caused to the destroyer, casualties were relatively light – nine killed and 30 wounded.

Halsey Powell's crew identified the attacker as a "Zeke," although it was almost certainly a "Judy" from the Suisei-tai. Seven D4Ys from the 701st Kokutai had taken off on tokko missions that day, with three from the 103rd Hikotai departing from Kokubu No. 1 airfield between 1250hrs and 1356hrs and four more being despatched from Kokubu No. 2 airfield between 1424hrs and 1505hrs. Their crews were tasked with attacking a carrier task force east of Kyushu/south of Shikoku. Given the timing, it was probably an aircraft from the former group, under the leadership of WO Takashi Harada, that found and attacked *Hancock* but hit *Halsey Powell* instead.

Hancock's sister-ship *Intrepid* also had a lucky escape during the Kyushu strikes. On the morning of March 18, while operating as part of TG 58.4, the carrier detected Japanese aircraft from around 0730hrs – almost two hours after the ship had launched its first strikes of the offensive, against the enemy airfield of Oita. At 0802hrs a "Frances" was shot down by USS *Yorktown* (CV-10) a safe distance away, and soon after another twin-engined aircraft bore in from the starboard side of *Intrepid*, with the carrier and other ships in the screen taking it under fire as it approached.

Just as it appeared that the tokko would hit the carrier, the bomber's tail was shot off and the aircraft flipped into the water and exploded, showering *Intrepid* with fragments and burning fuel. A fire was started in the ship's hangar bay but this was quickly brought under control. However, damage inflicted on the hangar bay "curtains" meant the ship's ability to rearm and re-spot aircraft that night below deck was impeded as it was unable to be effectively darkened. One sailor was killed in the attack and 44 wounded.

A small number of D4Ys undertook tokko operations against TF 58 during the four-day Kyushu strikes, with this radial-engined "Judy" of the Kikusui Butai's Suisei-tai coming very close to hitting *Essex* on March 19, 1945. The aircraft's starboard wingtip has clearly been blown off by antiaircraft fire, making it difficult for the pilot to accurately target the carrier with his dive-bomber. It appears that the D4Y's bomb-bay doors are missing too. *(NARA)*

G4M2E "Betty" (and MXY7 Ohka) 721-328 of the 711th Hikotai/721st Kokutai, Kanoya airfield, Kyushu, March 21, 1945

This aircraft was one of 15 motherships involved in the first combat mission of the MXY7 Ohka manned aerial bomb on March 21, 1945. The two white flashes on the bomber's tail indicated its assignment to the 2nd Chutai – the "Bettys" allocated to the operation came from the 711th Hikotai's 1st and 2nd Chutai. All of the motherships fell victim to US Navy F6F Hellcats well before they attained launch range for their Ohka weapons. (*Artwork by Jim Laurier, © Osprey Publishing*)

Gunners manning a quadruple Bofors 40mm cannon mount on *Hornet* open fire during the Kyushu operation in March 1945. This was the mounting on the port side of the flightdeck, just forward of the aft pair of 5in./38 single guns. Note the expended shells to the right of the photographs, and the ready rounds lining the gun tub. The 40mm gun was probably the most successful medium-range antiaircraft weapon of the war, and each of the Essex-class carriers had eight quadruple mounts – one mount each at the bow and stern, four atop the island, and two on the port side of the flightdeck next to the 5in./38 single guns. Each mount was controlled by its own Mk 51 director. *(NARA)*

F6F-5 Hellcat (BuNo unknown)/White 35 flown by Lt James Pearce, VF-17, USS *Hornet* (CV-12), Western Pacific, March 18–21, 1945

Lt Jim Pearce was possibly at the controls of this aircraft – he flew five different Hellcats during the March raids on Kyushu – when he led the VF-17 and VBF-17 divisions in the interception of the "Betty" motherships of the 711th Hikotai/721st Kokutai that attempted to target TG 58.1 on March 21, 1945. (*Artwork by Jim Laurier, © Osprey Publishing*)

Although *Intrepid* identified the tokko as being a "Betty," a series of photographs taken from on board the carrier during the attack clearly showed the aircraft to be a "Frances." The Ginga-tai had despatched eight bombers on tokko missions that morning, beginning with two aircraft from Kanoya at 0440hrs, one from Oita at the same time and five more from Chikujo between 0628hrs and 0710hrs. Each of the P1Y1s was armed with a single 1,764lb No. 80 Mk 5 Land Bomb, bar the Oita-based aircraft, which carried a torpedo. It would appear that a pair of the Chikujo-based tokko, possibly the aircraft commanded by 1Lt Akira Sakaguchi and Lt(jg) Noboru Ogawa that took off at 0700hrs and 0710hrs, respectively, were the ones that attacked *Intrepid* and *Yorktown*. Ever prone to overclaiming, the IJNAF declared that its conventional and tokko attacks had sunk a carrier and damaged two more on March 18, with another "flattop" sunk and a second vessel set on fire the following day.

Just before 1400hrs on the 21st a large force of enemy aircraft was detected on radar and Hellcats from VF-17 and sister-unit VBF-17, embarked in USS *Hornet* (CV-12), were vectored to intercept them. Future ace Lt Jim Pearce, who was one of the first pilots to engage the aircraft, quickly identified them as 18 "Bettys" flying in a "V-of-V" formation and escorted by fighters.

Perhaps falsely buoyed by the victory claims of March 18–19, and eager to land further blows on TF 58, Ugaki had ordered the unleashing

This was the scene at Kanoya airfield just prior to the departure of Lt Cdr Goro Nonaka's 15 G4M2e "Betty" motherships and their Ohka manned aerial bombs (and three pathfinder "Bettys") on a mission to attack TF 58 carriers operating off Japan on March 21, 1945. Virtually all of these bombers, from the Jinrai Butai, were shot down by defending US Navy fighters and no hits were scored. (NARA)

Only a small number of G4M2s were modified to carry the Ohka, and they were designated G4M2e Model 24Js once converted to do so. With an Ohka on board, the "Betty" was even more vulnerable than usual, and it proved an easy target for American fighters. Since the maximum range of the Ohka was only 20 nautical miles, it was extremely problematic to fly a slow, ungainly "Betty" bomber within range of a target. Despite an insufficient number of escorting "Zeke" fighters, that was exactly what the Jinrai Butai attempted to do on March 21, 1945. Here, the "Betty" crews sit at Kanoya waiting for the order to take off. (NARA)

of a new Japanese secret weapon – the manned MXY7 Ohka rocket-powered aerial bomb – against the Americans on the 21st. The Kanoya-based Jinrai Butai (Divine Thunder Unit) had been chosen to undertake the first attacks with the Ohka following its formation in October 1944 as the 721st Kokutai. The unit was assigned two Hikotai of G4M2E "Betty" motherships (from the 711th Hikotai) to carry the Ohka into action and two more Hikotai of "Zekes" to act as escorts.

The IJNAF had originally scheduled an Ohka mission for the 708th Hikotai on March 18 following the commencement of the US Navy

ABOVE LEFT
The Ohka-carrying "Bettys" were sitting ducks for the Hellcat CAP. This gun camera film still clearly shows the wings of the manned aerial bomb under the belly of the G4M2e as the bomber fills the Hellcat pilot's gunsight prior to him opening fire. Between them, VF-17 and VBF-17 (both embarked in *Hornet*), and VF-30 (embarked in *Belleau Wood*) claimed a total of 26 "Bettys" destroyed – more than were actually on the mission! *(NARA)*

ABOVE RIGHT
This still is from the famous sequence of photographs taken from the gun cameras of F6F-5 Hellcats of VF-17, VBF-17, and VF-30, which intercepted the disastrous attempt by the Jinrai Butai to attack the carriers of TF 58 off Kyushu on March 21. All 15 "Betty" motherships were shot down, most still with their Ohka on board, and the few that were released had been launched too far from their targets to pose any threat. *(NARA)*

strikes on Kyushu. However, the unit's airfield at Usa was attacked and the motherships (again from the 721st Kokutai) were caught on the ground. Almost all of them were destroyed, causing the cancelation of the mission. Finally, shortly after noon on the 21st, the Ohka was given its combat debut when 15 "Betty" motherships from the 711th Hikotai were led aloft from Kanoya by Lt Cdr Goro Nonaka. Three more G4M2s would act as pathfinders. They were accompanied by a 55-strong escort of "Zekes" that was quickly whittled down to just over 30-strong as technical and other problems took their toll. This was bad news for "Betty" crews, as their mount was already highly vulnerable to fighters due to the bomber's lack of armor or self-sealing fuel tanks.

Indeed, the G4M had been christened the "one-shot lighter" by Allied pilots in early 1942 due to its propensity to immediately catch fire when hit. When further encumbered with a 4,718lb Ohka in the bomb-bay, the "Betty" became a slow and lumbering sitting duck – the motherships'

ABOVE LEFT
Future ace Lt Jim Pearce led the VF-17 and VBF-17 divisions that were the first to intercept the Jinrai Butai formation, subsequently claiming two of them destroyed. *(Edward M. Young collection)*

ABOVE RIGHT
As Operation *Iceberg* approached, TF 58 headed north to the waters between Okinawa and Kyushu at the end of March 1945 for another series of raids against tokko airfields. Again, Japanese opposition to the operation was negligible, with a pair of "Judys" from the Kikusui Butai's 2nd Suisei-tai being the only tokko attackers on the 29th. Here, one of them gets shot down while attacking USS *Yorktown* (CV-10) off Tanegashima. *(NARA)*

maximum ceiling was just 16,400ft, which was almost 14,000ft less than a conventional G4M3. The IJNAF was fully aware of this vulnerability well before the Ohka made its combat debut, with Air Technical Arsenal Chief Vice Admiral Masao Wada warning that successful operations with the aerial bomb could only be carried out under conditions of local air superiority.

This was far from the case on March 21, with the "Zeke" fighter escort being quickly brushed aside by the Hellcat pilots, who then unceremoniously shot down all the "Betty" motherships in short order. A few of the Ohkas were jettisoned in panic as the motherships came under attack, but no successes were achieved as the G4M2Es were still almost 50 nautical miles away from TF 58 when they were intercepted – the aerial bomb's maximum range was just 20 nautical miles.

The following day TF 58 headed south for a series of strikes against Okinawa and the Ryukyu Islands ahead of the forthcoming invasion. The carriers returned to attack Kyushu on March 28–29, although by then US forces had already landed on some of Okinawa's outlying islands. Both the IJNAF and the IJAAF again refused to engage TF 58 on any significant scale, with the only tokko sent against the carrier being a pair of "Judys" from the 2nd Suisei-tai on the afternoon of the 29th. One of these narrowly missed *Yorktown* off Tanegashima, disintegrating from the combined fire of the ship's guns and a pair of pursuing Hellcats from *Langley*. One of the latter had the misfortune to be accidentally shot down by American gunfire, although the pilot was recovered.

TOKKO IN SOUTHEAST ASIA

On October 17, 1944, the British Pacific Fleet – centered on the aircraft carriers HMS *Indomitable* and HMS *Victorious* – launched the first in a series of strikes against the Japanese-held Nicobar Islands to the north of Sumatra, in the Dutch East Indies, in an attempt to draw some Japanese attention off the American landings on Leyte.

The IJAAF eventually responded to these raids 48 hours later when a twin-engined aircraft flew over the fleet without being intercepted at 0840hrs on the 19th. This was obviously a reconnaissance flight, for at 0930hrs a group of aircraft was detected on radar. After a failed attempt at interception by British Hellcats, the formation was intercepted by Corsairs from *Victorious* just ten nautical miles from the carriers shortly before 0950hrs. The aircraft were identified as nine "Oscars" at 7,000ft and three more providing top cover at 16,000ft. A 40-minute aerial battle ensued that resulted in four Oscars from the lower group and all three from the higher group being shot down for the loss of two Corsairs and a Hellcat – the latter had become involved in the engagement shortly after it had started. More importantly, the remaining Ki-43s were chased off by the fighters.

Japanese records show that the "Oscars" were probably the nine aircraft of the 1st Yasen Hoju Hikotai listed as departing on a tokko mission from Medan, on Sumatra, that morning. Essentially a depot or

ABOVE
HMS *Indefatigable* heads through the Suez Canal on its way to the Pacific in late 1944. The Seafires of 894 NAS are still wearing the standard roundels for the European theater. In late January 1945, *Indefatigable*, along with the carriers HMS *Indomitable*, HMS *Illustrious*, and HMS *Victorious*, carried out Operation *Meridian I* and *II* – a series of aerial strikes against the vital Japanese oil refineries, and associated infrastructure, in Sumatra. In opposition to these raids, seven Ki-67s from the 2nd Shichisei Kojun Hikotai were sent on a tokko mission against the British carriers on January 24. Seafires from 894 NAS (with the help of Hellcats from *Indomitable* and antiaircraft fire) downed all of the unescorted "Peggy" bombers before they could complete their attacks. (*Tony Holmes collection*)

holding unit for replacement aircraft, it also trained air- and groundcrew for front-line Hikotai throughout the Southwestern Area. It had also been known to take part in local air defense operations as required, hence the failed attempt at engaging the British warships on October 19. Although this mission had been an abject failure, the 1st Yasen Hoju Hikotai had created history on this date by undertaking the first official tokko mission attempted by the Japanese, beating the IJNAF's initial attempt off Leyte the following day. Despite not even getting within visual range of the Royal Navy ships, the IJAAF claimed that three of the "Oscars" had hit three British vessels, including an aircraft carrier and a destroyer!

The strikes on Nicobar prompted the IJAAF's 3rd Kokugun (which was responsible for all units in the area) to hastily form its own tokko-tai, as the Japanese feared that the arrival of the British carriers heralded an invasion of Sumatra. Coming under the umbrella of the Shinsho-tai, two such tokko-tai, known as the 1st and 2nd Kojun-tai, were formed from the heavy bomber-equipped 58th Sentai and the 1st Yasen Hoju Hikotai, with the intention of using them to repulse any Allied invasion. Although this did not eventuate, the commander of the 3rd Kokugun, Lt Gen Hayashi Kinoshita, nevertheless created more tokko-tai. Known as the Shichisei Tokubetsu Kogekitai, they were further subdivided into individual tokko-tai named after their parent units. Most of these did not see action prior to war's end, as they were intended to be expended in the event of an Allied invasion of the region that never came. There were, however, exceptions.

In late January 1945, the carriers HMS *Indomitable*, HMS *Illustrious*, HMS *Indefatigable*, and HMS *Victorious* carried out Operations *Meridian I* and *II* – a series of strikes against the vital Japanese oil refineries, and associated infrastructure, in Sumatra. The attacks, which took place on the 24th and 29th, were mostly successful, stopping all oil production in Sumatra until March. Even after repairs had been effected, the refineries never achieved more than 30 percent of their pre-strike capacity.

The first strike on January 24 took the Japanese totally by surprise, resulting in little fighter opposition being encountered over the target. This was not the case five days later, however, as the IJAAF managed to sortie four tokko-tai to search for the British fleet even as their aircraft were pummeling Japanese targets. Three of these, the Shichisei Shoki-tai (Ki-43s), Shichisei Shoju-tai (Ki-45s), and the 1st Shichisei Kojun Hikotai (Ki-67s), were recorded as having failed to find their targets prior to returning to their bases on Sumatra. Indeed, it would appear that the "Peggys" of the 2nd Shichisei Kojun Hikotai were the only aircraft to spot the enemy ships.

Radar operators on board several Royal Navy vessels began to pick up contacts from 0900hrs, resulting in the Seafires of 894 Naval Air Squadron (NAS) flying CAP over the task force being vectored towards three twin-engined aircraft. At 0940hrs Sub Lt J. W. Hayes shot down one of the bombers, while the remaining two escaped in cloud. Several other IJAAF aircraft also fled as they encountered the defending fighters, while two more Japanese aircraft detected at 1028hrs approximately 35 nautical miles from the fleet were left alone as their course led them away from the ships.

However, just as 15 of the fleet fighters were being recovered before noon, ships' radar detected more contacts 25 nautical miles south of the fleet. Seven Seafires from *Indefatigable* that were still on CAP to the north of the vessels were quickly redirected to meet the bogies, which they soon identified as seven low-flying twin-engined bombers. These aircraft were engaged just as they came within sight of the destroyers undertaking outer radar picket duty. Assisted by a trio of Hellcats scrambled from *Indomitable*, as well as antiaircraft fire from the ships, the Seafires despatched all seven enemy bombers into the sea before they could hit any of the vessels. No British fighters were lost in return, and the only damage suffered by any of the ships was self-inflicted – the bridge of *Illustrious* was struck by two 5.25in. shells fired from the cruiser HMS *Euryalus*, epitomizing the generally poor gunnery discipline displayed by the Royal Navy in the Pacific.

The bombers were variously identified as "Sallys," "Helens," or "Bettys," although a trawl through Japanese records indicates that these aircraft were almost certainly "Peggys" from the 2nd Shichisei Kojun Hikotai, led by Maj Hiroyuki Kato. Indeed, the latter was heard exhorting "Attack! Attack!" over the radio at 1358hrs (Tokyo time), which would roughly tie in with the British timeline. Despite being briefed to target the ships, the one pilot that actually got close enough to strike a British carrier inexplicably avoided hitting it! The crew of *Illustrious* reported seeing the aircraft pull up so as to clear the vessel's stern and island structure prior to crashing into the sea and exploding off the carrier's starboard bow.

Surviving IJAAF records did not state how many aircraft were involved in the attack by the 2nd Shichisei Kojun Hikotai, although they do list a total of 34 crew on board the aircraft that were lost in this attack, including Maj Kato. Given that a "Peggy" crew usually numbered six to eight men, the Japanese records would suggest that between four and six bombers attacked the task force off Sumatra on the 29th – less than the number reported by the Royal Navy.

Five months passed before the tokko from the 3rd Kokugun saw action once again. In May, the Allies launched Operation *Oboe* – a series of amphibious landings on the island of Borneo, south of the Philippines. Tied to Operation *Montclair*, which secured Mindanao and the Visayas Islands in the southern Philippines, Borneo was at the time seen as a strategic objective due to its natural resources and oil, although by this late stage in the war the occupying forces were already cut off from Japan and had no hope of resupply or reinforcement. The first landings were made on Tarakan on May 1, followed by North Borneo and Labuan on June 10. Preparations then commenced for the assault on Balikpapan, on Borneo's central east coast, on July 1.

The bulk of Allied ground forces involved in the fighting in Borneo were from the Australian Army's I Corps, although the ships supporting the offensive were mainly American. To prepare for the landings on Balikpapan, an intense Allied air and naval bombardment of the area was mounted, with 44 ships of the Minesweeping Group along with two cruisers and several destroyers of Covering Group TG 74.2 arriving offshore on June 15.

Up to this point, the Japanese aerial presence in Borneo had been virtually non-existent. However, this changed on June 25.

The tokko-tai involved were from the Shichisei Jinrai-tai, a unit formed from the Singapore-based and "Peggy"-equipped 61st Sentai. The latter had only moved to Singapore in February 1945, at which point it became the first unit assigned to the 3rd Kokugun that was trained in torpedo attack tactics. On June 19 the Shichisei Jinrai-tai received orders to target the Allied fleet gathering off Balikpapan, and the next day 61st Sentai commander Maj Shozaburo Hirakawa briefed his aircrew on a plan that called for the unit to attack using Type 91 torpedoes at night after first staging to the airfield at Surabaya, on Java, south of Borneo. It sortied eight aircraft (including one used to observe the results of the attack) from Surabaya at 1750hrs on June 25, encountering Allied shipping off Balikpapan. They arrived after dark on a moonlit night and claimed eight ships sunk, including an oiler and several cruisers or destroyers, in exchange for three aircraft lost in tokko attacks.

American reports painted a slightly different picture of the results achieved by the "Peggy" crews, however. Soon after 2020hrs, radar operators on board a number of US Navy picket ships began detecting contacts approaching over land from the southwest at a range of about 15 nautical miles. At 2030hrs the ships started opening fire on targets as the bombers, variously identified as "Peggys" and "Bettys" although most ships simply reported them as twin-engined torpedo-bombers, closed in from the starboard side. The high-speed transport USS *Cofer* (APD-62) bore the brunt of the attack, reporting that three "Bettys," launched torpedoes at it, two of which missed just ahead while the third narrowly missed the stern as the ship was turned hard to port in order to avoid the weapons. Another one was aimed at the destroyer USS *Cony* (DD-508), although it too missed. Meanwhile, one of the four "Peggys" sighted by the minesweeper USS *Sentry* (AM-299) made a tokko run on it and missed the bridge by a mere ten feet prior to crashing harmlessly into the sea a short distance away.

Where the two protagonists concur is in respect to the number of aircraft lost by the Japanese. *Sentry*'s after action report stated that three of the attackers were shot down in total, with the aircraft that narrowly missed the ship being claimed by its gunners. The second was credited to *Cofer*, while both ships and the light cruiser USS *Denver* (CL-58) claimed the third shared jointly between them and other vessels in the formation. The remaining aircraft withdrew, with the radar operator on board the light cruiser USS *Montpelier* (CL-57) plotting six contacts exiting the area. Shortly thereafter, at 2100hrs, the ships stood down from General Quarters.

By July 1945, with Okinawa secured and the Borneo campaign winding down, the Japanese feared that Malaya and Singapore would become the next objectives for an Allied invasion. Indeed, by early 1945 South East Asia Command had developed plans for the liberation of the British colonies of Malaya and Singapore, which had been captured by the Japanese in early 1942. Operation *Zipper* was scheduled for October 1945, with Commonwealth forces landing in northwest Malaya with two divisions and a brigade. Once a foothold had been gained, Operation *Mailfist* would commence, involving a further two divisions and another brigade landing in Malaya as soon as possible after *Zipper* and advancing south to retake Singapore.

Among the steps the Japanese took to reinforce Malaya and Singapore was to form more tokko-tai in July 1945 from the aircraft remaining in the area. By this time the local IJAAF units were in a sorry state, with many of the best aircraft having been withdrawn to Japan to defend the homeland or sacrificed in tokko attacks off Okinawa. Nevertheless, the 3rd Kokugun still managed to cobble together nine more tokko-tai from the various second-line units based in the region. However, they would be flying trainers or obsolete types, which made them little more than cannon fodder when intercepted by Allied fighters. Unsurprisingly, only one of the newly formed tokko-tai managed to give a relatively good account of itself in combat.

On July 24 the Royal Navy's TF 63, made up of four destroyers, five minesweepers, the heavy cruiser HMS *Sussex*, the battleship HMS *Nelson*, and the escort carriers HMS *Ameer* and HMS *Empress*, arrived off the coast

Ki-51 "Sonia" of the Shichisei Shodo-tai, Taiping airfield, Malaya, July 1945

When it became apparent that the Allies planned to eventually invade Malaya and Singapore, the IJAAF's 3rd Kokugun started forming its own tokko units. These include the Shichisei Shodo-tai, which was formed from the 3rd Kyoiku Hikotai and carried out the attack that sank the minesweeper HMS *Vestal* and hit the heavy cruiser HMS *Sussex* off Phuket, Siam, on July 25, 1945. (*Artwork by Jim Laurier, © Osprey Publishing*)

of Phuket, in Thailand, to commence Operation *Livery* – a feint to make the Japanese think landings were imminent. Minesweeping operations were also undertaken, and 24 Hellcats from each of the escort carriers carried out a series of attacks on targets in northern Malaya and southern Thailand, with a particular focus on Phuket and the Kra Isthmus. Over the next four days the Fleet Air Arm fighters flew more than 150 sorties, destroying in excess of 30 grounded Japanese aircraft and damaging rail and road links. On a less successful note, the minesweeper HMS *Squirrel* struck a mine on the first day of the operation and had to be scuttled.

The IJAAF quickly started making preparations to fight back, and on July 25 the Shichisei Shodo-tai received orders to attack the British fleet. Formed from the 3rd Kyoiku Hikotai, the "Sonia"-equipped unit was based at Taiping, in northern Malaya. At 0700hrs on the 26th, three Ki-51s took off in search of TF 63. However, these aircraft were forced to turn back when they encountered bad weather en route, leading the unit to try again later that morning with two "Sonias." This time they managed to locate the enemy vessels, and Cpl Toshiro Omura had commenced his attack on a carrier when his aircraft was hit by antiaircraft fire and crashed into the sea at 1030hrs. This is corroborated by Royal Navy records, which state that a "Sonia" was shot down while attacking *Ameer*. The lead aircraft, flown by Sgt Maj Isao Tokunaga, got off a sighting report before he again returned to base to plan the next attack.

The only British ship sunk by a tokko attack, the unlucky HMS *Vestal* was also the last Royal Navy vessel to be lost during the war. On July 26, 1945, it was targeted by a Ki-51 from the Shichisei Shodo-tai that had taken off from Alor Setar, in northwestern Malaya. The aircraft hit the vessel squarely amidships, causing severe damage and killing 20 crewmen. Unfortunately the minesweeper had to be scuttled, as to its proximity to enemy-held Phuket meant a recovery attempt was too risky.

This was duly launched at 1600hrs with five more "Sonias," the aircraft taking off from the base at Alor Setar, in northwestern Malaya. Once again Tokunaga was among the pilots, and despite the adverse weather conditions that caused the formation to become separated, they managed to locate TF 63 late in the day. The vessels detected the approaching tokko as they crossed the coastline at Phuket, with action stations being sounded at 1625hrs as two attackers were spotted, followed by three more behind them.

One of the pilots targeted the minesweeper HMS *Vestal* and hit it squarely amidships, despite the vessel opening fire with every gun it could bring to bear. The "Sonia" caused severe damage and killed 20 crew. With the ship being so close to enemy-held Phuket, it was deemed to be too risky to attempt to recover or repair *Vestal*, so the minesweeper was scuttled like its sister-ship *Squirrel* had been two days earlier. This meant that *Vestal* had the unhappy double distinction of being the only British ship sunk as a result of a tokko attack and the last Royal Navy vessel to be lost during World War II.

The heavy cruiser HMS *Sussex* was also targeted by two Ki-51s on July 26, one of which was shot down by gunfire during its attack run. The other managed to crash into the starboard side of the ship abaft its "Y" turret just above the waterline. However, the cruiser's thick belt armor, together with the "Sonia's" light construction, meant the damage sustained by the ship was limited to dents, scrapes, and scorch marks on the side of its hull. Some reports stated that the fixed undercarriage of the Ki-51 had actually made contact with the water prior to impact, resulting in the aircraft literally bouncing into the side of the cruiser. The "Sonia" would have also been slowed down by the water, thus further limiting the damage it caused to *Sussex*.

HONSHU

With Okinawa finally in Allied hands by June 22, 1945, despite the ferocious campaign waged by tokko from both the IJAAF and IJNAF (as detailed in the next chapter), the fast carriers turned their attention to Japan once again. On July 1 US Navy carriers of TF 38 departed Leyte and arrived off Honshu, the largest of Japan's three main islands, ten days later. They commenced flying strikes against targets on the mainland almost immediately. Royal Navy carriers of the British Pacific Fleet (now designated TF 37) arrived on July 16 after departing Manus ten days earlier.

From then on, the carriers roamed virtually at will off the Pacific coast of Honshu, and beyond, until war's end, their air groups attacking myriad targets. These included the surviving remnants of the IJN's once mighty fleet, now confined to various ports due a lack of fuel. They also struck at airfields, infrastructure, and other targets, while high above, USAAF B-29s continued their round-the-clock campaign to lay waste to Japan's cities and industry.

Japanese air operations in response to TF 38 were muted, with the focus being to continue building up strength by training a new cadre of kamikaze pilots to carry out attacks once American troops started to come ashore. This was illustrated by the fact that during July the IJAAF failed to mount a single tokko attack and just one such operation was carried out by the IJNAF, despite the fact that warships from both TF 37 and TF 38 were brazenly sailing just off the coast of Japan.

The IJNAF's only attempt at taking the fight to the Allies came on July 25 as the carriers struck the naval base at Kure and airfields in the Kobe, Osaka, and Shikoku regions. From 1730hrs, 12 "Grace" torpedo-bombers from the 7th Mitate-tai, also known as the Ryusei-tai after the Japanese name for the B7A, took off from Kisarazu, east of Tokyo. Each aircraft was carrying a single 1,764lb No. 80 Mk 5 Land Bomb, and the

USS *Hank* (DD-702) was in the thick of the action on several occasions during the tokko campaign, surviving a close brush with a "Zeke" (probably from the 5th Kenmu-tai) on April 11, 1945 while screening the fast carriers of TF 58. On August 9, while on "Tomcat" radar picket duty 45 nautical miles southeast of TG 58.3 and east of the Japanese port city of Sendai, *Hank* and sister-ship USS *Borie* (DD-704) found themselves in the midst of five tokko (probably rare, bomb-equipped, B7A "Graces" from the 2nd Ryusei-tai of the 7th Mitate-tai). One of the aircraft came so close to *Hank* that it drenched both ship and personnel forward with gasoline before the vessels combined to destroy it and the remaining four attackers. *(NARA)*

group was charged with attacking an enemy carrier task force reported 200 nautical miles southeast of Cape Daio, in Mie Prefecture. No successes were reported, however, with three torpedo-bombers being shot down by Hellcats from 1844 NAS embarked in HMS *Formidable* and another by an F6F-5P nightfighter flown by Lt(jg) R. Klose from VF(N)-91, assigned to the USS *Bon Homme Richard* (CV-31) air group, just before sunset. According to TF 37, the remaining attackers, which approached in three distinct groups, then retreated without engaging the fleet.

On the afternoon of August 9, just hours after B-29 44-27297 *BOCKSCAR* from the USAAF's 509th Composite Group had dropped a Fat Man nuclear weapon on Nagasaki, the destroyers USS *Benner* (DD-807), USS *Borie* (DD-704), USS *Hank* (DD-702), and USS *John W. Weeks* (DD-701) were on "Tomcat" radar picket duty 45 nautical miles southeast of TG 58.3 and east of the port city of Sendai. The task group had spent the day conducting strikes on northern Honshu that included targeting the airfield at Misawa and Ominato Harbor.

Just before 1500hrs *Borie* was struck by a Japanese dive-bomber that had approached undetected from its port quarter, the aircraft hitting the vessel between its mast and five-inch main gun director at bridge level. A large fire broke out around the superstructure and bridge, disabling the two main gun directors, torpedo directors, all radar, the signal bridge area, and two forward 40mm gun mounts. *Borie* also had the top of its forward stack sliced off in the attack and superstructure, forward deck house, and main deck area peppered with shrapnel on the right-hand side. This indicated that a bomb carried by the aircraft had passed through the destroyer from its port side to starboard, where the weapon exploded. Having suffered 48 dead and 68 wounded, *Borie* was forced to leave TG 58.3 and head, via Saipan, for repairs at Pearl Harbor.

The aircraft that hit the ship was identified as being a "Val," although sailors on both *Benner* and *Hank* stated that the vessel had been hit by a "Grace." Eyewitnesses from the latter ship also noted that the tokko had dropped a bomb prior to crashing.

Four more attacks developed in the 75 minutes after *Borie* had been hit, although all the tokko were shot down by the destroyers before they could inflict any damage. The identities of these aircraft were also disputed, with *Benner* stating it was targeted by a "George," two "Zekes," and a "Jack," while *Hank* identified them as three "Zekes" and a "Frank."

The IJNAF did indeed send out five aircraft against an enemy carrier task force in the same general area as TG 58.3 and at a time that would have put them over the destroyers during the mid-afternoon of August 9. These were five 1,764lb bomb-equipped "Graces" from the 2nd Ryusei-tai

The destroyer *Borie* was the second-to-last ship to be struck by a tokko during the war, being hit once during a series of attacks against a group of destroyers acting as radar pickets for TF 58 off northern Honshu on August 9. The destroyer's crew stated that their attacker was a "Val," although nearby vessels identified it as a "Grace," which was probably correct based on Japanese records. *Borie* suffered 48 dead and 68 wounded in the attack. *(NARA)*

of the 7th Mitate-tai – the same unit that had targeted TF 38 on July 25. On this day the attackers, led by Lt(jg) Matsuo Ibaraki, took off from Kisarazu at 1345hrs after being tasked with engaging ships 90 nautical miles east of Kinkasan. Kisarazu was home to the IJNAF's 5th Hikotai, which was part of the 752nd Kokutai. The latter unit was one of only two front-line Kokutai issued with a significant number of B7As.

Other tokko units also saw action on August 9, with a solitary "Lily" from the IJAAF's 255th Shinshu-tai targeting a carrier group off Kamaishi, in northern Honshu. Six "Judys" from the 4th Mitate-tai at Hyakurihara, in Ibaraki Prefecture, were tasked with attacking another carrier group east of Tokyo at about the same time that the Ryusei-tai departed Kisarazu. Finally, shortly after 1600hrs, another D4Y from this unit headed for the carriers off northern Honshu. Thanks to effective Allied fighter CAPs, no results were obtained from any of these attacks, with the last aircraft to be downed almost certainly being the "Judy" claimed by Ens J. C. Stires at 1820hrs while flying a Hellcat of VF(N)-91 from *Bon Homme Richard* – the latter was part of TG 58.4, which was also operating off northern Honshu.

The Japanese mounted a more concerted tokko effort on August 13, with the 4th and 7th Mitate-tai despatching four more "Judys" and "Graces" from the Suisei- and Ryusei-tai, respectively, against TF 38 early that afternoon, although again no results were obtained from their attacks. The IJAAF also increased its tokko efforts that day, with six "Nicks" from the 201st Shinshu-tai and a similar number of "Lily" bombers from the 253rd Shinshu-tai being ordered aloft. The tokko from both services were told to attack a carrier task force reported east of Cape Inubo.

Disaster struck the 253rd Shinshu-tai when US Navy fighter-bombers attacked its airfield at Nasu, north of Tokyo, just as the traditional ceremony for the departing pilots had been completed. All six fully fueled bombers were destroyed during a series of strafing passes made by 11 Hellcats from VF-94 and VBF-94, embarked in *Lexington*, whose pilots subsequently claimed that they "burned" 17 aircraft and probably destroyed five more in their attack on Nasu. The remaining tokko fared little better, with all the aircraft that approached TF 38 that day being shot down or chased away by the CAP or radar picket ships prior to them getting close to the task force. The "Grace" downed by fighters from *Randolph* at 1345hrs could have been a Ryusei-tai aircraft, while two "Judys" claimed by TF 38 pilots at 1630hrs were probably a pair of attackers from the Suisei-tai.

At 2000hrs the pilots of two of the Ki-45s from the 201st Shinshu-tai that had taken off at 1740hrs radioed that they were attacking enemy ships. No further transmissions were heard from either "Nick," although the crew of an IJNAF aircraft that was keeping an eye on TF 38 that day reported seeing "two balls of flames" soon after the Ki-45 pilots had made their final broadcast. Again, no Allied ships were damaged, and it is unclear whether the "Nicks" were shot down or simply missed their targets and crashed into the sea. At about the same time the nightfighter Hellcats of VF(N)-91 claimed two "Nicks" and two "Frances" shot down, with one more of each type as probable kills. It would seem likely that the 201st Shinshu-tai aircraft had fallen victim to the clinically effective 24-hour CAP that surrounded TF 38.

At noon on August 15, 1945, a pre-recorded speech by Japan's Emperor Hirohito was broadcast over Tokyo Radio, the head of state reading the Imperial Rescript on the Termination of the War and accepting the terms of the Potsdam Declaration. The announcement came too late, however, for a handful of aircrew from the 4th and 7th Mitate-tai that had taken off in 11 "Judys" and two "Graces" between 1050hrs and 1130hrs from Hyakurihara and Kisarazu, respectively. Four D4Ys and a single B7A subsequently returned to base, at which point their crews discovered that the war was over. The remaining airmen proceeded with their mission, ignorant to this fact, and were killed. At least one "Judy" was shot down by fighters from the light carrier *Belleau Wood* at 1252hrs – almost an hour after the Emperor's address.

CHAPTER 5
OKINAWA

With the Philippines effectively liberated by late February 1945 and US forces having landed on Iwo Jima on the 19th of that same month, Allied attention now turned to Okinawa – the largest and most developed of the Ryukyu chain of islands that stretches from southern Kyushu to Formosa. If it could be taken, Okinawa would provide the Allies with a key staging area and strategically critical launchpad for the invasion of the Japanese mainland. Located approximately 350 nautical miles south of Kyushu, the island was within range of most Japanese aircraft based in southern Japan. Units on Formosa had an even shorter distance to fly in order to reach Okinawa, which Vice Admiral Matome Ugaki had decided would be the next battleground for his kamikazes.

In an effort to improve the effectiveness of their air operations (which included tokko attacks) following the failed defense of the Philippines, the IJAAF and IJNAF made an attempt to unify their command structure with the creation of the 6th Air Army in early 1945. A consensus was also reached on the targets each service would concentrate on, as laid out in the Joint Central Agreement on Air Operations issued in March 1945 as part of the IJNAF's Directive No. 540. This called for units from both services to deploy to the East China Sea area, where the less-capable pilots of the IJAAF would concentrate on attacking transport convoys and their escorts. The IJNAF, meanwhile, would target enemy carrier striking task forces and other warships. Furthermore, the IJAAF was expected to provide as much assistance as possible to the IJNAF when the latter was attacking its far deadlier target set.

Undermining these grand plans for cooperation was the poor quality of aircrew, due to the paucity of training they had received,

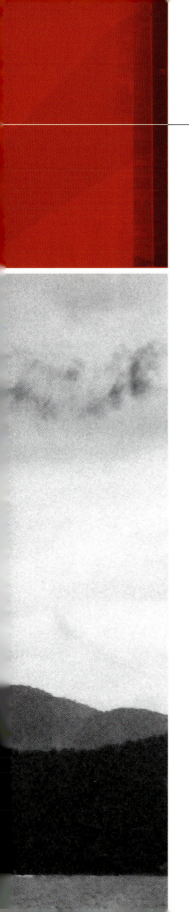

A "Zeke" trails a spectacular plume of smoke and flame after being shot down while attacking USS *Wake Island* (CVE-65) off Okinawa on April 3, 1945, this photograph being taken from its sister-ship USS *Tulagi* (CVE-72). *Wake Island* had been attacked by two "Zekes" from either the 2nd Kenmu-tai or the 252nd Kokutai, and although both were "splashed" by antiaircraft fire, one crashed close enough to damage CVE-65's hull plating and cause minor flooding. *(NARA)*

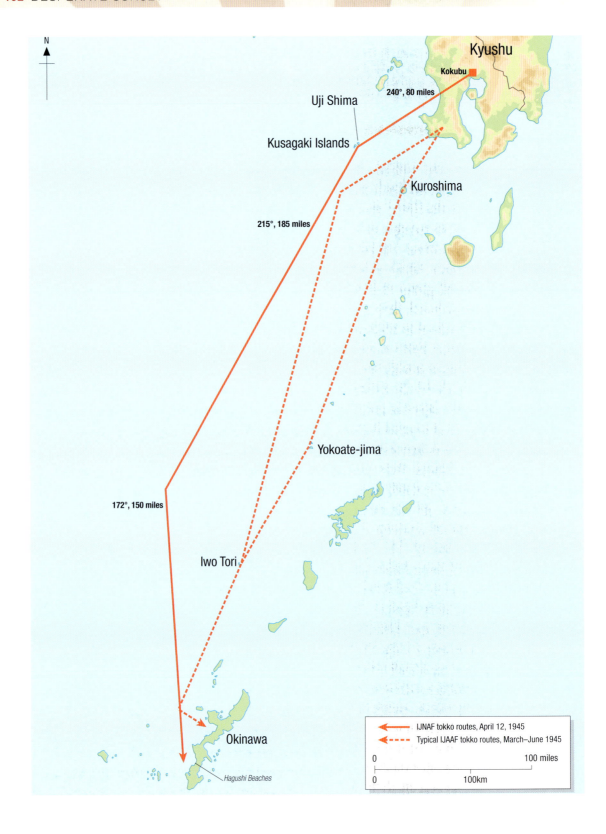

MAP LEFT
IJNAF and IJAAF tokko units would usually fly set routes from Kyushu to Okinawa due to the pilots' relative inexperience in overwater navigation. For largescale Kikusui missions the fighter escorts often acted as pathfinders, guiding the tokko to their targets off Okinawa. IJAAF aircraft typically took a more direct route south due to them lacking the range of IJNAF fighter and bomber types.

---

by this late stage in the war. Indeed, the number of combat-ready naval aviators had declined from the heady days at the start of the wider Pacific War to the point where the IJNAF stated in January 1945 that it did not expect its aircraft and crew strength to be ready for battle until May at the earliest. This decision, however, was taken out of the IJNAF's hands with the invasion of Okinawa, which commenced with the occupation of Kerama Retto – a small group of islands 17 nautical miles southwest of Okinawa – whose sheltered, deep waters were earmarked as a possible anchorage for ships involved in supporting the landings and subsequent battle. Seizure of Kerama Retto would also deny the IJN a base from which to launch its Shinyo suicide boats in attacks on Allied ships.

Following the March 19–20 strikes on Kyushu, TF 58 arrived off Okinawa to "soften up" Japanese positions prior to the actual landings, scheduled for March 26 at Kerama Retto and April 1 on Okinawa proper (Operation *Iceberg*). The presence of hundreds of carrier-based fighters in the area meant the tokko-tai were unable to muster more than token resistance in the days immediately leading up to the invasion of Kerama Retto, much less achieve any successes.

This all changed on the morning of the 26th when the destroyer USS *Kimberly* (DD-521), part of TU 51.1.13 assigned to TG 51.1, was approaching its assigned Radar Picket Station 9 to the southwest of Kerama Retto. At 0610hrs one of its SC-2 search radar operators spotted bogies that were soon visually acquired heading for the troop transports closing on Kerama Retto. The aircraft were identified as a pair of "Vals," one of which peeled off and commenced a long, circular diving approach on *Kimberly* from astern. The pilot of the aircraft managed to survive the barrage of gunfire fired at him by performing a series of radical maneuvers, which, according to the ship's after action report, consisted of "zooming, climbing, slipping, skidding, accelerating, decelerating, and even slow rolling." Despite trailing a stream of black smoke from where it had been hit, the "Val" honed in on the bridge from dead astern until it suddenly "went out of control and fell nearly vertically" onto the destroyer's aft 40mm gun mount.

Radar Picket Ships

Radar picket ships would play an important part in the battle against the tokko off Okinawa. It was correctly anticipated during the planning phase of Operation *Iceberg* that Japanese air attacks on the invasion fleet – both conventional and tokko – would be intense, and that an early warning system to alert ships of these attacks as they approached was required. Starting on March 26, a ring of 15 radar picket stations was established around Okinawa, using Bolo Point, just off Naha (the capital of Okinawa Prefecture and situated on the southwest coast of the island), as a reference point.

These radar picket stations were all located at different bearings and distances (between 15 and 90 nautical miles) from Point Bolo to provide all-round coverage of the approaches to Okinawa and the invasion fleet, and they remained operational until war's end. Each was manned by a destroyer and smaller supporting craft. At this point, radar picket ships were not fitted with special search radar, although they did embark fighter direction teams. In effect, they were acting as early warning radar platforms. The problem with this was that the pickets were too far apart to provide mutual protection, which in turn meant that they were vulnerable to mass kamikaze attack – losses on the picket stations were very heavy. This forced the US Navy to look for alternatives, all of which were still in the process of being evaluated as the war ended. These included using aircraft for early warning, submarines that could submerge when under kamikaze threat, and more-expendable destroyer escorts.

A typical radar picket station off Okinawa would have one of two destroyers or destroyer escorts with a fighter direction team on board to control the CAP overhead. The primary vessels would in turn be supported by two landing ships, usually Landing Craft Support (Large) – abbreviated to LCS(L) – or Landing Ship Medium (LSM) for additional antiaircraft firepower. As the battle progressed, some of the radar picket stations that saw the greatest incidences of attacks had the number of ships assigned doubled and dedicated CAPs maintained overhead.

Such defensive measures soon proved their worth, for the Japanese quickly took to targeting the ships assigned at the various radar picket stations – particularly during the massed Kikusui attacks – in a bid to knock out radar coverage for a particular sector in order to allow later waves of tokko to break through to the main fleet undetected. No fewer than ten destroyers and destroyer escorts were sunk and 32 damaged to varying degrees while fulfilling radar picket station duties. In addition, the landing ships assigned to the radar picket stations also took a battering, with two LCS(L)s being sunk and 11 damaged. Three LSMs were also lost and two more damaged by tokko attacks while supporting radar picket destroyers.

The impact, the explosion of the aircraft and its bomb, and the resultant fire killed four and wounded 57 crew. Damage to the ship itself was mostly confined to the aft 40mm gun and mounts as well as nearby 20mm guns in the same general area. *Kimberly* remained available for operations until April 1, when it headed to Mare Island Navy Yard to be repaired.

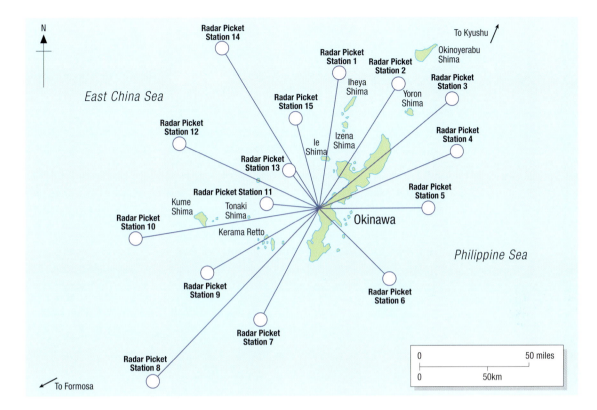

MAP ABOVE
The most intense and prolonged air-sea battle in naval history was fought off Okinawa from March to July 1945. Roughly a third of the Japanese sorties were conducted by some 1,900 tokko aircraft. The vast majority of kamikazes flew from bases in Kyushu, the Japanese home island located to the north of Okinawa. The American landing occurred on April 1 on the southwestern section of Okinawa, and this prompted a series of mass tokko attacks that began on April 6 and did not conclude until June 22. In order to provide early warning of imminent attacks on the invasion fleet, the US Navy established a number of radar picket stations as depicted on this diagram. These were manned by destroyers, and since they were the first ships encountered by tokko headed south, they bore the brunt of Japanese kamikaze attacks. The destroyers manning the northernmost stations suffered the worst. The US Navy used the Kerama Retto anchorage to shelter damaged ships and as a retreat at night, so this area was also a favorite kamikaze target.

Soon after DD-521 was struck, the destroyer-turned-high-speed transport USS *Gilmer* (APD-11), flagship of the Underwater Demolition Flotilla TG 52.11 and carrying teams of frogmen charged with reconnaissance and preparation of the landing beaches, sighted a pair of "Tonys" overhead heading on an almost reciprocal course from its starboard bow. One of these traced a wide arc above the ship and commenced an attack run from the same quadrant, being fired on by the ship as the pilot strafed APD-11 in return. The antiaircraft fire from

Gilmer, together with its hard turn to starboard at full speed, seemed to put the attacker off, for he only managed to skid across the ship's galley deck house superstructure prior to plunging into the water close aboard. Although one sailor was killed and three wounded, the damage caused by the Ki-61 was insignificant.

At 0700hrs the destroyer minelayer USS *Robert H. Smith* (DM-23) was narrowly missed by what its crew reported was another "Val," the aircraft overshooting the warship and plunging into the sea off its port beam – despite the pilot making a last ditch attempt at correcting his dive. The crash and subsequent underwater explosion of the aircraft's bomb caused only slight shrapnel and shock damage to DM-23, with no injuries sustained by its crew.

IJAAF records list two groups of tokko that were active that day, with four "Sonias" from the Sei 17th Hikotai, led by Capt Yokyu Ishado, and six "Tonys" of the 23rd Dokuritsu Chutai, led by 2Lt Yumeno Abe, being sent against ships off Kerama Retto from Ishigaki Island, 200 nautical miles southwest of Okinawa. According to IJNAF records, none of its aircraft participated in tokko missions that day.

More IJAAF tokko attacks were mounted on the morning of March 27, with nine "Sonias" from the Sei 32nd Hikotai (or "Bukoku-tai") and a further pair from the Sekishin-tai targeting the invasion fleet. The latter unit was a tokko-tai formed from the 49th Dokuritsu Chutai. It seems most likely that these aircraft were the ones that succeeded in hitting the battleship USS *Nevada* (BB-36), the light cruiser USS *Biloxi* (CL-80), the destroyer *O'Brien* (which had previously been struck by a tokko off

The battleship USS *Nevada* (BB-36) was hit by a single tokko (probably a "Sonia") on March 27, 1945 while participating in the pre-invasion bombardment of Okinawa. The aircraft hit near 14in. gun turret No. 3, but caused little damage. Aside from putting the turret out of commission, it demolished three 20mm gun mounts and both embarked Kingfisher floatplanes, and holed the aft deck area. The nearby exposed antiaircraft gun crews suffered nine dead and 46 wounded. *(NARA)*

Luzon on January 6) and the high-speed destroyer minesweeper USS *Dorsey* (DMS-1) between 0620hrs and 0624hrs. However, crews on board these vessels reported being attacked by either "Vals" or "Nates" (which, like the "Sonia," had fixed undercarriages).

The first ship to be attacked was *Dorsey*, whose crew stated that three "Vals" approached from the starboard bow while the vessel was sailing off Kerama Retto. One of the aircraft split away from the others and passed down DMS-1's starboard side, before approaching from astern and crashing into the main deck aft of the galley deckhouse at 0620hrs. The ship only sustained superficial damage, almost certainly because gunners had managed to shoot off the bomb attached to the aircraft's centerline before *Dorsey* was hit.

The veteran battleship *Nevada* came under attack three minutes later, BB-36 having famously been the only vessel on "Battleship Row" to get underway during the attack on Pearl Harbor. Part of Rear Admiral Morton L. Deyo's TF 54 Gunfire and Covering Force, the warship was hit by what its crew identified as being a "Nate" at 0622hrs. The aircraft struck the main deck near the No. 3 turret, demolishing three 20mm gun mounts and both embarked Vought OS2U Kingfisher floatplanes. The No. 3 turret was also put out of commission and the aft deck area holed in several places. Nine crew were killed and 46 wounded.

Biloxi also reported coming under attack at this time from a pair of "Vals" that approached the ship from its port bow and port beam. Although the lead aircraft was shot down into the sea, the second tokko crashed into the ship's waterline at Frame 140. Some flooding and a small fire resulted, but no major damage occurred as the aircraft's bomb failed to explode – a stray 40mm shell fired by a nearby ship that hit *Biloxi* in error during the attack also failed to detonate. As the ship's after action report noted, "the fates have been kind to us."

O'Brien was less fortunate. Its crew reported being attacked by two aircraft, identified as being either "Vals" or "Nates," as they sailed off Okinawa's Hagushi Beaches with *Nevada* and *Biloxi*. One of the tokko slammed into the destroyer's port side just aft of the after stack, with the impact and subsequent bomb detonation inflicting significant damage to the ship's topsides. It also knocked out the Combat Information Center (CIC) and forward fireroom, *O'Brien*'s top speed having to be reduced to 27 knots as a result. DD-725 also suffered heavy casualties, with 22 killed, 28 missing, and 76 wounded. The destroyer was subsequently sent to Mare Island

One of the most prevalent tokko was the D3A2 "Val," although numerous attacks by both the Ki-51 and Ki-27 were routinely blamed on the Aichi dive-bomber by shell-shocked sailors due to all three types have a fixed undercarriage and being powered by radial engines. This photograph shows an aircraft armed with a single 551lb Type 99 No. 25 Model 1 bomb on its centerline rack and single 140lb Type 99 No. 6 Model 1 weapons under each wing. It is being waved off by groundcrew from an airfield on Kyushu during an early Kikusui operation. *(Tony Holmes collection)*

Navy Yard to be repaired, remaining out of commission until mid-August.

Also hit that morning were the destroyer USS *Callaghan* (DD-792) and destroyer escort USS *Foreman* (DE-633). They were struck by what sailors identified as "Vals" at about the same time and locations as the previous vessels, with crews reporting that their attackers had dropped bombs immediately prior to crashing into their targets.

The IJNAF was also involved in despatching tokko that morning, with five "Frances" from the 1st Ginga-tai taking off from Miyazaki soon after 0300hrs followed by ten "Judys" from the 2nd Suisei-tai staging from Kikaijima Island just before 0600hrs. Both formations had been tasked with attacking TF 58's carriers off Okinawa, and neither met with any success.

At sunrise on March 28, just as the minesweepers of TU 52.4.1 were preparing for a day of clearing mines from the beaches of Kerama Retto, the destroyer minelayer USS *Adams* (DMS-27) sighted four aircraft nine nautical miles away to the west and started taking action to unmask its antiaircraft guns. The ship quickly opened fire when two of the aircraft, again identified as "Vals," bore in from its port side. Both attackers were shot down, although the second aircraft crashed close enough to scatter debris and fuel all over the vessel's deck and dent its port bow. These aircraft were most likely part of a group of five "Sonias," led by 2Lt Kunishiro Tsurumi, from the Sekishin-tai that were sent after ships near Kerama Retto that morning.

The tokko failed to inflict any damage on Allied ships over the next two days, with only the landing craft *LCI(G)-560* having a close shave at 0600hrs on March 29 when its mast was clipped by one of three attacking "Nates" – almost certainly aircraft from the Sei 41st Hikotai.

Undeterred, the IJAAF continued to generate early morning sorties, and at 0708hrs on the 31st – the day before the planned landings on Okinawa – the heavy cruiser *Indianapolis* spotted an "Oscar" as the fighter emerged from cloud cover near its starboard quarter. Gunners immediately opened fire as the Ki-43 commenced its dive, and although hits were scored by the 392 20mm shells fired, they only managed to deflect the attacker. The "Oscar" struck the cruiser's main deck aft and disintegrated, the aircraft's solitary bomb penetrating through the plating and passing out of its side before exploding just above the water. This served to reduce the damage inflicted on the ship, although some flooding resulted and nine crew were killed and 20 injured. The identification of the tokko as an "Oscar" concurs with IJAAF records, which indicate that the day's only such mission was carried out by three aircraft led by Capt Susumu Sasagawa of the Sei 39th Hikotai, also known as the "Soryu-tai."

The start of Operation *Iceberg* the next day was matched by a dramatic increase in tokko activity, with the IJAAF sending out 28 aircraft from six different groups and the IJNAF despatching ten aircraft from three groups. The latter included six Ohka-carrying "Bettys," although no hits were scored by the rocket-powered aerial bombs. The same could not be said for the conventional tokko, which succeeded in damaging no fewer than seven ships to varying degrees.

The most successful of the attackers were the seven Ki-61s led by 1Lt Toshimitsu Hirai of the Formosa-based 17th Sentai, the sole tokko-tai flying the inline-engined fighter that day. Crews from four of the damaged ships identified their attackers as "Tonys," these being the unfortunate *Adams* (struck for the second time in just four days), the attack transport USS *Hinsdale* (APA-120), and *LST-724* and *LST-884*, all of which were struck in the same general vicinity within a few minutes of each other at 0550hrs. *Hinsdale* had three holes punched into its port side just above the waterline – a seven-foot hole made by the "Tony's" fuselage, another caused by the explosion of one of its wing-mounted 132lb bombs, and a ten-inch hole caused by a second bomb that failed to explode. The aircraft's 12-cylinder Kawasaki Ha-40 inline engine and the unexploded bomb were found inside the ship, which further helped to confirm the identity of APA-120's attacker and the ordnance it was carrying. Fifteen crew were killed and a further 40 listed as missing or wounded following the tokko strike.

Meanwhile, *Adams* had been near-missed by its attacker, which splashed into the water aft of the ship after being hit by antiaircraft fire as the destroyer took evasive action. However, the explosion of the "Tony's" bombs as the fighter hit the water jammed the vessel's rudder in the hard right position and left it steaming in a right-hand circle. Adams was then attacked by two more aircraft, which the crew identified as "Hamps," although both were shot down without inflicting further damage.

Seafire III PR256 flown by Sub Lt R. H. Reynolds, 894 NAS, HMS *Indefatigable*, Pacific, April 1, 1945

Because of their limited range, Seafire IIIs were used for fleet defense only, and early on April 1, 1945, an inbound tokko raid was intercepted by the CAP from *Indefatigable*. One "Zeke" dove on the carrier, with Sub Lt Richard Reynolds on its tail. In spite of the Japanese pilot's determined evasion, and proximity to the barrage thrown up by the vessel, Reynolds continued attacking. Indeed, he only broke away seconds prior to the Japanese fighter hitting the ship. Twenty minutes later, he attacked a second "Zeke," and with two short bursts sent it down. He then chased a third, using up his remaining ammunition in ensuring its destruction. PR256 was subsequently decorated with its pilot's score (Reynolds also had two victories over German flying boats) and the nickname *Merry Widow* – both rare additions to an aircraft of the Fleet Air Arm. (Artwork by Chris Davey, © Osprey Publishing)

Sub Lt Richard Reynolds of 894 NAS became an ace at the start of the Okinawa operation when he destroyed three tokko to add to two German flying boats he had downed in August 1944. On the morning of April 1, 1945, while he was manning a CAP over British Pacific Fleet carriers off the Sakishima Gunto group of islands, Reynolds scored several cannon hits at long range on the "Zeke" that subsequently hit his carrier, *Indefatigable*. (Tony Holmes Collection)

These tokko could in fact have been late-model "Oscars" of the Sei 39th Hikotai (which had sortied six aircraft), their reduced wingspan giving them a similar planform to the clipped wings of the "Hamp."

LST-884, whose cargo included 60mm and 81mm mortar ammunition, was so badly damaged by the Ki-61 that it was taken out of service after being towed to Ulithi and eventually scuttled in February 1946. *Hinsdale* was also in a sorry state following the "Tony" strike, the transport ship having to be towed by the rescue tug *ATR-80* at just five knots to Kerama Retto. Once there, its cargo – equipment and stores needed ashore by the US Marines Corps – was shifted to USS *Pitt* (APA-223) and *Hinsdale* pressed into service as a receiving ship for survivors of vessels hit by kamikazes. APA-120 was eventually towed to

Ulithi, where a month of intensive work by repair ship USS *Vulcan* (AR-5) readied it for a return voyage to Brooklyn Navy Yard.

The British Pacific Fleet had arrived off the Sakishima Gunto group of islands, located between Okinawa and Formosa, on March 26 specifically to neutralize Japanese airfields and other military positions there as the landings on Kerama Retto began. The Royal Navy vessels spent the final three days of March refueling, before operations recommenced on the morning of April 1. At 0722hrs the radar picket destroyers reported bogies approaching the fleet, the aircraft having been detected at a distance of 65 nautical miles.

Although the CAP managed to shoot down at least one "Zeke," a second IJNAF fighter slammed into *Indefatigable* at 0728hrs despite one of the carrier's Seafires, flown by 894 NAS's Sub Lt R. H. Reynolds, scoring several cannon hits on it from long range. The aircraft, which the carrier's damage report states was armed with a 551lb bomb, hit the armored flightdeck abaft the island, with the explosion holing both and starting a fire that had been extinguished by 0742hrs. The crash also wrecked the radio room and sick bay within the island, as well as damaging the crash barriers on the flightdeck and riddling three parked aircraft with splinters.

This was the first occasion a British carrier, with its armored flightdeck, had been hit by a tokko. In the case of *Indefatigable*, although the flightdeck had been buckled where the aircraft had hit it, the armor plating had done its job by saving the hangar bay from damage. The flightdeck itself was soon operational again, the damage having been repaired in eight hours. Much has been made of this design difference between British and American carriers, with the latters' unarmored flightdecks allowing tokko to plunge through them into the hangar bay and other spaces and causing fire and mayhem belowdecks. However, the additional armor came at a price, with British carriers having a reduced aircraft capacity (103 aircraft for an Essex-class vessel versus 81 for

At 0728hrs, *Indefatigable* was hit by a bomb-armed "Zeke" from the 1st Taigi-tai, flying from Ishigaki Island. The tokko struck the carrier on the forward crash barrier where the flightdeck joined the island. The blast from the exploding bomb and the aircraft itself damaged the sickbay, a briefing room, and a second flightdeck crash barrier. Eight crewmen had been killed immediately and 16 wounded – six of the latter subsequently passed away. Here, sailors inspect a hole punched into the island by the detonation of the 551lb bomb. *(Jamie Seidel)*

Indefatigable's blackened island bears witness to the impact of the tokko, the explosion of its bomb, and the fuel "flash fire" that ensued. Sub Lt John Birtle of 887 NAS also fired at the "Zeke" just before it hit the carrier. "After diving down the flight deck the Zero pulled up into a vertical climb, at the top of which he did an immaculate stall turn and commenced another dive onto *Indefatigable*. I don't know how long I fired at it, three or four seconds maybe, but I saw strikes on the Zero and, fractionally before he hit, his port wing started breaking away. Discussing this with Erik Govaars (my flight leader) afterwards, we thought that he was trying to dive down the funnel – which the kamikazes were ordered to do if the lifts were not open; fortunately, they weren't at the time – and losing control at the last split second, the aircraft finished up diving into the base of the island." (Jamie Seidel)

Indefatigable and its sister-ships) and range (14,100 nautical miles at 20 knots versus 6,900 nautical range at the same speed).

The tokko that had targeted the British ships were from the IJNAF's 1st Taigi-tai, flying from nearby Ishigaki Island. The unit had sortied three bomb-laden "Zekes" at 0645hrs under the leadership of Lt(jg) Masatoshi Sakai, with a fourth fighter undertaking the escort-observer role. The Taigi-tai had been formed from the 205th Kokutai, which had itself been created from the remnants of three Hikotai that had been evacuated from the Philippines. The Formosa-based naval aviators were highly regarded by their enemies, who stated that they were more skilled and capable than their Japan-based counterparts. This assessment would be repeatedly borne out over the next few months as Formosa-based tokko achieved results out of all proportion with their numbers.

On April 2 seven groups of tokko (including four "Zekes" from the Kanoya-based 1st Kenmu-tai) had headed for Okinawa in search of Allied warships. Seven vessels were duly hit, with five of them falling victim to just one group that struck south of Kerama Retto at dusk. The successful group was almost certainly from the Sei 114th Hikotai, its eight "Nicks" being led by 2nd Lt Okiteru Takeda. The aircraft had spotted transports and their screen headed southward away from Okinawa on their nightly retirement out of range of the tokko threat. The Ki-45s managed to damage USS *Chilton* (APA-38), USS *Goodhue* (APA-107), USS *Henrico* (APA-45), and USS *Telfair* (APA-210) to varying degrees, while USS *Dickerson* (APD-21), hit by two aircraft that

ABOVE
The attack transport USS *Alpine* (APA-92) was hit twice by tokko, being struck off Leyte on November 18, 1944 and off Okinawa on April 1, 1945. On both occasions the ship was in the process of debarking troops and their equipment. Five crew were killed and 12 wounded off Leyte while 16 perished and 19 were wounded in the second incident, which also saw *Alpine* hit by a bomb dropped by the tokko prior to it crashing into the ship's Nos. 2 and 3 holds. APA-92 – still with a noticeable list to port following the attack on April 1 – is seen here anchored in Okinawan waters with the Diver-class rescue and salvage ship USS *Gear* (ARS-34) alongside. *(NARA)*

badly holed its main deck and then ignited a uncontrollable fire, was scuttled two days later. A total of 54 crew, including the captain, had been killed on board APD-21.

The after action reports and war diaries of these ships agreed that their attackers were twin-engined aircraft, although they differed when it came to type identification. The report from *Goodhue* was the most accurate, its crew identifying the tokko as a mixed formation of eight "Nicks" and "Frances," while *Telfair* stated its attackers were "Sallys," although none of this type were ever involved in such attacks on ships in 1944–45.

The attack cargo ship USS *Achernar* (AKA-53) had actually been the first vessel struck on April 2 when a lone "Sonia," and its bomb, hit it at 0043hrs, killing five crew and injuring 41. Just before dawn fellow attack cargo ship USS *Tyrrell* (AKA-80) was strafed by a "twin-engined plane" that then proceeded to clip the main mast, starboard yardarm support, and five-ton cargo boom before exploding when it crashed into the sea. Due to a smokescreen generated by the ship and poor light, the attacker was sighted very late and was neither identified nor fired upon.

MAP ABOVE
The battleground for the bitterly fought tokko campaign following the landings on Okinawa stretched from Kyushu in the northeast to Formosa in the southwest. Tokko-tai units that relied on IJAAF and IJNAF fighters for protection flew from airfields on Kyushu and on Formosa. Their targets were the American transport vessels anchored off the west coast of Okinawa and the carriers of TF 58 steaming to the east of the island. The tokko units and their escorts followed the Ryukyu Islands chain to their targets.

The morning of April 3 found *LST-599* off Kuba Jima, in the Kerama Retto group, awaiting its turn to land *LCT-876*, 29 officers, 164 men, and 424 tons of cargo for US Marine Corps fighter squadron VMF-322 on Okinawa. At 0610hrs lookouts sighted two single-engined aircraft, one of which turned to attack the vessel from its starboard beam. Diving at an angle of about 45 degrees from an altitude of 1,500ft, the tokko had its starboard wing shot away prior to plowing through *LCT-876* and penetrating the main deck of *LST-599*. The impact started a conflagration that was rapidly fueled by 300 barrels of gasoline earmarked for VMF-322 that had been stored topside. By 1130hrs the fires were under control following help from a number of nearby vessels. Remarkably, despite the damage inflicted on *LST-599*, casualties were relatively light – 21 wounded, including two from the LCT.

Examination of the wreckage, specifically the inline engine that was found below decks, led the crew of *LST-599* to conclude that their attacker was a "Tony." The sole Ki-61s undertaking tokko missions on this day were a flight of six 105th Sentai aircraft sortied from Matsuyama, in Formosa. Led by 2Lt Wataru Hasegawa, the "Tonys" had been escorted by five other aircraft from the Sentai.

The escort carrier USS *Wake Island* (CVE-65) and high-speed destroyer minesweeper USS *Hambleton* (DMS-20) both had a narrow escape that day when they were targeted at 1800hrs at separate locations. *Wake Island*, conducting air operations in support of the land campaign, was southeast of Okinawa when its crew spotted five enemy aircraft off the carrier's starboard side. Two of the tokko dove at the ship and both splashed into the sea alongside CVE-65, with the second aircraft being close enough to damage hull plating and cause minor flooding.

Wake Island's war diary described the attackers as "Oscars," although its after action report identified them as a pair of "Zekes." The only Ki-43-equipped tokko-tai active that day was the 22nd Shinbu-tai, which despatched three aircraft from Chiran, on Kyushu, during the afternoon. None managed to reach their targets, however, with all the "Oscars" succumbing to non-combat-related causes. Several IJNAF tokko-tai sortied "Zekes" on the 3rd, with three from the 3rd Taigi-tai taking off from Formosa at 1440hrs and 1510hrs, the 2nd Kenmu-tai despatching six from Kanoya at 1500hrs, and the 252nd Kokutai sending two aloft from Kokubu at 1535hrs. With the carrier's attackers approaching from the north, it would appear to have been one of the Kyushu-based tokko-tai that almost hit the vessel.

At about the same time that *Wake Island* was attacked, *Hambleton* encountered what its crew identified as a "Val" while sailing towards Ie Shima, off the west coast of central Okinawa, to take up its night patrol station in company with four other ships. The aircraft clipped the vessel's fantail with its starboard wing before disintegrating when it hit the water. There were no "Vals" on tokko missions that day, so perhaps *Hambleton*'s attacker was yet another "Sonia," for there were three different tokko-tai operating the perennially misidentified Ki-51 that day. All assigned to Kyushu-based units, six were from the Sei 32nd Hikotai at Nyutabaru, five were 23rd Shinbu-tai aircraft flying from Bansei (that took off at

B6N2 131-56 of the Kikusui-Tenzan Kokutai (formerly 131st Kokutai), Kushira airfield, Kyushu, April 6, 1945

This aircraft, assigned to the special attack Kikusui-Tenzan Kokutai, participated in Kikusui No. 1 – the first largescale tokko strike generated by the IJNAF and IJAAF in response to the invasion of Okinawa – on April 6, 1945. Each armed with a 1,764lb No. 80 Mk 5 Land Bomb, the "Jills" apparently targeted the destroyers *Bush* and *Colhoun*, which were manning Radar Picket Stations 1 and 2 (north of Okinawa), respectively, on this date. *Bush* was hit by two tokko and sunk, while *Colhoun* was struck by at least four aircraft and had to be scuttled a short while later. (*Artwork by Jim Laurier, © Osprey Publishing*)

1530hrs), and three were 62nd Shinbu-tai machines from Tachiarai. The "Sonias" headed for the waters west of Okinawa.

The fact that there were not more attacks by the Ki-51s that evening was due to ace Lt Thaddeus Coleman and his wingman Ens Richard Langdon from Hellcat-equipped VF-83, embarked in *Essex*, who were scouting for Japanese ships near the Osumi group of islands south of Kyushu when they reported encountering seven "Sonias" carrying bombs beneath their fuselages. They shot down all of them, thus accounting for a high proportion of the Ki-51 tokko sortied by the IJNAF on April 3.

The next two days were quiet, although it soon turned out that this was merely the calm before the storm for on April 6 the Japanese launched the first of the Kikusui massed tokko attacks, which officially lasted till the 11th. Aircraft started taking off primarily from airfields on Kyushu shortly after 1000hrs, continuing to sortie until the early afternoon. According to a United States Strategic Bombing Survey (Pacific) study published in 1946, over the first 48 hours of the offensive a total of 355 aircraft – 230 from the IJAAF and 125 from the IJNAF – were despatched on Kikusui No. 1. An additional 344 fighters and bombers undertook escort or conventional attack missions in support of the tokko.

The first vessel to be targeted on the 6th was the destroyer USS *Haynsworth* (DD-700), whose crew sighted what they reported to be a "Judy" pursued by a pair of Corsairs soon after 1245hrs as the ship steamed in company with TG 58.3 east of Okinawa and south of Tokunoshima. The dive-bomber managed to elude the fighters and targeted the destroyer from its starboard side, dropping a bomb that fell harmlessly into the ocean before crashing into the ship's radio transmitter room. The aircraft destroyed DD-700's radio and radar equipment and killed seven of its crew, with a further 25 being wounded.

Assuming the identification of *Haynsworth*'s attacker is correct, the "Judy" was one of 13 despatched by the 210th Kokutai's Suisei-tai from Kokubu airfield on Kyushu at 1020hrs. The aircrafts' crews had been instructed to target enemy shipping south of Tokunoshima.

The sheer number of attacks that day, and the fact that many of the tokko-tai were flying aircraft that could be easily mistaken for another type ("Jills" with "Kates," and "Zekes" with "Franks" and "Oscars," for example), has meant that the exact attribution of which ship was hit by what aircraft on April 6 is an almost impossible task. In *Haynsworth*'s case, however, identification was made easier by the fact that the 210th Kokutai's Suisei-tai was the sole Kyushu-based tokko-tai from the IJNAF to have sortied in the morning, with other units having taken off too late to have been responsible for that attack.

Another group of "Judys" active that day as tokko were three aircraft from the Formosa-based Chusei-tai, which left Shinchuku (Hsinchu) at 1500hrs in search of a carrier group spotted south of Ishigaki Island. This trio of dive-bombers was almost certainly part of the formation of four aircraft that penetrated cloud cover over British carriers soon after 1700hrs. One of these dived on HMS *Illustrious* from its port quarter, the carrier immediately turning under full helm and opening fire. The gunners achieved several hits on the tokko, causing it to disintegrate while still 500ft away. Most of the aircraft fell into the water 50ft from the ship, although one of its wings clipped the bridge and associated debris and fuselage parts crashed onto the flightdeck.

Even though the bulk of the aircraft had missed *Illustrious*, the explosion of its ordnance, which Japanese records state was a 1,764lb No. 80 Mk 5 Land Bomb, managed to cause damage when it detonated underwater. The carrier, already battered from near misses following earlier service in the Mediterranean (which left it with persistent propeller

A "Judy" from the Formosa-based Chusei-tai targeted HMS *Illustrious* while the carrier was sailing 200 miles east of the island on April 6, 1945, the dive-bomber plunging out of cloud cover on the port bow. Just 11 seconds passed from when it emerged from the overcast sky until it hit the water. In that time the ship's gunners achieved several hits on the tokko, causing it to disintegrate while still 500ft away. Most of the "Judy" fell into the water 50ft from the ship, although one of its wings clipped the bridge and associated debris and fuselage parts crashed onto the flightdeck. The plume of water seen here was caused by the explosion of the D4Y's 1,764lb No. 80 Mk 5 Land Bomb, which caused significant shock damage when it detonated underwater. *(Donor K. Henville/AWM)*

shaft vibration problems), was subsequently unable to make even its already reduced top speed of 24 knots without unbearable shaking throughout the ship. *Illustrious* had to be pulled off the line shortly thereafter, and when divers inspected the hull they discovered some of its outer plating was split and a number of the transverse frames to which they were attached had cracked. The carrier would need significant dockyard time to fix these faults, and it was still in Sydney undergoing repairs when the war ended.

As the shattered "Judy" plunged towards the sea, one of its wingtips clipped the front of the island – reportedly only nine feet from where the commander of *Illustrious*, Capt Charles Lambe, was standing. The glancing blow put a gash in a radar dome, as clearly seen here, but did little other damage. *(© IWM A 29571)*

Radar picket destroyers had been particularly badly hit on April 6, with those located on a direct path from Kyushu to Okinawa coming under heavy attack. The destroyer *Bush*, a veteran of operations off the Philippines, was manning Radar Picket Station 1 (north of Okinawa) when it was hit by two kamikazes and sunk with the loss of 87 dead and 42 wounded. The destroyer USS *Colhoun* (DD-801) on nearby Radar Picket Station 2 was struck by at least four kamikazes and had to be scuttled after midnight. A further 35 sailors lost their lives and 21 were wounded.

LST-447 was struck by what was reported to be a "Zeke" while in the anchorage at Ie Shima on April 6, 1945, the storeless vessel (it had discharged its cargo on the beach on Okinawa on D-Day – April 1) sinking the following day. *(NARA)*

While tokko were pummeling the radar picket destroyers, the bombardment force also came under sustained attack in the waters off Ie Shima. A total of four destroyers were hit and two were eventually declared total constructive losses, while the remaining two were repaired but did not return to service until after the end of the war. *LST-447* was also struck by what was reported to be a "Zeke" while in the anchorage at Ie Shima, the storeless vessel burning ferociously until it sank the following day. Finally, that evening, the Victory ships SS *Hobbs Victory* and SS *Logan Victory* – each of which was carrying 6,000lb of ammunition – were also hit while anchored off Kuba Island and 27 crew were killed. Both ships were abandoned and later scuttled on April 7.

Elsewhere, the high-speed destroyer minesweeper USS *Emmons* (DMS-22) was hit by no fewer than five kamikazes in quick succession, resulting in the ship having to be scuttled with the loss of 64 dead and 71 wounded. It had been covering small minecraft sweeping the channel between Iheya Retto and Okinawa when attacked, the destroyer USS *Rodman* (DD-456) also being hit. The leading tokko in the first wave to target the vessels had dived out of cloud at 1532hrs and crashed into *Rodman*'s port bow, its bomb exploding beneath the ship. Although 16 crew were killed or missing and 20 wounded, the destroyer's engineering plant remained operational.

Emmons immediately started to circle *Rodman*, providing the damaged vessel with defensive fire as more kamikaze aircraft commenced their attacks. Six tokko were downed by DMS-22, and a further

Newly commissioned Fletcher-class destroyer USS *Leutze* (DD-481) is shown in April 1944 while undertaking performance trials and crew training off the northwest Pacific coast. The ship is wearing a Measure 31, Design 16D camouflage scheme. Note the five 5in./38 single guns and the mid-war 40mm battery of five twin mounts. *Leutze* suffered a tokko attack on April 6, 1945 that inflicted such extensive underwater damage the destroyer had to be declared a constructive total loss. *(NARA)*

While screening minesweepers off Ie Shima at 1600hrs on April 6, 1945, the destroyers *Newcomb* and *Leutze* were set upon by a number of tokko – at least 40 were observed in the area. Although the ships' gunners struggled to acquire attacking aircraft in time to engage them effectively due to a low cloud ceiling, they were able to drive off or shoot down several tokko. Nevertheless, over a period of 90 minutes, DD-586 *Newcomb* was struck four times, inflicting the devastation seen here. Like *Leutze*, *Newcomb* was declared a constructive total loss immediately post-war. *(NARA)*

ABOVE
Immediately recalling its firefighting parties from *Newcomb* in the wake of the explosion aft, *Leutze* maneuvered clear of DD-586 to allow its crew to bring the flooding under control. Despite having its fantail almost severed, the destroyer was successfully towed to Kerama Retto for emergency repairs and then sent back to California. *(NARA)*

LEFT
This close-up of the stern section of *Leutze* in Kerama Retto on April 9, 1945 reveals the extent of the damage inflicted on the ship three days earlier in a tokko attack. DD-481 was alongside the burning USS *Newcomb* (DD-586), assisting its crew tackling fires started by three kamikaze hits, when a fourth aircraft struck the destroyer and skidded across its deck into *Leutze*. The tokko's bomb then detonated against DD-481's port quarter, inflicting the damage seen here. *(NARA)*

20 were claimed by US Marine Corps F4U Corsairs that also appeared overhead. Nevertheless, *Rodman* was hit twice more during an engagement that lasted three-and-a-half hours. As noted earlier, *Emmons* was also hit by five aircraft and damaged by four near misses in less than ten minutes from 1732hrs. At 1800hrs, with uncontrolled fires detonating ordnance on board the ship, the decision was made by the surviving crew to abandon DMS-22. It was sunk by gunfire from the high-speed destroyer minesweeper USS *Ellyson* (DMS-19) the following morning.

The destroyers USS *Newcomb* (DD-586) and USS *Leutze* (DD-481) would have shared a similar fate had it not been for outstanding damage control by their respective crews after both ships were hit while they too were screening minesweepers off Ie Shima at 1600hrs. Despite *Newcomb*'s gunners struggling to acquire attacking tokko in time to engage them effectively due to a low cloud ceiling, they were able to drive off or shoot down several enemy aircraft. Nevertheless, over a period of 90 minutes, the vessel was struck four times. Despite the ship having suffered serious engine damage, and with numerous fires raging above and below decks, the crew managed to keep the destroyer mobile. This in turn allowed it to maneuver out of the way of further crashing aircraft.

Leutze quickly came to the vessel's aid, and while alongside the burning *Newcomb*, assisting its crew tackling the fires started by three tokko hits, a fourth aircraft struck DD-586 and skidded across its deck into DD-481. Its bomb then detonated against *Leutze*'s port quarter, inflicting sufficient damage to almost sever the fantail. Recalling its firefighting parties from *Newcomb*, *Leutze* maneuvered clear to allow its crew to bring the flooding under control.

By the end of the action, 18 crew had been killed aboard *Newcomb*, with 25 more listed as missing and 64 wounded. *Leutze*'s casualties numbered one dead, seven missing, and 30 wounded. Both warships were towed to Kerama Retto for emergency repairs prior to being sent home. Neither destroyer would return to fleet service post-war, the level of damage they had suffered resulting in them being declared constructive total losses and sold for scrapping.

For Allied warships off Okinawa, April 6, 1945 would be the worst day of the Okinawa campaign. It had proven impossible for the CAPs to stop every kamikaze aircraft, despite 19 US Navy and four US Marine Corps carrier squadrons engaging IJNAF and IJAAF aircraft in running battles that began around noon and lasted into the early evening. Naval aviators claimed 275 Japanese aircraft shot down – the fourth highest one-day total of the war. Thirteen pilots became aces that day, including four who achieved "ace in a day" status by shooting down five or more aircraft. Ten pilots shot down four aircraft, and a further 17 downed three. Honors for the day went to the pilots of VF-83 and its sister-squadron VBF-83, who claimed 69 aircraft. VF-30 was the next highest scoring squadron, claiming 47 tokko shot down.

VF-82's aircraft action report gave a telling account of what the CAP pilots repeatedly encountered off Okinawa that day:

> Of all the enemy planes encountered, *not one returned fire*; all remained on course, boring in toward the surface vessels. The only evasive action offered was jinking, and the majority of the aircraft were obsolete models as can be seen by the list [of] destroyed. Primary danger to our pilots was collision or getting in the path of a friendly plane's fire.

Despite the naval aviators' best efforts, inevitably some tokko made it through to the fleet. While the ships' antiaircraft fire shot down many, 20 vessels had been hit and six sunk.

Although wildly over-estimating the number of American ships sunk or damaged, the IJN's Combined Fleet Headquarters judged Kikusui No. 1 to have been a success. Based on reconnaissance reports, the Japanese believed the tokko had sunk two battleships, two carriers, three cruisers, eight destroyers, and five transports, with many more ships damaged. Success was attributed to the strategy of massed, simultaneous attacks, and the fact that the recently lost airfields on Okinawa were not yet capable of supporting American fighter units. However, the Japanese lacked the personnel and aircraft to quickly mount another mass attack. Smaller Special Attack missions would be flown almost daily, but it would take another five days before a sufficient number of tokko units could be organized for the next Kikusui operation.

The drop off in attacks on April 7 meant that fewer ships were hit. The first vessel to be targeted was the destroyer USS *Bennett* (DD-473), manning the increasingly dangerous Radar Picket Station 1 north of Ie Shima. It had been sent there following the sinking of the destroyers *Bush* and *Colhoun* in this very location the previous day. Having already had a busy night vectoring its assigned nightfighters and using its own guns to shoot down or drive off a number of snoopers, the ship detected three bogies closing in from the northeast at 0846hrs. Fighter controllers on board DD-473 vectored their assigned CAP towards the contacts, who reported shooting down three "Vals." In actual fact one of these had only been damaged, and minutes after *Bennett* called off the CAP the sole surviving attacker crashed into the vessel's starboard side amidships, despite its antiaircraft guns belatedly opening fire. Electrical power to the ship was knocked out by the tokko, which also damaged the forward

ABOVE
At 1212hrs on April 7, 1945, *Hancock* was attacked by a single "Judy" from almost dead ahead when carrying out flight operations northeast of Okinawa as part of TG 58.3. The aircraft dropped a bomb squarely on the vessel's flightdeck forward as it raced overhead at an estimated altitude of 50ft, and the ensuing blast sent the D4Y cartwheeling into the carrier amidships. Some 62 crew were killed and 71 wounded by the tokko, with the former receiving a traditional burial at sea on April 9. Note the Marine burial party second from left in this moving photograph. *(NARA)*

engine room, killed seven crew, and injured 14. DD-473 limped to the anchorage at Kerama Retto for emergency repairs and then sailed back to Puget Sound Navy Yard, Washington, for an overhaul. The destroyer eventually returned to fleet service in August 1945.

Also hit at various times and locations off Okinawa that day were the battleship *Maryland*, the destroyer USS *Longshaw* (DD-559), the destroyer escort USS *Wesson* (DE-184), and the motor-minesweeper *YMS-81*. Despite all of their attackers being identified as "Vals," none were assigned to the tokko-tai that targeted the invasion fleet on April 7 according to Japanese records. The IJAAF's 74th and 75th Shinbu-tai did sortie seven and four similar-looking "Sonias" at 1230hrs from Kyushu's

Bansei airfield, although they were unlikely to have hit these ships, which were all struck in the mid-morning or at twilight.

Aircraft carriers also had their encounters on this day. At 1212hrs *Hancock* was attacked by a single "Judy" from almost dead ahead as the vessel carried out flight operations northeast of Okinawa as part of TG 58.3. The aircraft dropped a bomb squarely on the ship's flightdeck forward as it raced overhead at an estimated altitude of 50ft, with the ensuing blast sending the D4Y cartwheeling into the carrier amidships. The bomb penetrated into the hangar bay and destroyed three aircraft, while the "Judy" wrecked 13 more on flightdeck aft. Several of *Hancock*'s antiaircraft guns were also damaged and fires started, although these were extinguished within 30 minutes and the holed flightdeck patched up so that CV-19 could resume flight operations just an hour after it had been hit. Some 62 crew had been killed and 71 wounded by the tokko.

Later that afternoon USS *Sitkoh Bay* (CVE-86) was participating in the delivering of aircraft from Marine Air Group 31 to Yontan airfield, Okinawa, with three other escort carriers when, at 1513hrs, a single bogey was picked up on radar about 22 nautical miles away. The CAP was vectored towards the contact, but confusion soon reigned as the ships received conflicting information as to whether the contact was hostile or friendly. This meant that the aircraft was not intercepted until it revealed itself to be a "Frances" twin-engined bomber. The tokko was taken under fire by both the US Marine Corps Corsair CAP overhead *Sitkoh Bay* and the ships' antiaircraft guns as it dived on the carrier, and they combined to shoot the bomber down into the sea within about 100 yards of the vessel's port beam.

Two groups of P1Y1s had been assigned to tokko missions that day, although the timing of the attack on CVE-86 would indicate that the aircraft that targeted it was one of four from the 4th Ginga-tai that departed Kanoya at around 1245hrs.

Sporadic attacks continued over the followings days as the IJNAF and IJAAF concentrated their efforts on organizing the men and aircraft required for the next Kikusui offensive. These lulls were not without periods of intense action, however, with small groups of tokko still continuing to mount strikes on Allied ships off Okinawa. Among the units involved were the IJAAF's 42nd and 68th Shinbu-tai, equipped with obsolete "Nate" fighters, which flew tokko missions on April 8 and 9. The 68th was one of five Shinbu-tai formed from the Hitachi-based Kyodo Hiko Shidan

(Instructional Flying Division) during March, with the unit – equipped with 12 Ki-27s – completing its organization on the 23rd.

IJAAF records note that eight aircraft from the 68th Shinbu-tai took off from the unit's original base in Ibaraki Prefecture, north of Tokyo, and headed south via Sagami, Tenryu, Kakogawa, and Ashiya airfields until they finally arrived at Chiran on April 5 in time to launch their first attacks from 1730hrs on the 8th. Two hours earlier, four "Nates" from the 42nd Shinbu-tai had departed Kikaijima Island and headed for shipping to the northeast of Okinawa. There, three of the aircraft found the destroyer USS *Gregory* (DD-802) on patrol at Radar Picket Station 3 just after 1800hrs, the pilots timing their arrival to perfection as the overhead CAP that had previously been under the ship's direct control had just departed with sunset imminent after an uneventful day.

Splitting up to attack from different directions, the lead "Nate" (identified as a "Sonia," most likely due to its fixed undercarriage) slammed into the destroyer on its port side amidships near the waterline despite having pieces shot off by antiaircraft fire. The hit instantly knocked out all electrical power throughout the ship and cut its speed from 25 knots to just ten knots as the forward engine room and fireroom flooded. Despite this, the vessel still managed to thwart the remaining two Ki-27s, which both missed. Limping to Kerama Retto for emergency repairs and then on to US Repair Base San Diego, in California, DD-802 was still in overhaul there when the war in the Pacific came to an end.

On April 9 three aircraft from the 42nd Shinbu-tai and a single Ki-27 from the 68th Shinbu-tai (flown by unit commander 2Lt Iichi Yamaguchi) took off from Kikaijima Island at 1740hrs and again headed for Okinawa. Soon after 1845hrs the quartet attacked the destroyer USS *Sterett* (DD-407), *LCS(L)(3)-36*, and *LCS(L)(3)-24* as they manned Radar Picket Station 4. DD-407 was hit by the third aircraft in the group, resulting in the loss of steering control, all power to the guns and fire directors, all communications, and the rupturing of its forward fuel tanks. Like *Gregory*, *Sterett* limped to Kerama Retto, before proceeding to Pearl Harbor and then on to Bremerton Navy Yard, Washington, to be repaired. The destroyer rejoined the fleet in late August 1945.

Just a solitary "Sonia" from the 30th Shinbu-tai was sent to attack Allied ships on April 10, without result. As was so often the case during the kamikaze campaign in the Pacific, this was very much the calm before the storm. Tokko attacks began to ramp up on the 11th, with Japanese aircraft taking off from late morning. These included 13 "Zekes" of the 5th Kenmu-tai that sortied from Kanoya over a nine-minute period from 1215hrs.

Detailed analysis by historians Akira Kachi and Katsumi Hiragi has shed much light on the 5th Kenmu-tai's operations during the defense of Okinawa, and on this day it targeted the battleship *Missouri* and the destroyer USS *Kidd* (DD-661). Using available information found in Japanese and American archives, including the records of radio messages sent by tokko pilots, as well as interviews with surviving members of the 721st Kokutai (the unit that supplied the 5th Kenmu-tai with its pilots and aircraft), Kachi and Hiragi have determined that the unit would have initially flown from Kanoya to Kikaijima Island. From here they would have split into pairs and flown a fan-shaped search pattern to locate the two TF 58 task groups operating in that area.

According to Hiragi, *Kidd*, manning Radar Picket Station 11, was hit in the forward bow near the waterline on the starboard side by Lt(jg) Shigehisa Yaguchi at 1412hrs following an aborted attack run on the nearby destroyer USS *Black* (DD-666). The strike, which killed 38 crew and wounded 55, including the captain, Cdr H. G. Moore, knocked out the forward fireroom and eventually sent the destroyer back to San Francisco Navy Yard, via Ulithi, for repairs.

At 1443hrs another "Zeke" hit *Missouri* in an attack that has been immortalized by a photograph showing the "Mighty Mo" about to be struck on its starboard side by the tokko (see page 20). The aircraft crashed into BB-63 just below its main deck, resulting in the fighter's starboard wing being flung onto the ship. Like other battleships hit by kamikazes, the damage inflicted was superficial, mainly being confined to a fire in its five-inch No. 3 gun mount owing to spilt fuel from the wing. This was soon put out. Kachi believes that either PO2c Setsuo Ishino or PO2c Kenkichi Ishii from the 5th Kenmu-tai was responsible for this attack, the mutilated body of the pilot being found on board *Missouri* just aft of one of the 40mm gun tubs. Despite protestations from a number of the crew, the naval aviator was given a military burial at sea the next day on the orders of the ship's captain, Capt William M. Callaghan, who believed that the young pilot deserved such a ceremony after he had died as a warrior fighting for his country.

Along with *Kidd* and *Missouri*, the destroyers USS *Hank* (DD-702) and USS *Bullard* (DD-660) had brushes with "Zekes" on this day at

ABOVE
During the early afternoon of April 12, 1945, the destroyer escort USS *Rall* (DE-304) was performing anti-submarine screening duties in "Kamikaze Gulch" when it was attacked by a pair of Ki-27 "Nates." One of the aircraft managed to hit DE-304 amidships, although fortunately for the vessel the attacker's bomb passed through the other side of its hull before exploding. Photographs of the wrecked "Nate" sticking out from the hatch the aircraft slammed into suggest that *Rall*'s attacker was 2Lt Satoshi Yagyuu of the 69th Shinbu-tai. (NARA)

1352hrs and 1358hrs, respectively. Again, these aircraft were almost certainly from the 5th Kenmu-tai. The carrier *Enterprise* also had two close shaves, with one tokko striking a glancing blow at 1410hrs and a second hitting its flightdeck with part of a wing at 1501hrs when the aircraft's bomb exploded upon hitting the water. Although both were identified as "Judys" in the vessel's after action report, a photograph of the first attacker and subsequent examination of the tip of the second aircraft's aileron revealed that they were in fact A6M5s. Moreover, it would seem likely that the 5th Kenmu-tai was responsible for the first attack and possibly the second one too, although the latter could have been carried out by the tokko units of the 252nd or 601st Kokutai, both of which sortied aircraft from Kokubu soon after the 5th Kenmu-tai.

The IJAAF also had aircraft undertaking tokko missions that day, although on a smaller scale than the IJNAF. At sunset the destroyer escorts USS *Manlove* (DE-36) and USS *Samuel S. Miles* (DE-183) were attacked and near-missed by a pair of "Tonys" as they engaged in anti-submarine screening duties southeast of Okinawa, with both ships suffering a single crewman killed and equipment damaged from strafing. The attackers were from either the 19th or 105th Sentai, which sent out three and two aircraft, respectively, from bases on Formosa.

April 12 saw the start of the second Kikusui operation. Tellingly, the Japanese could only muster half the number of tokko involved in Kikusui No. 1, with 125 IJNAF and 60 IJAAF aircraft being sent out along with 195 fighters and bombers as escorts and conventional attackers. For the IJAAF, the tokko included "Sonias," "Nates," "Oscars," and "Franks" from Bansei, Chiran, and Miyakonojo, on Kyushu, as well as from Karenko (Hualien), on Formosa, while the IJNAF's "Zekes," "Vals," and "Kates" originated from Kanoya, Kokubu, and Kushira. The IJNAF also sortied eight "Bettys" from the Jinrai Butai for another crack with the Ohka rocket-powered aerial bomb – the first time MXY7s had been used since the opening day of the Okinawa campaign.

Although Kikusui No. 2 involved fewer aircraft, the tokko still managed to strike 18 ships and sink two in an action-packed afternoon on April 12 that saw almost all the vessels hit in a frenetic hour starting just before 1400hrs. Most of the attackers had taken off from their southern Kyushu bases at around noon, resulting in a relatively coordinated attack as they arrived off Okinawa at almost the same time.

The majority of the ships hit by aircraft that day claimed their attackers were either "Kates" or "Vals," which was perhaps not surprising given the two types represented more than a fifth (38 aircraft) of the total tokko despatched. Include the 34 "Sonias" (which, as we have seen, were almost always mistaken for "Vals") sortied that day and that figure rises to almost 40 percent of the attackers.

The destroyer escort USS *Rall* (DE-304) was on anti-submarine screening duties in what was already becoming known as "Kamikaze Gulch" – the triangle of water roughly bounded by Ie Shima, Kerama Retto, and the western shore of Okinawa – when Commander Task Force 51 issued a Flash Red warning for air attack at 1335hrs. The crew immediately went to action stations, and at 1440hrs, as the ship turned to the west following the completion of the easterly component of its patrol line, a radar operator picked up a bogey approaching from the north nine nautical miles away. It was part of a raid of approximately five to seven tokko originally detected almost 48 nautical miles from Okinawa.

Rall's crew soon visually acquired the first aircraft approaching from the starboard side, which was identified as a "Nate," and took it under fire as the pilot commenced a gliding dive towards the ship. As the first aircraft bore in, another one was sighted crossing the bow from starboard to port, before turning towards *Rall*. The vessel's port-side 20mm guns immediately opened fire and shot the tokko down into the sea. Meanwhile, the first aircraft had leveled out about 1,000 yards away just above the wave tops and, despite being hit numerous times, closed in on DE-304 and slammed into the destroyer escort amidships just above the main deck.

The tokko's engine and fuselage crashed directly through a hatch leading to one of its passageways, while the aircraft's solitary bomb punched through the starboard hull plating before exiting the port side of the ship and exploding about 15ft away, showering *Rall* with shrapnel. Despite the hit, which killed 21 and wounded a further 38 (most of the casualties came from the port-side gun crews), DE-304 managed to shoot down two more aircraft and survived a strafing attack from an "Oscar" before retiring to Seattle, Washington, via Ulithi, for repairs and an overhaul. It returned to the Pacific Fleet in August 1945.

The exact identity of *Rall*'s attacker has been aided by a photograph showing the tail (bearing the katakana character "ya") of what is clearly a "Nate" sticking out from the hatch the aircraft slammed into. A number of IJAAF tokko-tai were known to carry characters of part or all of their pilots' surnames on their tail, with several of the Hakko units seen in the Philippines and Shinbu-tai active off Okinawa adopting the practice. According to IJAAF records, the sole tokko-tai to use the "Nate" on April 12 was the 69th Shinbu-tai, whose four Ki-27s, under the command of 2Lt Toru Ikeda, departed Chiran at 1210hrs along with the "Oscars" of the 20th and 43rd Shinbu-tai and the "Sonias" of the 103rd Shinbu-tai.

Checking through the roster of 69th Shinbu-tai pilots who flew that day, the only aviator from the unit with "ya" as part of his name was 2Lt Satoshi Yagyuu. It would appear, therefore, that he was the pilot who struck *Rall* on the 12th. Born in Kani, near Nagoya, in Japan's central Gifu Prefecture, in 1922, Yagyuu had graduated from the Shibaura Institute of Technology prior to joining the IJAAF. Following training at the Akeno Kyodo Hiko Shidan, he was assigned to the 69th Shinbu-tai. Yagyuu and

ABOVE
Despite its gunners throwing up a wall of antiaircraft fire, the battleship USS *Tennessee* (BB-43) has just been struck by a "Val" off Hagushi Beaches on April 12, 1945. The vessel was part of Rear Admiral Morton L. Deyo's TG 54.1 Gunfire Support Group when it was attacked, with 19 Vals from the 2nd Hachiman-Goko-tai, 2nd Kusunagi-tai, and 2nd Shisei-tai and a similar number of "Kates" from the 2nd Hachiman-Goko-tai, 2nd Tokiwachuka-tai, and 2nd Goko-Shirasagi-tai hitting several ships. The D3A slammed into the signal bridge and slid aft along the superstructure, destroying several antiaircraft gun mounts and causing various electrical and structural damage. *(NARA)*

his unit were deployed to Chiran for their final missions. In his last letter home before the operation on April 12, he wrote "I do not desire the prosperity of the future. It is an honor to solely give one's life for my country." Following his death, Yagyuu was promoted two ranks to captain in line with Japanese military practice during World War II.

At about the same time *Rall* was being attacked, the battleships, cruisers, and destroyers of Rear Admiral Morton L. Deyo's TG 54.1 Gunfire Support Group were targeted by a large group of tokko – identified as "Vals" and "Kates" – while sailing off the Hagushi Beaches. The battleship USS *Idaho* (BB-42) had already shot down two D3As and two B5Ns intent on hitting it when a third "Kate" blew up so close to the vessel that it was showered by fragments from the aircraft. These punched holes to the vessel's port-side anti-torpedo blister, which in turn caused

ABOVE
Tennessee sails past the burning USS *Zellars* (DD-777), which had been hit shortly before BB-43 was struck by the "Val." The destroyer was attacked from its port quarter by what the crew identified as three "Jills" (almost certainly "Kates") flying just "15ft above the water." Gunners shot down two but the third came on despite being hit and crashed into the port side of the handling room for the No. 2 turret. Its bomb tore through several bulkheads and crossed the main deck on the starboard side prior to exploding. *(NARA)*

minor flooding and knocked out the rear SG surface search radar. The shock damage from the exploding aircraft also ruptured steam pipes in the No. 3 engine, which meant that it had to be secured. The ship's speed was reduced to 17 knots as a result. Ten of the crew were also wounded. BB-42 was sent to Guam to be repaired, and the battleship was back on the gun line off Okinawa by late May.

The nearby destroyer *Zellars* also came under attack from its port quarter by what the crew identified as three "Jills" flying just "15ft above the water." Gunners shot down two of them while they were still a safe distance away, but the third came on despite being hit repeatedly and slammed into the port side of the handling room for the No. 2 turret at 1450hrs. Its bomb tore through several bulkheads and crossed the main deck on the starboard side before exploding, temporarily knocking out all power forward and forcing the crew to secure the forward fireroom.

However, the damage and resulting fire were quickly contained, and within 50 minutes of being hit *Zellars* was underway towards Kerama Retto for emergency repairs, making 15 knots and being controlled via its after steering station. According to the destroyer's after action report, the crew charted a course by navigating with the ship's magnetic compass, relaying changes in direction to the steering station via "jury rigged sound-powered telephone lines and using judicious profanity for communications."

Seen here undergoing speed trials shortly after its commissioning in July 1944, USS *Purdy* (DD-734) was manning Radar Picket Station 1 with USS *Cassin Young* (DD-793) on April 12, 1945 when both vessels were attacked by a formation of about 25 tokko. The destroyers opened fire and, with the assistance of the carrier-based CAP, they succeeded in fighting off most of the attackers. Two, however, broke through to score hits on *Cassin Young* and a third was shot down so close to *Purdy* that its momentum propelled the aircraft into the destroyer. The tokko's bomb broke loose when it hit the ship, piercing the hull plating and then exploding. Fifteen sailors were killed and 25 wounded, and the destroyer suffered extensive damage. *(NARA)*

Zellars was sailing with USS *Tennessee* (BB-43) when the tokko attacked the fire support group, and the battleship was also targeted by five "Vals" and "Kates" from its port quarter. The Pearl Harbor veteran shot down four of the aircraft before it was taken by surprise by a D3A that initially banked to port and crossed the ship's bow before suddenly swinging back towards BB-43 from the starboard quarter in a maneuver that has been likened to an "end run" in American football. With gunners preoccupied engaging the other attackers as this occurred, only a few of the battleship's antiaircraft batteries managed to fire on the "Val" as it dove at the vessel at an approximately 50-degree angle. The tokko swerved slightly as it was hit by gunfire, before slamming into the signal bridge and sliding aft along the superstructure, destroying several antiaircraft gun mounts and causing various electrical and structural damage. Although 23 sailors were killed and 106 wounded, *Tennessee* was still able to remain on the line for a further two weeks.

Several IJNAF tokko-tai flew "Vals" and "Kates" on this day, departing their bases at Kokubu No. 1 and Kushira between 1100hrs and noon. These included 19 "Vals" from the 2nd Hachiman-Goko-tai (16 aircraft), 2nd Kusunagi-tai (two), and 2nd Shisei-tai (one) and the same number of "Kates" from the 2nd Hachiman-Goko-tai (ten), 2nd Tokiwachuka-tai (six), and 2nd Goko-Shirasagi-tai (three). The D3As each carried a single 551lb bomb, while the "Kates" were armed with a solitary 1,764lb No. 80 Mk 5 Land Bomb, and these tokko-tai appear to be the ones that targeted TG 54.1. Although a significant number of the D3As and B5Ns fell to the CAP before they reached the task group, the latter still had to endure attacks and suffer damage from the remaining "leakers."

The radar picket destroyers again came in for special attention on April 12, with Radar Picket Station 1 being the scene of more desperate combat as the destroyers USS *Cassin Young* (DD-793) and USS *Purdy* (DD-734), along with four smaller landing craft, came under attack from a group of some 25 IJNAF and IJAAF aircraft. The two destroyers were quickly damaged and forced to head to Kerama Retto for repairs, while *LCS(L)(3)-33* was sunk by a hit from a "Val." The Landing Craft Support (Large) had been attacked by three kamikazes, with its crew downing the first one and the second aircraft crashing close by after it had taken off the vessel's radio antenna prior to hitting the water. The third tokko struck *LCS(L)(3)-33*'s starboard side and started an uncontrollable fire, forcing the crew to abandon ship. The vessel

continued to circle slowly to port before eventually blowing up and sinking in front of the survivors.

Radar Picket Station 14 (the furthest north of all the picket stations) was manned by the destroyer *Mannert L. Abele* on April 12, and at 1345hrs its crew started engaging the first of several tokko groups that targeted the ship that day. At 1440hrs, two "Zekes" dove on the vessel and one of them succeeded in hitting the after fireroom on the starboard side. As the destroyer slowed to a stop, a new threat emerged at 1446hrs in the form of an aircraft described in *Mannert L. Abele*'s after action report as a "small mid-wing job with no projections, a large fuselage, stubby wings and painted light blue-gray or aluminum." This aircraft, which the report added was "skimming the water at a terrific speed on [the] starboard beam," plowed into the starboard side of the destroyer just above the waterline abreast the forward fireroom, causing a "terrific explosion and shock."

Being hit twice in six minutes in virtually the same location broke the ship's back, resulting in *Mannert L. Abele* sinking from amidships, with both its bow and fantail rising from the water. By 1449hrs the destroyer had slipped beneath the waves, taking 84 crew with it.

Survivors of this action had described their attacker as being a "buzzbomb," which was the term used by the Allies for the German V1 rocket-powered missile. However, the weapon that struck the destroyer was, of course, a manned Ohka. The unfortunate *Mannert L. Abele* would be the only ship to be sunk by an MXY7.

The destroyer USS *Mannert L. Abele* (DD-733), seen here sailing off the Virginia coast on August 1, 1944 just weeks after its commissioning, holds the unhappy distinction of being the sole vessel to be sunk by an Ohka manned aerial bomb. It was struck off Okinawa on the afternoon of the April 12, 1945, the weapon breaking the destroyer's back as it shuddered to a stop following a hit just six minutes earlier by a conventional "Zeke" tokko. DD-733 took 84 crew with it when the vessel sunk shortly thereafter. *(NARA)*

Further east at Radar Picket Station 2, off the northern tip of Okinawa, the destroyer USS *Stanly* (DD-478) was facing its own problems. The vessel had been kept busy since 1330hrs following a call to assist the tokko-damaged *Cassin Young* at neighboring Radar Picket Station 2 and take control of its CAP. *Stanly* was also occupied with fending off kamikaze attacks of its own, as well as vectoring CAP fighters assigned to Radar Picket Station 2 on several intercepts against other southbound tokko. Eventually, DD-748's crew spotted an unidentified aircraft that descended from a dogfight off the ship's starboard beam and "outran our Combat Air Patrol" before slamming into the destroyer's starboard bow just above the waterline.

Unlike *Mannert L. Abele,* this aircraft – referred to as a "buzzbomb" by *Stanly*'s crew, although it was of course another Ohka – ripped its way through the ship's hull and then exploded when it hit the water. The pilot and some wreckage were later recovered from inside the vessel, however. A second MXY7 made another run on DD-748 at 1458hrs, with the destroyer's antiaircraft guns scoring hits on the rocket-powered aerial bomb before it narrowly missed the after stack and crashed into the sea beyond.

Yet another Ohka targeted the high-speed destroyer minesweeper *Jeffers* at 1453hrs while it was steaming north from Radar Picket Station 12 to aid the stricken *Mannert L. Abele*. Its crew observed a twin-engined bomber 15,000 yards away at an altitude of 4,000ft drop an unidentified, smoking object that was initially thought to be a belly tank. Although the aircraft then flew away, a smaller machine was spotted coming straight at the warship at a "terrific speed" (estimated to be at least 350 knots) from the same direction as the high-flying bomber. Several hits were scored by *Jeffers*' 40mm gun batteries, and a hard turn to port caused the attacker to hit the water aft, bounce up, and then disintegrate upon striking the sea for a second time.

The weapons that hit *Mannert L. Abele* and *Stanly* and narrowly missed *Jeffers* were three of six Ohkas launched from the eight Jinrai Butai "Betty" motherships that had taken off from Kanoya between 1130hrs and 1230hrs. The G4M2Es had paid a high price for this relatively modest success, with five being shot down and a sixth example crash-landing back at Kanoya.

In other attacks on April 12, the destroyer minelayer USS *Lindsey* (DM-32) was targeted by a group of seven "Vals." Two hits forward removed 60ft of the bow back to the second five-inch gun mount,

The destroyer USS *Stanly* (DD-478) was manning Radar Picket Station 2, off the northern tip of Okinawa, on the afternoon of April 12, 1945 when it was targeted by two Ohkas. One ripped its way through the ship's hull and then exploded when it hit the water, its pilot and some wreckage later being recovered from within the vessel. The second MXY7 made a run on DD-748 shortly thereafter, with the destroyer's antiaircraft guns scoring hits on the rocket-powered aerial bomb before it narrowly missed the after stack and crashed into the sea beyond. *(NARA)*

resulting in 57 crew being killed or listed as missing and 57 wounded. The ship survived, however, and after being towed initially to Kerama Retto for emergency repairs and then on to Guam for the fitment of a temporary bow, *Lindsey* returned to Norfolk Navy Yard, Virginia, for a thorough overhaul.

It had been a day of intensive combat, with almost all the tokko strikes having taken place in the afternoon. By the end of the day US Navy pilots had claimed 144 Japanese aircraft shot down and their US Marine Corps compatriots 77. Again, despite these impressive totals, a number of tokko had managed to break through the CAPs to attack Allied ships, with 18 being hit and two sunk.

Following the frenetic attacks and heavy losses suffered by the Japanese on April 12, the 13th proved to be appreciably quieter. Only a handful of tokko were engaged and no significant damage inflicted on the battle-weary Allied ships. Among the vessels targeted on this date was the destroyer escort USS *Connolly* (DE-306) after it had been detached from anti-submarine screening duties in the early afternoon following a report by a US Navy patrol aircraft of a possible submarine contact in the East China Sea. As the ship approached the area at 1730hrs, its crew spotted five "Val" dive-bombers being attacked by American fighters. One of the

THIS PAGE and INSET
As this astonishing photograph reveals, the explosion of the forward five-inch gun magazine removed 60ft of *Lindsey*'s bow back to the second five-inch gun mount. Thanks to outstanding damage control, the destroyer minelayer remained afloat. *(NARA)*

RIGHT
The crew of one of *Lindsey*'s port forward 20mm guns pose by their weapon at Guam on June 16, 1945. They had stuck to their post until knocked off their feet by the force of the exploding magazine ahead of them on April 12. (NARA)

BELOW
Lindsey was initially towed to Kerama Retto for emergency repairs and then on to Guam for the fitment of a temporary bow. It is seen here at the latter location prior to this work being carried out, DM-32 being moored alongside the destroyer escort USS *Seid* (DE-256) and the station tanker USS *Quiros* (IX-140). When this photograph was taken wreckage from the explosion had been partially removed. The ship left for Norfolk Navy Yard on July 8, where permanent repairs were carried out. (NARA)

tokko managed to break off from the engagement and make a suicide run on the ship, striking the water close by after being shot down by *Connolly*'s antiaircraft fire. Although the resultant explosion temporarily knocked out the sonar and radar, the ship was otherwise undamaged.

Japanese records show that no "Vals" undertook tokko missions on the 13th, and although a handful of "Sonias" from the 30th, 46th, 74th,

75th, 103rd, 104th, and 107th Shinbu-tai were active, their takeoff times from Chiran, Bansei, and Kikaijima Island were either too early or too late to credit them with this attack. It would seem likely, therefore, that *Connolly* had in fact survived a jibaku attack.

Only two IJNAF aircraft had targeted Allied ships off Okinawa on April 13 – a solitary "Zeke" and its escort from the 9th Taigi-tai, which had taken off from Ishigaki Island with orders to attack British carriers sailing off Yonaguni Island. The tokko, flown by PO1c Takashi Yamazaki, and the escort fighter (whose pilot has not been identified) were almost certainly the aircraft shot down by Corsairs flown by Sub Lts D. A. Baldwin and G. S. P. Salmon of 1830 NAS, embarked in *Illustrious*, soon after they were detected by the fleet at 0645hrs.

The IJNAF was far more active the following day as the Japanese finalized their preparations for Kikusui No. 3, scheduled for April 16. A sizeable force of A6M2 tokko, with a 125-strong fighter escort (comprising both late-model "Zekes" and formidable "Georges"), departed Kanoya from 1130hrs in search of enemy carriers spotted "south of Tokunoshima" in the Satsunan Islands, between Kyushu and Okinawa. The tokko were from the 1st Showa-tai (ten aircraft), 2nd Tsukuba-tai (two), and 6th Kenmu-tai (six). Some of these machines were almost certainly the fighters encountered by Hellcats from VBF-17, embarked in *Hornet*, whose pilots claimed six shot down out of a formation of approximately ten aircraft at around 1400hrs.

Still, enough tokko leaked through to strike the fleet. More than ten (estimates vary) IJNAF aircraft encountered six destroyers that had formed a picket line 22 nautical miles ahead of TG 58.1 soon after 1345hrs and attacked. The tokko and fighters from *Hornet*'s CAP fought each other at close quarters, preventing the destroyers' gunners from effectively targeting the enemy aircraft. This in turn allowed the "Zekes" to target USS *Dashiell* (DD-659), USS *Hunt* (DD-674), and USS *Sigsbee* (DD-502). DD-659 suffered a near miss and DD-674 was struck at deck level, the tokko shearing off the mainmast and leaving its starboard wing embedded in the forward stack. The fuselage crashed into the water about 25 yards from the destroyer, whose crew soon doused several small fires following the impact.

Sigsbee suffered appreciably more damage, however, the destroyer being struck aft of its No. 5 gun turret. The impact, which killed 23 crew, knocked out the ship's port engine and left its starboard engine only

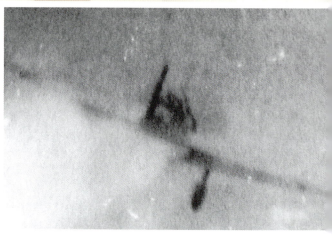

ABOVE LEFT
The successful pilots from 1771 NAS were photographed together after landing back on board *Indefatigable* following their one-sided clash with five Ki-51s off Formosa on April 12. They are, from left to right, Lt Bill Thomson, Lt Ward (Sub Lt Phil Stott's observer), Sub Lt Stott, and Sub Lt Miller (Lt Thomson's observer). *(Tony Holmes collection)*

ABOVE RIGHT
On April 12, 1945 the British Pacific Fleet's TF 57 moved west following a US Navy request to hit tokko airfields on Formosa. That morning a pair of Firefly I fighters flown by Lt Bill Thomson and Sub Lt Phil Stott of 1770 NAS, which was embarked in *Indefatigable*, were escorting a US Navy PBM Mariner flying boat on an air-sea rescue mission when they spotted five Ki-51 "Sonia" tokko. Breaking off, the Firefly pilots each shot down two (the fifth "Sonia" was claimed as probably destroyed). The demise of one of the four Ki-51s was caught on film by the camera gun fitted to Lt Thomson's aircraft. *(Tony Holmes collection)*

capable of being run at five knots. The steering gear was also wrecked and the ship began to take on water. Nevertheless, its commanding officer, Cdr Gordon Pai'ea Chung-Hoon, not only continued to fight his ship and direct antiaircraft fire, he also effectively mustered damage control parties that duly saved it. *Sigsbee* was towed south to Guam, where it was sufficiently patched up to allow the destroyer to be towed on to Pearl Harbor. Here, a new 60ft stern section was installed, after which DD-502 sailed to Philadelphia Navy Yard for an overhaul.

Taking off from Kanoya at the same time as the "Zekes" on the 14th were seven "Betty" motherships from the 708th Hikotai's Jinrai Butai, each carrying an Ohka. Any hope they had of replicating the success of April 12 was quickly dashed when all seven bombers were lost in quick succession without any hits being scored by the MXY7s. Two of the G4M2Es were shot down soon after 1300hrs by a pair of Hellcats from VBF-17's sister-unit VF-17 while the fighters were flying top cover for a strike and photo-reconnaissance mission over Kikaijima Island. Another "Betty" was reportedly "splashed" by TF 58's CAP 23 minutes later.

Soon after sunset, the battleship USS *New York* (BB-34) was hit off Okinawa's Nakagusuku Bay by what its crew reported was an "Oscar," the attacker clipping the ship's port mainmast, which sheared off its wing. The latter fell onto, and wrecked, one of the battleship's OS2U Kingfisher floatplanes spotted on a catapult, while the rest of the tokko crashed into the sea close aboard. Little damage was caused other than to the unfortunate floatplane, with two crew also being wounded. No Ki-43s participated in tokko missions that day, however, and while the IJNAF sent nine "Zekes" from the 2nd Shinken-tai after shipping off Kerama Retto during the afternoon of the 14th, the last fighter from this unit was recorded as having taken off at 1438hrs. This would have been too early for any of the A6M2s to have attacked *New York*, which was hit at 1930hrs. It would seem, therefore, that the battleship was the victim of a jibaku attack.

The next day the IJNAF and the IJAAF suspended daylight tokko missions in order to complete the final preparations for Kikusui No. 3. TF 58 chose April 15 to send fighter sweeps over the airfields on Kyushu, with TG 58.1 also despatching a strong force of fighters from VF-17, VBF-17, VF-30, and VF-82 to attack Kanoya airfield.

Kikusui No. 3 commenced shortly after dawn on April 16 when, at 0630hrs, 32 N1K2 "George" fighters from the 343rd Kokutai took off on an air superiority mission in an attempt to clear the skies of the US Navy and US Marine Corps CAP operating over Kikaijima and Amami Oshima Islands.

USS *Sigsbee* (DD-502) was one of three destroyers hit by "Zekes" on April 14, 1945 as they formed part of a six-ship picket line 22 nautical miles ahead of TG 58.1's carriers sailing south of Tokunoshima. DD-502 was the most badly damaged of the three, losing 60ft of its stern when it was hit aft of the No. 5 five-inch gun battery. Although 23 crew were killed, the destroyer's steering gear had been wrecked, and it was left with only one operational engine, the ship's commanding officer, Cdr Gordon Pai'ea Chung-Hoon, not only continued to engage the enemy and direct antiaircraft fire, but also effectively mustered damage control parties that saved *Sigsbee*. (NARA)

Soon after sunset on April 14, 1945, the battleship USS *New York* (BB-34) was hit off Okinawa's Nakagusuku Bay by what its crew reported was an "Oscar," the attacker clipping the ship's port mainmast which sheared off its wing. The latter fell onto – and wrecked – one of the battleship's OS2U Kingfisher floatplanes spotted on a catapult, as seen here. The rest of the aircraft crashed into the sea close aboard. Little damage was caused other than to the unfortunate floatplane. No Ki-43s participated in tokko missions that day, so it would seem that the battleship was the victim of a jibaku attack. *(NARA)*

The IJNAF forlornly hoped that this tactic would give the following tokko aircraft a threat-free run at the naval vessels off southern Okinawa. It did not.

Taking off in separate waves composed of "Zeke" fighter escorts, tokko, and conventional carrier-based and twin-engined bombers, the Special Attack aircraft were a collection of older A6M2/3s, "Kates," and "Vals" and more modern "Myrts" and "Frances." Many different units contributed tokko, including the 701st, 721st, and 732nd Kokutai. Two waves of 76 "Zekes," 50 assorted tokko types, ten "Judys," and eight "Frances" bombers headed for the American carriers, while a further

The destroyer escort USS *Bowers* (DE-637) was hit by a tokko on the morning of April 16, 1945 while it was on screening duties off Okinawa. This photograph, taken the following day, shows the wreckage of the ship's attacker still crushed against the superstructure between the vessel's No. 2 three-inch main gun and the bridge. The official US Navy caption for this shot identified *Bowers'* attacker as an "Oscar," although none flew that day as tokko, while the ship's after action report said it was a "Val" that struck the destroyer escort. *(NARA)*

52 "Zeke" fighters escorted ten "Kates," 19 "Vals," 12 "Frances," ten "Myrts," and an unknown number of "Zeke" tokko towards other vessels off Okinawa.

The IJAAF sortied 45 tokko that day – obsolete "Nate" fighters from the 40th, 42nd, 69th, 79th, 106th, 107th, 108th, and 109th Shinbu-tai, "Sonias" from the 75th Shinbu-tai, and Tachikawa Ki-55 "Ida" two-seat advanced trainers also from the 79th Shinbu-tai and the Sei 38th Hikotai.

Again, American fighters were up in force to repel this mass attack. US Navy squadrons claimed 157 aircraft destroyed and the US Marine Corps was credited with 46 victories, making this the third-highest scoring day of the campaign. Among the types shot down were four of six Ohka-carrying "Betty motherships" of the 708th Kokutai's Jinrai Butai, which again failed to score any successes.

BELOW
USS *Laffey* (DD-724), an Allen M. Sumner-class destroyer, was a salient example of the determination of the US Navy's warship crews to fight back against tokko attack. From 0744hrs on April 16, 1945, the vessel endured the most concerted kamikaze attack of the entire war when it engaged at least 23 aircraft (mostly "Zekes" and "Vals") during a two-hour period while manning Radar Picket Station 1. Hit by six aircraft and three bombs, the destroyer nevertheless survived. This photograph shows the damage sustained by the ship, including a destroyed rear 5in./38 turret that was hit by a "Val." Its bomb ignited the turret's powder magazine, destroying the gun mount and starting a major fire. Shortly thereafter, another "Val" crashed into the burning turret after it had been set alight by *Laffey*'s gunners. (NARA)

Remarkably, only ten ships were hit by tokko on April 16 thanks to the effectiveness of the CAP. The radar picket destroyers were again the favored targets, with the destroyer USS *Laffey* (DD-724) earning the dubious distinction of suffering the most concerted kamikaze attack of the entire war. From 0744hrs, the vessel engaged at least 23 aircraft during a two-hour period while manning Radar Picket Station 1. It was hit six times and grazed twice, with three bombs exploding on board and another two near misses being recorded. Despite this beating, *Laffey*'s engineering plant remained operable and the destroyer was able to maneuver in spite of rudder damage. The crew fought fires to save their ship, which was never in danger of sinking throughout the ordeal. Considering the scale of the attack, casualties on board were surprisingly moderate – 31 dead and 72 wounded. *Laffey* subsequently returned to Tacoma, Washington, to be repaired, after which it went on to serve with the fleet for a further 30 years.

Summoned to *Laffey*'s assistance, the destroyer *Bryant* (manning nearby Radar Picket Station 2) was also subjected to a coordinated attack by six "Zekes." The first three fighters closed on the warship in a shallow glide, one of the aircraft being downed by the port gun batteries and the CAP destroying a second. However, the third attacker, although being hit repeatedly and leaving a trail of smoke in its wake, struck *Bryant* just below the bridge near the main radio room. The aircraft's 551lb bomb then exploded, engulfing the bridge in flames and severely damaging communication, fire-control, and radar equipment. Fortunately, the damage control teams that were already standing by to assist *Laffey* extinguished the fires within minutes of the destroyer being hit, and soon *Bryant* was making 23 knots once again. Having had 34 sailors killed and 33 wounded, the badly damaged vessel was withdrawn to Kerama Retto shortly thereafter and eventually sent back to San Francisco to be repaired.

The destroyer *Pringle*, manning Radar Picket Station 14, was not so fortunate when it was targeted by three "Vals." Although the first two aircraft were destroyed by five-inch gunfire, the third tokko conducted a steep, high-speed diving attack that ended with it hitting the ship abaft the base of the forward stack. The solitary bomb carried beneath the "Val's" centerline duly exploded in the forward fireroom, with catastrophic results. Within two minutes *Pringle* had broken in two, the vessel sinking just three minutes later with the loss of 78 crew.

The high-speed destroyer minesweeper USS *Harding* (DMS-28) was immediately transferred to Radar Picket Station 14 to replace *Pringle*, and it

OPPOSITE
Survivors of *Laffey*'s April 16 action share their memories of the attack with each other while standing alongside the destroyed rear 5in./38 turret. It had been knocked out when an exploding bomb from a crashed "Val" ignited the turret's powder magazine. Of the 31 sailors killed that day, many of them were either manning the turret or working in the powder magazine directly below it. *(NARA)*

ABOVE
An unidentified Fletcher-class destroyer (its five-inch guns trained skyward) cuts across *Intrepid*'s bow shortly after the carrier was hit for the fourth, and last, time by a tokko. This action photograph was taken from the large cruiser USS *Alaska* (CB-1) on April 16, 1945, the aircraft having scored a direct hit near the aft elevator and penetrated through to the hangar bay, where a large fire broke out. *(NARA)*

RIGHT
Excellent damage control by *Intrepid*'s battle-hardened crew saw a blaze in the hangar bay extinguished in under an hour and the hole in the flightdeck soon repaired – the carrier was able to recover aircraft just three hours after the crash (which had killed eight crew and wounded 21). Effective damage control by US Navy personnel was critically important, and it helped to save many ships hit by tokko. *(NARA)*

too was attacked by four tokko shortly thereafter. Two were driven off and a third one shot down, but the fourth, despite being hit by antiaircraft fire, crashed so close to the vessel's starboard side that its bomb exploded under the hull and tore a huge gash from the keel up to the main deck. With 14 crew killed, eight missing, and nine wounded, *Harding* was towed to Kerama Retto. Upon its eventual return to Norfolk Navy Yard, *Harding* was subsequently declared a constructive total loss and sold for scrapping.

Although the radar picket ships were repeatedly attacked on April 16, only a small number of aircraft from Kikusui No. 3 were actually able to find TF 58. Nevertheless, *Intrepid* was hit for the fourth, and last, time by a kamikaze, the tokko scoring a direct hit near the aft elevator and penetrating to the hangar bay, where a large fire broke out. Excellent damage control by its battle-hardened crew saved the ship and managed to repair the hole in the flightdeck, allowing *Intrepid* to recover aircraft just three hours after the crash (which had killed eight crew and wounded 21). Nevertheless, CV-11 was pulled off the line the following day and forced to return to San Francisco for repairs. By the time these had been completed the war was over.

The crews from the ships that were hit reported that their attackers were "Vals," and the IJNAF did indeed have D3As in the air that morning assigned to tokko missions. The 3rd Hachiman-Goko-tai, for example, sortied 18 of the dive-bombers from Kokubu No. 2 airfield at 0630hrs. However, the IJAAF also sent "Nates," "Sonias," and "Idas" into action that day, all of which had fixed, spatted undercarriages like the "Val," thus complicating any attempt at identifying individual attackers.

Following the attack on April 16 weather conditions and the depletion of tokko units forced the postponement of the next Kikusui operation for 12 days. This gave US Navy ships off Okinawa a welcome reprieve. By then the kamikaze had damaged three fleet carriers – *Hancock*, *Enterprise* and *Intrepid* – sufficiently to force their withdrawal from *Iceberg*.

Being subjected to a tokko attack was nerve-wracking. The sailors manning ships on radar picket stations suffered the most as they bore the brunt of the attacks. On board other vessels in the fleet, waiting for the outcome of an attack was never easy. As Lt John Larkin, a pilot with Hellcat-equipped VF-83 embarked in *Essex*, recalled:

> It was something to live under, when we were the target of a kamikaze attack, which was a frequent occurrence during the Okinawa operation. You always heard the five-inch guns, which were the big ones, going "boom," "boom," "boom." Then after that you'd hear the 40mm start to go, then, finally, when they were really in close, you'd hear the 20mm go off. And at that point you just sort of waited for what was going to happen.

Even during this relatively quiet period in tokko operations, a small number of missions were undertaken on April 17 and 18 by both the IJNAF and IJAAF. The only result of note was the slight damage inflicted on the destroyer USS *Benham* (DD-796) following what its crew described as an "Oscar" crashing nearby as the vessel operated with the fast carriers of TF 58 at 0944hrs on the 17th. Four fighters had just strafed the destroyer USS *Colahan* (DD-658) when one of the aircraft abruptly pulled up and then dove straight at *Benham*. Although antiaircraft fire from several destroyers shot the tokko down about 50ft astern of DD-796, it disintegrated in a large explosion that killed one sailor, wounded 14 more, and knocked out the destroyer's radar – it appears that *Benham* was also hit by friendly fire.

As no Ki-43s undertook tokko missions that day, DD-796's attacker was almost certainly a "Zeke" from either the 252nd or 601st Kokutai. Both units sortied aircraft from Kokubu No. 1 airfield between 0640hrs and 0700hrs on April 17.

The lull in the action ended on the 22nd when the IJAAF sent out another force of tokko designed to arrive over the Okinawa beaches at dusk. From 1440hrs, the Chiran-based 80th and 81st Shinbu-tai despatched 11 "Idas" each, while the co-located 105th and 109th Shinbu-tai sent up another six and four "Nates," respectively, along with a single "Sonia" from the Sei 17th Hikotai. They were accompanied by a single "Ida" from the 79th Shinbu-tai at Kokubu. Later that afternoon, the Formosa-based tokko units chimed in with three "Tonys" from the 19th Sentai, these aircraft being flown by 2Lts Kuniomi Namibe, Hiroshi Ono, and Shigeru Sakamoto from Giran (Yilan) at 1635hrs, while a further five "Nicks" from the Sei 119th Hikotai left Touen (Taoyuan) 25 minutes later.

A tokko (almost certainly a "Zeke" from either the 252nd or 601st Kokutai) crashes near the stern of USS *Bataan* (CVL-29) during an unsuccessful kamikaze attack on the morning of April 17, 1945. This photograph was taken from the battleship USS *South Dakota* (BB-57), which, like CVL-29, was assigned to TG 58.3 at the time. *(NARA)*

F4U-1D Corsair (BuNo unknown)/White 26 flown by 1Lt Jeremiah O'Keefe, VMF-323, Yontan airfield, Okinawa, April 1945

O'Keefe scored all seven of his aerial victories in two actions on April 22 and April 28, 1945. On April 22 he became an "ace in a day" in his first combat, together with Majs George Axtell and Jefferson Dorroh, and was awarded the Navy Cross for his efforts. It appears that his victims were all IJAAF tokko, specifically "Nates" and "Sonias." *(Artwork by Jim Laurier, © Osprey Publishing)*

The southbound force ran headlong into seven Corsairs of VMF-323, led by unit CO Maj George Axtell, on CAP duties near Aguni Shima. Axtell identified the aircraft as a force of approximately 35 bomb-carrying "Vals," and in short order VMF-323 claimed 24.5 victories from among the obsolete aircraft flown by poorly trained pilots – three Corsair pilots, including Axtell, were credited with 17 kills between them. Despite being whittled down, the surviving tokko nevertheless gave a relatively good account of themselves once they arrived off Okinawa shortly after 1830hrs, diving out of thick cloud and sinking the minesweeper USS *Swallow* (AM-65) off Kerama Retto and *LCS(L)(3)-15* at Radar Picket Station 14, as well as damaging the destroyers USS *Hudson* (DD-475) and USS *Isherwood* (DD-520) and the minesweeper USS *Ransom* (AM-283).

Of the three damaged ships, *Isherwood* was the most severely hit when its attacker slammed into the No. 3 turret and exploded, together with its bomb. Most of the five-inch gun crew (typically numbering nine sailors) within the mount were killed or wounded, as were personnel in the turret's ammunition handling room. Although most of the fires started by the tokko and its bomb were quickly put out, one that could not be doused in time caused an aft-mounted depth charge rack to explode 25 minutes after the ship had been hit, killing many more crewman – including most of the sailors manning the aft engine room, which was

Flying from the newly captured airfield at Yontan, on the west coast of Okinawa, VMF-323 enjoyed its best day against tokko on April 22, 1945 when squadron commanding officer Maj George Axtell (left), squadron executive officer Maj Jefferson Dorroh (center), and 1Lt Jeremiah O'Keefe (right) all became "aces in a day" by collectively shooting down 17 aircraft. Their victims were a mixed force of "Nates," "Idas," and "Sonias," which the US Marine Corps pilots misidentified as "Vals." (NARA)

demolished. *Isherwood* limped into Kerama Retto later that evening, where the debris from the attack was removed and emergency repairs commenced. The attack and the explosion of the depth charges had killed 42 crew and wounded a further 41. Once temporarily patched up, DD-520 headed for San Francisco via Ulithi and Pearl Harbor. It did not return to fleet service until shortly after VJ-Day.

Like Maj Axtell of VMF-323, the crews on board the ships attacked that day identified their attackers as "Vals," although the writer of *Hudson*'s after action report noted that the vessel's attacker "may possibly have been smaller than a Val, but very closely resembled one." Clearly, the "Idas," "Nates," and "Sonias," all of which had fixed undercarriages, had been misidentified in the heat of battle.

As the tokko from Kyushu carried out their attacks, the Formosa-based aircraft also started arriving off Okinawa. At 1813hrs the destroyer

USS *Wadsworth* (DD-516) detected three contacts closing from the west while manning Radar Picket Station 10, the vessel opening fire at 1829hrs and rapidly shooting an aircraft down. Although one of the remaining two tokko broke off the engagement and left the area, the other aircraft dove at the ship from port aft, overshooting and crashing into the sea 15ft off the starboard amidships with a "terrific explosion" as the destroyer's gunners repeatedly hit it with 20mm and 40mm rounds.

Shortly thereafter, at 1855hrs, the minesweeper USS *Gladiator* (AM-319) sighted what its crew initially thought was a USAAF P-51 Mustang fighter as it patrolled off Kerama Retto, only to quickly realize it was actually a Japanese "Tony" when the aircraft swept in on an attack run from the vessel's starboard quarter, strafing as it bore in. As with *Wadsworth*, the ship's antiaircraft gunners repeatedly hit the Ki-61, although it too continued on as if unaffected, flying over AM-319's fantail and plunging into the water off the port beam. No damage was done, although one of the 40mm gun crew was killed and five others wounded by strafing.

This "Tony" was probably one of the three aircraft that *Wadsworth* had previously encountered at Radar Picket Station 10, although the destroyer had identified the trio as "Judys." No D4Ys were tasked with tokko attacks that day, however, and it is likely that the inline engine of the Ki-61s confused *Wadsworth*'s crew into thinking that they were being engaged by early-model "Judys," which had a similar engine configuration.

The last aircraft to reach Okinawa on April 22 were the five Sei 119th Hikotai Ki-45s led by 2Lt Akira Takegaki. Two of them made attack runs on the destroyer escort *Sederstrom* and the destroyer minelayer *Shea* at 1929hrs and 1936hrs, respectively, as the ships patrolled their assigned screening stations. According to *Sederstrom*'s crew, the tokko that clipped and showered the vessel's bridge and forecastle with fuel and fragments as it narrowly missed the ship was one of eight "Frances" spotted immediately prior to the attack, although the after action report admitted that "darkness made identification difficult." *Shea*, on the other hand, identified the attacker that passed directly over its No. 2 turret from starboard to port before splashing into the sea alongside as a "Nick." The destroyer minelayer's topsides were covered in fuel and aircraft parts following the crash, although no damage or casualties were sustained.

Following this brief spike in tokko activity, there was no further aerial action off Okinawa until Kikusui No. 4 commenced on April 27.

Like all IJNAF and IJAAF fighter pilots tasked with defending vulnerable tokko from attack by marauding Allied CAPs off Okinawa, the naval aviators of the 303rd Hikotai suffered at the hands of US Navy Hellcat and Corsair units. Flying from Kagoshima, the 303rd had supplied fighter escorts for the disastrous Ohka debut mission on March 21, 1945. Although all the "Bettys" and their manned flying bombs were lost that day, the "Zeke" pilots were credited with four US fighters destroyed and three probables. The 303rd continued to escort tokko during the numbered Kikusui missions generated following the invasion of Okinawa on April 1. *(Tony Holmes collection)*

The IJNAF could muster only 65 kamikaze aircraft and the IJAAF barely 50 for this latest offensive. All of the attacks launched on this day were aimed at Allied shipping in the waters immediately surrounding Okinawa, for TF 58 had temporarily sent its carriers further south, thus placing them out of range of the tokko.

The operation started slowly when, at 0550hrs, the Sei 36th Hikotai and 80th and 109th Shinbu-tai each sent a solitary "Frank," "Ida," and "Nate" towards Okinawa from Chiran, although this token force achieved nothing of note. It appears that a handful of IJAAF and IJNAF tokko sortied in the afternoon too, hoping to arrive over the ships at dusk. The weather that evening was mainly clear, with scattered cloud at lower levels and an almost full moon. The ships off Okinawa spent most of the night at General Quarters, with aerial contacts showing up on radar.

At 2145hrs the 15,200-ton cargo ship SS *Canada Victory* was off Hagushi Beaches unloading its dangerous cargo of ammunition under a smokescreen generated by smaller vessels when one of the latter ran out of fog oil. An unknown Japanese aircraft took advantage of the lifting of the smokescreen and, with little warning, slammed into the vessel near its aftermast and came to rest within its No. 5 hold. The subsequent explosion blew out *Canada Victory*'s side and it started sinking stern first. The order to abandon ship was issued at 2200hrs, by which point two armed guards and one merchant marine had been killed and 12 crewmen wounded. *Canada Victory* was the third, and last, Victory ship to be sunk off Okinawa in a tokko attack, these vessels carrying a total of 24,000 tons of ammunition (including most of the 81mm mortar shells needed for the invasion) between them when they were lost.

As the cargo ship sank two nautical miles west of Tokashiki Island, more drama was playing out offshore following the detection of a number of bogies on radar at around 2130hrs. Classified as "Raid 5," this group was estimated to number between three and five aircraft and was observed on radar orbiting about ten to 13 nautical miles off Hagushi Beaches, before splitting up. Ships in the area noted that one tokko had blinking running lights on as the aircraft orbited, using the scattered cloud as cover. After they had split up they each chose targets, and between 2201hrs and 2207hrs the destroyer USS *Ralph Talbot* (DD-390), the destroyer escort *England*, and the high-speed transport USS *Rathburne* (APD-25) came under attack in rapid succession.

As with the aircraft that hit *Canada Victory*, the attackers were not seen until very late. Although this meant that the ships' gunners could not engage the tokko, aiming a fast-flying aircraft at a moving vessel in total darkness also took great skill. A near miss caused slight damage to *England*, while *Rathburne*'s attacker clipped the water during the final stage of its low-level attack before plowing into the ship's port bow at the waterline and then bursting out the starboard side. The aircraft's bomb did likewise, subsequently exploding underwater. This in turn caused the flooding of three compartments, although no significant damage was inflicted on the ship. Nevertheless, *Rathburne* was withdrawn from the line and sent to Kerama Retto to be patched up, before heading for San Diego.

A veteran of the attack on Pearl Harbor, and of numerous campaigns in the Pacific that followed (which included being badly damaged at the battle of Savo Island on August 8, 1942), *Ralph Talbot* was targeted by two attackers. The first crashed into its starboard side next to the No. 4 turret, its right wing sweeping through the deck aft, causing casualties and starting a small fire on the fantail. The aircraft's engine and fuselage slammed into the hull near the waterline, opening a hole in the plating before rupturing fuel tanks and damaging ammunition magazines and crew quarters. The second tokko was a near miss, crashing into the sea off

D3A2 "Val" RI-215 of the Dai 2nd Seito-tai, Kamikaze Attack Corps, (Hyakurigahara Kokutai), Kokubu airfield No. 2, Kyushu, April 1945

Major training units stationed in Japan all fielded tokko formations for the Okinawa campaign. Hyakurigahara Kokutai formed the Dai 2nd Seito-tai (Orthodoxy Unit), which flew sorties on April 6 and 28, May 25, and June 3, 1945. Note that this aircraft's white surround to the hinomaru national insignia has been painted out to reduce visibility. Bomb load consists of a Type 99 No. 25 Ordinary Bomb Model 1 and four Type 99 No. 6 Ordinary Bomb Model 1s, two beneath each wing – the maximum possible bomb load for the D3A2. (Artwork by Jim Laurier, © Osprey Publishing)

DD-390's port quarter. Damage control parties had brought flooding under control by 2213hrs, shortly after which the destroyer headed for Kerama Retto for repairs. On May 20 it got underway once again and returned to the Hagushi Beaches anchorage, where the destroyer joined the antiaircraft screen.

Although the crew of *Canada Victory* barely had time to see their attacker, which was therefore never identified, sailors on board the other ships targeted that night stated that their tokko were single-engined fighters. Indeed, *England*'s after action report identified the aircraft that near-missed it as being a "Tojo." This would tally with the five "Franks" led by 2Lt Itsuo Fukui from the Sei 33rd Hikotai that took off from Touen, on Formosa, at 1835hrs – the Ki-84 and Ki-44 shared a similar planform and profile, which meant that they were frequently misidentified. The Sei 33rd Hikotai was formed after students from the Akeno Kyodo Hiko Shidan had been transferred to Hattoku, on Formosa, in mid-April, the unit launching its first attack on the 16th of that month.

April 28 was considerably busier, with the Japanese choosing to launch the bulk of Kikusui No. 4's 115 aircraft that day. The CAP again played a key part in whittling down the attackers, which was probably why only a relatively small number of ships were hit. At 1600hrs, eight cannon-armed F4U-1Cs from VMF-311 departed Yontan airfield to the northeast

Ki-27 "Nate" of the 76th Shinbu-tai, Chiran airfield, Kyushu, April 1945

The "Nate" was hopelessly obsolete as a fighter by 1945, but when specially modified with the addition of bomb lugs to mount a 1,102lb bomb on the centerline it became a deadly opponent during the tokko campaign off Okinawa. A large number of Ki-27s were hastily rounded up from flying training units and deployed in specially formed Shinbu-tai during April 1945. The 76th Shinbu-tai was one such outfit, and it expended six aircraft on April 28 and three on May 11. This Ki-27 is depicted here with olive brown upper surfaces, although Shinbu-tai "Nates" were also painted dark green, dark blue, and dark gray for dawn and dusk operations. (Artwork by Jim Laurier, © Osprey Publishing)

of Okinawa on CAP, and before long they were vectored towards a formation of bogies that pilots identified as eight "Vals." Six of them were quickly shot out of the sky. It would appear that these aircraft were part of a force of 19 D3As (13 from the 3rd Kusanagi-tai and a further six from the Dai 2nd Seito-tai) that had taken off Kokubu No. 2 airfield between 1514hrs and 1543hrs.

Despite these losses, seven of the "leakers" went on to attack the destroyers USS *Daly* (DD-519) and *Twiggs* manning Radar Picket Station 2 soon after 1730hrs. *Daly* claimed five tokko shot down, but in return was peppered with shrapnel that killed three crew, including the chief medical officer, as one of the stricken "Vals" hit the water and exploded off the port beam. Meanwhile, *Twiggs* was near-missed by two more attackers, with the exploding ordnance from one of these aircraft blowing in the hull plating between the main and first platform deck and damaging the starboard propeller. The destroyer remained watertight, however. DD-591 would not be so lucky when it next encountered tokko on June 16.

Although Allied sailors often mistakenly claimed that they had been attacked by "Vals" during the long-running kamikaze campaign of 1944–45, this was almost certainly not the case on this occasion, as *Daly* and *Twiggs* were targeted just as the IJAAF's tokko-tai were departing their Kyushu bases.

Three sailors peer into the cavernous 30ft hole extending from the bridge deck down to the bulkhead deck that marked where a Ki-27 had struck the evacuation transport USS *Pinkney* (APH-2) while the ship was at anchor off Kerama Retto at 1930hrs on April 28, 1945. *(NARA)*

The "Nate" was the principal aircraft type committed to Kikusui No. 4, with the 67th, 76th, 77th, 106th, 108th, and 109th Shinbu-tai despatching six, six, eight, three, one, and two examples, respectively, from Chiran. They were joined at 1615hrs by a solitary "Sonia" from the Bansei-based 102nd Shinbu-tai and seven "Franks" from the 61st Shinbu-tai at nearby Miyakonojo.

This force was almost certainly the one encountered north of Amami Oshima by four divisions of Corsairs from VF-84 embarked in the carrier *Bunker Hill*, which had been assigned CAP duties near Kikaijima Island. The F4U pilots identified their targets as 20 "Nates," six "Franks," and two "Tojos" and attacked. Following the one-sided melee that ensued, the US Navy fighter pilots were credited with 12 "Nates," four "Franks," and a "Tojo" shot down.

The few remaining IJAAF aircraft pressed on with the mission, and it was possibly one of the surviving "Nates" that hit the 11,500-ton evacuation transport USS *Pinkney* (APH-2) while at anchor off Kerama Retto at 1930hrs. The impact on the after end of the superstructure not only ruptured water lines, electrical conduits, and steam pipes, but also started a large fire that quickly "cooked off" ammunition. Fortunately, most of the crew and many wounded patients were in the No. 5 hold watching a film when the tokko hit, thus escaping with their lives. Nevertheless, 18 crew were still killed in the initial attack, along with 16 patients.

Rescue tugs and landing craft quickly moved in to help with firefighting, although the ship continued to burn for three hours. By the time the blaze had finally been extinguished all wards in the amidships hospital area had been burned out and *Pinkney* had developed a heavy list to port. A hole some 30ft in diameter extending from the bridge deck to the bulkhead deck marked the impact of the aircraft. Temporary repairs took eight days to complete, and on May 9 the ship headed to Saipan en route to San Francisco. *Pinkney* returned to the Pacific Fleet five months later.

Despite being used as an evacuation transport, APH-2 had been painted gray like a regular warship, and among all the other vessels off Okinawa it was impossible to tell that the ship was engaged in medical and evacuation work. The same could not be said for the 6,000-ton hospital ship USS *Comfort*

(AH-6), which had weighed anchor for Guam earlier that day filled with wounded from *Iceberg*. Barely an hour after *Pinkney* was hit, *Comfort* was south of Okinawa "fully illuminated as a hospital ship and carrying out full hospital ship procedure" when, at 2041hrs, a Japanese aircraft made several passes at low level across its bow and stern before plunging into the vessel's starboard side. It plunged through three decks and exploded in the surgery area, killing all the doctors and nurses working in the operating room at the time. In all, six doctors, six nurses, nine army medical corpsmen, one navy crewman, and seven patients were killed in the attack, with a further 38 army and navy enlisted personnel wounded.

Comfort's after action report did not identify the aircraft that attacked the ship, although it noted that the body of an IJAAF first lieutenant was found among the debris scattered throughout the damaged areas below deck. Given that AH-6 was south of Okinawa heading southeast when hit, it would suggest that the vessel's attacker was from one of the Formosa-based tokko-tai sortied that day. Aircraft despatched included four "Franks" from the Sei 34th Hikotai at Taichu (Taichung) at 1740hrs, four 105th Sentai "Tonys" that took off from Giran, and four "Nicks" of the Sei 119th Hikotai from Touen, with both of the latter groups departing at 1800hrs. The roster of pilots from these units, however, showed that 105th Sentai tokko flight leader Isao Nakamura was the only IJAAF first lieutenant to participate in the late afternoon mission. If *Comfort*'s after action report is indeed correct, it would make him the pilot who struck the defenseless ship.

Shortly before *Comfort* was hit, the destroyer *Wadsworth*, which had narrowly missed being struck by a tokko just six days earlier, had another close shave when, at 2007hrs, one of a pair of torpedo-bombers clipped the ship after it had dodged a torpedo only moments before. The crew identified the attackers as "Myrts," but these highly valuable reconnaissance aircraft did not carry torpedoes and were not used in tokko missions due to their paucity in number. It was highly likely that the destroyer had instead encountered a "Kate" or "Jill," with examples of the former being employed on tokko missions that day. However, the six Kushira-based aircraft from the Hachiman Shinchu-tai, Shirasagi Sekichu-tai, and Seiki-tai that took off between 1535hrs and 1635hrs were carrying 1,764lb Type 2 No. 80 Mk 5 Land Bombs instead of torpedoes, leaving a pilot (probably flying a "Jill") intent on committing jibaku likely to be responsible for targeting the *Wadsworth*.

A6M2 "Zeke" of the 5th Shichisei-tai, Kyushu, April 1945

In early April 1945, the second Genzan Kokutai sent its A6M2s and A6M2-Ks from its airfield in Genzan (now Wonsan in North Korea) to Kyushu, from where it flew tokko missions as the 5th Shichisei-tai against Allied warships off Okinawa. The last of the unit's aircraft were expended during a mission flown on the afternoon of April 29. *(Artwork by Jim Laurier, © Osprey Publishing)*

During the afternoon of April 29 the IJNAF sent out four groups of Kanoya-based tokko against the recently returned carriers of TF 58 that were again operating in the dangerous waters off Okinawa. The aircraft started departing at 1413hrs, with five from the 4th Tsukuba-tai taking off first, followed by four more from the 5th Shichisei-tai between 1417hrs and 1419hrs and, finally, eight from the 5th Showa-tai between 1420hrs and 1426hrs. Despite all the attackers being identified as "Zekes," the aircraft from the 5th Showa-tai were actually two-seat A6M2-K trainers drawn from the Yatabe Kokutai – they were all flown by a single pilot, however. The four early-model A6M2s from the 5th Shichisei-tai, meanwhile, represented the very last aircraft from the Genzan Kokutai, which had flown its surviving fighters to Kyushu from Genzan (Wonsan in today's North Korea) in early April so that they could participate in tokko attacks.

These groups were followed aloft (between 1442hrs and 1459hrs) by the 9th Kenmu-tai, which consisted of ten more "Zekes" from Kanoya. Unlike the aircraft of the previous units sortied that day, the fighters assigned to the 9th were new A6M5s drawn from the 721st Kokutai. Following the decimation of the Ohka-carrying "Betty" motherships of the Jinrai Butai, the "Zekes" from the 721st were no longer needed for bomber escort missions. They would now be pressed into service as tokko instead. The 721st's aircraft probably proceeded to Okinawa separately from the previous units owing to their later takeoff times and heavier all-up weight, as they were each laden down with a heavier

1,102lb Type 2 No. 50 Model 1 Ordinary Bomb, rather than solitary 551lb bombs carried by the remaining single-seat "Zekes."

One or more of these groups would have been the aircraft that found TGs 58.3 and 58.4 sailing northeast of Okinawa just before 1700hrs. Three attackers were claimed by a CAP from the carrier *Yorktown*, while the fighters under the control of the destroyers manning nearby Radar Picket Station 4 knocked down two more. Nevertheless, the remaining tokko proceeded to badly damage the screening destroyers USS *Hazelwood* (DD-531) and USS *Haggard* (DD-555) while they were en route to a radar picket station.

The former was struck first, having managed to maneuver out of the way of the first two A6Ms that targeted it before being hit by a third that dove out of cloud cover astern of the destroyer and smashed through the after stack and crashed into the base of the bridge. The subsequent explosion of the aircraft's bomb and flaming gasoline from its ruptured tanks caused heavy casualties (46 dead, including the ship's commanding officer, Cdr V. P. Douw, and 26 wounded).

A short while later *Haggard* was targeted by a tokko in a shallow diving attack to starboard. Despite the aircraft being repeatedly hit by the destroyer's antiaircraft weapons, it crashed close aboard and penetrated the hull near the waterline. Moments later its bomb exploded in DD-555's engine room, allowing water to pour in through a gaping hole in the destroyer's side. As the vessel began to settle, a second tokko attacked, although it was quickly downed by the ship's gunners. Thanks

On April 29, 1945, USS *Hazelwood* (DD-531) was targeted by three "Zekes" while en route to a radar picket station. Although the ship managed to maneuver out of the way of the first two tokko, a third dove out of cloud cover astern of the destroyer and hit the No. 2 stack, before crashing into the base of the bridge. The explosion of the aircraft's bomb and flaming gasoline caused heavy casualties. Although badly damaged, *Hazelwood* was eventually repaired post-war and returned to fleet service. (NARA)

Hazelwood's signal bridge, pilot house, radio room, chart house, and captain's sea cabin were all totally destroyed by the "Zeke" hit on April 29, as were the directors for the main battery and 40mm guns. The 40mm guns and their tub can be seen lying on the main deck behind the No. 2 turret. Finally, the SC and SG radar antennae were also destroyed when the mainmast was crushed by the No. 2 stack as it collapsed into the forward superstructure. *(NARA)*

to fast and skillful work by *Haggard*'s seasoned damage control parties, the flooding was stopped and the ship saved from sinking – by which point 13 crew had been killed and 38 wounded. Unlike DD-531, which was subsequently repaired and returned to fleet service, DD-555 was declared a constructive total loss shortly after reaching Norfolk Navy Yard in August 1945 and was sold for scrapping.

The destroyer minelayer USS *Harry F. Bauer* (DM-26) and destroyer USS *Cowell* (DD-547) were also near-missed while on Radar Picket Station 4 that same evening.

The Japanese had by this time started to step up night tokko operations in an effort to avoid both the increasingly effective CAP (during the month of April US Navy carrier-based pilots had claimed 937 aircraft shot down – 590 of them during the four Kikusui attacks – and carrier- and land-based US Marine Corps pilots had been credited with 279 kills) and ever-present antiaircraft fire that proved hard to penetrate during daylight hours.

The destroyer minelayer USS *Shannon* (DM-25) was narrowly missed by an unidentified aircraft at 0248hrs on April 29. Nocturnal tokko enjoyed better luck during the early hours of May 1, however, when the Liberty ship SS *S. Hall Young* and the minelayer USS *Terror* (CM-5) were struck while anchored in Nago Bay at 0345hrs and off Kerama Retto at 0400hrs, respectively. The former had just offloaded the first tranche of groundcrew for the USAAF's P-47N Thunderbolt-equipped 318th FG on Ie Shima the previous day, although it was still packed with 530 tons of ammunition and rockets when the tokko crashed into the vessel's No. 5 hold. Thankfully, these were stored elsewhere on the ship, and the resulting fire from the strike was extinguished before it could spread to the ammunition – only 12 trucks and various other supplies and equipment were lost.

Terror was not so lucky, its attacker spotting the ship through a hole in the smoke screen that had been thrown up when tokko were detected in the general area. Coming in on the ship's port beam, the pilot banked tightly around the stern before approaching at such high-speed from the starboard quarter that only one of the minelayer's stern batteries managed to open fire. When the aircraft hit the ship's superstructure one of its bombs exploded, while the second weapon penetrated the main deck before detonating. The tokko's engine ripped through the ship's bulkheads before finally coming to rest in the wardroom. Fire immediately broke out within the superstructure, although this was soon contained and eventually extinguished. The ship's magazines had also been hastily flooded to prevent any possible explosions. Although CM-5 had suffered no engineering damage, the tokko had killed 48 crew and wounded 123. *Terror* was eventually sent back to San Francisco, via Eniwetok and Pearl Harbor, to be repaired. The vessel headed back to the Pacific Fleet in mid-August 1945.

CM-5's after action report stated that the ship had been attacked by a "Judy," adding that there was a second unidentified aircraft present overhead at the same time. The only tokko missions undertaken by the Japanese on the night of the April 30/May 1 were flown by a single "Tony" from the 19th Sentai at 2330hrs and a pair of Ki-61s from the 23rd Dokuritsu Chutai at 0410hrs – all three had taken off from Ishigaki Island. However, IJAAF records show that the 19th Sentai's Sgt Tsuneo Kurita turned back due to bad weather en route, and he was lost after engaging enemy nightfighters or bombers over his airfield. With the pair from the 23rd Dokuritsu Chutai having departed Karenko too late to attack *S. Hall Young* and *Terror*, the identity of the aircraft that hit these ships is set to remain a mystery.

The relative quiet of the first two days of May was shattered on the 3rd when Kikusui No. 5 commenced. It was timed to precede a major

Ki-43-III "Oscar" of the 18th Shinbu-tai, Kyushu, April 1945

A little-known tokko unit formed from the 10th Hiko Shidan, the 18th Shinbu-tai sent six of its "Oscars" to Okinawa waters on the afternoon of April 29. No results of note were achieved by these aircraft. It also sortied a solitary Ki-43 (possibly its last tokko) on May 4 as part of Kikusui No. 5. The increased fighter escort allocated to the tokko that day resulted in 17 ships being hit, four of which sunk, despite eight fast carrier-based US Navy squadrons and five land-based US Marine Corps Corsair units claiming 167 Japanese aircraft destroyed between them. (Artwork by Jim Laurier, © Osprey Publishing)

counterattack by the IJA's 32nd Army on Okinawa on May 4. The first IJAAF tokko-tai committed to Kikusui No. 5 went into action from Formosa during the late afternoon, with five "Franks" and a "Nick" of the Sei 35th and 123rd Hikotai from Taichu, four "Tonys" from the 17th Sentai at Karenko, and five "Oscars" from the 20th Sentai at Ryutan (Longtan) all being sortied. Accompanying this contingent were a "Kate" and two "Vals" of the Shinten-tai and a "Jill" from the Kiichi-tai, all of which took off from Shinchuku, also on Formosa. This mission had been planned as a rare coordinated inter-service attack, with all aircraft taking to the skies between 1600 and 1640hrs. The raid was timed to perfection, with the tokko targeting ships on radar picket stations west-southwest of Okinawa from 1830hrs just as the evening sun began to set.

The aircraft were initially spotted nearing Radar Picket Station 9 by the destroyer USS *Bache* (DD-470) and the high-speed destroyer minesweeper *Macomb*, which were manning the station along with the support ships *LCS(L)(3)-89*, *LCS(L)(3)-111*, and *LCS(L)(3)-117*. At 1809hrs *Bache* reported radar contact with several groups of bogies, and the CAP was vectored to intercept the one heading for the ships. However, communications difficulties prevented an effective interception from taking place, and at 1828hrs three "Tonys" were sighted emerging from the scattered cloud to starboard. These made individual runs on the ships that were then sailing in column formation, with *Bache* leading *Macomb*.

ABOVE
USS *Aaron Ward* (DM-34) was laid down as an Allen M. Sumner-class destroyer and converted into a destroyer minelayer before commissioning. The ship endured an intensive kamikaze attack on Radar Picket Station 10 on May 3, 1945, this photograph – taken in the Kerama Retto anchorage the following day – showing the damage inflicted on the ship's aft section after it suffered five tokko hits or near misses. DM-34 was eventually declared a constructive total loss and scrapped. *(NARA)*

The first two attackers targeted DD-470, with the lead aircraft being shot down at long range and the second splashed under heavy fire just off the destroyer's port quarter at 1829hrs. The final tokko found his target, crashing into and tearing off *Macomb*'s No. 3 turret and five-inch gun from the mounting at 1830hrs. The impact also ignited a fire, although this was quickly extinguished. The ship avoided further damage when a bomb from the aircraft passed through its superstructure before exploding in the water off the port quarter.

There is little doubt that the fighters involved in this attack were three of the four Ki-61s from the 17th Sentai that had been led aloft from Karenko by 2Lt Michiyasu Shimoyama at 1640hrs. The mystery of the fate of the fourth "Tony" was resolved when *LCS(L)(3)-111* picked up a US Navy pilot from Radar Picket Station 9's CAP who had been shot down by friendly antiaircraft fire from the ships during the action. He confirmed that his division of fighters had encountered a single Ki-61

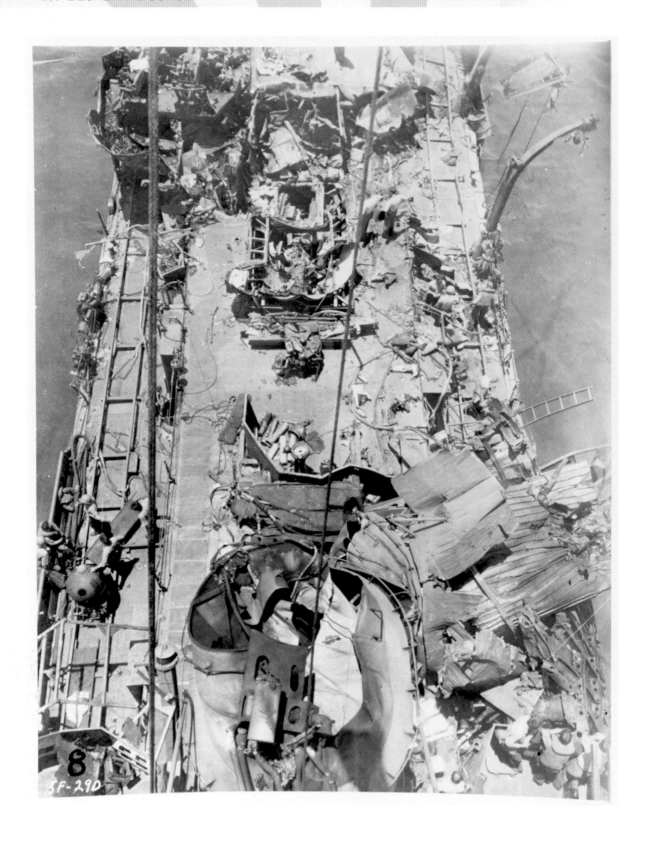

flying at altitude while the remaining three approached at low level, the lone "Tony" subsequently being downed while the others made their attacks. This solitary aircraft could have been Shimoyama's, who was possibly observing and reporting on his wingmen's progress when he was intercepted and shot down before he could carry out his own attack run.

If attribution of the attacks on *Bache* and *Macomb* was relatively straightforward, the same cannot be said for the engagement fought by the five vessels manning Radar Picket Station 10 some 26 nautical miles northwest of Radar Picket Station 9. Soon after *Bache* and *Macomb* had come under attack, the destroyer minelayers USS *Little* (DM-803) and USS *Aaron Ward* (DM-34) and support ships *LSM(R)-195* and *LCS(L)-14*, *LCS(L)-25* and *LCS(L)-83* were also targeted by the first of at least 20 tokko over the next 40–50 minutes. *Aaron Ward* was hit at 1841hrs, having shot down two aircraft, and moments later *Little* was struck on its port side. Within four minutes three more tokko had crashed into DM-803, breaking the keel, demolishing the amidships section, and splitting open all three after machinery spaces. At 1855hrs *Little* broke up and sank, taking 62 crew with it. A further 49 were wounded.

Aaron Ward somehow managed to stay afloat despite absorbing five hits that inflicted grievous damage and killed 42 crew. Left dead in the water and suffering severe flooding aft, DM-34 was only saved from sinking by the efforts of its damage control parties. Towed to Kerama Retto later that night, and eventually patched up enough to sail back to New York, *Aaron Ward* was declared a constructive total loss and sold for scrapping in July 1946.

Like *Little*, *LSM(R)-195* was also sunk in the attack on Radar Picket Station 10 while trying to come to the aid of the stricken destroyer minelayers, its commanding officer, Lt(jg) W. E. Woodson, noting in his after action report:

> Two planes were observed approaching, the closest identified as a "Nick." This plane was taken under fire by the ship's 5in./38 mount and both 40mm guns as it circled and approached from the starboard side. The other plane started an attack run on our port side, coming in at a very low altitude and maneuvering violently to confuse our two port 20mm gunners who had taken him under fire. This plane was strafing on its way in and hit the port side, ripping the main deck all the way into amidships.
>
> The subsequent explosion and degree of damage inflicted on *LSM(R)-195* indicated that this plane carried a bomb. The rockets that were loaded in the

OPPOSITE
This elevated view taken from *Aaron Ward*'s mainmast reveals the level of destruction inflicted on the warship by the tokko attack, which killed 42 crew. The photographer has trained his camera aft, and much of the damage visible here was caused by a final bomb-laden tokko, which made a high-speed, low-level approach and crashed into the base of the No. 2 stack at 1920hrs. The subsequent explosion blew the aircraft, the stack, the searchlight, and two gun mounts into the air. They all came to rest across the deck aft of stack No. 1. *(NARA)*

launchers topside began exploding in every direction as the fire spread from one broken rocket motor to another, causing a great deal of shrapnel and fragments to be in the air at all times. These rockets were propelled only short distances, with numerous hits about the deck causing fires. The plane or bomb had also penetrated the forward assembly room, causing assembled rockets to be propelled throughout the ship, and the area surrounding it.

With *LSM(R)-195*'s fire main and auxiliary pumps having been knocked out by the tokko, the surviving crew (nine having been killed and 16 wounded from a complement of 81) were forced to abandoned the vessel. It subsequently sank after being rocked by several large explosions.

With Radar Picket Station 10 having endured a sustained attack in fading light, there is little chance of assigning responsibility for individual ship strikes to specific aircraft. For example, the ships' after action reports identified at least nine of the protagonists as "Vals" and a further five as "Zekes" despite IJNAF records listing only two of the attackers as D3As and none as A6Ms. Only one of the attackers was identified as an "Oscar" and none were said to be "Franks," although five of each type were sortied that afternoon. Furthermore, *LSM(R)-195*'s CO stated that his vessel was hit by a "Nick," which had to be from the 23rd Hikotai as it was the only Ki-45 tokko in the area that day.

Adding to the confusion surrounding what aircraft hit which ship is the varying times the vessels logged certain events, with the crew of *Aaron Ward* recording the first attackers diving on them at 1830hrs, while survivors from *Little* stated that both ships were simultaneously targeted at 1843hrs.

The following morning dawned bright and clear, and Kikusui No. 5 soon swung into action once again. The IJAAF marshaled all the aircraft it could muster – around 50 "Nates," "Oscars," "Tonys," "Franks," and "Nick" fighters at Chiran, Bansei, and Miyakonojo airfields. Most of the 11 depleted tokko-tai units involved (the 19th, 20th, 24th, 42nd, 60th, 66th, 77th, 78th, 105th, 106th, and 109th Shinbu-tai) could only contribute a few aircraft to the attack. The IJNAF also committed 75 mostly obsolete tokko aircraft, which, for the first time, included reconnaissance seaplanes. Three Aichi E13A1 "Jakes" and 15 elderly Kawanishi E7K2 "Alfs" from the Ibusuki-based Dai-ichi Kashira-Ku (a maintenance training unit) and Kotohira Suishin-Tai, respectively, were among the 28 seaplanes that joined a group of "Zeke" and "Kate" tokko aircraft. Finally, the Jinrai Butai also sortied seven "Bettys" and their Ohka charges.

A large attacking force headed from bases in Kyushu at 0500hrs, the tokko force having an escort of 48 "Zekes," mostly from the 203rd Kokutai, with an additional 35 IJAAF fighters – probably "Franks" drawn from the 101st, 102nd, or 103rd Sentai. Once again, the IJNAF sent out a fighter sweep ahead of the tokko force, with 35 N1K2s from the 343rd Kokutai, along with 15 IJAAF fighters, pushing south to Kikaijima and Amami Oshima Islands in an effort to pave the way for the attackers, who were themselves given a close escort of fighters. For maximum effect, all the attacks were concentrated on warships and transports supporting US troops fighting on Okinawa.

The increased fighter escort appeared to have an effect that day, for despite eight fast carrier-based US Navy squadrons and five land-based US Marine Corps Corsair units claiming 167 Japanese aircraft destroyed between them, the tokko still managed to hit 17 ships, sinking four of them.

The carnage began soon after 0700hrs, and once again the northern radar picket ships bore the brunt of the attack. The first vessel sunk was the destroyer USS *Luce* (DD-522), assigned to Radar Picket Station 12 to the northwest of Okinawa. At about 0740hrs the tokko had been intercepted by the CAP in the immediate vicinity of *Luce*, and although most of the aircraft were shot down, two (identified as either "Zekes" or "Oscars") succeeded in attacking the destroyer from its port side. DD-522 managed to splash one of the aircraft, although the explosion from its bomb caused the ship to suffer a total power failure. Unable to bring its guns to bear in time, the destroyer was struck in the aft section by the

Ki-84 pilots of the 100th Hikoshidan (comprised of the 101st, 102nd, and 103rd Sentai) had the task of escorting tokko units to Okinawa, clearing a path through the American CAPs for the kamikaze pilots. Among the operations they participated in was Kikusui No. 5 on May 4, 1945. On this particular occasion their efforts appeared to have had an effect, for despite US Navy fighter squadrons and US Marine Corps Corsair units claiming 167 Japanese aircraft destroyed between them, 17 ships were hit and four sunk. *(Tony Holmes collection)*

second kamikaze, knocking out its port engine, flooding engineering spaces, and jamming the rudder. At 0814hrs *Luce* started to list heavily to starboard, at which point the order was given to abandon ship. Of the 335 personnel on board, 149 were killed and 94 wounded.

Despite having 32 (soon increased to 48) fighters on CAP nearby, the destroyers USS *Morrison* (DD-560) and USS *Ingraham* (DD-694), along with *LSM(R)-194*, *LCS(L)-21*, *LCS(L)-23*, and *LCS(L)-31* had also come under sustained attack at Radar Picket Station 1. The ships' guns, together with the enlarged CAP, kept the attackers at bay for more than an hour until 0825hrs, when *Morrison* was hit by two "Zekes" in rapid succession. The fighters crashed into a stack and the bridge, causing heavy casualties among the crew and knocking out most of the ship's electrical equipment.

At about the same time, a mixed formation of Corsairs from VF-83 and VF-85 encountered slow-flying seaplanes at low level – seven E7K2 biplanes were soon shot down. VF-83 claimed a further seven "Alfs" destroyed shortly thereafter, although overclaiming was a distinct possibility given the fact that only 13 such aircraft were sent aloft that morning and at least three succeeded in hitting their targets.

The victim of the successful trio of seaplanes was the already stricken *Morrison*, which was hit by the first "Alf" at 0834hrs and two more shortly thereafter. The seaplanes had attacked from astern, and despite their slow speed they had managed to avoid being shot down by antiaircraft fire sent their way. In fact, the pilot of the second "Alf" had actually alighted on the water in order to force the defending CAP to overshoot, before taking off again and slamming into the luckless *Morrison*. The explosions from the heavier 1,102lb bombs carried by the seaplanes proved fatal, resulting in the destroyer sinking at 0840hrs with the loss of 152 men – more than half its complement.

Ingraham enjoyed better fortune, its gunners downing four tokko before the fifth aircraft crashed into the ship above the waterline on the port side. A solitary bomb carried by the attacker penetrated the hull plating and exploded in the generator room. Down by 14ft at the bow and with only one gun left operable, DD-694 (which had had 15 crew killed and 36 wounded) was withdrawn from the line and eventually sent to Hunter's Point, California, to be repaired.

The second vessel sunk at Radar Picket Station 1 was *LSM(R)-194*, whose crew reported being hit by a bomb-toting "Tony" at 0838hrs despite no Ki-61s actually being a part of the tokko force in the air that morning. *LSM(R)-194* was the second of three LSM(R)-188-class Landing Ship Medium (Rocket) ships to be sunk in little more than 24 hours, thus attesting to the prescience of the after action report for the period April 2–20, 1945 tabled by Cdr Dennis L. Francis, commander of TG 52.21's Flotilla Nine. In this document, he indicated that these ships were not particularly suited to radar picket duty:

> Since their primary function is to deliver rockets during invasion operations, it seems feasible that subjecting them to continual enemy air attack will allow this secondary duty to seriously effect [sic] their ability to perform their primary function due to damage. They have no great value in combating enemy aircraft due to the absence of air search radar, adequate director control for the 5in./38 main battery, and director control for the 40mm single guns. The fact that they carry a considerable quantity of explosive rockets in their magazines presents another hazard. In general, it is believed that assigning them to picket duty should be avoided since it means risking the operation of a limited number of specialized ships in a role that could be performed by any number of other landing craft whose primary function is more closely coincident with screening operations.

BELOW LEFT
The Fletcher-class destroyer USS *Morrison* (DD-560) was sunk with heavy loss of life on May 4, 1945 while manning Radar Picket Station 1, the vessel being hit by two "Zekes" and three "Alf" seaplanes. Seen here on October 24, 1944 after being damaged while assisting in the firefighting efforts to save the ill-fated light carrier USS *Princeton* (CVL-23) off Luzon, *Morrison* sank with the loss of 152 men. *(NARA)*

BOTTOM LEFT
LSM(R)-194 unleashes a salvo of rockets while undertaking its designated shore bombardment role during the early stages of the invasion of Okinawa. LSMs often found themselves at the radar picket stations off Okinawa in an effort to bolster the antiaircraft capability of the destroyers normally assigned there. Not well suited to this role, they suffered accordingly when tokko started targeting the radar picket ships. Hit shortly after *Morrison* went down, *LSM(R)-194* was sunk on May 4, 1945 while also assigned to Radar Picket Station 1 during Kikusui No. 6. It was the second of three LSM(R)-188-class ships to be sunk in little more than 24 hours. *(NARA)*

Unlike *LSM(R)-194*, *LCS(L)-31* survived the carnage of May 5 despite being hit by three tokko that killed nine and wounded 12. Prior to having its forward twin 40mm mount, aft fire director, and two 20mm mounts destroyed, the ship had claimed six aircraft destroyed. Crewmen on board *LCS(L)-31* and *Ingraham* had identified their attackers as "Vals" – survivors from *Morrison* also stated that the ship had initially been targeted by D3As. However, like *LSM(R)-194*'s mysterious "Tony," there were no "Vals" in the air as tokko that morning.

In fact, the high-speed destroyer minesweeper USS *Hopkins* (DMS-13) and minesweeper USS *Gayety* (AM-239) noted in their after action reports that they too had been targeted by tokko that morning. The likelihood was that these ships were actually attacked by "Nates" from one of six Shinbu-tai that saw action with the aircraft that day. Another possibility was that the drop tanks and/or bombs carried beneath the wings of the "Oscars" and "Franks" were mistaken for the fixed undercarriage of the "Val."

Also hit that morning was the light cruiser USS *Birmingham* (CL-62) in the Hagushi Beaches anchorage. At 0840hrs, an "Oscar" was shot down some 4,000 yards ahead of the light cruiser *St. Louis* as it flew at low level towards *Birmingham*. Simultaneously, a second Ki-43 quickly closed on the anchorage from a height of about 4,000ft, before pushing over into a vertical dive on CL-62. The aircraft was inside the elevation limit stops and cut out cams for most of the ship's heavy-caliber antiaircraft guns, thus reducing its defensive fire to just 20mm weapons. These failed to stop the "Oscar" from penetrating through the main deck to starboard, the aircraft exploding as it crashed through the sick bay and ruptured the main, second, and third decks. Bulkheads were also blown in and a large five-foot hole appeared in the starboard side below the waterline, flooding the armory, four living compartments, and three ammunition magazines before damage control parties could stem the ingress of water. By then, a total of 51 crew had been killed and 81 wounded.

The first of seven lumbering G4M2E motherships from the Jinrai Butai arrived off Okinawa just as the earlier tokko onslaught had started tapering off. At 0854hrs the destroyer minelayer *Shea* was manning Radar Picket Station 14, having already fought off two tokko from the early morning raids, when its crew sighted a "Betty" emerging from the smoke haze drifting northwest from the fighting near Okinawa's Hagushi Beaches. The bomber was engaged by the CAP under *Shea*'s control and quickly crashed in flames, although almost immediately after it had hit the water the ship's crew sighted an Ohka closing from the starboard side. Despite gunners scoring a number of hits on the rocket-powered aerial bomb, they could not prevent it from punching through the ship's thin bridge superstructure and exploding about 20ft off the port side.

The weapon badly damaged *Shea*, knocking out its two forward five-inch gun batteries and forward port 20mm weapons, jamming the gun director, and leaving the ship without a functioning communications system. Thirty-five crew had been killed and 91 wounded. The ship was removed from the front line and eventually sent back to Philadelphia Navy Yard the following month to be repaired.

The "Betty" that had launched the Ohka was one of six Jinrai Butai motherships lost that day. A second example also managed to launch its rocket-powered aerial bomb prior to falling to American fighters off Tori Shima soon after 0935hrs, its target being a nearby minesweeping group consisting of several vessels led by *Gayety* and *Hopkins* – both ships had already survived attacks by conventional tokko earlier that morning. The Ohka pilot attempted to mask his approach on *Gayety* by feigning a run on one of the smaller motor minesweepers sailing nearby, although this did not prevent the MXY7 being successfully targeted by the minesweeper's automatic gunfire. It duly disintegrated and fell into the sea close aboard at 0947hrs without its explosives detonating.

The final vessel sunk on May 4 was *LSM(R)-190*, which had been supporting *Shea* at Radar Picket Station 14 when it too was hit. The following detailed account by the ship's Executive Officer, Lt(jg) George T. Harmon, was included in the after action report:

> The attack on *LSM(R)-190* began at 0808hrs with a 'Dinah' [almost certainly a Ki-45] flying over the stern dropping a bomb, which missed. This plane was hit by our automatic weapons. Thereupon the plane turned over, returned and dived into the 5in./38 mount, setting it on fire. Shrapnel resulting from the plane crash severely injured the CO, Lt Richard J. Saunders, rendering him prostrate and immediately killed the Gunnery Officer, Ens Stuart C. Bjorklund. As the wounded skipper slipped in and out of consciousness, *LSM(R)-190* continued steaming under the last order given to the helm prior to the crash – full right rudder at flank speed. Reacting quickly, Radioman William J. Nuber, standing Phone Talker watch

on the bridge, took over the wheelhouse and conned the ship until relieved by the wounded Communications Officer, Ens Lyle Tennis.

The 5in./38 mount was practically knocked off its foundation and set on fire, and the latter spread to the handling room and after storage space. The sprinkler system to the magazines and the after rocket assembly room were ordered turned on and fire hoses broken out from amidships and played on the 5in./38 mount. However, as the fire mains had been ruptured, pressure was negligible, and the damage control parties commenced breaking out lines from the auxiliary fire pump.

A second kamikaze attacker approached low above the water from the port beam, then crashed into the upper level of the engine room. Wreckage of this plane remained stuck into the side of the ship. Fires broke out in the engine room and the crash disabled the auxiliary fire pump. Smoke was so thick that it was impossible to see the engine controls. Engineering Officer Lt(jg) Gordon Etter remained in the engine room until permission was granted to abandon the area as fires turned it into a virtual blast furnace.

A third Japanese plane came after *LSM(R)-190* at about 0824hrs as the ship attempted evasive maneuvers and zigzagging at flank speed. The twin-engined fighter crossed from port to starboard at about mast head height and dropped a bomb that missed widely by some 700 yards. By now the ship was all but defenseless, with every gun out of action except the starboard abaft 20mm. Two minutes later a fourth plane attacked in 'sneak' fashion, releasing a bomb that hit the Mk 51 Director tub. A fifth plane, a "Val," dove from a considerable height pursued by Corsairs of the CAP that had arrived on the scene. This plane crossed from port aft of the starboard 20mm, causing no damage.

As the fires were now beyond control and the ship had developed a decided port list, it was decided to abandon ship. The body of Ens Bjorklund and the wounded CO were carried down from the Conn by officers Etter and Tennis and placed in life rafts. Twenty minutes later (0850hrs approximately) the ship went down. As the abandoned, burning *LSM(R)-190* sank beneath the waves, those in the water felt the violent explosions from the rocket ship.

Fourteen crew had been killed and 18 wounded during the various attacks that sank *LSM(R)-190*.

Further south on May 4, the British Pacific Fleet's aircraft carriers and battleships were off Sakishima Gunto for yet another series of strikes against Japanese targets there. Codenamed *Iceberg II*, the morning strikes hit the airfields on Ishigaki and Miyakojima Islands, and were followed up by Royal Navy battleships shelling the bases with air-burst rounds. It was felt that the latter would be more effective against enemy aircraft and dug-in antiaircraft guns than cratering coral runways with conventional bombs, the damage from which could be quickly repaired.

However, this meant that the carriers were shorn of a significant portion of the fleet's antiaircraft firepower, and at 1130hrs TF 57 (as the British Pacific Fleet was known during *Iceberg II*) paid the price. The action started soon after 1100hrs when four groups of bogies were detected on radar in rapid succession closing in on the fleet from multiple directions and at varying altitudes. Some aircraft were decoys to draw out the CAP, and they turned away once the Fleet Air Arm fighters appeared. Nevertheless, at 1125hrs, Corsairs shot down one of four "Zekes" from the third of these groups.

Unfortunately, the pilots' inability to engage the remaining IJNAF fighters proved telling, for these turned out to be "Zekes" from the 17th Taigi-tai that had been led off from Giran, on Formosa, by 1Lt Itsuji Yagi at 0945hrs. At least two of the three surviving tokko reached the fleet by making their approach at low level, thus avoiding detection until 1131hrs when one crashed onto the flightdeck of *Formidable*. Moments later a

On May 4, 1945 the British Pacific Fleet's aircraft carriers and battleships were off Sakishima Gunto for strikes against Japanese targets. With the battleships attacking airfields, the carriers were shorn of a significant portion of the fleet's antiaircraft firepower, and at 1131hrs a "Zeke" from the 17th Taigi-tai approached at low level, avoiding detection, and crashed onto the flightdeck of *Formidable*. (© IWM A 29717)

Corsair II JT537 flown by Sub Lt D. J. Sheppard, 1836 NAS, HMS *Victorious*, Pacific, May 4, 1945

Sub Lt Don Sheppard used JT537 to destroy a "D4Y" tokko during an attack on the British Pacific Fleet on May 4 – the aircraft was almost certainly a "Zeke" participating in Kikusui No. 5, which had commenced that same day. The fire from his six 0.50in. guns caused the tokko to break up and crash into the sea before the pilot could target the Royal Navy carriers. One "Zeke" did manage to penetrate the CAP, however, and crash into the flightdeck of *Formidable*. (*Artwork by Chris Davey, © Osprey Publishing*)

second "Zeke" skidded along the flightdeck of *Indomitable*, trailing smoke and flames, before plunging into the sea.

The latter vessel, which was the flagship of the British Pacific Fleet's air operations commander, Admiral Philip Vian, was lightly damaged, while *Formidable*'s armored flightdeck was moderately dented over an area of 20ft by 24ft and lightly holed by a bomb that had detonated when it hit the vessel. The ordnance had been released from the "Zeke" seconds before it struck the ship, killing eight crew and wounding 55. Seven Avengers and a Corsair were destroyed by fire, with damage inflicted on *Formidable*'s antiaircraft guns, radars, electrical systems, and center boiler room – the latter had been hit by a large piece of flightdeck armor that had been blown into the bowels of the ship when it was struck by the aircraft. Nevertheless, once the dent had been filled with wood and concrete and covered by thin steel plates tack-welded in place, the carrier was able to resume flight operations at 1700hrs despite the damage.

There were other tokko launched against the British carriers that day, although no further hits were achieved and several aircraft were successfully intercepted. These included a "Judy" from the Chusei-tai that had sortied from Shinchuku, also on Formosa, at the same time as the morning flight from the 17th Taigi-tai. This lone D4Y was almost certainly the "Hamp"

ABOVE
Formidable's armored flightdeck was moderately dented and lightly holed by the "Zeke's" bomb. The ordnance had been released from the fighter seconds before it struck the ship. Seven Avengers and a Corsair were destroyed, with further damage inflicted on the ship's antiaircraft guns, radars, electrical systems, and center boiler room. Flight operations were suspended for almost six hours while repairs were carried out. (© IWM A29312)

claimed by the 894 NAS Seafire pilot Sub Lt Richard H. Reynolds, embarked in *Indefatigable*, at 1120hrs. At 1252hrs two Seafires from 887 NAS flown by Sub Lt C. M. Miseldine and CPO William Daniel, also from *Indefatigable*, claimed a "Val," which, by all accounts, would have been the solitary aircraft from the Shinten-tai that departed Shinchuku at 1050hrs crewed by CPO Kiyoka and PO1c Ishida.

The Japanese continued sending Formosa-based tokko against TF 57 as the fleet withdrew following the attack on Sakishima Gunto, with two more "Zekes" following a similar number of IJAAF "Tonys" from the 19th Sentai aloft from Giran at 1600hrs. The quartet of aircraft headed for the area south of Miyakojima. The IJAAF also sent tokko against the fleet off Okinawa at this time, with three "Franks" from the Sei 120th

ABOVE LEFT
The crumpled and charred remains of the "Zeke" from the 17th Taigi-tai. *Formidable* had just launched two Corsairs for bombardment-spotting duties and 11 Avengers on the flightdeck were in the process of being moved forward to allow other aircraft to land back on board when the "Zeke" attacked at 1131hrs – its presence had remained undetected until that point. The pilot initially strafed the flightdeck without opposition from the ship's antiaircraft batteries, before turning sharply and plunging into the forward section of the carrier – despite *Formidable*'s hard turn to starboard. *(The Stratford Archive)*

ABOVE RIGHT
This dramatic photograph was taken at 1900hrs on the evening of May 4, 1945 as a Ki-61 from the 105th Sentai dove at USS *Sangamon* (CVE-26) from the port quarter. The Ki-61 only managed to knock off the vessel's radio antennae before crashing into the sea. *(NARA)*

Hikotai and a "Nick" from the Sei 123rd Hikotai from Hattoku (Bade) joining two more Ki-61s from the 105th Sentai. It was unclear if these six tokko were escorted, although at dusk a division of cannon-armed Corsairs from VMF-311 led by 2Lt William Brown encountered what were reported as eight "Tonys" and three "Dinahs" approaching the anchorage at Kerama Retto. All 11 aircraft were shot down without loss.

If the group of aircraft engaged by VMF-311 were indeed the Formosa-based IJAAF tokko, then the unit's claim that they were all shot down was incorrect, for soon after 1900hrs the escort carrier *Sangamon* was targeted by a lone "Tony" as the vessel left Kerama Retto after rearming and headed south to rejoin its task group. The Ki-61 – almost certainly one of the two 105th Sentai aircraft flown by either 2Lt Hara or Sgt Nakajima

At 1933hrs, *Sangamon* was targeted by a Ki-45 almost certainly from the Sei 123rd Hikotai, the aircraft crashing through the flightdeck amidships before exploding. The resulting blaze caused extensive damage, with fierce fires being started on the flightdeck, in the hangar bay (seen here), and on the fuel deck. By 2230hrs the fires were finally under control and the ship headed to Kerama Retto so that temporary repairs could be made. Although *Sangamon* had been saved from sinking, it was not repaired post-war. (NARA)

– dove for the ship from the port quarter, knocking off its starboard radio antennae as it narrowly missed the hard-turning carrier and plunged into the sea 25ft off the vessel's starboard beam.

The danger was not over yet for the *Sangamon*, however, with unidentified aircraft still reported in the immediate vicinity. The carrier launched a pair of Hellcat nightfighters from its embarked air group in response, and they had just disappeared into the rapidly darkening sky when, shortly after 1930hrs, the crew spotted a twin-engined aircraft to the west. Gunners opened fire on it, only for the bogey to disappear into cloud cover and then reappear directly astern, diving for the carrier. The tokko, which was now identified as a "Nick," was taken under fire again and both of its engines were hit. Nevertheless, the pilot somehow still managed to slam into *Sangamon* at 1933hrs.

The "Nick," which was probably the aircraft flown by Cpl Saburo Mizukoshi from the Sei 123rd Hikotai, crashed through the flightdeck amidships and exploded. Fires immediately broke out on both the flightdeck and in the hangar bay. At 1940hrs the bridge was evacuated,

ABOVE
Sangamon's flightdeck was littered with the charred remains of Avengers and Hellcats, and both of its elevators were blown out of place by explosions in the hangar bay. Thirty-six crew had been killed and 21 seriously wounded in the attack. *(NARA)*

RIGHT
As this photograph clearly shows, both of *Sangamon*'s aircraft elevators were blown off their mountings by exploding ordnance. The only functional radio on board the ship at this time was in the last surviving aircraft – a Hellcat parked adjacent to the island superstructure with most of its starboard wing missing. *(NARA)*

with the exception of the skipper, Capt Maurice E. Browder, his orderly, the ship's navigator, and the helmsman. By 1955hrs all communications and control from the bridge had been lost, which left varying the speed of the engines as the only means to steer until control was reestablished at 2015hrs. The fire threatened armed and fueled aircraft on the flightdeck aft, and the decision was made to jettison them all by means of lines attached to a screening destroyer. A total of 16 perfectly serviceable aircraft were sent over the side this way, while the magazines were flooded to prevent a catastrophic explosion.

The raging fires had been extinguished by 2200hrs with the help of surrounding ships, although radio equipment and radar gear were still inoperable – hand signals, searchlights, and the radios of a damaged Hellcat still on the flightdeck were the only way the ship could communicate with the outside world. *Sangamon*, which had had 36 crew killed and 21 seriously wounded, returned to Kerama Retto for emergency repairs, before heading to Ulithi, Pearl Harbor, and then on to Norfolk Navy Yard for an overhaul. Work on repairing the carrier was halted with the end of the war and the vessel was decommissioned in late October 1945.

There was no tokko activity on May 5, but in the predawn hours of the following day the IJAAF despatched "Oscars" from the 49th and 51st Shinbu-tai (three and one aircraft, respectively), while the 55th and 56th Shinbu-tai sortied three and four "Tonys" each. The fighters took off from Chiran and Bansei, on Kyushu. At 0823hrs, what was almost certainly one of the Ki-43s (although it was identified as a "Zeke") found the 2,175-ton survey ship USS *Pathfinder* (AGS-1) as it worked alone in the northern waters of Sesoko Harbor off Okinawa's Motobu Peninsula. The fighter crashed into the vessel's capstan and rear 76mm gun, killing one sailor and starting fires that set off ready ammunition. Fortuitously, however, the bomb carried by the tokko failed to explode.

Twelve minutes later, the 12,610-ton seaplane tender USS *St. George* (AV-16) was at anchor at Kerama Retto when aircraft mechanic Louis (Jack) Norvelle Tickle spotted a "Tony" just before it made an attack run on the ship. The Ki-61 crashed into a Martin PBM Mariner flying boat positioned on the aft seaplane deck, before being swung around onto the main deck. Three crew were killed by the tokko and the ship's seaplane crane was wrecked, although the vessel was otherwise lightly damaged and remained on station. A barge crane was employed to lift seaplanes

On May 6, 1945, the seaplane tender USS *St. George* (AV-16) was at anchor in Kerama Retto when a lone Ki-61 from either the 55th or 56th Shinbu-tai suddenly made an attack run on the ship. The "Tony" hit a Martin PBM Mariner flying boat positioned on the aft seaplane deck, before crashing into the main deck. Three sailors were killed by the tokko and the ship's seaplane crane was wrecked. This photograph was taken from the seaplane tender USS *Chandeleur* (AV-10), which was also anchored in Kerama Retto. *(NARA)*

that needed repairing onto its aft deck. *St. George* also oversaw the emergency repairs carried out on numerous destroyers and destroyer escorts that sought refuge at Kerama Retto after being damaged by tokko.

Bad weather curtailed the activities of the tokko on May 7 and 8, but an improvement in conditions, along with renewed strikes on Sakishima Gunto by the British Pacific Fleet on the 9th, brought out Formosa-based aircraft yet again. TF 57's carriers were located by a high-flying reconnaissance aircraft just before noon, and having managed to avoid interception by the Seafire CAP, it radioed coordinates for the vessels back to Formosa. By 1500hrs four "Zekes" from the 18th Taigi-tai, led by Ens Junsai Kurose, were on their way from Giran. These were detected at 1645hrs some 24 nautical miles from the fleet and intercepted by Seafires while still 13 nautical miles out.

The British fighters were only able to shoot down one of the tokko, with the surviving "Zekes" also managing to dodge yet more Seafires encountered closer to the carriers before undertaking their final attack runs. Two of the IJNAF fighters hit the flightdeck of *Victorious*, the first soon after 1650hrs and the second six minutes later, while at 1705hrs another struck *Formidable*.

Despite all three surviving "Zekes" having successfully attacked TF 57, once again the aircraft had inflicted little lasting damage on the carriers thanks to the effectiveness of their armored flightdecks. Furthermore, only three crew were killed on *Victorious* and one on *Formidable*. The former also lost four Corsairs that were parked on the deck to the second

ABOVE
Renewed strikes on Sakishima Gunto by the British Pacific Fleet on May 9, 1945 brought out Formosa-based tokko yet again, with three of four "Zekes" sortied by the 18th Taigi-tai finding their targets when two hit *Victorious* and one struck *Formidable*. This photograph was taken on the latter carrier just minutes after it had been hit, with fires raging among aircraft ranged aft and the flightdeck strewn with debris from the "Zeke." According to the ship's Action Damage Report, "the aircraft crashed on the flightdeck slightly to starboard of the centre line, abreast the after end of the Island, at 1709, and was disintegrated. It was a single-engined aircraft. It carried what appeared to be overload tanks under each wing and either a 250lb bomb or a heavy shell which only detonated partially on hitting the flight deck." (© IWM A 29313)

ABOVE LEFT
Formidable's Action Damage Report also provided details on how the fires on the flightdeck were dealt with. "With the fires on deck, the ship was maneuvered to bring the wind on the starboard side and speed was reduced to 15 knots until the fires were under control. Those were tackled by the Flight Deck Fire Parties using foam only, and were under control by 1725hrs and finally extinguished ten minutes later. As the fire was exceptionally fierce (two of the Corsairs had full drop tanks), it was considered that the hot deck might cause a major fire in the hangar below, and at 1710hrs the order was given to spray 'C' Hangar. This was smoothly carried out." (© IWM A 29314)

ABOVE RIGHT
This Corsair II was one of six aircraft destroyed on the flightdeck of *Formidable* on May 9. A further five Corsairs and Avengers were also damaged to varying degrees, the fire that consumed the aircraft being fueled by full drop tanks hung beneath two of the fighters that were hit by the lone "Zeke" or by shrapnel from its exploding bomb. Aside from the destroyed aircraft, the carrier's armored flightdeck had been left relatively unscathed by the impact of the tokko. (© IWM A 29725)

hit, while the explosion of the first aircraft opened up a small hole on the flightdeck and destroyed one of its two catapults. Once the hole was patched over the carrier resumed flight operations at 1830hrs. *Formidable*, meanwhile, had had six Corsairs and Avengers destroyed and five more damaged on the flightdeck, which had otherwise been left unscathed by the impact of the tokko beyond a dent and some blistering and charring.

Taking advantage of the improved conditions on May 9, the Formosa-based tokko-tai also launched sorties against ships off Okinawa. That evening, the destroyer escort USS *Oberrender* (DE-344) was on screening duties midway between Kerama Retto and Ie Shima when, at 1850hrs, an aircraft that its crew had been tracking on radar appeared out of the darkening western sky in a dive towards the ship. Return fire set its engine alight and, eventually, ripped off one of its

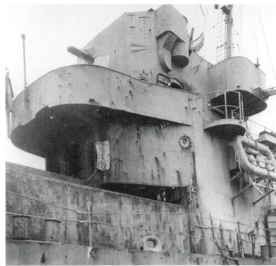

ABOVE
The destroyer escort USS *England* (DE-635) enters Philadelphia Navy Yard in July 1945 for repairs – that were never carried out – after being struck by a bomb-laden "Val" from the Shinten-tai off Okinawa on May 9, 1945. DE-635 was a famed submarine-killer, sinking six Japanese submarines in 12 days in the South Pacific during May 1944. *(NARA)*

ABOVE RIGHT
A close-up of *England*'s damaged bridge, which also boasts a detailed scoreboard of its anti-submarine and antiaircraft record – the latter comprises one twin- and two single-engined tokko. The Formosa-based "Val" clipped the ship's starboard boat davit and spun into the forward superstructure, spraying the bridge and three-inch guns with shrapnel and fuel as it exploded. A total of 37 crew were killed and 25 wounded. Shortly after VJ Day, the US Navy decided that the vessel was not worth repairing and the destroyer escort was decommissioned in October 1945 and scrapped a year later. *(NARA)*

wings, but parts of the disintegrating fighter, which it identified as a "Zeke," still managed to hit the ship.

Unfortunately for the destroyer escort, those parts included its bomb, which tore into the forward fireroom and exploded. The detonation instantly knocked out both of DE-344's engines and started a raging fire, although this was eventually extinguished and the ship towed to Kerama Retto. Eight crew had been killed and 54 wounded in the attack, which had left the vessel so badly damaged that the US Navy decided *Oberrender* was beyond repairing and decommissioned it in July. Stripped of all worthwhile equipment, the hulk was sunk as a gunnery target four months later.

The destroyer escort *England* was also on screening duty further south off the northwestern coast of Kerama Retto that same evening when, at 1854hrs, lookouts sighted several aircraft closing in from the west that had previously been tracked on radar. The lead bogey was identified as a "Val,"

DESPERATE SUNSET

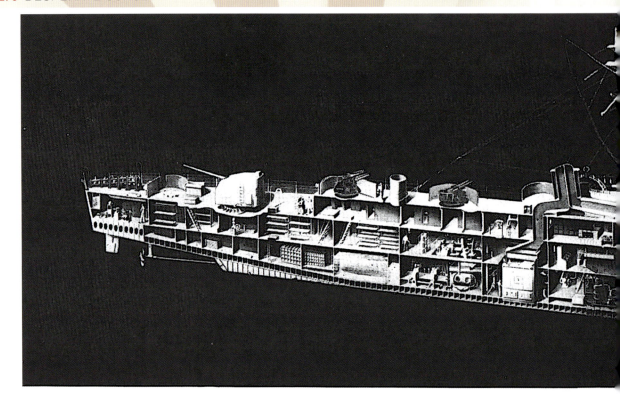

1—STEERING GEAR ROOM
2—CREW'S BERTHING
3—40MM AMMUNITION MAGAZINE
4—PASSAGE
5—CREW'S BERTHING
6—DEPTH CHARGE PISTOL STOWAGE
7—STOREROOM
8—AMMUNITION HANDLING ROOM
9—STOREROOM
10—CREW'S BERTHING
11—STOREROOM
12—40MM AMMUNITION
13—PASSAGE AND VENT SPACE
14—CREW'S W.C.
15—CREW'S BERTHINNG
16—SERVICE FUEL OIL
17—CONTAMINATED OIL
18—CREW'S WASHROOM
19—PASSAGE
20—PASSAGE
21—PASSAGE
22—AFT ENGINEROOM
23—AFT ENGINEROOM
24—GENERAL WORKSHOP
25—UPTAKE SPACE
26—AFT FIREROOM
27—AFT FIREROOM
28—SHIP'S ENGINEER'S OFFICE
29—VENT
30—FORWARD ENGINEROOM
31—FORWARD ENGINEROOM
32—UPTAKE SPACE
33—CODING ROOM
34—UPTAKE SPACE
35—RADIO ROOM
36—GALLEY
37—FORWARD FIREROOM
38—FORWARD FIREROOM
39—PILOT HOUSE
40—PASSAGE
41—RIFLE AND PISTOL LOCKER
42—CAPTAIN'S BATH
43—PANTRY
44—SCULLERY
45—SERVICE FUEL OIL
47—WARDROOM MESSROOM
48—CREW'S MESSING AND BERTHING
49—PASSAGE
50—SERVICE FUEL
51—GYRO I.C. ROOM
52—FUEL OIL OR BALLAST

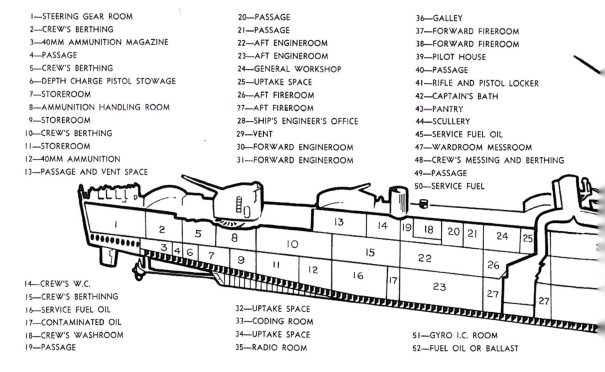

OKINAWA 277

53—WARDROOM STATEROOM
54—PASSAGE
55—PASSAGE
56—FUEL OIL OR BALLAST
57—CONTROL ROOM
58—CREW'S MESSING AND BERTHING
59—FRUITS AND VEGETABLES
60—STOREROOM
61—MEAT ROOM
62—STOREROOM
63—C.P.O. QUARTERS
64—SUPPLY DEPARTMENT STORES
65—STOREROOM
66—STOREROOM
67—5-INCH/38 HANDLING ROOM
68—SUPPLY DEPARTMENT STORES
69—STOREROOM
70—MANIFOLD AND PORTABLE PUMP STATION
71—PAINT AND INFLAMMABLE LIQUID STOREROOM
72—RODMETER COMPARTMENT
73—PASSAGE
74—UNDERWATER SOUND ROOM NO. 1
75—UNDERWATER SOUND ROOM NO. 2
76—CHAIN LOCKER
77—PEAK TANK
78—WINDLASS ROOM
79—BOATSWAIN'S STORES
80—BOATSWAIN'S STORES AND LAMP ROOM
81—PEAK TANK

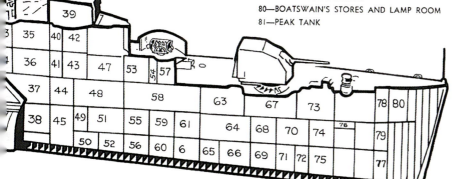

This US Navy cutaway artwork shows the inner workings of a John C. Butler-class destroyer escort, 83 of which were built. Among the latter was USS *Oberrender* (DE-344), which was struck in the forward fireroom (labeled 37 and 38 in this artwork) by a bomb from a "Zeke" tokko during the evening of May 9, 1945 while the vessel was on screening duties midway between Kerama Retto and Ie Shima. The ship's gunners had managed to down the fighter before it hit DE-344, but parts of the aircraft and, critically, the bomb still struck the vessel. When the ordnance exploded it knocked out both engines and started a raging fire that left *Oberrender* badly damaged. Indeed, the US Navy decided it was beyond repairing. *(NARA)*

"Zeke" vs Carrier

This tokko pilot has put himself in a perfect position to strike a serious blow against the US Navy with his bomb-armed "Zeke." The target below him is an Essex-class carrier whose crew has been late in spotting the suicide aircraft making a diving attack – the IJNAF pilot may have used cloud cover to mask his approach, or closed on the carrier at wave-top height before pulling up into a steep climb and then bunting over into his death dive.

   The ship's antiaircraft gunners have begun to engage the "Zeke" with 20mm and 40mm cannon, as well as a handful of 5in./38 rounds (two twin mounts flanked either side of the carrier's island), but at this late stage in the attack it is very doubtful that this will stop the tokko from striking the vessel. Indeed, if the Zero-sen pilot does not flinch at the last moment, he will hit the ship. If skilful enough, he will release his 551lb bomb before striking the carrier as close to the rear aircraft elevator as possible – one of the vulnerable spots he has been trained to hit. Given the large number of aircraft spotted on the flightdeck, all of which are probably fully fueled and armed, ready for their next launch cycle, this carrier is about to receive serious damage that could threaten the ship itself. (*Artwork by Jim Laurier, © Osprey Publishing*)

which carried out a gliding dive on the vessel. Despite being severely damaged by antiaircraft fire, the tokko clipped the ship's forward boat davit with its port wing, which swung the rest of it into the superstructure. The single weapon being carried by the dive-bomber blew up and the usual conflagration followed, killing 37 crew and wounding 25 before the fires had been extinguished and the ship towed to Kerama Retto.

England eventually made it back to Philadelphia Navy Yard in mid-July 1945, but as with *Oberrender*, it was decided the vessel was not worth repairing and the destroyer escort was decommissioned in October and scrapped a year later. This was a seemingly ignominious end for a ship that had previously achieved the unparalleled exploit of sinking six enemy submarines in the space of 12 days in May 1944 during operations in the Southwest Pacific – a feat of arms for which the ship had received a Presidential Unit Citation.

The three "Vals" that *England* had encountered were almost certainly the trio of aircraft from the Shinten-tai that had been led aloft from Giran by Lt(jg) Takashi Katayama at 1630hrs on May 9. Other than the aircraft that struck DE-635, the remaining two D3As were shot down by CAP fighters as they attempted to follow the lead "Val" in the attack on the destroyer escort.

No "Zekes" were assigned to the tokko-tai that targeted ships around Okinawa that day, so the aircraft credited with knocking *Oberrender* out of the war was either a "Judy" from the Chusei-tai or a "Frank" from the Sei 33rd, 34th, or 35th Hikotai, all of which sent out single aircraft from Taichu. The Chusei-tai had sortied a pair of "Judys" from Giran at 1550hrs, placing them near Okinawa at the time *Oberrender* was hit. IJAAF records do not state the takeoff times of the "Franks," however, making it impossible to determine if they too could have been responsible for the attack.

Despite IJAAF and IJNAF claims for a significant number of Allied ships sunk or damaged through tokko attacks, the Japanese high command could find no evidence that the American hold on Okinawa was weakening. To the contrary, US forces appeared to be expanding the number of airfields on the island and bringing in more land-based air support. The Combined Fleet Headquarters hastily ordered a renewed effort against shipping off Okinawa supporting the invasion in the form of Kikusui No. 6. A significant problem now facing the Japanese was the declining number of fighters available to escort the tokko to Okinawa.

For this new offensive, which would start on May 10, the IJNAF prepared a mixed force of 18 "Judys" and 26 "Zekes" from the 721st Kokutai for an

B6N2 131-64 of the Kikusui-Tenzan Kokutai (formerly 131st Kokutai), Kanoya airfield, Kyushu, May 1945

The B6N2 proved to be very effective in the tokko role thanks to its speed, range, and ability to carry either a torpedo (this aircraft is depicted with a Type 91 air-dropped weapon) or bomb(s). At least eight "Jill"-equipped kokutai formed tokko units, most of which flew from airfields on Kyushu. B6N2s armed with Type 91s routinely carried out lone attacks at dusk, rather than participating in massed Kikusui operations. *(Artwork by Jim Laurier, © Osprey Publishing)*

"Valencia's Flying Circus" was the name Hellcat-equipped VF-9 gave to Lt Eugene Valencia's division on board *Yorktown*. High-scoring ace Valencia had trained the members of his division in his own mutually supportive tactics, which proved highly effective. The division claimed a combined total of 36.5 victories during the Okinawa campaign (20 of these claims came during two missions on May 4 and May 11) and a wartime total of 50, the majority of them tokko. These pilots are, from left to right, Lt(jg)s Harris Mitchell, Clifton Smith, James French, and Lt Eugene Valencia. *(NARA)*

attack on the carrier groups (in the event only the fighters participated in the mission). A second combined force consisting of ten "Jills" from the Kikusui Raio-tai, six P1Y2-S "Frances" nightfighters from the 9th Ginga-tai, five "Zekes," two reconnaissance seaplanes (an "Alf" and a "Jake"), and four Ohka-carrying "Bettys" from the Jinrai Butai would target shipping around Okinawa. The escorts for both formations were 65 "Zekes" from the 203rd and 252nd Kokutai, along with a handful of other fighters from several unidentified units. The IJAAF's 6th Army Air Force committed seven "Peggy" bombers, with 15 "Franks" as escort, and 36 single-seat fighters ("Oscars," "Nates," "Tonys," and "Franks") drawn from 12 tokko-tai.

Only a small number of missions appear to have been flown on the first day of the new offensive, with the destroyer USS *Brown* (DD-546) being the sole vessel to suffer any damage. The ship was performing screening duties west of Okinawa when an aircraft was sighted closing on its starboard quarter just above the wave tops at 0843hrs. This was taken under fire and shot down shortly thereafter at close range. Three minutes later, another aircraft was sighted on the starboard beam following a similar flight profile and it too was shot down. Both aircraft were

BELOW
On the morning of May 11, 1945, USS *Evans* (DD-552) came under a sustained attack while manning Radar Picket Station RP 15 with USS *Hugh W. Hadley* (DD-774). Fighting for their lives for more than an hour, the crew on board *Evans* reported that the ship was targeted by "Oscars," "Jills," "Tonys," "Kates," and "Vals." *Evans* was hit four times, while the *Hugh W. Hadley* endured bomb, tokko, and Ohka strikes. In return, gunners from *Hugh W. Hadley* claimed 12 tokko destroyed and *Evans* 19. *Evans* had had 32 crew killed and 27 wounded, while *Hugh W. Hadley*'s complement suffered 30 fatalities. *(NARA)*

identified as "Jills," and a subsequent search of the water where they had crashed yielded the bodies of three Japanese airmen and other debris.

Assuming the three naval aviators were recovered from the same tokko, allied with the fact that no attempt was made by either aircraft to drop torpedoes, it would suggest that the attackers targeting *Brown* were two B6Ns from the Kikusui Raio-tai. These aircraft had been led aloft from Kushira by Lt(jg) Saburo Umetani at 0500hrs, each "Jill" being armed with a single 1,764lb bomb.

The following day saw a much larger force of aircraft sent against Allied ships off Okinawa. As usual, the attackers had to run a gauntlet of defending American fighters despite the presence of "Zeke" and "Frank" escorts. During a morning CAP off Kikaijima Island, Corsair pilots Lts Doris "Chico" Freeman and John M. Smith from VF-84, embarked in *Bunker Hill*, encountered a substantial force of "Nates" and quickly claimed seven destroyed, along with a single "Oscar." The Ki-27s were from the 65th, 70th, 76th, and 78th Shinbu-tai and the Sei 41st Hikotai, which had combined to sortie 11 aircraft from Chiran between 0635hrs and 0641hrs.

Despite proving little more than cannon fodder for the Corsairs, some of the obsolete fixed-undercarriage fighters appear to have reached their targets, for the destroyer USS *Evans* (DD-552) reported being attacked by "Vals" despite none being utilized as tokko that day. The vessel was manning Radar Picket Station 15 with USS *Hugh W. Hadley* (DD-774) when the two destroyers came under constant attack for more than an hour by what *Evans* reported were "Oscars," "Jills," "Tonys," "Kates," and "Vals." Both ships were badly damaged but survived, with DD-552 being struck four times by aircraft and DD-774 being hit by a bomb, two aircraft, and an Ohka.

The ships' gunners had mounted a stout defense, aided by the Japanese pilots' decision to conduct individual attacks that allowed each vessel to mass its firepower on successive targets. *Hugh W. Hadley* claimed 12 kamikazes destroyed and *Evans* 19. The latter ship had had 32 crew killed and 27 wounded, while *Hugh W. Hadley*'s complement suffered 30 fatalities. Although neither destroyer had been sunk, they were both declared constructive total losses after being towed back to San Francisco and subsequently scrapped.

One of the best-known strikes of the entire tokko campaign – the attack on TF 58's flagship, *Bunker Hill* – took place on this day. In addition to Lts Freeman and Brown whittling down the "Nate" force earlier that morning, other *Bunker Hill* pilots were also heavily involved in countering

OPPOSITE
Essex-class carriers proved very resilient to bomb and tokko damage. Here, *Bunker Hill* burns following the successful attacks of Lt(jg) Seizo Yasunori and Ens Kiyoshi Ogawa from the 7th Showa-tai on May 11, 1945. The attack resulted in the highest casualty toll on board a US Navy ship as the result of a tokko attack, with almost 400 killed – including 22 pilots from Corsair-equipped VF-84, who were burned or suffocated below decks following the attack and resulting fire.

the participants of Kikusui No. 6. Several of the Corsair pilots had returned, and were in their ready rooms, when, at 1005hrs, a pair of "Zekes" flown by Lt(jg) Seizo Yasunori and Ens Kiyoshi Ogawa took the carrier by surprise and slammed into its flightdeck. The two pilots were part of the group of six A6M5s from the 7th Showa-tai that had been led aloft from Kanoya by Yasunori at between 0640hrs and 0653hrs, each toting a single 1,102lb Type 2 No. 50 Model 1 Ordinary Bomb.

The first "Zeke," flown by Yasunori, plowed through the 34 fully fueled and armed F4Us and SB2Cs of VF-84 and VB-84, respectively, ranged on the flightdeck ready for their next mission. The IJNAF fighter destroyed a number of them before sliding over the side, while Ogawa's aircraft crashed through the flightdeck and exploded in the hangar bay. The resulting conflagration gutted the hangar bay and other spaces below, killing 393 crew and wounding a further 264 from its complement of 2,600 – the highest number of casualties suffered as a result of a tokko attack. Among those killed were "Chico" Freeman and 21 other pilots from VF-84, who were either burned or suffocated when the fire started by the detonation of Ogawa's bomb swept through the squadron's ready room.

Both "Zeke" pilots had dropped their bombs before crashing into *Bunker Hill*, although Yasunori's weapon tore through the ship and exploded relatively harmlessly to one side of the carrier. Ogawa and his fighter were found relatively untouched by the fire, which allowed both his identification and the retrieval of his personal effects, thus enabling the accurate attribution of the deadly attack.

OPPOSITE
Four bomb-equipped "Zekes" of the Kanoya-based 7th Showa-tai had found TF 58 without being detected by radar. With their approach masked by low cloud cover, the pilots used the element of surprise to attack *Bunker Hill* – the "Zekes" of Yasunori and Ogawa struck the ship within 30 seconds of each other. The intense black smoke indicates that fully fueled aircraft on the flightdeck have been set ablaze, and that the crew's epic efforts to save their ship have begun. *(NARA)*

Its stacks marked with shamrocks, the destroyer USS *The Sullivans* (DD-537) stands by to render assistance to *Bunker Hill* shortly after it was hit. *The Sullivans* duly closed up with the carrier and picked up 166 members of its crew who had been forced over the side when the fires on board the ship were burning out of control. *(NARA)*

Kiyoshi Ogawa

Born on October 23, 1922 in Usui District (now known as Takasaki City), Gunma Prefecture, Kiyoshi Ogawa was the youngest child in his family. He was subsequently educated at the private Waseda University, located on the northern side of Tokyo's Shinjuku Ward, and after graduation he became a gakuto (a college student who was later a soldier or officer during his academic years). Ogawa received his military instruction as part of the 14th Class of Naval Flight Reserve Students, with basic training at Takeyama and subsequent flying training taking place at Tsuchiura and Yatabe, in Ibaraki Prefecture.

Following graduation, he was commissioned and assigned to the A6M5-equipped 306th Hikotai of the 721st Kokutai at Kanoya. Here, Ogawa volunteered for his fateful tokko mission, writing in his last letter to his parents, "Beyond those boundless white clouds, I will make my attack with a calm feeling. Not even thoughts of life and death will come to mind. A person dies once. It will be an honorable day to live for the eternal cause."

Also targeted that day were the destroyer USS *Douglas H. Fox* (DD-779), the destroyer minelayer *Harry F. Bauer*, and four support ships, all of which were manning Radar Picket Station 5 due west of Okinawa. In fact, these vessels were engaged by tokko before Radar Picket Station 15 had come under sustained attack. Four aircraft were spotted at 0800hrs, and *Harry F. Bauer* narrowly avoided being struck by one of them. *LCS(L)(3)-88* was bombed by another tokko, the vessel having its commanding officer, Lt C. L. Bigos, killed. DM-26's after action report noted that its attackers were "Zekes," while *LCS(L)(3)-88*'s crew identified

The May 11, 1945 attack on *Bunker Hill* was the closest the tokko would come to sinking a US Navy fleet carrier. The first "Zeke" hit aft, creating havoc among the F4U Corsairs from VF-84 and the SB2C-3 Helldivers from VB-84 that were parked in rows here ready for their next mission. The pilot released his bomb prior to striking the carrier, and after penetrating parts of the ship, it exploded, causing horrendous casualties to exposed personnel. The second "Zeke" struck the base of the island, the bomb from this aircraft penetrating as far as the gallery deck (between the flightdeck and hangar deck) prior to exploding. The bomb started a fire in the hangar among the aircraft that were parked there, and this blaze, combined with the one raging on the flightdeck, came close to destroying the ship. (© *HU 51238*)

them as "Oscars." Signalman Arthur R. Martin wrote the following account of the attack on the latter vessel:

> On our second radar picket patrol, in company with USS *Douglas H. Fox* (DD-779), USS *Harry F. Bauer* (DM-26) and *LCS(L)(3)-52*, *LCS(L)(3)-109* and *LCS(L)(3)-114*, we encountered an attack on May 11, 1945 involving one Japanese "Betty" bomber and four "Oscar" single-engined fighters. In this attack, we assisted in splashing one of the latter planes, but another one circled our picket patrol and sneaked in on us. During this attack, our 20mm gunner clipped off his wing, which diverted his line of attack and subsequently sent him on into our fantail section. Our aft twin 40mm finally hit him point blank, splashing him, but the explosion (or the skill of the Japanese pilot) enabled a 200lb bomb to drop from the plane, hitting the aft end of the ship. This explosion resulted in the loss of nine men killed and seven injured. All men on the gun that splashed him were killed.
>
> We had our steering disabled, along with a severely damaged aft end. We also had a dangerous fire aboard that was extinguished by the very able leadership of our Engineering Officer, Lt(jg) White. All hands concurred that this officer certainly deserved a citation for his personal bravery. Because of the loss of our captain in the attack, nobody proceeded to single him out for a decoration.
>
> We were towed into Kerama Retto harbor, the location of all damaged ships – there were many here at this stage of the war. We tied up alongside a badly damaged destroyer, where we stayed for about a month, until our departure for

A wounded sailor is transferred from *Bunker Hill* to the light cruiser USS *Wilkes-Barre* (CL-103), Capt Robert L. Porter having brought his warship alongside the burning carrier *Bunker Hill* at 1115hrs (just over an hour after the vessel had been hit). He placed *Wilkes-Barre*'s bow hard against CV-17's starboard quarter, shortly after which the cruiser took on persistent fires with ten separate streams of water while 40 men, trapped astern in *Bunker Hill*, scrambled to safety down onto CL-103's deck. *Wilkes-Barre* also transferred firefighting gear, rescue breathing apparatus, and "handy-billies" (portable pumps) to *Bunker Hill* in exchange for the carrier's wounded and dying. At 1534hrs, when the fires on board CV-17 had finally been brought under control and the cruiser's assistance was no longer required, *Wilkes-Barre* cleared the blackened carrier. *(NARA)*

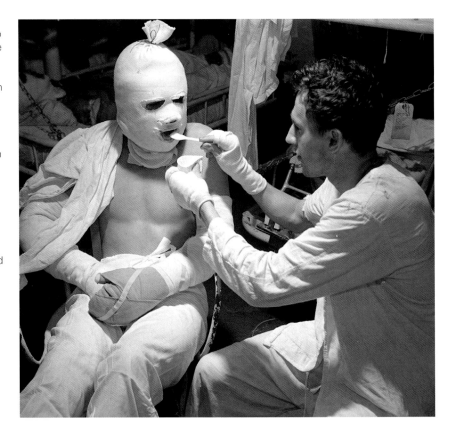

A sailor with minor burns to his hands feeds a shipmate with his head and arms in pressure bandages after they had suffered fuel "flash fire" burns when their ship was hit by a tokko during May 1945. Ignited aviation fuel from crashed aircraft, or fighters and bombers on the flightdeck of carriers, exacted a heavy toll on Allied seamen during the tokko campaign. These patients were photographed on board the hospital ship USS *Solace* (AH-5), which joined the invasion fleet for Okinawa at Ulithi Atoll in mid-March 1945. It subsequently arrived at Kerama Retto on the 27th of that same month and commenced receiving patients from various tokko-hit ships shortly thereafter. Over the next three months, the ship evacuated seven loads of casualties (totaling more than 400 patients per evacuation) to the Mariana Islands. *(NARA)*

Saipan. From there we went to Eniwetok, and subsequently to Pearl Harbor, where we were told we would get repaired.

Having lost his flagship, TF 58 commander Vice-Admiral Marc A. Mitscher transferred his flag to *Enterprise* and headed north to launch two days (May 13–14) of attacks on the tokko airfields in southern Kyushu in yet another effort to reduce this persistent threat. The day before this 48-hour blitz, a solitary "Kate" from the Kushira-based 3rd Seiki-tai that took off at 0500hrs was the only tokko listed in IJNAF records to have originated from Kyushu. The aircraft and crew were drawn from the Hyakurihara Kokutai, with Ens Tokukazu Odagiri and Shoji Horie and PO Shosaku Murata manning the torpedo-bomber.

However, at least one other B5N took off that morning on a tokko mission, as reported in a story published in *The Japan Times* in 2015. Takehiko Ena, who, like the aforementioned aircraft and crew, originally hailed from the Hyakurihara Kokutai, told of how he had to ditch his aircraft near uninhabited Kuroshima Island just south of Kyushu when its engine failed soon after departing from Kushira. The three-man crew duly spent more than two months there before being rescued by an IJN submarine. That was in fact Ena's second attempt at a tokko attack, for on April 28 (presumably while serving with the 1st Seiki-tai) he had had to abort a mission due to technical problems with his "Kate." Ena, therefore, had the possibly unique distinction of having survived two tokko missions.

With TF 58's targeted strikes on airfields on Kyushu virtually halting attacks on ships off Okinawa, it fell to Formosa-based tokko-tai to continue with the offensive. On May 12 two of these, the Sei 120th and 123rd Hikotai, sent a pair of "Franks" and a "Nick," respectively, to Okinawa in search of enemy warships. The Ki-84s were flown by Sgt Mitsuo Hagino and Cpl Kazufumi Tokyoku, with the latter being noteworthy as he was an ethnic Korean pilot. During the course of this mission he became one of more than 21,000 ethnic Koreans to die fighting for Imperial Japan, and whose sacrifice is now honored in the Honden building within the controversial Yasukuni Shrine – the latter commemorates those who died in the service of Japan.

The pair were almost certainly the tokko who spotted the battleship *New Mexico* entering the Hagushi Beaches anchorage soon after sunset. Its crew identified them as a "George" and a "Frank" and shot the lead aircraft down into the sea. Taking advantage of the antiaircraft fire being directed at his leader's Ki-84, the wingman managed to breech the battleship's defenses and slam into its starboard 20mm gun tubs and funnel. The crash and subsequent explosion of the "Frank's" bomb damaged BB-40's superstructure, put three of its nine boilers out of action, and started several fires. Having suffered heavy casualties when struck by a tokko off the Philippines on January 6, 1945, *New Mexico*'s 1,100-strong crew again experienced a significant loss of life – 54 killed (and 119 wounded) – following this attack.

With Kyushu's airfields targeted by TF 58's strikes on May 13, it was again left to the Formosa-based tokko to keep up the pressure on the invasion fleet off Okinawa. That afternoon, six "Judys" of the Chusei-tai took off from Giran at 1530hrs and headed northeast. They were joined by three "Sonias" from the Sei 31st Hikotai and three "Oscars" from the Sei 26th Hikotai, both units being based at Hattoku.

The latter could have been the pair of aircraft shot down by the destroyer escort USS *Bright* (DE-747) at 1919hrs as it performed anti-submarine screening duties midway between Okinawa and Aguni-jima.

ABOVE
Two famous photographs of an A6M5, its starboard horizontal stabilizer and part of its rudder shot away by antiaircraft fire, plummeting towards the sea near *Essex* on the morning of May 14, 1945 as the US Navy fast carriers mounted a 48-hour offensive against known airfields on Kyushu. This fighter could be one of those from the 6th Tsukuba-tai, 8th Shichisei-tai, or 11th Kenmu-tai that sortied that morning. *(NARA)*

The first of these fighters, which the crew identified as "Zekes," disintegrated from the ship's fire as it bore in. Nevertheless, the aircraft was close enough for its wing and attached bomb to carry on and strike DE-747's fantail, the resulting explosion destroying its aft steering room and jamming the rudder hard left. Although casualties were light, with only two men wounded, the vessel had to be towed to Kerama Retto for emergency repairs to be effected, before being sent home to Portland, Oregon, for a more thorough overhaul.

Also hit that evening was the destroyer *Bache* at Radar Picket Station 9 – the same location where the ship had escaped serious damage just ten days earlier. It was approached by a tokko force that the destroyer's radar operators estimated consisted of 12 aircraft, including seaplanes that were identified as Mitsubishi F1M "Petes" and at least one twin-engined bomber. Although most were shot

Lt(jg) Shunsuke Tomiyasu of the 6th Tsukuba-tai utilizes a diving profile to attack his target, the carrier *Enterprise*, on May 14, 1945 during TF 58's two-day offensive against Kyushu. When a ship was struck by a tokko, the most severe damage was caused by the explosion of the bomb (in this case a highly destructive 1,102lb Type 2 No. 50 Model 1 Ordinary Bomb), not by the impact of the aircraft. The ship was struck aft of the forward elevator and knocked out of the war. *(Tony Holmes collection)*

TOP LEFT
The resulting explosion from Tomiyasu's 1,102lb bomb blew *Enterprise*'s forward elevator 400ft into the air – it can clearly be seen atop the column of smoke rising from CV-6's flightdeck. The weapon also killed 12 crew and wounded 72. Although the veteran carrier's machinery escaped the attack unscathed, allowing it to steam as normal, the ship's ability to conduct flight operations was compromised and two days later it headed for Puget Sound Navy Yard to be repaired. *(NARA)*

LEFT
The attack on *Enterprise* was witnessed by other TF 58 carriers in the immediate vicinity, with this photograph being taken from *Essex* as the vessels were underway east of Tanegashima, in the Osumi Islands. *Essex* had enjoyed better luck when it was targeted by at least one of the 28 "Zekes" sortied from Kanoya between 0525hrs and 0630hrs that morning. *(NARA)*

down by CAP fighters, at 1850hrs *Bache* was hit by one of three "Vals" that managed to break through and attack the warship. It would be tempting to attribute this attack to the "Sonias" of the Sei 31st Hikotai, although with the information available it is not possible to say so with any degree of certainty.

The aircraft struck near the vessel's after stack, catapulting the tokko down onto the main deck amidships. Its solitary bomb exploded seven feet above the main deck, killing 41 crew and wounding 32. Despite all steam and electrical power being lost, damage control parties managed to extinguish several fires within 20 minutes of the destroyer being hit.

Shunsuke Tomiyasu

A mistranslation of the identity documents found on Shunsuke Tomiyasu's body, which was recovered on board *Enterprise* after he had hit it on May 14, 1945, meant that for years he was mistakenly referred to as "Tomi Zai" until research by historian and translator Kan Sugahara uncovered his real identity.

Tomiyasu was a native of Nagasaki, having been born there in 1922, before his family moved to Tokyo when he was six years old. He graduated from Waseda University in March 1943 with a degree in politics and economics and briefly worked in Shinkyo (Changchun), Manchuria, prior to joining the IJN in the 13th Class of Reserve Students in September of that year. Tomiyasu received his flying training on the "Zeke" at Tsukuba airfield and was commissioned as an Ensign in May 1944.

After several transfers and a promotion to lieutenant (junior grade), he was assigned back to the Tsukuba Kokutai on March 1, 1945 as an instructor for the 14th Class of Reserve Students. Tomiyasu volunteered to become a tokko pilot when the Kokutai organized its first such unit on March 28. In his final letter home, he told his family that, "I do not expect to return alive," adding that "I am surely determined to achieve excellent battle results." In his letter, Tomiyasu also beseeched his parents and sister to "live with great enthusiasm and cheerfulness. Worries will cause everyone to be discouraged."

With fire hoses snaking all over *Enterprise*'s flightdeck, damage control parties get to work clearing debris in the wake of Tomiyasu's clinical strike. The gaping hole left by the missing forward elevator immediately ended CV-6's war. Each of the carrier's three elevators was 48ft by 44ft in size and had a lifting capacity of 17,000lb. (NARA)

Bache was towed to Kerama Retto later that evening, prior to being sent to the New York Navy Yard to be repaired.

The IJNAF at last fought back against TF 58 on the morning May 14 when it despatched 28 "Zekes" from Kanoya between 0525hrs and 0630hrs in search of its tormentors. All were equipped with 1,102lb

An unidentified destroyer prepares to retrieve two crewmen from *Enterprise* who were blown overboard when the carrier was hit on May 14. The sailors were spotted standing on a large section of wreckage. *(NARA)*

Type 2 No. 50 Model 1 Ordinary Bombs for increased destructive power, and they were escorted by 40 more A6M5s in a bid to keep TF 58's numerous fighters at bay. Of the 28 tokko that took off, six dropped out for various reasons. Although only one vessel was ultimately hit, it was the flagship of TF 58, the veteran carrier *Enterprise*. At 0657hrs Lt(jg) Shunsuke Tomiyasu of the 6th Tsukuba-tai rolled his "Zeke" onto its back and crashed into the forward flightdeck of CV-6 while the task force was underway east of Tanegashima, in the Osumi Islands.

The resulting explosion from the aircraft's bomb blew *Enterprise*'s forward elevator 400ft into the air. It also killed 12 crew and wounded 72. Although capable of steaming as normal, the ship's ability to conduct flight operations was compromised and it detached from TF 58 two days later and headed for Puget Sound Navy Yard to be repaired. Like many of the ships damaged at this late stage in the war, CV-6 returned to fleet service too late to see any further action.

Radar Picket Station 9 was targeted once again on May 17, with the destroyers USS *Douglas H. Fox* (DD-779) and USS *Van Valkenburgh* (DD-656) and their support vessels coming under a coordinated attack by at least 11 tokko from Formosa shortly before sunset. DD-779's crew claimed five shot down before being hit by one aircraft (and its bomb) and sprayed with fuel from a second machine. Although seven crew were killed and 35 wounded, fires that broke out on board the ship were expeditiously extinguished and effective damage control measures allowed

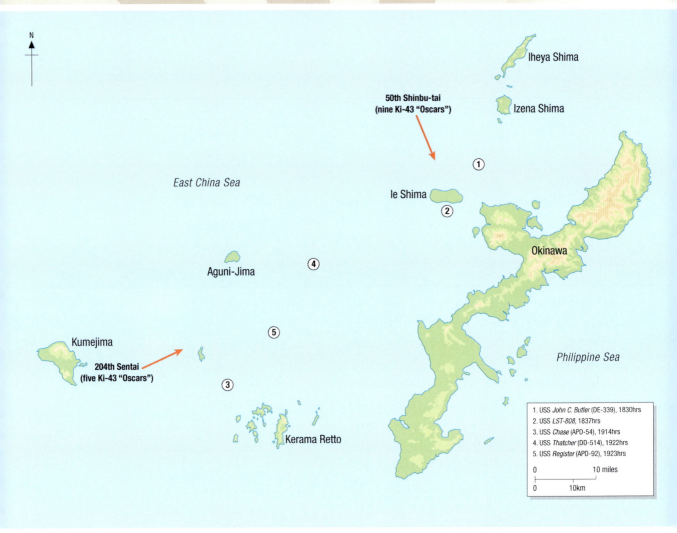

MAP ABOVE
During the evening of May 20, 1945, tokko aircraft from both Kyushu and Formosa were involved in a successful "sandwich" attack on ships west of Okinawa. Nine Ki-43s of the 50th Shinbu-tai took off from Chiran, on Kyushu, at 1603hrs and five more from the 204th Sentai set out from Hattoku, on Formosa, at 1650hrs. All 14 aircraft arrived off Okinawa as sunset approached and quickly commenced their attacks, hitting and damaging five ships.

the destroyer to make it to Kerama Retto under its own power. It later returned to San Francisco for repairs to be effected.

Douglas H. Fox noted in its after action report that three of the ship's attackers were "Vals," with the rest being unidentified, while *Van Valkenburgh*'s crew stated that they had been targeted by a "Jill" and an "Oscar." IJAAF records show that two "Sonias" from the Sei 31st Hikotai and four "Oscars" from the Sei 26th Hikotai were active that day, although their takeoff times from Hattoku and Karenko, respectively, are not known. The IJNAF also sortied a solitary "Judy" from the Chusei-tai, based at Shinchku, although its time of departure was 0415hrs – too early to have participated in the attack at Radar Picket Station 9.

The first notable strike in several days by aircraft from Kyushu occurred on May 18 when eight Ki-43s of the 53rd Shinbu-tai at Chiran took off for Okinawa at 1650hrs. Shortly thereafter, at 1723hrs, 2Lt Kimio Odatsume led three Ki-61s from the 19th Sentai aloft from Giran, on Formosa. Two aircraft from the latter unit found the high-speed transport USS *Sims* (APD-50) screening an area off the west coast of central Okinawa at 1930hrs, and the attackers split up before attempting to dive on the vessel simultaneously from both sides. *Sims* reversed course with a hard turn to port, which placed both aircraft on its port side – one approaching from amidships and the other from astern.

Despite gun crews scoring hits on the "Tonys," their pilots managed to get close to the ship before they were downed near the signal bridge in quick succession. The subsequent explosions lifted and shook *Sims*, rupturing oil and fuel lines (specifically to the forward fireroom) and causing considerable damage to its machinery and radar equipment. Nevertheless, the ship's crew soon had *Sims* operational again to the point where the vessel was able to resume patrolling.

The tokko-tai attempted another "sandwich" attack on ships off Okinawa during the afternoon of May 20, and again aircraft from both Kyushu and Formosa were involved. The 50th Shinbu-tai (which was also known as the Yamabuki-tai) despatched nine Ki-43s from Chiran at 1603hrs under the leadership of 2Lt Kazuo Saito and the 204th Sentai sortied five more "Oscars," led by 2Lt Yoshio Kurihara, from Hattoku at 1650hrs. All 14 aircraft arrived off Okinawa as sunset approached and quickly commenced their attacks, hitting and damaging five ships.

At 1831hrs the destroyer escort USS *John C. Butler* (DE-339) sighted what its crew reported were "eight to ten enemy aircraft flying in small groups approaching from the north." They were mostly identified as "Zekes," although its after action report also conceded that one was "possibly an Oscar." Five of the fighters attacked between 1832hrs and 1840hrs, and the furious antiaircraft barrage put up by the crew accounted for all of them. Two, however, came close enough to clip the vessel's mast and associated antennae. DE-339 also suffered minor shock damage from explosions as the aircraft crashed nearby, resulting in its sound gear for anti-submarine warfare being temporarily knocked out.

The remaining Ki-43s went after shipping off Okinawa and the southern coast of Ie Shima. One of the vessels at the latter location was the 4,080-ton *LST-808*, which had been purposely grounded on a reef to prevent it sinking after being hit by an aerial torpedo two nights before while supplying fresh water and fog oil to the ships assigned picket duty around Okinawa. It had only a skeleton crew on board when, at 1837hrs, an aircraft crashed into the ship's forward superstructure, plunged through the main and boat decks and then exploded on the tank deck. Gutted by the resulting fire, which was only put out close to midnight, *LST-808* was abandoned after being declared beyond repair.

More attacks started developing to the southwest soon after *LST-808* was hit. West of Okinawa, the high-speed troop transports USS *Chase* (APD-54) and USS *Register* (APD-92) and the destroyer USS *Thatcher* (DD-514) were on screening duties some eight nautical miles apart when they were approached by a group of aircraft that was estimated to be ten-strong by the crew of APD-92. All three ships were attacked in quick succession, with *Chase* sustaining shock damage at 1914hrs when a tokko crashed just off the port bow and its bomb or bombs exploded, while *Register* had its kingpost lopped off by its attacker at 1923hrs.

Thatcher was not so fortunate, being hit by an aircraft on its main deck just aft of the superstructure at 1922hrs. Fourteen crew were killed and 53 wounded. The impact left the ship without power or steering control

In addition to LSMs, the other class of ships most often used to support the destroyers at radar picket stations were Landing Craft Support (Large). This photograph shows *LCS(L)(3)-121* and *LCS(L)(3)-123* at sea, and both were attacked from the air while on radar picket duties. The former was damaged by a near miss from a bomb on May 23, 1945. *(NARA)*

from the bridge, knocked out both radars and the gyro-compass, and rendered all external communications inoperable. Once a number of fires had been extinguished, the crew found a 6ft-by-9ft hole between the keel and the bilge. Eventually able to limp into Kerama Retto under its own power, *Thatcher* was placed in the drydock there and repaired sufficiently enough to allow it to rejoin TF 58 on July 13.

Despite the ships' crews unanimously identifying their attackers as "Zekes," they were almost certainly targeted by the two groups of "Oscars" assigned to tokko missions that day. Due to the ships' relative locations and the direction their attackers were traveling when first sighted, the Yamabuki-tai was probably responsible for the attacks on *John C. Butler* and *LST-808*, while it would appear that the 204th Sentai attacked *Chase*, *Register*, and *Thatcher*.

Another lull in the action followed until May 25, when the Japanese launched Kikusui No. 7, which proved to be the last mass kamikaze attack mounted in significant numbers. In preparation for this latest offensive the IJNAF marshaled 65 tokko and the IJAAF 100. Subsequent Kikusui attacks would see a steadily diminishing number of kamikaze aircraft employed. A lack of aircraft, attacks on airfields (between April 17 and May 11 B-29s of the Twentieth Air Force bombed 17 airfields on Kyushu and Shikoku), and poor weather caused the two-week gap between Kikusui No. 6 and this new campaign.

The IJAAF and the IJNAF were now running short of aircraft and pilots for both tokko and conventional missions. The IJNAF in particular was facing a paucity of fighters for air defense and for escort missions. Having been particularly badly hit in the aerial battles on May 11, it had taken the IJNAF more time to prepare aircraft and pilots for the next mass attack.

The first tokko missions of Kikusui No. 7 had actually started on the night of the 24th when eight Kyushu K11W trainer/anti-submarine aircraft from the Shiragiku-tai departed Kanoya between 1926hrs and 1950hrs. The aircraft, which were normally manned by a crew of three, had only their pilots on board for their final missions. IJNAF records indicate that each aircraft carried a single 551lb No. 25 Model 1 Bomb. A few hours later, the high-speed troop transports USS *Barry* (APD-29) and *Sims*, the destroyer escort USS *O'Neill* (DE-188), and the destroyers *Cowell* and USS *Guest* (DD-472) reported encounters with enemy aircraft that attempted to crash into them between 0025hrs and 0230hrs, the vessels sustaining varying degrees of damage.

Ki-84-I "Frank" of the 58th Shinbu-tai, Miyakonojo airfield, Kyushu, May 1945

Manned by pilot graduates from the Akeno Kyodo Hiko Shidan, the 58th Shinbu-tai expended ten Ki-84s in attacks on ships off Okinawa between May 25 and 28, 1945. Although the "Frank" was the best fighter available to the IJAAF from mid-1944, and units equipped with the aircraft often escorted tokko in attacks on ships off Okinawa, it was also eventually used in the kamikaze role following the establishment of several tokko-tai. When flying such missions the "Frank" usually carried a 551lb bomb under one wing and a drop tank under the other. (Artwork by Jim Laurier, © Osprey Publishing)

Barry, on patrol 35 miles northwest of Okinawa when it was targeted, succeeded in shooting down one of its attackers before a second aircraft penetrated its defensive barrage and struck the ship below the bridge. Fuel from the tokko's tanks ignited when its bomb exploded, and the resulting fire was made worse by fuel oil escaping from *Barry*'s ruptured tanks. When fire threatened the forward magazine, which the crew could not reach in order to flood it, the order was given to abandon ship some 40 minutes after the tokko had struck. Although no one had been killed, 28 crew were wounded by shrapnel. APD-29 did not sink, however, thanks to the firefighting efforts of crews from other warships including *Sims*, and the vessel was eventually towed to Kerama Retto. There, the damage it had sustained was deemed to be beyond practicable repair, although as will be noted later in this chapter, *Barry* would still have a part to play in the story of the tokko.

The after action reports of the ships attacked provide further clues to the identity of the aircraft involved, with *Cowell* recovering a cockpit door from the fragments that showered the vessel after a tokko exploded in midair close aboard. *O'Neill* salvaged a window from the wreckage scattered across its superstructure, the crew describing the attacker that exploded or crashed close to the ship shortly after midnight as being "considerably wooden in construction." The K11W had crew access doors built into its fuselage aft of the wing, and the K11W2 anti-submarine variant was made primarily of wood due to worsening material shortages in Japan.

The pilots of VMF-323 sit on the wing of one of the squadron's Corsairs at Yontan. The unit claimed seven "Tojos" shot down on May 25, 1945, but these were almost certainly Ki-84 "Franks" from several tokko-tai that sortied that day with their fighter escorts. *(Tony Holmes collection)*

Some of the ships identified their attackers as "Vals," although none undertook any tokko missions on May 24 or 25. It is again likely that the fixed undercarriage of the attackers as they approached at night led to the K11Ws of the Shiragiku-tai being mistaken for D3As. The modest performance of the Kyushu aircraft, which cruised at just 95 knots, was the reason why the attacks developed five to six hours after their departure. Indeed, *O'Neill*'s after action report specifically noted the slow approach speed of its attacker as the aircraft closed on the ship.

More tokko took to the air as dawn broke, with most of them departing from the IJAAF's bases at Chiran, Bansei, and Miyakonojo in southern Kyushu. These included 63 "Franks," "Nates," "Oscars," and "Tonys" from 18 different Shinbu-tai, as well as three Ki-67 To-Go from the 62nd Sentai at Tachiarai in northern Kyushu. Once again, American fighters took their toll on the attackers and their escorts, with Okinawa- and Ie Shima-based US Marine Corps and USAAF pilots claiming 76 shot down. Nevertheless, the tokko struck a further seven vessels that morning, sinking two, with the mostly overcast skies and intermittent rain over Okinawa proving helpful to the Japanese pilots, who were able to use the cloud cover to mask their approach.

The majority of the ships that were targeted identified their attackers as "Zekes," "Tojos," "Georges," and "Oscars," although only the latter type was utilized that day as tokko. Any attempt to assign attribution to

A contemporary news photograph purporting to show an IJAAF tokko unit composed of recently trained university students taking their Ki-43-III fighters to the front in the spring of 1945. These machines are each equipped with two 200-liter drop tanks and no bombs, which does indeed suggest that the "Oscar" pilots were setting out on a flight to their new front-line base (probably on Kyushu), rather than a one-way suicide mission. *(Tony Holmes collection)*

an individual attack with any certainty is complicated by the similarities between the four aforementioned types and the "Frank," which *was* heavily involved in tokko missions that morning.

One exception was the attack on *LSM-135*, which had been ordered to render assistance to the minesweeper USS *Spectacle* (AM-305) off Ie Shima after the latter had been struck by what it reported as a "George" at approximately 0805hrs. Twenty-five minutes later, *LSM-135* had just finished picking up approximately 15 survivors from the water and was raising its bow ramp to look for more when two "Tonys" were spotted approaching at mast height from astern. Although the second aircraft ultimately broke off its run, the lead fighter carried on through the gunfire and slammed into the vessel's conning tower. This spun the Ki-61 round, sending the remnants of the aircraft and, more tragically, fuel through the landing ship's forward crew compartment and well deck. The fuel caught fire and rapidly spread out of control, *LSM-135*'s firefighting capability having been knocked out by the impact of the tokko.

The landing ship quickly developed a list to starboard and then began settling by the stern. The survivors soon abandoned *LSM-135*, 11 of their shipmates having been killed, including the commanding officer, Lt Harry L. Derby. Tragically, several of the survivors from *Spectacle* had also lost their lives (to add to the 29 that perished in the original attack on the minesweeper), for they had been receiving treatment in the

The high-speed troop transport USS *Bates* (APD-47) burns after being struck by two aircraft and near-missed by two bombs off Ie Shima on the morning of May 25, 1945. Its crew identified their attackers as a trio of "Vals," which initially bombed the vessel and then attempted to crash into it. Despite the ship being towed into a nearby anchorage by the tug USS *Cree* (ATF-84) while still on fire, the blaze raged out of control and it capsized later that day. By the time the order was given to abandon ship, 21 crew had been killed. *(NARA)*

forward crew compartment when the aircraft hit. The fires were eventually extinguished and *LSM-135* was subsequently towed to Ie Shima, where it was declared a total loss. *Spectacle* was also towed to Ie Shima and then sailed to Kerama Retto on one engine to receive temporary repairs. Sent to Puget Sound for further damage assessment in August, it was declared a constructive total loss and sold for scrapping.

The "Tony" that had struck *LSM-135* would have been from either the 54th, 55th, or 56th Shinbu-tai, these Chiran-based units having sortied aircraft from 0500hrs. The 54th contributed six aircraft, led by 2Lt Hiroshi Kasai, to the roster of tokko that morning, while the 55th and 56th despatched two Ki-61s each under the leadership of 2Lts Toshio Ito and Mototake Ikeda, respectively. All three units had been formed as tokko operations increased in size in response to the amphibious landings on Okinawa in early April, with the 54th and 55th Shinbu-tai being staffed by pilot graduates from the Akeno Kyodo Hiko Shidan – the latter was also the source of its aircraft. The 56th drew its men and machines from the Hitachi Kyodo Hiko Shidan.

Witnessing the devastating attacks on *LSM-135* and *Spectacle* at close quarters was the destroyer escort USS *William C. Cole* (DE-641). The ship had narrowly escaped being hit shortly after 0800hrs when one of two aircraft (which the crew identified as "Oscars") that targeted the vessel scraped its wingtip on DE-641's torpedo tubes and crashed into the sea off its starboard side. The ship's gunners then took the second tokko under fire moments before it slammed into *Spectacle*.

William C. Cole also came under attack from the second of the two "Tonys" that had initially approached *LSM-135*, shooting it into the sea soon after the latter was fatally hit.

Also sunk that day was the high-speed troop transport USS *Bates* (APD-47), which was targeted at 1115hrs while on patrol just two miles south of Ie Shima. As there were no active air raid warnings when the vessel was attacked, the ship's crew initially thought that the three aircraft they spotted approaching the newly operational airfield at Ie Shima as if preparing to land were friendlies. Realizing their error too late, the gunners on board APD-47 hastily took the aircraft, which they identified as "Vals," under fire as they commenced their dives.

The first tokko to attack dropped a bomb that only just missed the ship, the weapon rupturing the starboard hull plating when it detonated. The aircraft duly crashed into the starboard side of the fantail moments later. Almost simultaneously, the second tokko struck the pilothouse. Shortly thereafter, the third aircraft dropped a bomb that achieved a near miss amidships, port side. The resulting explosion ruptured yet more hull plating. The ship lost power, and with it pressure for the fire mains, allowing the conflagration that started with the crash of the tokko to rage out of control. By the time the order was given to abandon ship, 21 crew had been killed. Towed to the anchorage at Ie Shima by the tug USS *Cree* (ATF-84) while still on fire, *Bates* eventually capsized and sank at 1923hrs.

The IJNAF undertook a relatively lackluster tokko operation that morning, with bad weather thwarting several groups of aircraft seeking TF 58's carriers off Okinawa. The 3rd Seito-tai was the sole tokko-tai flying the "Val" on May 25, and only a single aircraft carried out its mission after taking off from Kanoya. This means that *Bates'* attackers were not D3As. The fact that the aircraft dropped bombs before crashing into the ship means that they might have been "Nates," 14 of which were assigned to tokko missions on the 25th. A large number of the obsolete Nakajima fighter trainers were modified to carry 551lb or 1,102lb bombs when assigned the kamikaze role.

Although limited in scope, the IJNAF attacks that morning did result in a rarity – a captured tokko pilot. Soon after 0430hrs, 12 "Frances" from the 10th Ginga-tai took off from Miho, in northern Kyushu, their task being to find and attack the carriers of TF 58. These aircraft were joined by two more P1Ys from the same unit that took off from Miyazaki. Bad weather forced 11 of the Miho-based aircraft to turn back, but the bomber of 1Lt Kaoru Hasegawa, who was accompanied by pilot WO Minato Yoshida and PO1c Shuichi Koyama, pressed on, joined by one of the Miyazaki-based P1Ys. At 1004hrs they were engaged by the battleship *West Virginia* at a range of more than four nautical miles, the vessel conducting gunfire support operations off eastern Okinawa at that time. Hasegawa elected not to attack the warship but to continue searching for the carriers instead.

Nine minutes later, the destroyer *Callaghan* was performing antiaircraft screening duties at the entrance to Nakagusuku Bay, on the southeastern tip of Okinawa, when its crew spotted a pair of bombers they identified as "Bettys" emerging from the low cloud. The ship opened fire, shooting one aircraft down in flames and damaging the other as the bombers flew directly over the destroyer. Approaching the crash site of the latter aircraft, *Callaghan*'s crew found two wounded aviators clinging on to the debris of the aircraft and duly rescued them. These turned out to be Hasegawa and his pilot Yoshida, although the latter succumbed to his injuries at 1555hrs.

Kaoru Hasegawa later wrote an autobiography that included details about his life in the IJNAF, revealing that he had previously been tasked to fly three earlier tokko missions. The first two had been abortive attempts to repeat Operation *Tan No. 2* – the March 11, 1945 attack on Ulithi that damaged the carrier *Randolph* (see Chapter 4) – while the third was a strike on American carriers off Kyushu on May 14 that was aborted after aircraft from TF 58 struck Kanoya before the bombers could take off.

Hasegawa later formed friendships with the surviving crew of *Callaghan*, and attended several reunions of the ship's association from the late 1990s. During the course of researching his autobiography, he also discovered the identity of the crew from the accompanying Miyazaki-based "Frances" that was shot down by the ship. It turned out to be the aircraft of Lt(jg) Hirozo Oguchi, who, with pilot PO1c Class Fukusaburo Iwashina and observer/rear gunner CPO Isamu Hirano as his crew, had also radioed back to Kyushu that TF 58 had been located when the P1Ys were fired upon by *West Virginia*. It is believed that Oguchi's aircraft, which had been hit hard by *Callaghan*'s gunfire and was observed to be smoking from its port engine and wing, subsequently crashed out of sight of the ship.

At 0330hrs on May 26 the 21st and 78th Shinbu-tai each sent out a single "Nate" from Kikaijima Island to harass TF 58 off Okinawa.

No results were obtained, although the seven Ki-61s of the 110th Shinbu-tai that departed at 1318hrs that same day enjoyed better luck. This unit had been formed in early April with men and aircraft from the 5th Rensei Hikotai, a training unit assigned to the 5th Kokugun in China. Led by 2Lt Hayato Tanaka, the unit, which was also known as the Keppu-tai, originally consisted of 12 pilots and aircraft based near Beiping (Beijing). The 110th Shinbu-tai had eventually been transferred to Kyushu in May, and its seven remaining aircraft were despatched on May 26 to undertake the unit's final mission.

Two of the "Tonys" found and attacked the 300-ton coastal patrol craft/submarine chaser *PC-1603* at 1540hrs as it lay at anchor in Kimmu Bay, on the east coast of Okinawa. One struck the ship on its port side just forward of the pilot house and the second attacked from the starboard side and achieved a direct hit on the pilot house at main deck level – three crew were killed and 15 wounded. After several of the 76mm shells for *PC-1603*'s main gun exploded, the ship was abandoned at 1620hrs. The burned out hulk was subsequently towed to Kerama Retto, where it was scuttled. The wreck was subsequently donated to the Government of the Ryukyu Islands for use as a breakwater in 1957.

Kikusui No. 8, on May 27–28, involved 60 aircraft from the IJNAF and 50 from the IJAAF. Among the latter were Ki-79b two-seaters – essentially a dedicated advanced trainer version of the Ki-27. Having previously been exempt from tokko missions, these aircraft stood even less chance of survival than the highly vulnerable "Nates" if intercepted by Allied fighters. Nevertheless, 14 ships were hit and a destroyer sunk during Kikusui No. 8.

The morning of May 27 dawned cloudy over Okinawa, much as it had been during previous days. Although the weather grounded the American CAP, such conditions did not deter the tokko, who once again used the overcast to their advantage. The attacks started from 0740hrs, with five ships being targeted in quick succession east of Okinawa in a rough line extending from Radar Picket Station 5 west to Nakagusuku Bay.

Bogies were first reported just before 0730hrs, and ten minutes later the converted hydrographic survey ship USS *Dutton* (AGS-8) sighted three aircraft to the north of it while sailing from Nakagusuku Bay to nearby Kinmu Bay. Two of these (which its crew identified as "Vals") broke off and attacked the ship, one being driven off by gunfire before the second aircraft, approaching from the port side, clipped the bridge, carrying off the forward starboard section. It then crashed into the sea off the starboard beam and exploded underwater. Although one sailor was blown overboard when the aircraft hit the bridge, the damage inflicted on the 340-ton vessel was otherwise restricted to holing in the hull above the waterline.

As *Dutton* was being attacked, its crew observed two friendly ships to the north and east, identifying one as a destroyer escort and the second as a destroyer minelayer. One of these vessels was probably the high-speed destroyer minesweeper USS *Forrest* (DMS-24), which was steaming in a southeasterly course when it was attacked at 0738hrs by what were described in the ship's after action report as three "Vals." Gunners shot down two of the aircraft and convinced the pilot of the third tokko to abandon his run by disappearing into cloud cover. At 0745hrs the nearby destroyer *Daly*, which was closing with *Forrest* for increased protection, opened fire on yet another "Val" that again targeted DMS-24. It was unclear if this was the aircraft that had previously attempted to attack *Forrest*, although the author of the ship's after action report believed this to be the case.

Despite being hit repeatedly by 20mm gunfire as it bore in, the tokko slammed into the vessel's bow on its starboard side near the waterline at 0747hrs. The crash and resultant bomb explosion caused flooding and damage, although this was reduced by the incomplete detonation of the weapon as evidenced by the subsequent recovery on board the ship of the bomb's tail cone, which still contained undetonated explosive material. Nevertheless, five crew were killed and 13 wounded, and *Forrest* was forced to head to Kerama Retto to be repaired.

Four minutes before DMS-24 had been hit, another aircraft again identified as a "Val" was spotted emerging from cloud cover to the port side of the high-speed destroyer minesweeper USS *Southard* (DMS-10) off Nakagusuku Bay – the vessel had only arrived off Okinawa, from Saipan, earlier that day. The tokko then disappeared back into the overcast, only to re-emerge off the ship's starboard astern in a diving attack. DMS-10's gunners immediately opened fire, causing the pilot to veer off to the right before recommitting to his attack run and crashing into the sea near the ship's bow, causing light shrapnel damage. This was *Southard*'s second encounter with kamikazes, as it had been hit by an aircraft while conducting minesweeping operations off Lingayen on January 6, 1945. On that occasion a tokko had crashed into the vessel aft of its stacks, the aircraft's engine embedding itself in the ship while the fuselage ricocheted off the starboard side of the main deck, ripping a trough six feet wide in the process.

Meanwhile, almost 24 nautical miles away, similar events were being played out. The destroyers USS *Anthony* (DD-515) and USS *Braine* (DD-630) were manning Radar Picket Station 5 with *LCS(L)-13*, *LCS(L)-82*, *LCS(L)-86*, and *LCS(L)-123* when, at 0730hrs, bogies were detected closing in from the south. These aircraft were soon identified as four "Vals," which attacked the destroyers from 0744hrs. One was shot down in flames and another near-missed *Anthony* as both ships turned hard to port to unmask their starboard antiaircraft weapons.

Two minutes later *Braine*'s luck ran out when it was hit by a pair of aircraft in quick succession. Although the first attacker had been set aflame by

Pilots from the IJAAF's 72nd Shinbu-tai pose for the camera on May 26, 1945. Three of the five aviators are 17 years old and the other two are 18 and 19 years old. They are, from left to right in the front row, Tsutomu Hayakawa, Yukio Araki, and Takamasa Senda, with Kaname Takahashi and Mitsuyoshi Takahashi behind them. Flying Ki-51 "Sonias" from Bansei, all five pilots were killed on May 27 when they attacked radar picket ships including the destroyer USS *Braine* (DD-630). The latter was hit twice – 66 sailors were killed and 78 wounded. Although badly damaged, the vessel survived and was subsequently repaired post-war. *(Tony Holmes collection)*

antiaircraft fire as it made a run on *Anthony*, its pilot managed to retain sufficient control to turn in the direction of *Braine* and crash into the forward handling room from almost dead ahead as the destroyer reversed its initial turn to port. Immediately following this hit, the second aircraft slammed into the starboard side amidships, tearing into the vessel's sickbay. The first attacker's bomb exploded in the wardroom, demolishing it, the CIC, and the No. 2 handling room and badly damaging the bridge structure. The detonation of the second aircraft's bomb blew away its after stack and badly damaged the torpedo shack and superstructure up to the after part of the galley. *Braine*'s crew had also suffered heavy casualties in the attacks, with 66 being killed and 78 wounded. It took until noon to quench the fires raging throughout the ship, which then retired to Kerama Retto for emergency repairs to be carried out prior to the vessel being sent to Boston Navy Yard for an overhaul.

Although all of the attackers that morning were identified as "Vals," only two groups of tokko engaged TF 58 during daylight hours on May 27 and they were from the IJAAF. At 0600hrs, the 72nd Shinbu-tai had sortied nine "Sonias" from Bansei and the 431st Shinbu-tai had despatched five "Nates" from Chiran. Both tokko-tai had been tasked with attacking warships to the west of Okinawa, although as it turned out the vessels hit that day were all sailing on the eastern side of the island.

The attacks on *Anthony* and *Braine* have been attributed to the "Sonias" of the 72nd Shinbu-tai, and given the number of tokko seen by the various ships that morning it is possible that some of its aircraft also targeted *Dutton* and *Southard* too.

The 72nd Shinbu-tai is best known for a well-circulated photograph of five of its pilots taken by a Japanese press photographer the day before the unit's fateful mission on May 27, 1945. In that shot, Cpl Yukio Araki cradles a puppy while Cpls Tsutomu Hayakawa, Takamasa Senda, Kaname Takahashi, and Mitsuyoshi Takahashi look on in their flying gear. All five men were aged between 17 and 19 years old.

Among the younger ones in the group, Yukio Araki had only turned 17 on March 10. A native of Kiryu, in Gunma Prefecture, he had joined the IJAAF's Air Service Youth Pilot Training Program as part of its 15th Class at the age of 15, commencing his training in September 1943 at Tachiarai airfield. In 1944 he was posted to Heijo (today Pyongyang, in North Korea) before volunteering with his entire class of trainees from the 23rd Rensei Hikotai (Learning Squadron) to be tokko pilots in February 1945. Flying back to Japan the following month, he bade his family a final farewell during an overnight visit before heading back to Heijo and eventually on to Bansei on May 25. The following day he wrote a final letter to his family in which he vowed to achieve great success in battle.

A tokko slammed into this unidentified Landing Craft, Infantry (Rocket) – possibly *LCI(R)(3)-119*, which was hit on the night of May 28, 1945 by a Nakajima A6M2-N "Rufe" floatplane fighter shortly after the vessel's gunners had claimed a "Betty" shot down. Fortunately for the ship's crew, the tokko had failed to detonate the hundreds of five-inch spin-stabilized rocket warheads on board. LCI(R)s were not known for their ability to sustain and survive such catastrophic damage. *(NARA)*

A tokko pilot of a B6N2 "Jill" from the Kikusui-Tenzan Kokutai inscribes the message "Hitchin" ("Determined to Sink," indicating his determination to sink an enemy vessel) on his aircraft's tail in chalk prior to taking off on his final mission from Kanoya airfield in late May 1945. The vertical inscription near the bottom of the rudder reads "Yamamoto," probably indicating the pilot's name. *(Photo by Yasuo Tomishige/The Asahi Shimbun via Getty Images)*

The tokko attacks continued that night, with more K11W trainers from the Tokushima-Shiragiku-tai and Shiragiku-tai being sent southward to harass the fleet. At 0010hrs *LCS(L)(3)-119* claimed a "Betty" shot down before a Nakajima A6M2-N "Rufe" floatplane fighter slammed into it seven minutes later. Earlier that night the high-speed transports USS *Loy* (APD-56) and USS *Rednour* (APD-102) and the destroyer escort USS *Eisele* (DE-34) also reported encounters with at least four Japanese aircraft while sailing 14 nautical miles west of Zampa-Misaki. *Loy* succeeded in shooting one of them down, while a second tokko inflicted modest shrapnel damage when it exploded nearby. A third machine was driven off, but the fourth aircraft hit *Rednour*'s fantail, blowing a ten-foot hole in the main deck. With three crew killed and 18 wounded, APD-102 was forced to head to Kerama Retto for emergency repairs. It subsequently returned to San Pedro, California, for an overhaul. *Loy* and *Rednour* identified their respective attackers as "Jills" and "Oscars."

Japanese aircraft were active throughout the night, and at 0545hrs on the 28th crewmen on board the Attack Personnel Transport Ship USS *Sandoval* (APA-194) saw what they identified as a "Pete" floatplane crash into the cargo ship SS *Mary A. Livermore* while both vessels were anchored in Nakagusuku Bay. Although various floatplane types were indeed used in kamikaze missions in the final months of the war, no "Petes" were involved in tokko operations on the 28th according to Japanese records. The IJNAF did, however, sortie other floatplanes that day in the form of "Jakes" and "Alfs," but these departed Ibusuki at 0600hrs – too late to have been responsible for the Nakagusuku Bay tokko attack.

They were accompanied that morning by 39 aircraft scraped together by 12 IJAAF tokko-tai at Chiran and Bansei. These machines departed southern Kyushu between 0500hrs and 0545hrs, and although better weather meant the defending American fighters were able to make several intercepts, a handful of them still got through.

The action started just before 0655hrs when at least five twin-engined aircraft attacked vessels manning Radar Picket Station 15. Their principal targets were the destroyers USS *Drexler* (DD-741) and USS *Lowry* (DD-770), which had arrived there a little over two hours before. Three of the attackers were shot down, including one by the CAP, but the remaining two slammed into either side of *Drexler* in quick succession – the first tokko to hit the destroyer had actually tried to crash into *Lowry* but had missed. *Drexler* lost all power and a large gasoline fire immediately broke out. Despite the heavy damage, the ship's gunners kept firing and two more aircraft were downed. At 0703hrs DD-741 was hit with such ferocity by a twin-engined aircraft that the destroyer rolled onto its beam ends and sank in less than a minute. The rapidity at which *Drexler* went under resulted in a heavy loss of life amongst its 357-strong crew – 158 dead and 52 wounded. The ship's commanding officer, Capt Robert L. Wilson, was one of those wounded.

At 0742hrs another twin-engined aircraft was sighted approaching Ie Shima from the north by crewmen on board the fleet tug USS *Tekesta* (AT-93). The vessel was at Ie Shima's southern anchorage at the time assisting in repairs on *Spectacle*, which had been struck by a tokko three days earlier. Gunners on board the tug identified this aircraft as a "Frances" and took it under fire, scoring several hits on its starboard engine prior to

Hajime Fujii

The story of the 45th Shinbu-tai's leader on May 28, 1945 has been covered in some detail in Japan post-war. Unlike most of the young, inexperienced tokko pilots sent on the one-way missions, 1Lt Hajime Fujii was 30 years old at the time of his death. A former infantryman in the IJA, he had been wounded in combat in China prior to becoming an instructor at the Kumagaya Army Aviation School. Here, Fujii served as a company commander, being responsible for students' character building and mental instruction. When the call came for pilots to undertake tokko missions, he immediately volunteered. His application was repeatedly rejected, however, on the grounds that he was married with two children.

Fujii's wife Fukuko initially opposed her husband's desire to take part in kamikaze operations, but as his determination to join the tokko-tai grew and the reason for the rejection of his application became apparent, she took the drastic step of killing herself and her daughters to pave the way for him. On the night of December 14, 1944, having drowned the sisters in the frigid waters of the Arakawa River near the Kumagaya Aviation School, she then took her own life. Only then was Fujii's next application (said to be written in his own blood) accepted, and he duly joined the 45th Shinbu-tai when it was formed with personnel and aircraft from the Hokota Kyodo Hiko Shidan in early February 1945.

---

the tokko crashing into the mainmast of the nearby transport SS *Brown Victory*. Although most of the aircraft fell into the water to the vessel's starboard side, resulting in little damage being inflicted on the ship (which was fully loaded with drums of fuel), the resulting explosion of its bomb(s) killed four crew and wounded 16.

Further to the southeast in Nakagusuku Bay, *Sandoval* was itself the target of a tokko attack when a low-flying "Tony" crashed into its wheelhouse on the port side at 0737hrs, starting a fire and killing five crewmen, including the executive officer. The commanding officer, Cdr Richard C. Scherrer, was also among the 29 men wounded (three of whom later died) by the strike. Despite the damage inflicted on the bridge, the ship's crew effectively joined other vessels in the anchorage in defending against further air attacks. Indeed, *Sandoval*'s gunners assisted in the shooting down of what they reported was a "Frances" at 0755hrs and observed another "Tony" crash into the nearby transport SS *Josiah Snelling* at 0815hrs.

The Ki-61s that hit *Sandoval* and *Josiah Snelling* could have been from the 54th Shinbu-tai, which sortied three aircraft flown by 2Lts Shinichi Nakanishi, Takami Kamigaki, and Masamitsu Takai, or the solitary fighter from the 55th Shinbu-tai flown by 2Lt Yasuo Ooiwa – all four had taken off from Chiran at 0500hrs. One of the "Tonys" was reportedly shot down at 0718hrs by the CAP near Radar Picket Station 15, while the remaining three went on to attack the vessels in Nakagusuku Bay.

Also taking to the air at the same time as the Ki-61s were nine "Nicks" from the 45th Shinbu-tai under the leadership of 1Lt Hajime Fujii. One crashed soon after takeoff, leaving eight to complete the mission. The 45th Shinbu-tai were the only tokko-tai flying a twin-engined type that day, and given their time of departure and when the ships on Radar Picket Station 15 came under attack, it would appear that the unit was almost certainly responsible for the sinking of *Drexler* – even though its crew identified their attackers as "Frances" bombers. *Lowry*'s after action report erroneously described the tokko as "Dinahs."

The 45th Shinbu-tai was also probably responsible for hitting SS *Brown Victory* off Ie Shima, while the "Frances" shot down over Nakagusuku Bay by gunners from several vessels, including *Sandoval*, at 0755hrs was also likely to have been another "Nick" – its demise would account for seven of the eight aircraft sortied by the unit.

By the time Kikusui No. 8 had been launched, the land battle for Okinawa was beginning to wind down. Kamikaze attacks also started to tail off as the Japanese realized the battle to save the island was all but lost and attention turned to preparing the tokko-tai for the American invasion of Japan. This shift in emphasis meant that May 28 was the last occasion where more than five ships were hit by aerial tokko in one day. Nevertheless, sporadic attacks continued through to month-end.

Soon after midnight on May 29 the destroyer USS *Shubrick* (DD-639) was hit by what its crew stated was one of a pair of twin-engined aircraft as the vessel headed for Radar Picket Station 16 – neither the IJAAF or IJNAF reported having any twin-engined tokko in the air that night, however. The bomb carried by the aircraft punched a 30ft hole in the starboard side of the vessel, which suffered further damage when one of its depth charges exploded. Although it initially appeared that the ship would sink, damage control parties finally got the flooding under control and *Shubrick* was towed to Kerama Retto. The destroyer had had 35 crew killed and 25 wounded in the attack. The damage inflicted on the ship was so bad that DD-639 was declared a constructive total loss shortly after its return to Puget Sound in August 1945.

The rest of the day passed quietly until shortly after dusk, when the high-speed transport USS *Tatum* (APD-81) was alerted to the presence of enemy aircraft approaching from the south as the vessel patrolled its screening station east of Ie Shima. At 1922hrs lookouts spotted four enemy aircraft circling in pairs off the port and starboard quarters, and they then proceeded to dive on the ship in quick succession. Although gun crews shot down three of the tokko, the lead aircraft skidded into the side of APD-81 and caused moderate damage after first hitting the water just off the starboard bow. Its bomb (described as a 551lb weapon in *Tatum*'s after action report) was jarred loose when the tokko skipped off the surface of the water and pierced the ship's starboard hull but did not explode, sparing the high-speed transport from more damage and limiting casualties to just three wounded.

The crew believed they had been attacked by "Val 22s" (late-model D3A2s), adding that none of the Japanese aircraft had strafed the ship. However, Japanese records state that the day's only tokko were a pair of "Kates" from the Shinten-tai that took off at 1610hrs from Shinchuku and five "Oscars," led by 2Lt Shiro Ishibashi, from the 20th Sentai that departed Giran. There is no mention of when the Ki-43s took off, although it would be expected that their mission was timed to roughly coincide with that of the Shinten-tai in order to take advantage of the setting sun.

Given the B5Ns were each armed with a single 1,760lb No. 80 Mk 5 Land Bomb and an unexploded 551lb weapon was recovered on board *Tatum*, the latter would suggest that the ship's assailants were the Ki-43s from the 20th Sentai. Typically, "Oscars" could carry two 551lb bombs (or one bomb and one auxiliary fuel tank for long-range missions) under their wing hardpoints, which would explain why sailors on board APD-81 mistook the fighters' underwing stores for the "Val's" fixed undercarriage sponsons during the dusk attack.

Late May and early June at last gave the warships sailing off Okinawa some respite from more than two months of near-constant tokko attacks. On May 31 only a solitary "Lily" from the Sei 15th Hikotai attempted to engage vessels in the area, while on June 1 the 20th Sentai sortied another pair of "Oscars" to Okinawa from Formosa and a single 433rd Shinbu-tai Ki-79b took off from Kyushu. No hits on Allied ships were registered by the tokko on either date, however.

Kikusui No. 9 commenced on June 3, this latest offensive (which officially ran until the 7th) having been postponed for several days because of poor weather. The IJNAF could muster only 20 tokko aircraft (mostly "Vals"), while the IJAAF sent out 30, again primarily "Nates." A force of 65 "Zekes" was also sortied as escorts for the kamikazes. While the Fast Carrier Task Force, now designated TF 38 after Admiral Halsey had taken over from Admiral Raymond Spruance on May 27, made regular strikes on the Kyushu airfields, US Marine Corps Corsair and USAAF Thunderbolt squadrons took over responsibility for the air defense of Okinawa, flying both CAPs north of the island and regular fighter sweeps over Kyushu.

The IJAAF sortied 22 "Nates" and five "Oscars" from Chiran between 1019hrs and 1030hrs, while the IJNAF despatched three "Vals" from the Kokubu-based 4th Seito-tai at 1040hrs. The returns were paltry, with the cargo vessel USS *Allegan* (AK-225), moored in Nakagusuku Bay, and *LCI(L)-90* sailing in Chimu Bay being the only vessels to suffer any damage. *Allegan* was unable to identify its attacker, which crashed into the water nearby and shook the ship with an underwater explosion at 1345hrs. *LSM-120*'s crew, which also saw the tokko, identified it as a "Nate," while personnel on *LSM-156*, moored alongside *Allegan*, reported it as a "Val."

At about the same time *LCI(L)-90* (a veteran of amphibious landings in French North Africa, Sicily, Anzio, and Normandy, prior to participating in *Iceberg*) was hit by a "Val" that had originally appeared to

At dusk on June 5, 1945, the heavy cruiser *Louisville* suffered its third tokko hit in five months, having been struck twice during the liberation of the Philippines. Its last attack was carried out by a Formosa-based Ki-61 from the 17th Sentai, which destroyed one of the ship's floatplanes and the after stack. Four of *Louisville's* eight boilers were also knocked out by the shock of the impact. (NARA)

ABOVE
On June 6 USS *J. William Ditter* (DM-31) was attacked by aircraft approaching from the east soon after 1700hrs while patrolling the waters off southeast Okinawa, its crew identifying the attackers as "Nates" and "Oscars." Two fighters struck DM-31, and although the first tokko inflicted little damage, the second aircraft blew open the forward engine room and after fireroom (seen here), killing ten crew and wounding 27. DM-31 had to be towed to Kerama Retto for repairs. Upon returning home later in the year *J. William Ditter* was declared a constructive total loss and sold for scrapping. *(NARA)*

be diving on a land target before switching to drop its bomb near the vessel. The pilot followed up the impromptu attack by crashing into the after starboard side of the pilot house, killing one crewman and wounding seven others. There is some doubt about whether the aircraft that struck *LCI(L)-90* was even a tokko, given its attack profile.

The next tokko attacks took place on June 5 when four "Tonys" from the 17th Sentai took off from Hattoku, on Formosa, led by 2Lt Seiji Inamori. At least two of these aircraft reached southern Okinawa just before 1930hrs, where they spotted the battleship *Mississippi*, the heavy cruiser *Louisville*, and the destroyer USS *Rooks* (DD-804) just as the latter two ships were preparing for a night of illumination duties in support of anti-explosive motor boat operations. The overcast weather and fading light meant the tokko were not seen until the last minute, and their engagement by the ships' gunners was further delayed by the enemy aircraft initially being mistaken for friendly fighters until just before they started their attack runs.

Both of the larger ships were hit, with *Louisville* losing a floatplane (only its central float remained on the catapult after the attack) and after stack and having four of its eight boilers knocked out by the shock of the impact. *Mississippi* was hit on its starboard quarterdeck just above the armored "blister." The heavy cruiser, which had been struck by tokko on two previous occasions off the Philippines, had eight sailors killed (the entire crew of a quad 40mm gun mount) and 45 wounded. The battleship – also a survivor of a tokko strike off the Philippines six months earlier – had just one killed and six wounded.

Two more vessels were hit on June 6 when the destroyer minelayers *Harry F. Bauer* and USS *J. William Ditter* (DM-31) were attacked by aircraft approaching from the east soon after 1700hrs as they patrolled the waters off southeast Okinawa. The former reported being attacked by "Bettys" and "Vals," while the latter identified the tokko as a mixture of "Nates" and "Oscars." Two fighters struck DM-31, the first glancing off its No. 2 stack before plunging into the sea and the second hitting the vessel port amidships just below the main deck. Although the first tokko had inflicted little damage, the second aircraft blew open the forward engine room and after fireroom, killing ten crew and wounding 27. The warship lost all power and had to be towed to Kerama Retto for repairs. Eventually sailing back to New York Navy Yard in July, *J. William Ditter* was subsequently declared a constructive total loss two months later and sold for scrapping in July of the following year.

The IJAAF established several tokko-tai units equipped with Ki-84s, and these usually carried a 551lb bomb under one wing and a drop tank under the other. Some of the escorting fighters would also carry a bomb for conventional attacks. This aircraft is possibly from the Sei 33rd Hikotai, which flew "Franks" on tokko missions from Hattoku, on Formosa. *(Tony Holmes collection)*

Harry F. Bauer appears to have enjoyed more luck than *J. William Ditter* on June 6, with the closest a tokko came to hitting the vessel being a "Val" that crashed into the water just ten yards to starboard directly off the bridge. Some localized flooding occurred within the forward emergency diesel room, but no further damage was done and no casualties were reported. The warship duly returned to Kerama Retto and eventually left for Leyte, and it was not until June 23 (some 17 days after the attack) that the flooded compartment was pumped out to reveal the cause of the damage – an unexploded 551lb bomb that had penetrated the hull. The space was hurriedly flooded again and isolated while a bomb disposal team was called in to render the weapon safe.

The only tokko in the air on June 6 were from the IJAAF, and they included ten Chiran-based Ki-79bs from the 113th Shinbu-tai (also known as the Tenken-tai) led aloft by 2Lt Masaharu Takano. Each of these aircraft carried a single 551lb bomb beneath the fuselage centerline, and they were almost certainly the "Nates" seen by *J. William Ditter* and identified as "Vals" by *Harry F. Bauer*'s crew. There were no "Oscars" among the attackers from Kyushu and certainly no "Bettys" (or any other twin-engined types for that matter). Instead, 14 "Tonys" from four other tokko-tai accompanied the 113th Shinbu-tai, and two of them could have been the aircraft that struck DM-31, as evidenced by the fuze cap found by the vessel's on-board bomb disposal officer. These identified the weapon as being an IJAAF 220lb bomb.

Later that same afternoon the Formosa-based tokko-tai despatched four "Oscars" from the 20th Sentai and a similar number of "Franks" from the 29th Sentai and Sei 33rd Hikotai, but no results were obtained by either unit.

On June 7 the Sakishima Gunto group of islands were targeted again, this time by the US Navy escort carriers of TU 32.1.1. The action started soon after 0630hrs, and the vessels were already at routine General Quarters when a previously undetected "Zeke" dove on the escort carrier *Natoma Bay* from astern, strafing as it bore in. As the pilot neared the bridge he steepened his dive and slammed into the forward flightdeck, the fighter's engine, propeller, and bomb tearing a 12ft-by-20ft hole in it. Fortunately for the ship, the ordnance being carried by the tokko exploded in the space between the flightdeck and forecastle, damaging the latter and destroying the anchor windlass, as well as setting a Wildcat attached to the catapult on fire – the burning aircraft was quickly shot off into the sea. Casualties were light as a result, with one officer being killed and four personnel wounded.

A short while later a second "Zeke" that had managed to sneak in over the task unit by tailing a section of returning Wildcats made a strafing run on USS *Sargent Bay* (CVE-83) from astern. Hit by the escort carrier's antiaircraft fire, the fighter disintegrated as it passed overhead and crashed into the sea forward of the ship. The falling pieces of the aircraft and the rounds it had fired when closing on CVE-83 wounded six crew and damaged two Wildcats, although both fighters were quickly repaired.

The two "Zekes," flown by 21st Taigi-tai pilots CPO Kazuyoshi Hashizume and PO1c Sadao Yanagihara, had taken off from Ishigaki Island at 0500hrs shortly after the approaching American task unit was detected by the IJNAF.

Poor weather conditions meant the Kyushu-based tokko-tai were kept on the ground until 1650hrs on June 7, when the 63rd Shinbu-tai sortied six "Sonias" from Chiran. Some of these aircraft were almost certainly the tokko that targeted the destroyers *Anthony* and *Walke* at 1900hrs while they manned Radar Picket Station 1. *Anthony*'s crew reported that they were attacked by a pair of "Nates" or "Vals," both of which were shot down. The lead aircraft crashed close enough to the destroyer to hole its port side, with part of the aircraft sailing over the ship and ending up in the sea off its starboard side. The ensuing splash doused *Anthony* with water, burning fuel, aircraft components, and parts of the pilot. The sheer

The destroyer USS *William D. Porter* (DD-579) claimed the dubious honor of being sunk by a tokko despite not suffering a direct hit. On June 10, 1945, while manning Radar Picket Station 15 off Aguni Shima, the vessel was attacked by a "Nate" from either the 112th or 214th Shinbu-tai. The aircraft's bomb exploded underwater after crashing into the sea nearby, lifting the rear of the destroyer out of the water and holing the hull sufficiently to flood the after engine and firerooms. Damage control parties were unable to stem the flooding and DD-579 eventually sank two-and-a-half hours after it had been attacked. *(NARA)*

volume of water that hit the ship was sufficient to carry the burning fuel with it when it washed away. Five men were swept overboard, but all were quickly recovered with no loss of life.

Clearer skies on the 8th saw the IJAAF again target warships off Okinawa, sending up seven "Oscars" and six "Franks" from five Kyushu-based tokko-tai at dawn. These sorties all ended in disappointing failure, however, with not a single ship being damaged by tokko that day.

Instead, it was left to the obsolete "Nates" of either the 112th or 214th Shinbu-tai to show how it was done when they took off from Chiran on June 10, with one slipping through the CAP at Radar Picket Station 15 off Aguni Shima to attack the destroyer *William D. Porter* just before 0830hrs. The aircraft appeared out of low cumulus cloud to the ship's starboard side before banking into a left-hand turn across its bow and making a run from the port side. The tokko was under fire throughout this maneuver, being targeted by *William D. Porter* and the accompanying destroyers *Aulick* and USS *Cogswell* (DD-651) and the support ships *LCS(L)-18*, *LCS(L)-86*, *LCS(L)-94*, and *LCS(L)-122*. Somehow the pilot still managed to hit the water just off the ship's stern, where his bomb blew up immediately beneath *William D. Porter*.

The explosion lifted the rear of the destroyer out of the water and holed the hull enough to allow water to flood its after engine and firerooms. The shock also ruptured steam lines in the after part of the ship, further complicating damage control efforts. *LCS(L)-86* and *LCS(L)-121* came alongside to help pump out the water flooding the rear of the destroyer, but their efforts were in vain as the list continued to worsen and DD-579 settled by the stern. At 1045hrs *Aulick* noted that the stricken destroyer's deck was awash from amidships, and abandon ship was ordered at 1110hrs. *William D. Porter* sank down some ten minutes later. All 273 crew survived the incident.

Cdr C. M. Keyes, the vessel's commanding officer, noted in the after action report that the aircraft had not been detected by the radars on any of the ships in the immediate area until it was just 7,000 yards away. One of the support ships recovered several wooden and fabric pieces from the water that were said to be from the crashed tokko, suggesting that it was made primarily of these materials. Keyes believed that this could have explained why the aircraft had avoided radar detection. This does not adequately explain things, however, for the "Nate" (and the "Val," for that matter) was primarily of metal construction, with the only significant fabric elements being the control surfaces in line with common practice at the time.

The support ships *LCS(L)(3)-86* and *LCS(L)(3)-122* maneuvered in close to *William D. Porter* initially to offer assistance and then, when it became clear the ship was beyond saving, to take on board the vessel's entire 273-strong crew. *LCS(L)(3)-122* had itself suffered minor damage from a tokko near miss that same day. (NARA)

Groundcrew from the Kikusui-Tenzan Kokutai at Kanoya airfield ease a Type 91 air-dropped torpedo beneath a B6N2 prior to the aircraft flying a tokko mission at dusk in late May 1945. The previous month, on April 6, the Kikusui-Tenzan Kokutai had participated in Kikusui No. 1 – the first largescale tokko strike generated by the IJNAF and IJAAF in response to the Allied invasion of Okinawa. *(Photo by Yasuo Tomishige/The Asahi Shimbun via Getty Images)*

Radar Picket Station 15 came under renewed attack on June 11, with the 215th Shinbu-tai despatching a "Nate" and the 56th and 159th Shinbu-tai a single "Tony" each from Chiran, none of which succeeded in damaging Allied warships. The afternoon mission, involving nine "Sonias" and an "Oscar" from the 64th and 144th Shinbu-tai, respectively, enjoyed better luck. The ten aircraft took off from Bansei soon after 1600hrs, and some of the Ki-51s were probably the "Vals" that ships at Radar Picket Station 15 and in Nakagusuku Bay reported being attacked by later that evening.

Shortly before 1900hrs the destroyers *Aulick* and *Cogswell*, which had witnessed *William D. Porter* sunk the previous day, were on duty with *Ammen* (which had survived a tokko hit off the Philippines in November 1944) and a cluster of support ships when they detected incoming bogies. Although the CAP shot down three of the reported seven Japanese aircraft, three more attacked the support ships, with one slamming into *LCS(L)(3)-122* at the base of its conning tower to starboard and starting a fire on board. Its bomb passed through the vessel and exploded upon hitting the water off the port side, showering the ship with shrapnel. After a heroic firefighting effort that eventually earned its commanding officer, Lt Richard M. McCool, the Congressional Medal of Honor, *LCS(L)(3)-122* was towed back to Kerama Retto with 11 crew dead and 29 wounded. Soon repaired, the vessel duly served with the occupation service in the Far East through to February 1946, when it returned to the USA.

The anchorage at Nakagusuku Bay also came under attack at around this time, with the Dock Landing Ship USS *Lindenwald* (LSD-6) reporting that a "Val" made a run on it at 1908hrs from the port side as the vessel lay at anchor. The aircraft pulled up at the last moment, barely clearing the top of the ship, before veering to the left and crashing into the water ahead of LSD-6. Another tokko clipped a cargo boom on board the nearby Liberty Ship SS *Walter Colton* and crashed close by. Both ships also sustained damage when inadvertently hit by antiaircraft fire from vessels around them, while some of the crew and an armed guard on the *Walter Colton* were wounded by shrapnel.

No more tokko appeared in the skies off Okinawa until June 19, although at 2030hrs on the 16th the destroyer *Twiggs* was hit by a "Jill" in a jibaku attack as it was on duty off western Okinawa. The vessel had just been struck in the port side by a torpedo dropped by the aircraft and had barely recovered when the B6N pilot, evidently determined to finish the ship off, circled back around and slammed into it aft. His sacrifice, and that of his crew, was probably superfluous for the torpedo was what caused the most damage, having hit near the forward five-inch guns and started a fire that raged out of control. When the blaze reached the magazine for the No. 2 turret at around 2130hrs the ammunition stored within it promptly blew up, sinking the destroyer within minutes and taking 152 of its crew with it, including the commanding officer, Cdr George Philip Jr.

As the land battle petered out the Japanese launched Kikusui No. 10 on June 21. This final Kikusui attack had been delayed due to poor weather (June is typically wet in Japan), the offensive having originally been scheduled for June 14, then postponed to the 16th and, finally, delayed indefinitely. When the weather eventually cleared on June 21, Kikusui No. 10 commenced. For this last attack against US ships off Okinawa, the IJNAF could muster only 30 tokko aircraft and the IJAAF just 15. The operation itself was pointless, as by this time the battle for Okinawa was effectively over, but it went ahead nonetheless.

The first aircraft to see action were the four "Franks" from the 26th Shinbu-tai that departed Miyakonojo, on Kyushu, for Okinawa at 1615hrs. These fighters were flown by 1Lts Hachirou Sagara and Kiyoji Kimura and 2Lts Fukujiro Nagashima and Tadao Nishinomiya. They were almost certainly the aircraft that arrived over Kerama Retto two hours later, when the seaplane tenders USS *Curtiss* (AV-4) and USS *Kenneth Whiting* (AV-14) were hit in rapid succession by two tokko that appeared from the west at 1842hrs, the pilots having used the islands of Geruma and Fukaji to mask their low-level approach. There were several friendly aircraft in the air at the time, which further complicated the aerial picture to the benefit of the tokko, and the first inkling the ships' crews had of the enemy's presence was when the attackers were sighted visually.

Curtiss's after action report identified its attacker as either a "Frank" or a "George," while *Kenneth Whiting*'s crew reported that their ship was struck by an "Oscar" and identified the attacker that hit *Curtiss* as a "Tony." The tokko that targeted AV-4 had initially made a climbing turn on its starboard side, before crossing the bow and diving from the vessel's port quarter. Its longer run-in meant the fighter was repeatedly hit by gunfire and crashed close aboard the port side, only wounding five men. AV-14 had got off lightly, but *Curtiss* (which had survived a

Groundcrew from a US Marine Corps fighter squadron carefully dismantle an Ohka found at Yontan following the capture of the airfield. The manned aerial bomb was based around a massive 2,645lb Tekkou armor-piercing warhead in the nose of the aircraft, as seen here following the removal of the nose fairing. The final Ohka attack of Operation *Iceberg* occurred on June 22, 1945 – the day the Allies declared the battle for Okinawa to be over. Six "Betty" motherships and their Ohkas from the Jinrai Butai were sortied and two returned to base with technical problems. The remaining four were all shot down by US Marine Corps or USAAF fighters well before they got within launching range of the Allied ships. (*NARA*)

jibaku attack during the Pearl Harbor raid), then anchored to the starboard side of *Kenneth Whiting*, was not so lucky. Its attacker made a more direct approach at low level before slamming into the hull to starboard. The aircraft and its bomb punched two holes through the hull plating prior to the weapon detonating on the third deck, killing 35 and wounding 21.

Almost simultaneously, another pair of aircraft approached from the west and took the crew of the tug USS *Lipan* (ATF-85) equally by surprise as it towed the hulk of the high-speed troop transport *Barry* out to sea via the north entrance of Kerama Retto harbor, with *LSM-59* sailing alongside. *Barry* had been deemed beyond repair following a tokko strike in the early hours of May 25, and following its arrival in Kerama Retto the hulk had been stripped of everything serviceable. In fact, the vessel had only been officially decommissioned earlier in the day, and it had been decided that the ship would serve as experimental tokko "bait" off Ie Shima after being equipped with randomly flashing lights to simulate antiaircraft guns being fired in an effort to decoy the attacking pilots.

The first of the aircraft slammed into the port quarter of *LSM-59* at 1841hrs, ripping a path through its tank deck into the engine room and tearing a hole out the bottom of the ship. All electrical power was lost, both main engines were destroyed, and a fire broke out at the stern. Although the blaze was quickly extinguished, the ship was beyond saving as a result of the underwater damage and it sank at 1854hrs with the loss of two crew.

Meanwhile, the pilot of the second fighter flew past *Barry*'s stern and then banked to port to approach from the ships' starboard quarter, initially aiming for *Lipan* before turning his attention to the larger vessel and crashing into its superstructure. Despite being fitted with additional buoyancy in an effort to improve survivability in its new role as a decoy, the hulk quickly started taking on water and sank in the early hours of the following morning.

All things considered, the four "Frank" pilots from the 26th Shinbutai had achieved quite impressive results, sinking two ships (although one was admittedly a derelict hulk unable to defend itself), badly damaging a third, and near-missing a fourth.

A noteworthy detail of this attack was the wildly differing identities of the attackers reported by witnesses, with *Lipan*'s crew stating that both the tokko they encountered were "Jacks." The survivors from *LSM-59* claimed the second aircraft was a "Judy" – its lookouts had in fact failed to spot the aircraft that hit the ship. Meanwhile, crewmen on board two other vessels that witnessed the attack, the minesweeper USS *Steady* (AM-118) and the destroyer escort USS *Swearer* (DE-186), identified the tokko as an "Oscar" and a "Grace" and an "Oscar" and a "Hamp," respectively, clearly illustrating how fraught an exercise attempting to analyze the identity of attackers from solely perusing US or Allied sources can be.

The IJNAF was involved in more tokko attacks that evening, with eight K11Ws taking off from Kyushu between 1900hrs and 2000hrs. Later that night, five "Pete" floatplane fighters from the tokko unit formed by the 12th Koku Sentai departed Ibusuki at 2330hrs and headed for Okinawa. At about that same time, an aircraft was shot down by the destroyer escort USS *Halloran* (DE-305) as it patrolled the waters off Okinawa, the tokko crashing in flames just 75 yards short of its target following a strafing and failed attack run. The aircraft's bomb exploded when it hit the water, riddling the vessel's superstructure with fragments and killing four and wounding 18 of the crew. The blast also knocked out DE-305's radars and most of its radio antennae. The primary suspect for this attack would be one of the K11Ws, although the author of *Halloran*'s after action report and war diary failed to identify the ship's attacker.

Shortly after midnight *LSM-213* was hit by another Japanese aircraft forward of its conn while sailing in Kimmu Bay, the vessel suffering severe hull and fire damage. The tokko, which also killed three crew and wounded 35, was identified by survivors as being a "Val." It was, however, almost certainly another one of the K11Ws.

On June 22, 1945 the Allies declared the battle for Okinawa to be over, with major ground combat operations having ended on that date. Nevertheless, the Japanese still sent another wave of tokko into action that day, with 11 "Franks" from the 27th and 179th Shinbu-tai being joined by six "Betty" motherships and their Ohkas and seven "Zekes" from the Jinrai Butai on what proved to be the final kamikaze missions off Okinawa. All had departed by daybreak, with the Ki-84s flying from Miyakonojo and the IJNAF aircraft, escorted by 65 "Zekes," from Kanoya.

Of the "Betty" force, only four managed to press on with the mission after two aborted with technical problems, and they were all shot down by US Marine Corps or USAAF fighters before they were able to reach a suitable launch position. Despite this, the tokko still managed to hit one ship and near-miss a second vessel. The latter was the high-speed destroyer minesweeper *Ellyson*, whose attacker crashed just off its starboard bow at 0930hrs while the ship was on a screening patrol with the destroyer escort *Foreman* – one sailor was killed and four wounded. *LST-534* was not so fortunate, the landing ship being hit while beached in Nakagusuku Bay unloading supplies at around the same time. The vessel was struck in the forecastle area, with the aircraft's bomb penetrating the deck and blowing a hole in the bottom of the hull. With an uncontrollable fire raging on board, *LST-534* slowly settled on the shallow seabed and was totally gutted. Thirty-five crew had been wounded in the attack, while three sailors from a shore party that happened to be on board when the ship was hit were killed.

Their attackers were identified as "Zekes," and, crucially, an assembly data plate from the tokko that hit *LST-534* was retrieved by the crew. It confirmed that the ship had been hit by a Nakajima-built A6M2.

The June 22 mission essentially marked the end of the tokko campaign over Okinawa, with both the IJAAF and the IJNAF now focused on rebuilding their aircraft and pilot numbers for the forthcoming invasion of Japan. Small-scale attacks nevertheless continued off Okinawa until war's end, although these were few and far between and nowhere near the scale and intensity of April or May. Nevertheless, ships continued to be hit and lives lost.

For example, on the evening of July 19 the destroyer *Thatcher* was at anchor in Nakagusuku Bay having repairs completed following a tokko attack on May 20 when, at 1950hrs, lookouts spotted a pair of aircraft approaching from the south. They had just passed close astern when the pilot of one of them did a wingover and dove at the vessel from its port side. The tokko struck the ship on that side above the waterline amidships before glancing off into the bay. Most of the aircraft ended up in the water alongside the destroyer, burning as it sank, although one wing remained on board after having struck a lifeboat. Two men on board were wounded in the attack, which the ship's after action report stated was carried out by an "Oscar."

Ki-43s had indeed been tasked with tokko missions that day, four 204th Sentai aircraft led by 2Lt Yasunari Oda having departed Karenko, on Formosa, at 1705hrs. This was the only success achieved by the tokko on July 19, despite the IJAAF having also despatched single "Sonias" from the Hattoku-based Sei 31st and 71st Hikotai at 1630hrs. In one of the coincidences that war throws up, the 204th Sentai was almost certainly the unit responsible for the May attack on *Thatcher* that sent the vessel to

USS *Callaghan* (DD-792) had the unfortunate distinction of being the last ship to be sunk by the tokko, after being struck by a slow-flying Yokosuka K5Y Willow biplane trainer of the 3rd Ryuko-tai soon after midnight on July 29, 1945. The bomb carried by the aircraft exploded and started a fire that soon reached the handling room for the No. 3 turret, which blew up. Forty-seven crew went down with the ship when it sank shortly after 0230hrs. *(NARA)*

the drydock at Kerama Retto and then on to Nakagusuku Bay for the final repairs to be completed.

Things remained quiet off Okinawa until 0031hrs on July 29 when the destroyers *Callaghan*, *Cassin Young* and USS *Pritchett* (DD-561), manning Radar Picket Station 9A, were alerted that bogies were closing on them from the southwest. *Callaghan*, which was steaming in column formation behind *Pritchett*, was hit by a biplane trainer at 0038hrs as both ships executed a hard turn to starboard. The aircraft had approached *Pritchett* from the port side, before suddenly turning and flying in between both ships until it struck *Callaghan* from the starboard side. The bomb carried by the attacker exploded and started a fire that soon reached the handling room for the No. 3 turret, which blew up.

At 0140hrs the destroyer's commanding officer, Cdr Charles M. Bertholf, ordered abandon ship and the vessel sank soon after 0230hrs, with an underwater explosion rocking the area as it did so – 47 crew went down with the ship. *Callaghan* had the unhappy distinction of being the last vessel to be sunk by an aerial tokko attack.

This photograph of the stern of USS *Pritchett* (DD-561) shows shrapnel and other damage inflicted when the bomb carried by a Yokosuka K5Y1 Willow of the 3 Ryuko-tai exploded as the aircraft crashed into the sea alongside the destroyer on the night of July 29. The ship had been manning Radar Picket Station 9A with the destroyers *Callaghan* and *Cassin Young* when all three vessels were attacked. *(NARA)*

As the destroyer was being abandoned, more attacks on nearby ships commenced. Other aircraft had been circling out of range after *Callaghan* had been hit, with *Cassin Young* shooting one down at 0047hrs and a nightfighter claiming a possible "Betty" soon after 0130hrs. Another aircraft made a run on *Pritchett* from its starboard side at 0143hrs, crashing just six feet off its port stern. The tokko's bomb then exploded, bowing the hull, damaging the superstructure and depth charge racks, and killing two crew.

More attacks by biplanes developed the following night, with *Cassin Young* being the target as it screened off Nakagusuku Bay. The high-speed troop transport USS *Horace A. Bass* (APD-124) was also attacked off Hagushi Beaches, the latter vessel being clipped by a tokko soon after 0200hrs. The underwater explosion that followed when the aircraft hit the water peppered the ship with shrapnel, killing one crewman and wounding a further 15.

A little over an hour later, *Cassin Young* was hit by a second biplane that approached the vessel from astern. Having flown partway along its starboard side, the pilot then struck the warship's aft boat davit at main deck level, knocking out the radars and radios, and communication with the forward fireroom. With their vessel ablaze, the crew hurriedly jettisoned its torpedoes and some 40mm ammunition to prevent their possible detonation from the fire. By 0345hrs, 20 minutes after the hit, this danger had passed, although *Cassin Young*'s starboard propeller shaft remained frozen, leaving only the port engine operational. Despite having suffered serious damage, and the loss of 22 crew (with 45 wounded), the destroyer managed to make its own way to Nakagusuku Bay for emergency repairs to be carried out.

The attacks on both nights were attributed to slow-flying biplanes, identified as "Type 93s" or "Willows" in the various ships' after action reports. The IJNAF did indeed sortie six Yokosuka K5Y Willow intermediate trainers from the 3rd Ryuko-tai that night, the aircraft staging from Giran, on Formosa, via Ishigaki or Miyakojima Islands, although no time of departure for the group was listed. These were presumably the tokko that attacked *Cassin Young* and *Horace A. Bass*, although no information is available on the seemingly similar aircraft types that had attacked *Callaghan* and *Pritchett* the previous night. IJNAF documentation notes that other tokko units – namely the 1st and 2nd Ryuko-tai – had been formed with eight "Willows" each, although neither appear in records as having participated in any missions.

The after action report compiled by *Cassin Young*, which was close to the ships targeted on both nights, also gave further insight into several aspects of the attacks. These included the fact that the biplanes were accompanied by larger, faster aircraft that its crew believed acted as guides and attack directors, reporting the results back to wherever the tokko had taken off from. The report's compiler also theorized that the controlling aircraft had used radar or homing devices to find the ships, although it was also noted that the attackers often relied on the moonlight to spot their targets. Finally, the report stated that the larger aircraft presented as better targets on radar than the biplane attackers, making it easier for nightfighters to intercept them. This had indeed been the case on the night *Callaghan* was sunk.

This was in stark contrast to the actual attackers, which presented "poor tracks" on radar – several of the ships that were engaged over the two nights noted that the "Willows" were little more than "fuzzy" tracks on their radars. The range at which they were detected was also short owing to their wood-and-fabric construction, low-altitude approach, and slow speed, which was estimated at about 95 knots. The latter also limited the effectiveness of the ships' defensive tactic of making sudden evasive turns at speed when attacked, while the efficacy of the antiaircraft fire was also negated by the construction of the biplanes. *Cassin Young*'s crew also observed that the "Willows" did not burn as readily when hit (unlike more modern types, the K5Y's wings did not contain fuel tanks). These factors probably contributed to the relative success of the attacks, despite the "Willow's" obsolescence and poor condition – *Cassin Young*'s after action report described the aircraft as being in "dilapidated" condition based on the wreckage recovered, which included a tire that was "thoroughly worn and threadbare."

There was another pause in attacks until after the two nuclear bombs had been dropped on Hiroshima and Nagasaki and US Navy ships started operating off Japan again. At 1800hrs on August 13, two "Zekes" from the 2nd Jinrai Bakusen-tai (formed from the remnants of the 721st Kokutai) took off from Kikaijima Island loaded with a 1,102lb Type 2 No. 50 Model 1 Ordinary Bomb each and headed once again for Okinawa. Flown by Lt(jg) Shiro Okajima and PO1c Minoru Hoshino, the "Zekes" found the attack personnel transport USS *La Grange* (APA-124) at anchor in Nakagusuku Bay at 1945hrs and crashed into it in quick succession. Although the second fighter only managed to clip the ship before crashing alongside and exploding, showering it with debris, fragments and burning fuel, the lead "Zeke" smashed through the superstructure prior to its bomb exploding, causing severe internal damage and killing 21 crew and wounding 89.

La Grange was the last ship to be hit by a kamikaze during World War II, although its attackers were not the final tokko pilots to die off Okinawa. Following Emperor Hirohito's radio broadcast to the Japanese people at noon on August 15, 1945, declaring that the nation would capitulate and accede to the terms of the Allies' Potsdam Declaration, Vice Admiral Matome Ugaki wrote in his diary that as he had not received an order from the IJN high command to cease fighting. He duly decided that he would head to Okinawa on one last tokko mission, stating he was taking responsibility for the failure of his pilots to turn the tide of the war.

Initially, a small cadre of pilots and observers from the 701st Kokutai at Oita were rounded up for the mission, although once the remaining crews on the base heard about the operation they insisted on joining Ugaki. In the end, 11 D4Ys and 23 men took off at 1700hrs, each aircraft

Having removed his rank insignia, Vice Admiral Matome Ugaki prepares to climb aboard the 701st Kokutai D4Y idling behind him at Oita on August 15, 1945 prior to leading the last tokko mission of World War II. This operation was mounted after Emperor Hirohito's radio broadcast to the Japanese people at noon that same day stating that the nation would capitulate and accede to the terms of the Allies' Potsdam Declaration. Prior to taking off, Ugaki wrote in his diary that he was taking responsibility for the failure of his pilots to turn the tide of the war. *(Tony Holmes collection)*

carrying a half-tank of fuel and a 1,102lb Type 2 No. 50 Model 1 Ordinary Bomb. Ugaki's aircraft – almost certainly a D4Y3 or a D4Y4 coded 701-122, given it was the "Judy" he posed in front of for his final photographs – took off with three aircrew on board (the others had two, as was standard for the D4Y). Aside from Ugaki, WO Akiyoshi Endo also climbed into the rear crew position occupied by the Vice Admiral. The identity of the pilot remains unknown.

Ugaki's hopes for striking one last blow against the enemy were ultimately dashed, for despite radioing at 1830hrs that the remaining aircraft (three had turned back due to mechanical maladies) had encountered the enemy fleet and were attacking, no ships were hit off Okinawa that evening. The D4Y of Ens Takashi Isommura and CPO Takao Goto crashed into a small hillock on one of the islands off Okinawa that evening, having possibly mistaken it for a building in the fading light. Bits of the wreckage and Goto's life vest remain on display at the National Museum of the USAF in Dayton, Ohio, having been donated by a US serviceman who was on the unidentified island when the aircraft crashed.

As for Ugaki himself, the still-smoldering remains of a "Judy" cockpit section containing three men was found on a sandbar at Iheya Jima, 20 miles northwest of the northern tip of Okinawa, by the crew of *LST-926* on the morning of August 16. A short sword was found on the

A common scene at many Japanese airfields in the weeks after the war had ended was the removal of propellers from any aircraft that might be used for unauthorized tokko missions (like Vice Admiral Ugaki's) after the ceasefire. This photograph was taken at the IJNAF's base at Atsugi, near Tokyo, and it features a variety of aircraft including "Zeke" fighters and "Frances" and "Judy" bombers – all effective tokko types. (*NARA*)

ABOVE
A group of IJAAF pilots conduct a brief ceremony before a "mission." This event was actually a staged re-enactment at Chofu airfield, west of Tokyo, in November 1945 for a USAAF film crew making a documentary about the tokko campaign. Immediately behind the pilots is an apparently serviceable Ki-51, complete with a propeller, while a clearly derelict Ki-27 is off to the right. *(NARA)*

body of a man wearing a dark green uniform. Ugaki was said to have been in possession of such a weapon as he boarded the aircraft at Oita, reportedly removing his gold braid and rank insignia as he did so. All three bodies were buried in the sand near to the wreckage. In the end, the final tokko mission was perhaps a summation of the entire campaign, with eager young men dying needlessly for little tactical or strategic gain while fighting for a cause that was already lost.

THE NUMBERS

The exact number of tokko that targeted Allies ships from October 1944 until war's end is difficult to determine with any accuracy. It is generally accepted that almost 4,000 Japanese aircrew died during the course of 3,000 kamikaze missions. This figure includes 2,525 IJNAF and 1,388 JAAF personnel. Only one-third of crews involved in the 3,000 missions managed to actually carry out an attack on a ship. Those that achieved this feat had roughly a 36 percent chance of success. A total of 367 tokko hit their target or managed a near miss close enough to inflict damage. Overall, each kamikaze aircraft had about a 9.4 percent chance of hitting a target, and if it did, it caused an average of 40 casualties.

The cost of the tokko campaign to the US Navy and its Allies was 66 vessels sunk or never repaired and almost 400 damaged to some degree. Of the vessels that never returned to service, only 39 were sunk outright by a kamikaze. Personnel casualties from these attacks totaled approximately 15,000, with this figure including 6,190 killed and 8,760 wounded.

Such losses meant that the US Navy had to take the kamikaze campaign very seriously. Indeed, the threat posed by tokko was graphically spelt out in early February 1945 in a report using data collated from October 12 to November 30, 1944. Its author calculated that more than half of the 108 kamikaze attacks undertaken during this seven-week period resulted in some kind of damage being inflicted on the ships that were targeted. Furthermore, 5.1 percent of targets hit had been sunk and 47.4 percent had suffered some form of damage. Following the carnage inflicted on Allied ships during the bloody campaign to retake the Philippines it quickly became obvious to senior naval officers in the Pacific that tokko attacks posed a far greater threat than conventional attacks – a kamikaze attack was seven to ten times more likely to cause damage than a conventional attack. From October 1944 through to April 1945, the average number of aircraft required to score a hit on a ship was 37 for conventional attacks and 3.6 for kamikaze attacks.

Although the Japanese had ultimately been defeated in the Philippines, the IJNAF and the IJAAF had proven without doubt that the kamikaze was a viable weapon that could have tactical effects on the enemy. Between 500 and 600 aircraft had been lost in tokko attacks, but they had damaged

140 vessels, of which 17 were sunk or scuttled. As significant as these losses where, however, they had no operational or strategic impact on the final outcome of the campaign in the Philippines.

The kamikazes' stunning debut in the Philippines was as good as it got for the Japanese. By the time Operation *Iceberg* commenced on April 1, 1945, it was clear to the Allies that the tokko's overall effectiveness was declining. This was primarily because attacks were now being mounted by novice pilots and both the US Navy and, on a much smaller scale, the Royal Navy had become better at countering the threat. Improved fighter CAPs and increased antiaircraft armament combined to take a heavy toll on the kamikazes between February and May 1945, when an estimated 1,100 tokko sorties were flown. Roughly 500 kamikazes were downed by fighters and 420 destroyed by antiaircraft fire, thus inflicting no damage on Allied ships. This meant that around 180 tokko hit a target. In percentage terms, 84 percent of kamikazes were missing their target by 1945.

Although the number of sunk and damaged ships dramatically increased in the final months of the Pacific War, this was because of the sheer number of aircraft being used as kamikazes – particularly during the numbered Kikusui operations. Aside from the 32 ships sunk between January and August 1945, many damaged vessels were declared constructive total losses and sold for scrapping at war's end. Even with this level of success, it soon became clear to the Japanese that such totals were not going to stem the Allied advance in the Pacific.

Despite the fact that kamikazes were dealing real blows to the US Navy, an obvious side effect was that these operations were also causing huge losses to the Japanese. Ultimately, suicide operations were unsustainable. It is important to note that even in April 1945, the heaviest month of kamikaze attacks, only 35 percent of Japanese sorties were conducted by kamikazes.

Two key problems undermined the effectiveness of tokko attacks. Firstly, pilots tasked with hitting ships exhibited poor or non-existent target recognition skills when selecting targets. In the heat of battle, having successfully penetrated the increasingly effective CAP off Okinawa, inexperienced pilots were targeting the first ships they saw – usually destroyers manning radar picket stations – and ignoring more important targets like loaded troops transports or supply ships bringing in men and materiel for *Iceberg*. The bold statistics bear this fact out. Between February and May 1945, 38 percent of tokko attacks were against destroyers and 45 percent targeted smaller vessels. Although this tactic adhered to the Japanese strategy of reducing the effectiveness of the US Navy's critically important radar picket line off Okinawa in order to give subsequent kamikaze aircraft a better chance of hitting more lucrative targets, this proved to be fundamentally wrong since it gave pilots with limited skills the difficult job of hitting the type of vessel best able to defend itself through maneuvering and accurate antiaircraft fire.

The second problem lay with the weapon itself. Although an aircraft that hit a ship could cause appreciable destruction, it typically lacked sufficient terminal speed to penetrate into the bowels of a ship and inflict telling damage. When a vessel sank as a result of a tokko attack, it was usually because of the detonation of the aircraft's bomb(s), rather than the impact of the aircraft itself. Although kamikazes took a toll of small warships, they had little impact on cruisers and battleships because of their armored decks and turrets. Kamikazes inflicted shocking topside damage and killed a considerable number of sailors manning exposed antiaircraft gun batteries, but they were found sorely lacking in destructive power when it came to sinking large warships.

This was not the case, however, when aircraft carriers were targeted. One of the tokko's key weapons was fire, and carriers were crammed full of combustible items in the form of fuel lines and aircraft loaded with fuel and ordnance. Escort carriers proved particularly vulnerable, lacking the damage-control crews and firefighting capabilities found in the larger fleet carriers. The Japanese knew this, and carriers proved to be the most important target for the kamikazes due to their combustibility. Furthermore, US Navy carriers had unarmored flightdecks, and the resulting fires caused by tokko penetrating into the hangar bay before their ordnance exploded forced a number of vessels out of action for weeks at a time.

Ultimately, despite the kamikazes' proven successes against both large and small carriers, the Fast Carrier Task Force managed to conduct combat operations for more than 70 days within easy range of Japanese airfields on Kyushu and still maintain sea and air control over Okinawa and surrounding islands.

Despite the carnage caused by the kamikazes, they failed to change the course of the war. As a military weapon, the kamikaze was ineffective in achieving its goals. The initial attacks did not deter US forces from coming ashore at Leyte, and even as the IJNAF and IJAAF dramatically

An unidentified tokko pilot ties a knot in his cloth hachimaki headband marked with a red naval rising sun insignia. Typically, such headbands usually only featured the red hinomaru, flanked either side by kanji symbols that read "Divine Wind." He has tucked a Hamada hand gun into the straps used to secure his float vest over his one-piece summer flight suit. (© NYP 69993)

stepped up the formation of tokko-tai, they proved powerless to stop the invasion of Luzon. Even at Okinawa, with the implementation of the Kikusui campaign, the efforts of the kamikazes failed to slow the pace of the American advance towards Japan. As a military weapon the kamikaze had been a failure. The unbroken morale of Allied sailors exposed to them during the final 11 months of the Pacific War proved that the tokko had also failed as a psychological weapon. Staring defeat in the face, yet unwilling to surrender, Japanese airmen had no other option but to resort to suicide attacks.

BIBLIOGRAPHY

BOOKS

Chambers, Mark and Holmes, Tony, Osprey Combat Aircraft 119 – *Nakajima B5N "Kate" and B6N "Jill" Units* (Osprey Publishing, 2017)

Francillon, René, *Japanese Aircraft of the Pacific War* (Putnam, 1987)

Hobbs, David, *The British Pacific Fleet: The Royal Navy's Most Powerful Strike Force* (Seaforth Publishing, 2011)

Ichimura, Hiroshi, Osprey Aircraft of the Aces 85 – *Ki-43 "Oscar" Aces of World War 2* (Osprey Publishing, 2009)

Millman, Nicholas, Osprey Aircraft of the Aces 100 – *Ki-44 "Tojo" Aces of World War 2* (Osprey Publishing, 2011)

Millman, Nicholas, Osprey Aircraft of the Aces 103 – *Ki-27 "Nate" Aces* (Osprey Publishing, 2013)

Millman, Nicholas, Osprey Aircraft of the Aces 114 – *Ki-61 and Ki-100 Aces* (Osprey Publishing, 2015)

Model Art No. 451, *Imperial Japanese Army Air Force Special Attack Units* (Model Art, 1995)

Model Art No. 458, *Imperial Japanese Navy Air Force Kamikaze Special Attack Units* (Model Art, 1995)

Morison, Samuel Eliot, *History of United States Naval Operations in World War II: The Liberation of the Philippines* (University of Illinois Press, 2002)

Rielly, Robin L., *Kamikaze Attacks of World War II: A Complete History of Japanese Suicide Strikes on American Ships, by Aircraft and Other Means* (McFarland, 2012)

Smith, Peter C., *Kamikaze – To Die for the Emperor* (Pen & Sword, 2015)

Stanaway, John, Osprey Aircraft of the Aces 26 – *Mustang and Thunderbolt Aces of the Pacific and CBI* (Osprey Publishing, 1999)

Stern, Robert, *Fire from the Sky: Surviving the Kamikaze Threat* (Naval Institute Press, 2010)

Stille, Mark, Osprey Duel 76 – *US Navy Ships vs Kamikazes 1944–45* (Osprey Publishing, 2016)

Tagaya, Osamu, Osprey Combat Aircraft 22 – *Mitsubishi Type 1 Rikko "Betty" Units of World War 2* (Osprey Publishing, 2001)

Tillman, Barrett, Osprey Aircraft of the Aces 10 – *Hellcat Aces of World War 2* (Osprey Publishing, 1996)

Young, Edward M., Osprey Aircraft of the Aces 109 – *American Aces against the Kamikaze* (Osprey Publishing, 2012)

Zaloga, Steven J., Osprey New Vanguard 180 – *Kamikaze: Japanese Special Attack Weapons 1944–45* (Osprey Publishing, 2011)

WEBSITES

https://www.fold3.com/

http://arawasi-wildeagles.blogspot.com

http://www.usni.org/magazines/navalhistory/2008-04/who-knocked-enterprise-out-war

http://www.kamikazeimages.net/

http://www.j-aircraft.com/research/rdunn/hms_aust/first_kam.htm

http://www.navsource.org/

http://www.ibiblio.org/hyperwar/USN/rep/DamnNeck/index.html

http://ww2db.com/person_bio.php?person_id=305

http://www.japantimes.co.jp/news/2015/05/19/national/history/former-airman-survived-two-wwii-kamikaze-missions/#.VpMa5Pl97IV

http://www.aviationofjapan.com/2015/07/nate-special-attackers-ki-27-aces-extra.html

http://www.armouredcarriers.com

INDEX

Page numbers in **bold** refer to maps and illustrations.

Abdell, Capt E. W. 119
ace pilots 72, 79, 132, 173, **200**, 206, 212, **241**, **242**, 280
after action reports **100**, 135, 182, 193, 197, 203, 205, 218, 222, 225, **234**, 242, 243, 246, 249, 253, 257–258, 261, 262, 263–264, 294, 298, 299, 312, 319, 323, 327, 331, 332
aircraft: Germany: Messerschmitt Bf 110 63; Japan: Aichi B7A "Grace" 147, 185–186, **186**, 187, 188, 189; Aichi E13A "Jake" 258, 281, 309; Aichi Type 99 D3A "Val" 7, **7**, **8**, 16, 41, 48–50, **49**, 51, 71, **71**, 72, 86, 87, **90**, **91**, 93, 106, 109, 110, 123, 126, 127, 128, 131, 137, **139**, 141, 144, 187, 193, 196, 197, 198, **198**, 205, 213, 219, **221**, **222**, 224, 226–230, **234**, 234–235, **235**, 239, 241, 242, **246**, 247, 254, 258, 262, 264, 267, **275**, **279**, **281**, 283, 291, 299, 302, 304, 305, 312, 315, 316, 317, 319, 322; Kawanishi E7K "Alf" 258, 260, 309; Kawanishi H8K2 "Emily" 164–165; Kawanishi N1K1-J "George" 147, 231, 233, 289, 299; Kawasaki Ki-45 "Nick" 25, 44, **63**, 63–64, **111**, **112**, 113, 115, **123**, 130–131, 135, 139, 140, 141, 143, 145, 179, 188, 189, 202, 240, 243, 249, 254, 257, 268, 269, 289, 311; Kawasaki Ki-48 "Lily" 34, 44, 64, 104, 117, 121, 122–123, 125, 127, 145, **145**, 188, 312; Kawasaki Ki-61 "Tony" 16, 33, **40**, **44**, 60–62, 113–114, 132, 144, 195–196, 199, 200, 205, 219, 240, 243, 249, 253, 254–257, 262, **268**, 268–269, 271, **272**, 279, **281**, 295, 300, 301, 302, 304, 310–311, **313**, 315, 322, 323; Kyushu K11W 297, 298, 299, 327; Mitsubishi A5M "Claude" 45; Mitsubishi A6M Zero "Zeke" 19, **21–22**, 29, 33, 37, 45–46, **46**, 72, 73, 75, 77, 79–82, **80**, **81**, **83**, 85–86, 87, 88–90, 95, **96**, 97–99, **98**, 106, 115, 117, **118**, 119, **120**, 125–126, 129, 132–133, 135–136, **136**, 137, 141, 146, 150, 152, 153, 154, 155, 156, 157, **158**, **174**, 175, 176, **186**, **191**, **200**, **201**, 202, 205, 217, 218, 219, 221, 225, 231, 233, 234–235, 237, **244**, **250**, 258, 259, 260, **265**, 265–266, **266**, **268**, 272, **278**, 281, 283, 285, **286**, **290**, **291**, 292–293, 295, 299, 312, 317, 327, 328, 332, **335**; Mitsubishi F1M "Pete" 290, 309, 327; Mitsubishi G3M "Nell" 146; Mitsubishi G4M1/2 "Betty" **9**, 10, 11, **11**, 12, **12**, 13–15, **14**, 64, 65, **65**, 70, 73, **74**, 113, 142, 145–146, 159, **172**, **173**, **174**, **175**, 175–177, 181, 226, 232, **244**, 258, 262–263, 281, 287, 303, 308, 315, 316, **324**, 327; Mitsubishi J2M "Jack" 132; Mitsubishi Ki-46 "Dinah" 28, **37**, 113, 268, 311; Mitsubishi Ki-51 "Sonia" 49, **50**, 50–51, 52, 72, **108**, **109**, 110, 122, 123, 125, 127, 128, 131, 134, 135, 137, 139, 141, **183**, 183–185, **184**, 196, 198, **198**, 203, 205–206, 216, 219, 220, 230–231, **232**, 235, 239, 240, **241**, 248, 294–295, **306**, 307, 317, 322, 328; Mitsubishi Ki-67 "Peggy" 25, 44, 64, **103**, 103–104, 122, 142–143, 145, 146, **178**, 179, 180, 181, 281; Nakajima A6M2-N "Rufe" **307**, 308; Nakajima B6N "Jill" 34, **35**, 41, 55, **56**, 56–57, 70–71, 102, 110, 132, 135, 153, 154, 155, 156, 160, 206, 249, 254, **280**, **281**, 281–283, **308**, **320–321**, 322; Nakajima C6N "Myrt" 28, **28**, 147, 161, 162, 166, 234, 249; Nakajima J1N "Irving" 126, 129, 136; Nakajima Ki-27 "Nate" 44, 49, 51–52, **52**, 72, 197, 198, **198**, 215–216, **218**, 219, 220, 235, 239, 240, **241**, 244, **247**, 248, **248**, 262, 283, 299, 302, 303–304, 306, 312, 313, 315, 316,

317, 318, **318**, 319, 322, **336**; Nakajima Ki-43 "Oscar" 16, 19, 41, **41**, 46–48, **47**, 59, 61, 93, 104, **105**, 106, 107, 108, **108**, 109, 110, **114**, 115, 116, **118**, 118–119, **119**, **122**, 123, 125, 126, 127, **133**, 135, 139, 140, **140**, 142, 143, 177, 178, 179, 198–199, 200, 219, 220, 233, **234**, 239–240, 254, **254**, 262, 271, **281**, 283, 287, **294**, 295–296, 299, **300**, 312, 313, 315, 316, 318, 322, 323, 328; Nakajima Ki-44 "Tojo" 121, 141, 152, 246, 248, 299, **299**; Nakajima Ki-49 "Helen" 34, 121; Nakajima Ki-79b 52, **52**, 304, 312, 316; Nakajima Ki-84 "Frank" 41, **59**, 59–60, 123, 146, 147, 219, 244, 246, 248, 249, 254, 258, 259, 262, 267–268, 279, 281, 283, 289, **298**, 299, **299**, 300, **316**, 317, 318, 323, 326, 327; Nakajima Type 97 B5N "Kate" 7, 16, **27**, 34, 54–55, **55**, 57, 137, 219, 221, **221**, **222**, 224, 234–235, 249, 254, **281**, 288–289, 312; Tachikawa Ki-9 "Spruce" 35–36, **36**; Tachikawa Ki-55 "Ida" 235, 239, 240, 244; Yokosuka D4Y "Judy" 17, 19, 33, 49, 52–54, **81**, **82**, 85, **99**, **100**, **101**, 102, 106, 114–115, **119**, **120**, 129, 135, 137, **149**, 150, 154, 155, 156, 157, 160, 167–168, **168**, **170**, 171, **171**, **176**, 188, 189, 198, 207, **208**, **214**, 215, 218, 234, 243, 253, 266–267, 295, 327, 333, **335**; Yokosuka K5Y "Willow" **329**, 329–332; Yokosuka MXY7 Ohka "Baka" 64–65, **65**, **66–67**, **172**, 174, **174**, 175–176, 225, **225**, 226, **227**, **324–325**; Yokosuka P1Y "Frances" 7, **8**, 34, 39, 41, 44, 57–59, **58**, 64, 92, 94, 103, 115, 121–122, **122**, **123**, 161, **161**, **163**, **164**, 165–167, 171, 173, 189, 198, 215, 234–235, 281, 302–303, 310, 311, **335**; UK: Fairey Firefly **232**; Supermarine Seafire **178**, 180, **200**, 272; US: Boeing B-17: 16; Boeing B-29: 64, 153, 164, 185, 186, 297; Curtiss SB2C Helldiver 285, **286**; Grumman F4F/FM-2 Wildcat **9**, 10, 53, 131, 139, 140, 317; Grumman F6F Hellcat 53, **87**, 97, 103, 121, **155**, 157, **172**, **173**, **175**, 176–177, 180, 183, 186, 188, 189, 206, 231, 232, **244**, 269, 271; Grumman TBF/TBM Avenger 82, 86, **87**, 131, 266, **267**, **268**, 274; Lockheed P-38 Lightning 53, 104, 107, 109, 112; Marine PBM Mariner 271, **272**; North American P-51 Mustang 153; PBY Catalina 144; Republic P-47 Thunderbolt 53, 121, 253, 313; Vought F4U Corsair 53, 118, 177, 207, 231, 241, **241**, **244**, 246–247, 248, **254**, 259, **259**, 260, 264, 265, **266**, 272–274, 283, 285, **286**, **299**, 313; Vought OS2U Kingfisher 197, 233, **234**

air superiority mission tactics 233–234
air tactics for tokko attacks 21–25, **22–23**, **25**
Allied convoy attack at Lunga Point, Guadalcanal 13–16
Allied strategy 9–10, 21, 69, 111, 117, 153, 167, 182, 185, 338
amphibious landings on Borneo *see* Operations: *Oboe*
Anazawa, 2Lt Toshio **47**
anti-flash clothing **124–125**
anti-submarine screening **218**, 219, 289
antiaircraft fire **79**, **83**, **84**, 85, 92, 95, 102, 125, 139, 141, 142–143, 152, 171, **191**, 193, 195–196, **221**, 226, 232, **233**, 240, 252, 262, **290**, 295, 322, 332
Araki, Cpl Yukio **306**, 307
Arima, Rear Adm Masafumi **17**, 17–19
armor penetration 32, 33
armor protection **61**, 201
Australian Army I Corps 181
Axtell, CO Maj George 241, 242, **242**

battle of Iwo Jima, the 57
battle of Leyte Gulf, the 57, 74–86, **78**, **79**, **80**, **81**, **82**, **83**
battle of Midway, the 10, 49, 53
battle of Okinawa, the 23, 27, 33, 191–328, **192**, **195**, **196**, **200**, **201**, **202**, **203**, **204**, **208**, **209**, **210**, **211**, **214**, **218**, **221**, **222**, **223**, **225**, **228–229**, **230**, **233**, **234**, **235**,

236–237, **238**, **240**, **242**, **244**, **248**, **251**, **252**, **255**, 256–257, **259**, **261**, **265**, **267**, **268**, **269**, **270**, **272**, **273**, **274**, **275**, **281**, **282–283**, **284–285**, **286**, **287**, **290**, **291**, **292**, **293**, **294**, **296**, **299**, **301**, **307**, **313**, **314**, **316**, **318**, **319**, **320–321**, **324–325**, 340
battle of Santa Cruz, the **7**, 8, 16
battle of Savo Island, the 245
battle of the Solomons, the 7
Bogan, Rear Adm Gerald F. 86
burials at sea **102**, **214**, 217

Callaghan, Capt William M. 217
camouflage schemes **210**, 248–249
CAPs (combat air patrols) 21, **26–27**, 27, 28, **31**, 44, 64, 70, 79, 88, 97, 109, 118, 130, 132, **175**, 188, 189, **194**, 201, 212, 213, 215, **223**, 226, 237, 246–247, 251, 254, 259, 272, 283, 309, 311, 313, 322, 338
cargo ships 244–245, 309, 310, 322; Liberty ships 73, 74, 110, 116, 126, 127, 131, 145, 252–253, 322; Victory ships 209, 245
carrier design differences 201–202
carriers as targets for tokko attacks 37–39, **39**, 339
Chandler, Rear Adm Theodore E. **137**
Chung-Hoon, Cdr Gordon Pai'ea 232, **233**
Cole, Capt William M. 109, 114
Combined Fleet Headquarters 161, 162, 166, 213, 279
command structures 191
constructive total loss declarations 3**14**, **38**, **210**, 212, 238, 252, **255**, 257, 283, 301, 311, 315, 338
convoy ship attacks 13–16, 110, 116, 126–127, 131, 145
cruisers and damage impacts 41

damage impacts 36–41, **38**, **39**, **40**, 52, 60, 65, **69**, 71–72, 77, 80, **80**, 81–83, **83**, 85, 118–119, **123**, 126, **134**, 134–135, **139**, 140, 143–144, 146–147, **149**, **154**, **155**, 156, **157**, 157–159, **163**, 165, 169, 171, 184–185, 186–187, 337–339; at Leyte 77, 80, **80**, 81–83, **83**, 85, 88–89, **91**, 92–93, 95, **96**, **98**, **99**, 99–100, **101**, 103, 108, 109–110, 112, 115–116; at the Battle of Okinawa x**196**, 199, 201, 204–205, 208, **208**, **210–211**, 212, 215, 217, 220, **222**, 231–232, **233**, **235**, 237, 241, 243, 245, 247, 249, 251–252, **252**, 253, **255**, 255–257, **256**, 262–264, 266, **267**, **268**, 269–271, **270**, 272–274, **273**, **274**, **277**, 283, 285, **286**, 289, 290, **291**, 293, 295–297, 298, 300, 302, 305, 306, 308, 309, 310, 311, 313–315, **314**, 316, 317, **318**, 322, 323, 326, 327, 328, 329–331, **330**, 332
damage report for the USS *Abner Read* **91**
Dechaineux, Capt Emile **71**, 72
destoyers and damage impacts 39–41
Deyo, Rear Adm Morton L. 197, **221**
Doolittle raid, the 61
drawbacks in plane performance and design 45, 48, 52–53, 54–55, **55**, 58, 62

Egusa, Lt Cdr Takashige 7, 8, **8**, 161
engines 11, **39**, 44, 51, 53, 60, 62, 63, 64, 114, 147; Homare 11: 57, 58, 60, 166; Kinsai 49; Mamoru 11: 56; Sakae 11: 54, 56, 57
Essex-class carriers **96**, **172**, **278**, **282–283**
experience levels of pilots 31, 338

fighter escorts for tokko formations **30–31**
film documentary about the tokko campaign **336**
first battle of the Philippine Sea ("Great Marianas Turkey Shoot"), the 7, 54, 57
"flash fire" burns **288**
Fleming, Capt Robert 136, **136**
Formosa offensive, the 149–153, **150**, **151**
Fuchida, Cdr Mitsuo 54–55, 160–161
Fujii, 1Lt Hajime **310**, 311
Fukudo me, Vice Adm Shigeru **76**

Guadalcanal, capture of 10–16, **12**
Gulf of Tonkin Incident, the 153

hachimaki headband **340**
Halsey, Adm William F. 69–70, **70**, 76, 312–313
Helmet for my Pillow (book) 11
Hiragi, Katsumi 217
Hirohito, Emperor 189, 332
homing devices 331
Honshu campaign, the 185–189, **186**, **187**

identification of aircraft 49, 50–51, 72, 94, 102, 107, 110, 113, 114, **118**, 119, 125, 126, 128, 132, 135, 140, 142, 145–146, 147, 152, 156, 157, 159, 160, 171, 173, 180, 181, 187, **187**, 198, **198**, 205, 207, 216, 218, 219, **234**, 242, **242**, 243, 246, 249, 253, 262, 294–295, 299–300, 302, 312, 313, 327
IJA (Imperial Japanese Army), the 254
IJAAF (Imperial Japanese Army Air Force), the 7, 8, 16, 17, 25, 34, 41, 60–61, 63, 104, 114, 117, **151**, 167, **168**, **169**, 177, 185, 191, **192–193**, 196, 297, 337, 339–340; 6th Hikodan (Flying Brigade) 72; Sentai (Air Flotilla) 123; 1st 146; 11th 146; 12th Koku 327; 17th 199, 254, 255, **313**, 315; 19th 219, 240, 253, 267, 295; 20th 104, 115, 254, 312, 317; 26th Koku 17; 29th 113, 317; 31st 140; 33rd **122**; 45th 128; 54th 107; 58th 179; 61st 181; 62nd 299; 72nd 146; 73rd 146; 75th 117, 118, 125; 83rd 125; 95th 121; 101st **59**, 259, **259**; 102nd 259, **259**; 103rd 259, **259**; 105th 205, 219, 249, 268, **268**; 200th 146; 204th **294**, 295, 297, 328; 208th 117, 128, **145**; 246th 121; tokko units: 3rd Kokugun-tai 178–179, 181, 183, **183**, **184**; 4th Kokugun-tai 146; Banda-tai 104; Chusei-tai 279, 295; Fugaku-tai 103, 104, 123, 142, 145; Gokoku-tai 115, 143; Hakko-tai 115; 1st tai 105, **105**, 107; 3rd Yasukuni-tai 104, 107, 115; 5th Tesshin-tai 110, 122–123, 127, 135, 137; 6th Sekicho-tai **108**, **109**, 110, 135, 137, 140; 7th Tanshin-tai 115, 123; 9th Ichisei-tai **133**, 135, **140**, 142; 10th Jungi-tai 125, 127; 11th Kokon-tai 135, 139, 140, 143; 12th Shinshu-tai 128, 131, 140, 188, 189; Hakko Dai 2-tai 104; Ichyu-tai 115, 117; Kyoko-tai 117, 118, 121, 123, 125, 145, **145**; Seika-tai 123, 125, 143, 146; Shichisei Jinrai-tai 181; Shichisei Shodo-tai 183, **183**, **184**; Shinbu-tai 214–215, 216, 220, 231, 235, 240, 244, **247**, 248, **254**, 258, 271, **272**, 283, **294**, 295, **298**, 299, 301, 303–304, 306, 310, **310**, 311, 312, 316, 318, 322, 326, 327; 72nd **306**, 307; Yasukuni-tai 115 *see also* IJN, the; IJNAF, the
IJN (Imperial Japanese Navy), the 7, 9, 13, 160, 213; Kamikaze Special Attack Corps: 1st Kamikaze Special Attack Corps 19, 72, 75; Hazakura-tai 87–88, 90; Kikusai-tai 121, 168; Shikishima-tai 85; Taigi-tai 202, 205, 231, 265, **265**, 266, 272; Wakazakura-tai 118, 125; 2nd Kamikaze Special Attack Corps 87; 11th Shomu-tai 110; Reisen-tai 93,

150; Shinpei-tai 93; Shisei-tai 87, 93, 94, **221**, 224; Tenpei-tai **90**, 93, 94; 3rd Kamikaze Special Attack Corps: Baika-tai 93 ; Byakko-tai 95; Kasagi-tai 103; Oka-tai 93, 128; Sakon-tai 95; 4th Kamikaze Special Attack Corps: Katorai-tai 102; 5th Kamikaze Special Attack Corps: Gufu-tai 115; Kusunagi-tai 121–122, **123**, **221**, 224, 247; Shippu-tai 103; Chihaya-tai 114–115; Gekko-tai 129; Hachiman-tai 135, **221**, 224, 239, 249; Jinrai Butai 174, **174**, **175**, **176**, 219, 226, 235, 258, 262, 263, **324**, 327; Kenmu-tai 202, 205, 217, 218, 231, 250, **290**; Kongo-tai 117, **118**, 119, **120**, 122, 126, 127, 129, 133, 134, 135, 136, 137, 141; Kotohira Suishin-tai 258; Kyokujitsu-tai **134**, 135; Niikata-tai 149, 150, **152**; Seiki-tai 288, 289; Seito-tai **246**, 247, 302; Shichisei-tai 250, **250**, **290**; Shinken-tai 233, 267; Shinten-tai 254, 312; Shiragiku-tai 297, 308; Tokiwachuka-tai **221**, 224; Tokushima-Shiragiku-tai 308; Tsukuba-tai 231, 250, **290**, 293

IJNAF (Imperial Japanese Naval Air Force), the 7, 8, 10, 13, 16, 17, 25, **25**, 32, 41, 45, 56, 70, 106, 110, 115, 117, 128, 142, **151**, 167, **168**, **169**, 185, 191–193, **192–193**, 198, 297, 337, 339–340; Azusa Tokubetsu Butai 162; Hikotai: 1st 153; 1st Yasen Hoju Hikotai 177–178; 1st Kojun-tai 179; 2nd Kojun-tai 179; 2nd Shichisei Kojun Hikotai 179, 180; 3rd Kyoiku 183, **183**; 5th 188; 23rd 258; 32nd 196; 102nd **90**; 103rd 171; 254th 153; 303rd **244**; 306th **286**; 310th 153; 703rd 70; 708th 70, 174–175, 232; 711th **172**, **173**, 174, 175; Sei 15th 312; Sei 17th 196, 240; Sei 26th 289, 295; Sei 31st 289, 291, 294–295, 328; Sei 32nd 205; Sei 33rd 246, 279, **316**, 317; Sei 34th 249, 279; Sei 35th 254, 279; Sei 36th 244; Sei 38th 235; Sei 39th 199, 200; Sei 41st 198, 283; Sei 71st 328; Sei 114th 202; Sei 119th 240, 243, 249; Sei 120th 267–268, 289; Sei 123rd 254, 268, 269, **269**, 289; Kikusai Butai 168, **171**, 213, 219; Azusa-tai 168; Ginga-tai 168, 173, 198, 215, 302; Suisei-tai 168, **170**, **176**, 177, 198, 207; Kokutai: 4th 10, 11; 33rd **49**; 103rd 171; 121st 161; 141st 162; 201st 19, 79, **80**, 81, 133, 147; 203rd 259, 281; 205th 202; 210th 207; 252nd 205, 218, 240, **240**, 281; 343rd 233, 259; 405th 64; 601st 153, 218, 240, **240**, 701st **90**, 99, 102, 168, 171, 234, 332–333; 703rd 13; 705th (Misawa) 11, 13; 707th 13; 708th 235; 721st **172**, **173**, 174, 175, 217, 234, 250–251, 279–281, **286**, 332; 732nd 234; 762nd 168; 763rd 70; Genzan 250, **250**; Hyakurihara 288; Kikusui-Tenzan (131st) **27**, **56**, **206**, **280**, **308**, **320–321**; Tsukuba **292**; Yatabe 250; Mitate-tai 154, 156, 185–186, **186**, 188; 2nd Mitate-tai 34, 153–154, 160; 2nd Kogekitai 154–156, 157, 160; 2nd Ryusei-tai 187–188; 3rd Kogekitai 154, 157; 4th Kogekitai 154, **157**, 159; 5th Kogekitai 157, 159; 4th Mitate-tai 188, 189; 7th Mitate-tai 185, **186**, 188, 189 *see also* IJAAF, the; IJN, the

Ikeuchi, 1Lt Sadao 128, 141
insignia and emblems **36**, **90**, **172**, **200**, 220, **246**, **285**, **340**
invasion of the Philippines (October 1944 – January 1945), the 17, 19, 69–70, **78**, 79
Iwo Jima invasion, the 153–160, **154**

Japanese military strategy 8–9, 16–19, **18**, 27–29, 160–162, 167, **168**, 191, 338–339; tactics for tokko attacks 21–25, **22–23**, **25**
Japanese plan to attack the US Pacific Fleet *see* Operations: *Tan No. 2*
jibaku (suicide) attacks 9, **9**, 10, 16, 73, **74**, 92, 94, 110, 128, 326
John C. Butler-class destroyer artwork **276–277**

Kachi, Akira 217
Kerama Retto islands 193, **195**, 197, 205, the
Kiefer, Capt Dixie **150**, 152
Kikusui operations **27**, 27–28, 31, 219, 231, 233, 239, 243–244, 246–247, 338, 340; No.

1: **206**, 206–219, 213, **320**; No. 2: 219–231; No. 3: 231–243; No. 4: 243–253; No. 5: 253–279, **254**; No. 6: **261**, 279–297; No. 7: 297–301; No. 8: 304–312; No. 9: 312–323; No. 10: 323–324
Koreans in the Japanese imperial forces 289
Kumagaya Army Aviation School **310**
Kyushu airfields strikes 167–177, **168**, **169**, **170**, **172**, **173**, **175**, 313

Larkin, Lt John 239
Leckie, Robert 11
Leyte, invasion of 71–73
Liberty ships 73, 74, 110, 116, 125, 126, 127, 131, 145, 252, 322; SS *S. Hall Young* 252–253
Lingayen Gulf **133**, **134**, 134–135, **136**, 139, 144
losses 7, 8, 12, 15, 33, 35, **38**, **39**, 39–40, **40**, 41, 44, 49–50, 51, 54, 55, 57, 60, 64, 65, **71**, 73, 77, **80**, 80, 82, 83, **87**, **88**, 90, **91**, 92, 95, **97**, **99**, 100, 102, **102**, 104, 106, 108, 109, 110, 116, 117, 119, **119**, **120**, 121, 126, 127, 128, 131, **134**, **136**, **138**, **139**, 141, 142, 143, 144, 145, 152, **155**, 156, 159, 165, 168, **168**, **170**, 171, **184**, 187, **194**, **196**, 197, 199, **201**, 203, **203**, 209, 212, 215, 217, **223**, 224, **225**, 227, 237, **237**, **238**, 245, 253, 257, **259**, 259–260, **261**, 262, 264, 266, 271, **272**, 275, **279**, **281**, 283, 285, 289, 290, **291**, 300, 302, 305, 306, 308, 310, **314**, 315, 323, 328, 329, 330, 332, 333, 337
Luzon, invasion of 128–147, **133**, **134**, 340

MacArthur, Gen Douglas 69
Malaya and Singapore, British liberation of 182–185
"Material Condition Able" 88
medical assistance **288**
military honours 10, 15, **241**, 322
Mindoro invasion, the 41, **41**, 117, **118**, 118–128, **120**, **122**, **123**, **125**
minesweeping operations 183, **210**
MTBs (Motor Torpedo Boats) 117, 123, 126

Nicobar Islands strikes 177
night missions 59
night tokko operations 252–253
Nimitz, Adm Chester W. 69
Nishizawa, WO Hiroyoshi 72, 79, 82
nuclear bomb drops 186, 332

obsolescence 41, 44, 49, **49**, 50, 52, **52**, **55**, 182, 213, 215, 235, **247**, 258, 302, 318
obsolete aircraft for tokko operations 41, 44
O'Hare, Lt Edward H. "Butch" **9**, 10
O'Keefe, 1Lt Jeremiah **241**, **242**
Okinawa, capture of 191–195, **192**, **195**
Onishi, Vice Adm Takijiro 8–9, **18**, 19, **76**, 77
Ono, 2Lt Masayoshi 117, 118
Operations: *Iceberg* (April – June 1945) **192–193**, 193–194, 199, 338; *Meridian I and II* (January 1945) **178**, 179–180; *Montclair* 180; *Oboe* (May – August 1945) 180–182; *Tan No. 2* 160–167, **161**, **163**, **164**, **166**, 303; *Zipper* 182
ordnance 31–32, **32**, 34–35, **47**, **52**, 53, **55**, 56, 59, 62, 103, **103**, 108, 118, **122**, 146; A6M5 "Zeke" Type 99 No. 25 Model 1: 32, **32**, 48; MXY7 Ohka manned aerial bomb

44; Type 2 No. 50 Model 1: 33, **100**, 103, 154, 251, 285, **290**, 293, 332, 333; Type 2 No. 80 Mk 5: 33–34, 154, 165, 173, 185, 207, 224, 249, 312; Type 3 No. 6 Mk 6: 147; Type 91 air-dropped torpedo 160, 181, **280**, **320–321**; Type 98 No.25: 32–33, **33**; Type 99 No. 3 Mk 3: 147; Type 99 No. 6 Model 1: **90**, **198**, **246**; Type 99 No. 25: 32, **90**, **198**, **246**, **297**, **298**, **312**, 316

Outerbridge, Cdr William W. **111**, 113

Pacific, The (TV show) 11
Pearce, Lt Jim 173, **173**, **176**
Pearl Harbor attacks, the **8**, **111**, 197
performance 44, 45, 51, 52, 53, **56**, 57, 59–60, **61**, 62, **174**, 175–176
production 57, 58, 63, 65, 147, **158**

Rabaul, fall of **9**, 9–10
radar detection 11, 21, **23**, 25, **27**, **36**, 274, 319, 331–332
radar picketing **194**, **195**, 209, 216, 225, 261, **261**, **296**, 306, 339
rate of fire **86**, **94**, **158**
reconnaissance **28**, 28–29, 161, 162, 164–165, 177, 213
records of missions 196, 199, 203, 213, 216, 220, 258, 279, 294–295, 309, 312, 331
removal of propellers **334–335**
repairs and maintenance **14**, 16, 39, 72, 79, **98**, **101**, 106, 108, **119**, 121, 127, 134, 140, **140**, 141–142, 144, **152**, 153, 167, **170**, 194, 201, 208, 214, 216, 220, 222, 227, **230**, 232, 239, 246, 252, 253, 260, 263, 266, **267**, 272, **275**, 279, 290, **291**, 292, 294, 301, 305, 306, **306**, 308, 309, **314**, 315, 322, 328
rescues **287**, **293**, 300, 303
Reynolds, Sub Lt Richard **200**, 201, 267
Roosevelt, Franklin D. 69
Royal Navy, the 201, 264–265, 338; Naval Air Squadrons: 887 NAS 267; 894 NAS **178**, 179, **200**, 267; 1770 NAS **232**; 1771 NAS **232**; 1830 NAS **231**; 1836 NAS **266**; Task Forces: TF 57 **232**, 265, 272; TF 63 182–183, 184 *see also* ships

Sakita, CPO Sei 87
"sandwich" attacks 295–296
SC-744 submarine chaser 106–107
scrapping of ships **38**, 49, **53**, 144, 212, 238, 252, **255**, 257, 275, 279, **279**, 301, 315, 338
scuttling of ships **11**, 12, 16, **111**, 112, **112**, 113, **120**, 126, 127, **129**, 130, **206**, 209, 211, 304, 338
Second Battle of the Philippine Sea, the *see* battle of Leyte Gulf, the
Seki, Lt Yukio 79, **80**, 82
ships: Japan: *Akagi* 161; *Junyo* 7; *Kumano* 97; *Nachi* 95–96; *Shokaku* 7; *Soryu* 53; *Yamato* 77; *Yasoshima* 97; *Zuikaku* 7; Australia: HMAS *Arunta* 71, 134; HMAS *Australia* 41, **69**, 71, **71**, **72**, **73**, 134, 137, **138**, **139**, 139–140, **140**, 141–142, **142**; HMAS *Shropshire* 71, **72**, **73**, 92; HMAS *Vampire* 50; HMAS *Warramunga* 71, 72; UK: HMS *Ameer* 182, 183; HMS *Cornwall* **8**, 49; HMS *Dorsetshire* 7, **8**, 49; HMS *Empress* 182; HMS *Euryalus* 180; HMS *Formidable* 186, 265, **265**, 266, **267**, **268**, 272–274, **273–274**; HMS *Hermes* 7, 49; HMS *Illustrious* 179, 180, 207–208, **208**, 231; HMS *Indefatigable* **178**, 179, 180, **200**, **201**, 201–202, **202**, 232, 267; HMS *Indomitable* 177, **178**, 179, 180, 266; HMS *Nelson* 182; HMS *Squirrel* 183; HMS *Sussex* **44**, 182, **183**, 184–185; HMS *Vestal* 51, **183**, 184, **184**; HMS *Victorious* 34, 54, 177, **178**, 179, **266**, 272; US: USS *Aaron Ward* 50, **255**, **256–257**, 257, 258; USS *Abner Read* 49, **91**, 92, 93, 94; USS

Achernar 203; USS *Achilles* 104; USS *Adams* 198, 199; USS *Alaska* **238**; USS *Allegan* 313; USS *Allen M. Summer* 136; USS *Alpine* **203**; USS *Ammen* 92–93, 94, 322; USS *Anderson* 92, 93, 94; USS *Anthony* 306, 307, 317–318; USS *Arizon* 55; USS *Aulick* 107, 108, 318, 319, 322; USS *Bache* 254, 257, 290–292; USS *Barry* 297–298, 326; USS *Bataan* **240**; USS *Bates* 302; USS *Belknap* 144, 146; USS *Belleau Wood* **87**, 88, **88**, 89, **89**, 90, **175**, 189; USS *Benham* 239, 240; USS *Benner* 186, 187; USS *Bennett* 213–214; USS *Biloxi* 196, 197; USS *Birmingham* 262; USS *Bismarck Sea* **157**, 159; USS *Black* 217; USS *Bon Homme Richard* 186, 188; USS *Borie* 186–187, **187**; USS *Bowers* **234**; USS *Braine* 306, **306**, 307; USS *Bright* 289–290; USS *Brooks* 136; USS *Brown* 281–283; USS *Brush* 152; USS *Bryant* 125–126, 237; USS *Bullard* 217–218; USS *Bunker Hill* 33, 37, **39**, 46, 86, 248, **282–283**, 283–285, **284–285**, **286**, **287**; USS *Burns* 40, **129**, 130; USS *Bush* 93, 127, 128, **206**, 209, 213; USS *Cabot* 86, 97, 99–100; USS *California* 136; USS *Callaghan* 198, 303, 329, **329**, 331; USS *Caribou* 106; USS *Cassin Young* **223**, 224, 226, 329, 330–331, 332; USS *Chandeleur* **272**; USS *Chase* 296, 297; USS *Chilton* 202; USS *Claxton* 92–93, 94; USS *Cofer* 181, 182; USS *Cogswell* 318, 322; USS *Colahan* 239–240; USS *Colhoun* **206**, 209, 213; USS *Colorado* 48, **105**, 106; USS *Columbia* **40**, 41, 137, 141; USS *Comfort* 248–249; USS *Connolly* 227–230, 231; USS *Cony* 181–182; USS *Cowell* 252, 297, 298; USS *Cree* 302; USS *Curtiss* 323–326; USS *Daly* 247, 305; USS *Dashiell* 231; USS *De Haven* 50; USS *Denver* 182; USS *Dickerson* 202–203; USS *Dorsey* 197; USS *Douglas H. Fox* 286, 287, 293; USS *Drayton* 109, 110; USS *Drexler* 64, 309, 311; USS *DuPage* 143; USS *Dutton* 304–305, 307; USS *Edwards* **114**, 115; USS *Eisele* 308; USS *Ellyson* 211, 328; USS *Emmons* 209–211; USS *England* 49, 245, 246, **275**, 275–279, **279**; USS *Enterprise* 8, 46, 88, **88**, 218, 239, 288, **290**, **291**, **293**; USS *Essex* 35, **53**, 54, 95, **99**, **100**, **101**, 101–103, **102**, 152, **171**, 206, 239, **290**, **291**; USS *Evans* **281**, 283; USS *Fanshaw Bay* 79; USS *Flusser* 109; USS *Foote* 125; USS *Foreman* 198, 328; USS *Forrest* 305; USS *Franklin* 17, 19, 70, **87**, **88**, 88–89, **89**, 90, **149**, 167–168, **168**; USS *Gambier Bay* 77; USS *Gansevoort* 127, 128; USS *Gayety* 262, 263; USS *George F. Elliott* 10–12, **11**; USS *Gilligan* 143, 144, 146; USS *Gilmer* 62, 195–196; USS *Gladiator* 243; USS *Goodhue* 202, 203; USS *Gregory* 52, 216; USS *Guest* 297; USS *Haggard* 251–252; USS *Hall* **120**; USS *Halloran* 327; USS *Halsey Powell* 169, **170**, 171; USS *Hambleton* 205; USS *Hancock* 86, 97, 169, **170**, 171, **214**, 215, 239; USS *Hank* 186, **186**, 187, 217–218; USS *Haraden* **118**, **119**, 119–121; USS *Harding* 237–238; USS *Harry F. Bauer* 252, 286, 287, 315, 316; USS *Haynsworth* 207; USS *Hazelwood* 251, **251**, **252**; USS *Helena* 13; USS *Helm* 134, 159; USS *Henrico* 202; USS *Hinsdale* 199, 200–201; USS *Hodges* 25, 141; USS *Hoel* 77, 79; USS *Honolulu* 72; USS *Hopewell* **120**; USS *Hopkins* 262, 263; USS *Horace A. Bass* 330, 331; USS *Hornet* 7, 8, 16, 55, **172**, **175**, 231; USS *Howorth* 121; USS *Hudson* 241, 242; USS *Hugh W. Hadley* **38**, 65, **281**, 283; USS *Hughes* 64, 115–116; USS *Hull* **11**, 12; USS *Hunt* 231; USS *Idaho* 221–222; USS *Independence* **84**, 86; USS *Indianapolis* 48, 198–199; USS *Ingraham* 260; USS *Intrepid* 86–87, 94, **96**, **97**, 97–99, 171, 173, **238**, 238–239; USS *Isherwood* 241–242; USS *J. William Ditter* **314**, 315; USS *Jarvis* 12; USS *Jeffers* 65, 226; USS *John C. Butler* 295, 297; USS *John W. Weeks* 186; USS *Johnston* 77, 79; USS *Juneau* 13; USS *Kadashan Bay* 140; USS *Kalinin Bay* 79, 82–83, **83**, 85; USS *Kenneth Whiting* 323, 326; USS *Keokuk* 156, 157; USS *Kidd* 29, 217; USS *Killen* 94; USS *Kimberly* 193–194; USS *Kitkun Bay* **24**, **53**, 54, 79, **80**, **81**, **82**, 85, 140–141; USS *La Grange* 46, 332; USS *Laffey* **235**, **236**, 237; USS *Lamson* 112, 113–115, **114**, **119**; USS *Langley* 151, 177; USS *LeRay Wilson* 25–27, 142–143; USS *Leutze* **210**, **211**, 212; USS *Lexington* **9**, 10, 55, 95, 188; USS *Liddle* 115; USS *Lindsey* 226–227, **228–229**, 230; USS *Lipan* 326; USS *Little* 257, 258; USS *Long* 135–136; USS *Longshaw* 214; USS *Louisville* **53**, 54, **133**, **134**, 134–135, 137, **137**, **313**, 315;

USS *Lowry* 309, 311; USS *Luce* 259–260; USS *Lunga Point* **157**, 157–159; USS *Macomb* 62, 254–255, 257; USS *Maddox* 152–153; USS *Mahan* 64, **112**, 112–113; USS *Manila Bay* 133–134; USS *Manlove* 219; USS *Mannert L. Abele* 65, 225, **225**; USS *Marcus Island* 121, 140; USS *Maryland* 48, 107, 108, 214; USS *Mississippi* 141, 142, 315; USS *Missouri* **21**, 29, 217; USS *Moale* **120**; USS *Montpelier* 48, 106, 182; USS *Morrison* 260, **261**; USS *Mugford* 110; USS *Nashville* 41, **(41)42–43**, 48, 118–119; USS *Natoma Bay* 133, 317; USS *Nevada* 7, 196, **196**, 197; USS *New Jersey* 96; USS *New Mexico* 60, 136, **136**, 289; USS *New York* 233, **234**; USS *Newcomb* **210**, **211**, 212; USS *Oberrender* 39–40, 274–275, **276–277**, 279; USS *O'Brien* **111**, 113, **120**, 137, 196–198; USS *Ommaney Bay* **37**, 40, 64, **122**, **123**, **129**, 130; USS *O'Neill* 297, 298, 299; USS *Orestes* 127, 128; USS *Pathfinder* 271; USS *Paul Hamilton* 121; USS *Pensacola* **7**; USS *Petrof Bay* 76, 77, 86; USS *Phoenix* **73**; USS *Pinkney* 248, **248**; USS *Pitt* 200; USS *Porcupine* 51, 126, 127–128; USS *Portland* 13; USS *President Jackson* **12**; USS *Princeton* **261**; USS *Pringle* 127, 128, **237**; USS *Pritchett* 329, 330, **330**, 331; USS *Purdy* **223**, 224; USS *Rall* 52, **218**, 219–220; USS *Ralph Talbot* 245–246; USS *Randolph* 39, 59, **163**, **164**, 165, **166**, 188, 303; USS *Ransom* 241; USS *Rathburne* 245; USS *Rednour* 308; USS *Register* 296, 297; USS *Reid* 116; USS *Reno* 70–71; USS *Richard P. Leary* 72, 136; USS *Richard W. Suesens* 143, 146; USS *Robert H. Smith* 196; USS *Robinson* 143; USS *Rodman* 209–211; USS *Rooks* 315; USS *Salamaua* 60, 146, 147; USS *Samuel B. Roberts* 77; USS *Samuel S. Miles* 219; USS *San Francisco* **12**, 13–15; USS *San Jacinto* 88, 90; USS *Sandoval* 309, 310–311; USS *Sangamon* 62, 64, 76, 77, **268**, 268–271, **269**, **270**; USS *Santa Fe* **149**; USS *Santee* 46, 76, 77, 85, 86; USS *Saratoga* 57, **154**, **155**, 155–156, 157, 159; USS *Sargent Bay* 317; USS *Saufley* 107–108; USS *Savo Island* 131, 133–134; USS *Sederstrom* 64, 243; USS *Seid* **230**; USS *Sentry* 182; USS *Shamrock Bay* 140; USS *Shannon* 252; USS *Shea* 65, 243, 262–263; USS *Shubrick* 311; USS *Sigsbee* 231–232, **233**; USS *Sims* 50, 295; USS *Sitkoh Bay* 215; USS *Smith* 16; USS *Solace* **288**; USS *Sonoma* 73, **74**; USS *South Dakota* **240**; USS *Southard* 305–306, 307; USS *Spectacle* 300–301, 309; USS *St George* 271–272, **272**; USS *St Lo* **24**, 46, 79, **80**, 81–82, 85; USS *St Louis* 48, 106, 262; USS *Stafford* 133–134; USS *Stanly* 226, **227**; USS *Steady* 327; USS *Sterett* 52, 216; USS *Suwannee* 76, 77, 85–86; USS *Swallow* 241; USS *Swearer* 327; USS *Tatum* 311–312; USS *Tekesta* 309–310; USS *Telfair* 202, 203; USS *Tennessee* **221**, **222**, 224; USS *Terror* 252–253; USS *Thatcher* 296–297, 328–329; USS *The Sullivans* **285**; USS *Ticonderoga* 95, **100**, 102, 103, **150**, 151–152, **152**, 153; USS *Tulagi* **191**; USS *Twiggs* 35, 121, 247, 322–323; USS *Tyrrell* 203; USS *Van Valkenburgh* 293–294; USS *Vulcan* 201; USS *Wadsworth* 243, 249; USS *Wake Island* **191**, 205; USS *Walke* 112, 136, 317; USS *Ward* **111**, 111–113, **112**; USS *Wesson* 214; USS *West Virginia* 119, 303; USS *White Plains* 79, **79**, 80; USS *Wilkes-Barre* **287**; USS *William C. Cole* 301–302; USS *William D. Porter* 41, **318**, 318–319, 322; USS *Yorktown* 55, 171, 173, **176**, 177, 251, **280**; USS *Zeilin* 35, 146–147; USS *Zellars* 55, **222**, 222–224

shortage of experienced airmen 7, 8, 338
Sino-Japanese War (1938), the 54
Sprague, Rear Adm Thomas 75, 76
Stump, Rear Adm Felix B. 118, 130, 133
submarine support 162–163
supplies and reinforcements 13

target effectiveness of kamikaze attacks 337, 338
Technical Manual of the US Army 33
technical specifications **66–67**

tokko pilots **76**, **77**
tokko-tai (Tokubetsu Kogekitai) units 8, 9, 16, 17–18, 19, 21–27, **23**, **25**, **27**, 29–32, 34–41, **36**, **37**, **39**, 46, 149 *see also* IJAAF, the; IJNAF, the
"Tomcat" radar picket duty 186
training 21, 23, 36, 54
trials and testing 54, 56, 60

Ugaki, Vice Adm Matome **161**, 161–162, 164, 173–174, 191, 332–336, **333**
underwater explosions 41
United States Strategic Bombing Survey (Pacific) study 206
US Army, the 109, 111, 112
US Marine Corps 200, 235, **242**, 252, **324**, 327; 5th Tank Battalion 157
US Navy, the **38**, 338; Bombardment and Fire Support Group 134; Fleet Composite (VC) Squadron 27: 131–132; Landing Craft **307**, 318; *LCI(G)-560:* 198; *LCI(L)-90:* 5; *LCI(R)(3)-119:* **307**; LCS (Landing Craft Support) **194**, 224, **296**; *LCS(L)-31:* 262; *LCS(L)(3)-88:* 286–288; *LCS(L)(3)-121:* **296**; *LCS(L)(3)-122:* **319**, 322; *LCS(L)(3)-123:* **296**, 306; *LCT-1075* (landing craft tank) 116; LSM support ships 260, 287, 319, **319**; *LSM-59:* 326–327; *LSM-120:* 313; *LSM-135:* 300–301, 302; *LSM-156:* 313; *LSM-213:* 327; *LSM(R)-190:* 263–264; *LSM(R)-194:* 260–261, **261**; *LSM(R)-195:* 257–258; LSTs 62, 115, 121; *LST-447:* 209, **209**; *LST-460:* 125; *LST-472:* **120**, 121; *LST-477:* 156–157; *LST-534:* 328; *LST-599:* 204–205; *LST-724:* 199; *LST-750:* 126; *LST-808:* 296, 297; *LST-809:* 156; *LST-876:* 204; *LST-884:* 199, 200; *LST-926:* 333; Minesweeping and Hydrographic Group 135; MTB Squadron 21 117, 123, 126; Pacific Fleet 161; PT Boats: PT-75: 123; PT-300: 123, 125; PT-332: 126; Support Carrier Group TG 52.2: 157; Task Forces: TF 11: 10; TF 17: 16; TF 37: 185; TF 38: 19, 70, 76, 86, 87, 95, 137–138, 149, **150**, 151, 152, 185, 188, 189, 312–313; TG 38.2: 86, 87, 96, 97; TG 38.3: 95, 96, 101; TG 38.4: 88; TF 54: TG 54.1: 221, 224; TF 58: 29, 167, 168, 171, 173, **176**, 177, 193, 198, 232, 238, 289, 292–293, 302; TG 58.1: 231, **233**; TG 58.3: **214**, 215, **240**, 251; TG 58.4: 188, 251; TF 74: 71, 72; TF 77: TG 77.2: 105–106, 107; TG 77.4: 75–77, 92; TG 74.2: 181; TG 78.3: 118 *see also* ships

Victory ships 209 *see also* cargo ships
"volunteers" for tokko operations 17, 19, **76**

weaponry 45, 68, **72**, **138**, **230**; Japan: Ho-3 20mm cannon 63; Ho-5 20mm cannon 60, **63**; Ho-103 12.5mm machine gun 47, 59–60; Ho-203 37mm cannon 63; Type 2 13mm machine gun 58; Type 99 20mm No. 25 Model 1 cannon 58, 75, **80**; US: 5in./38 dual-purpose gun 94, **96**, **210**, **278**; 20mm Oerlikon cannon 82, 86, **86**, **88**, **89**, **96**, **101**, **158**, **278**; 40mm Bofors cannon 84, **96**, **172**, **278**

Yasukuni Shrine, the 289